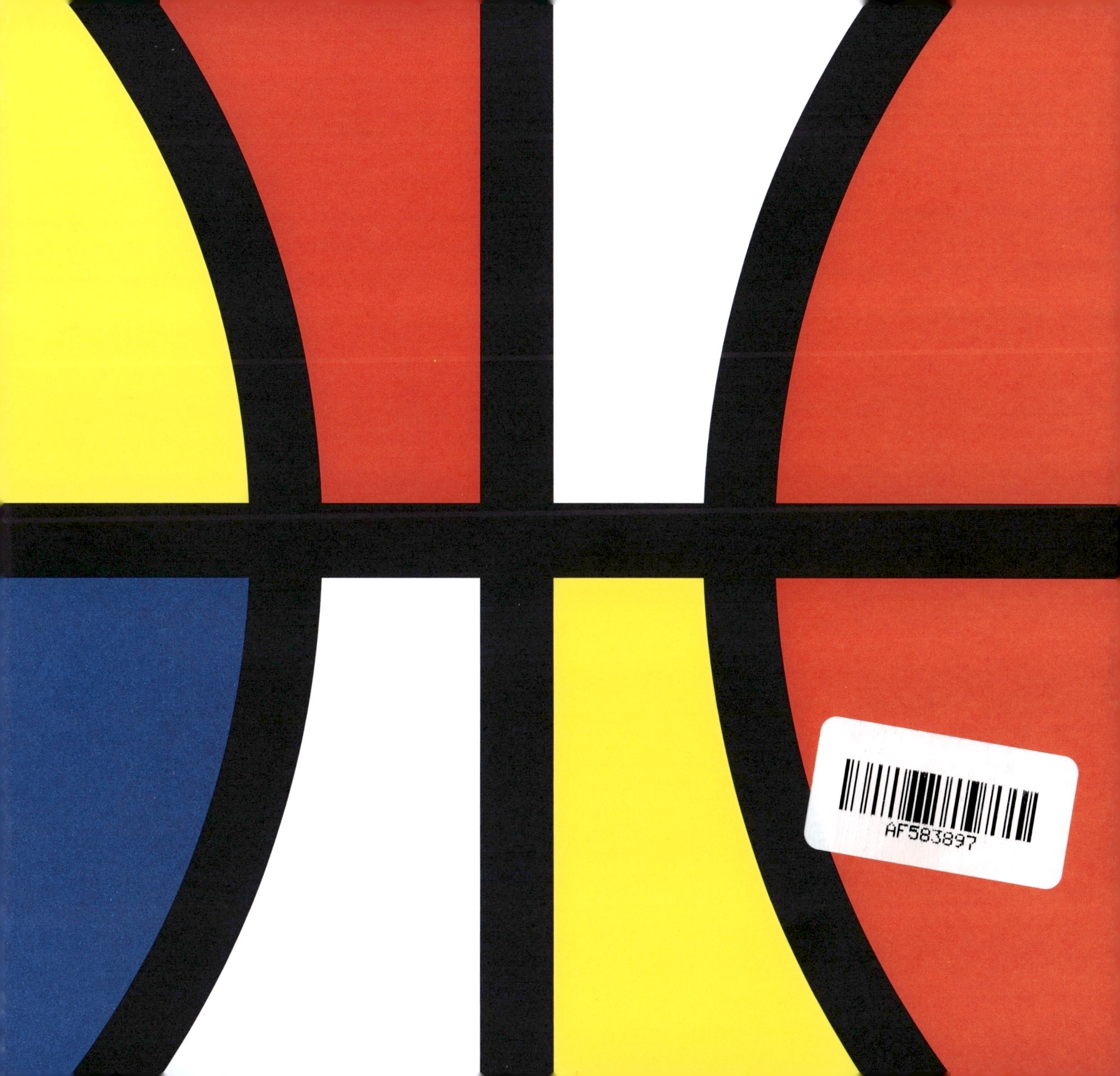

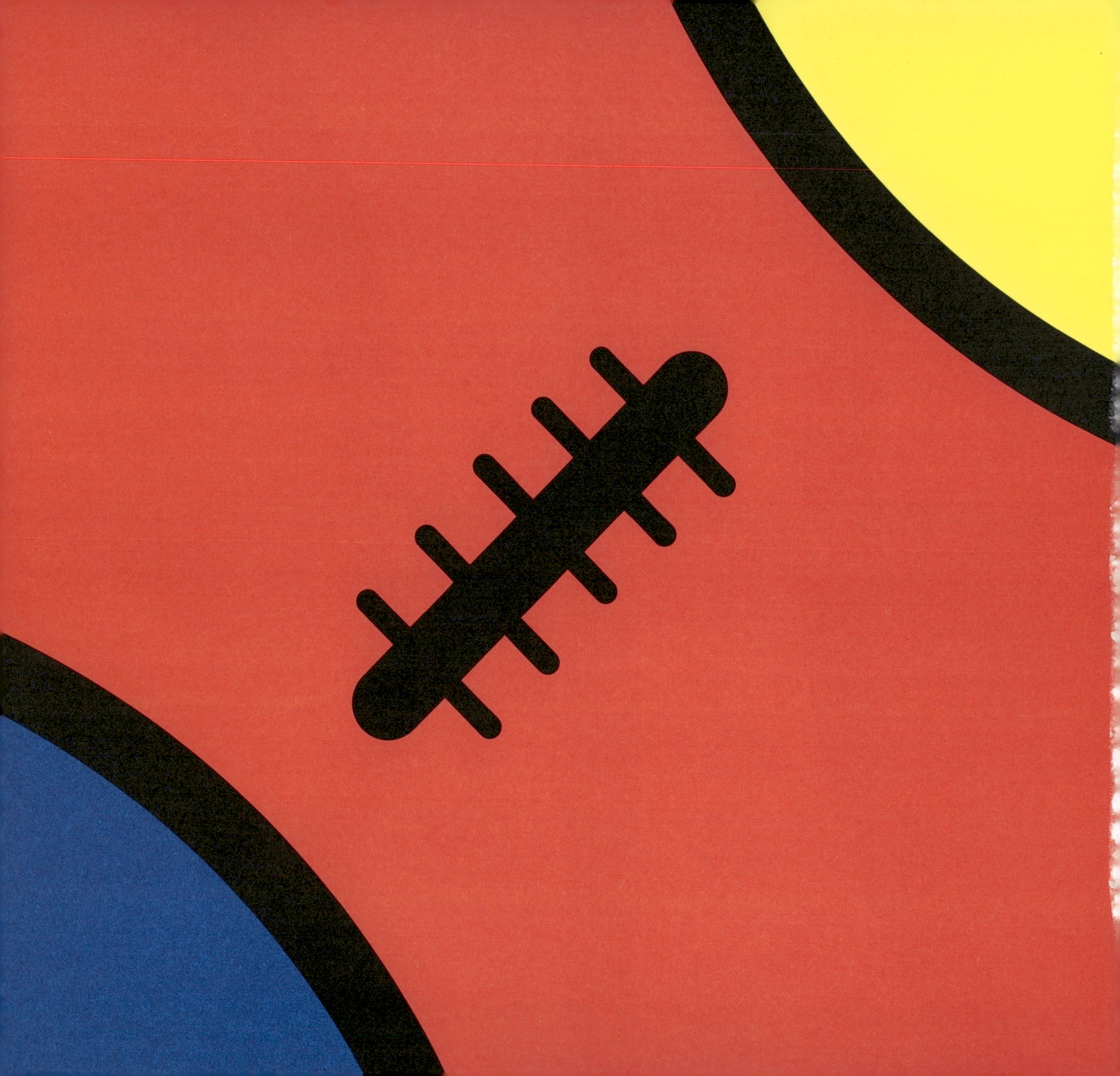

ART BUT MAKE IT SPORTS

EPIC MATCHUPS WHERE ART AND SPORTS COLLIDE

By LJ Rader

CHRONICLE BOOKS
SAN FRANCISCO

Grateful acknowledgment is made to the Getty and the photographers, teams, and institutions who supplied photographs for this book. They are credited on the pages where their photographs appear. All art images are reproduced with permission or licensed under CC0 with the exception of art on the following pages: P. 15 licensed under CC0 3.0 *The Resurrection*. P. 29 licensed under CC0 1.0 *Winged Victory of Samothrace*. P. 33 licensed under CC0 4.0 *The Sower (Sower at Sunset)*. P. 36 reproduced with permission *Hommage à Wayne Thiebaud*. P. 39 licensed under CC0 3.0 *Aeneas, Anchises and Ascanius*. P. 49 licensed under CC0 1.0 *Christ Healing the Blind*. P. 68 licensed under CC0 4.0 *Lamentation*. P. 89 licensed under CC0 3.0 *The Incredulity of Saint Thomas*. P. 91 licensed under CC0 1.0 *The Death of Sapphira*. P. 93 licensed under CC0 2.0 *The Girl I Left Behind Me*. P. 99 licensed under CC0 2.5 *Vaison Diadumenos*. P. 101 licensed under CC0 4.0 *Group of two male figurines carrying a female figurine of the early Spedos variety*. P. 105 licensed under CC0 3.0 *Diagoras carried in triumph by his sons to Olympia*. P. 119 licensed under CC0 4.0 *Paix aux chaumières, guerre aux palais*. P. 131 licensed under CC0 3.0 *Two Goats*. P. 132 licensed under CC0 3.0 *Der Gestürzte*. P. 133 licensed under CC0 1.0 *A Matador*. P. 143 licensed under CC0 2.0 *Ancient Greek Votive offering*. P. 157 licensed under CC0 1.0 *Divinity Lotus*.

Library of Congress Cataloging-in-Publication Data available.

ISBN 978-1-7972-3683-4

Manufactured in China.

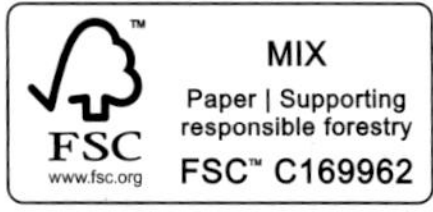

Design by Maggie Edelman.

10 9 8 7 6 5 4 3 2 1

Chronicle books and gifts are available at special quantity discounts to corporations, professional associations, literacy programs, and other organizations. For details and discount information, please contact our premiums department at corporategifts@chroniclebooks.com or at 1-800-759-0190.

Chronicle Books LLC
680 Second Street
San Francisco, California 94107
www.chroniclebooks.com

CONTENTS

FOREWORD

The first Art But Make It Sports post I ever saw popped up on my Instagram feed in the fall of 2020. It was deep into the pandemic, and sports teams were playing in empty stadiums. Everything felt sterile; the World Series took place in front of cardboard cutouts of fans instead of real ones. Football games were so quiet that you could hear quarterbacks call plays on TV. NBA stars finished out the season in a closed campus in Orlando, living in Disney World purgatory, and WNBA players had been sequestered in prep-school purgatory at IMG Academy in Bradenton, Florida.

There was no humanity surrounding the games; no electricity enveloping the field, no roar after a majestic dunk. No mass euphoria, no shared heartbreak. Everyone watched at home on their own individual screens.

And then I saw a side-by-side of a photo of Vanderbilt football kicker Sarah Fuller and the painting *Salome with the Head of Saint John the Baptist* by Benjamin West, after Guido Reni. The post was so funny and so accurate that I felt the same spark a sold-out stadium ignites. I started following the account it came from, and it was like watching the game with my smartest friend. The humanity of sports flooded back into my life.

It is my true honor to write the foreword to LJ's book five years later. He has done something very special here. He has turned the churn of social media into something we can hold. He has shown us new ways of looking at sports' greatest moments and the art world's greatest achievements. And he has given us insight into how he works his magic.

But back to Sarah Fuller and Salome. The news cycle moves so quickly that it's easy to forget how livid guys online were when Fuller kicked for a college football team. But LJ's work preserves the conversations that surround a moment. He is not only a meme lord, he's one of the most important historians of our time. He etches cultural responses into the permanence of the internet like music onto vinyl, or early drawings onto the walls of caves.

Art But Make It Sports is also subversive—the picture of Fuller shows her holding a helmet. In the painting, Salome holds the head of Saint John on a plate. Quite the message to angry men on the internet. LJ clearly knows how to be on the right side of history, which is not something I can say for everyone in the sports world.

There is alchemy to what LJ does. He finds an image and then matches its essence. But he's doing much more than simply matching shapes to shapes. When finding a comparison, he considers the title, the artist, the time period, and the subject matter. He turns a moment and a work of art into one moment of recognition.

And it all comes from his own brain. An AI model could never understand the nuance and layers. As LJ consistently proves, sports and art mirror each other. Sports imitate art, isn't that how the saying goes?

I'll let Oscar Wilde speak here: "The third doctrine is that life imitates art far more than art imitates life," Wilde wrote in his essay "The Decay of Lying." "This results not merely from life's imitative instinct, but from the fact that the self-conscious aim of life is to find expression, and that art offers it certain beautiful forms through which it may realize that energy."

Isn't the whole point of sports to also find expression? To feel? To watch dramas play out until the whistle blows or the buzzer sounds or the opponent is out of chances?

Art and sports both offer beautiful forms to realize people's inherent desire for meaning. The first time I saw a Titian painting above the altar in a church in Venice, it felt like watching the Red Sox win the World Series. And when Damar Hamlin's heart stopped on the field in Buffalo after a hard hit, I felt the same devastation brought on by John Singer Sargent's *Gassed*, a painting of British soldiers who had been blinded by a mustard gas attack in World War I.

Even if you can't play sports or make art, you can appreciate both. And with every post from Art But Make It Sports, LJ shows us how. He helps us reach emotions we didn't even know we had. His work is delightful, surprising, and deeply human, just like the most thrilling game or arresting painting.

If I had to pair this book with an image of an athlete, it would be Serena Williams, Tom Brady, or Simone Biles. LJ has invented an art form, and he's the GOAT of his medium. This book is his trophy, and now it's yours too.

—Charlotte Wilder, sports journalist, host of *The Sports Gossip Show*, and author of *The Wilder Things* newsletter

A NOTE FROM THE AUTHOR

When I first started the ArtButMakeItSports account, someone remarked that it was "everything I didn't know I needed." Since you're holding this book now, there's a good chance you also subscribe to this notion, and I cannot tell you how much it means to me that you consider my work necessary and worth supporting.

We live in the time of AI, where human ingenuity faces erosion and replacement by computerized slop. Social media outlets are overrun with ads, hate speech, and content that is designed to dumb us down and drive us apart. I take pride in the fact that I never use AI for any of the matchups. I try to treat all moments with tact, grace, and sensibility, and ultimately aim to successfully bridge the gap between two factions that are often seen as diametrically opposed. And while ArtButMakeItSports maintains the same core identity today as it did when I started the account in late 2019 as a dumb way to keep my friends, family, and myself entertained, it's grown to mean something more, both for myself and the community that supports it.

Although I never intended for this to be the case, what started as a mindless endeavor now seemingly carries weight, and I feel the responsibility to not only continue creating content but to also go deep into the aspects that have allowed it to stand out among the current landscape. A book affords me the opportunity to do just that: a canvas to talk through my process and thinking behind posts; introduce readers to new art, artists, and sports moments; and continue to provide not only entertainment but also education.

By conducting a survey of popular moments in sports through the lens of art history, both with imagery and extended text, this book will breathe even more life into the account and hopefully continue to be everything you didn't know you needed, without the constraints of a social media platform.

A few items worth noting before we dive in. This book was restricted to public domain art. The public domain lacks a significant number of both female artists and artists of color. This means that the diversity of imagery and representation that I champion on the day to day of my account doesn't fully come through as much as I'd like. This also means you won't see much art from roughly the last hundred years.

Despite the restrictions on the art side, I would like to give a big shout-out to Getty Images. I get comments on a weekly basis in the realm of "Why don't you write a book?" and other people often respond, "The licensing of sports imagery would be a nightmare." And while on the surface that might be the case, the fine folks at Getty Images have been amazing to work with, and have played a major role in allowing this book to become a reality.

Finally, there were a ton of pairings that ended up on the cutting room floor for one reason or another. The book has limited space, so if you enjoyed it but wish I had done x, y, or z sports image, let me know! The more feedback I get, the more chance I'll write a sequel!

INTRODUCTION

Many people have asked, “Why ArtButMakeItSports and not SportsButMakeIt-Art?” I’m sure this is because it’s clear the focus is on finding an art equivalent to the sports image, so one would assume the sports should come first.

The answer is rooted in the evolution of the account. For the first year or so, the entire feed was just images of artwork with sports-related commentary layered on top. I would travel to museums, snap photos of a few interesting pieces, and then come home and caption and post in bulk. I’d click “add image to Instagram stories,” write out the text on top of the image, click “save image,” and then crop the blank black areas on both sides—an extremely simple process emblematic of my commitment to minimalism. (Even as my methods have changed, I’m relying on my knowledge/memory of art first, so I’m taking the art I know and making it into sports.)

At my best, I’d make up some sort of pun or extended metaphor; but at a minimum my goal was to come up with something humorous. That approach lasted well over a year, until I realized that a lot of the time, where I was saying, “This piece of art looks like so and so player or team,” I could simply just use the image of so and so.

As the side-by-sides started to dominate the feed, the account began to grow, and I homed in on what’s become my process for the last few years.

Left: *Macbeth and Banquo meeting the witches on the heath*, 1855, Théodore Chassériau. Musée d’Orsay.

Right: *The Irritating Gentleman*, 1874, Berthold Woltze. Digital image by Dorotheum. Private collection.

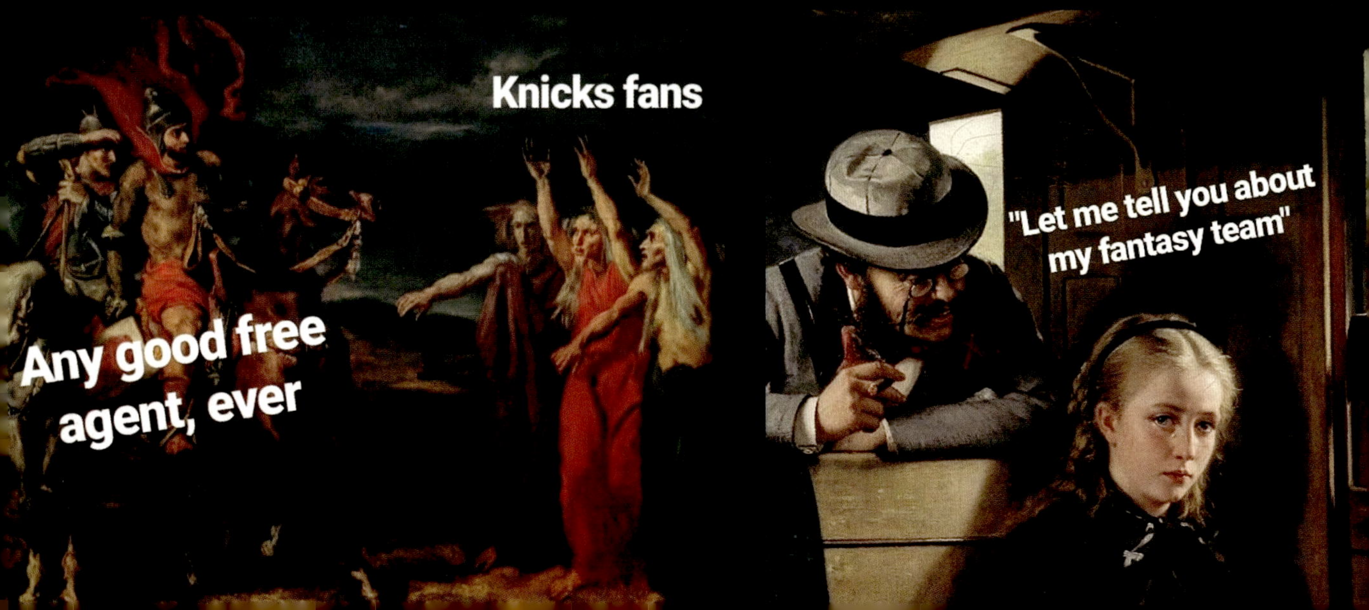

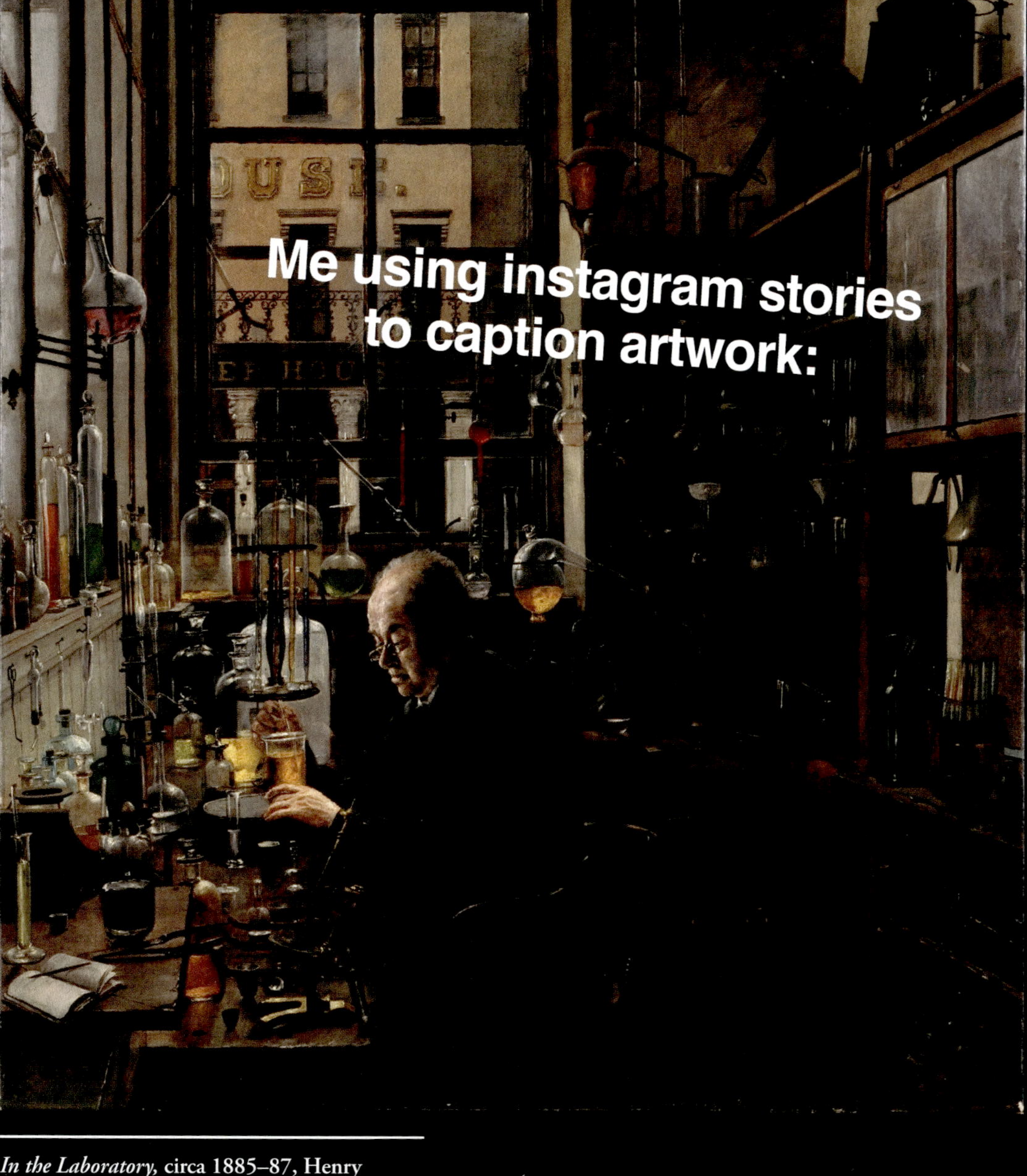

In the Laboratory, circa 1885–87, Henry Alexander. Metropolitan Museum of Art.

I'm lucky enough to travel, both for work and with friends and family. Wherever I go, I make it a priority to see local art. I go room to room, usually at a fast pace, taking pictures of works I think could at some point be used (mostly avoiding landscapes and portraits, unless they're particularly unique). After I'm done, I upload them into a folder on my phone called "Meme Fuel," composed of all the art photos I've taken, committing the most interesting ones to memory.

On the sports side of it all, I used to have to be watching a game or scrolling through social media to find content, but the ArtButMakeItSports community has grown to the point where they've become my eyes and ears, either tagging me in or DMing me viral sports images. It's then a matter of deciding:

- Is this moment unique and/or worth spending the time on to find the perfect comparison? Will it move the needle with my followers?
- If it's a screenshot, do I want to wait to see if a professional photo drops?
- Is there a better angle that I could work with?

Man Reading a Letter to a Woman in a distinguished interior (detail), 1670–1674, Pieter de Hooch. Digital image by Google Arts & Culture. Kremer Collection.

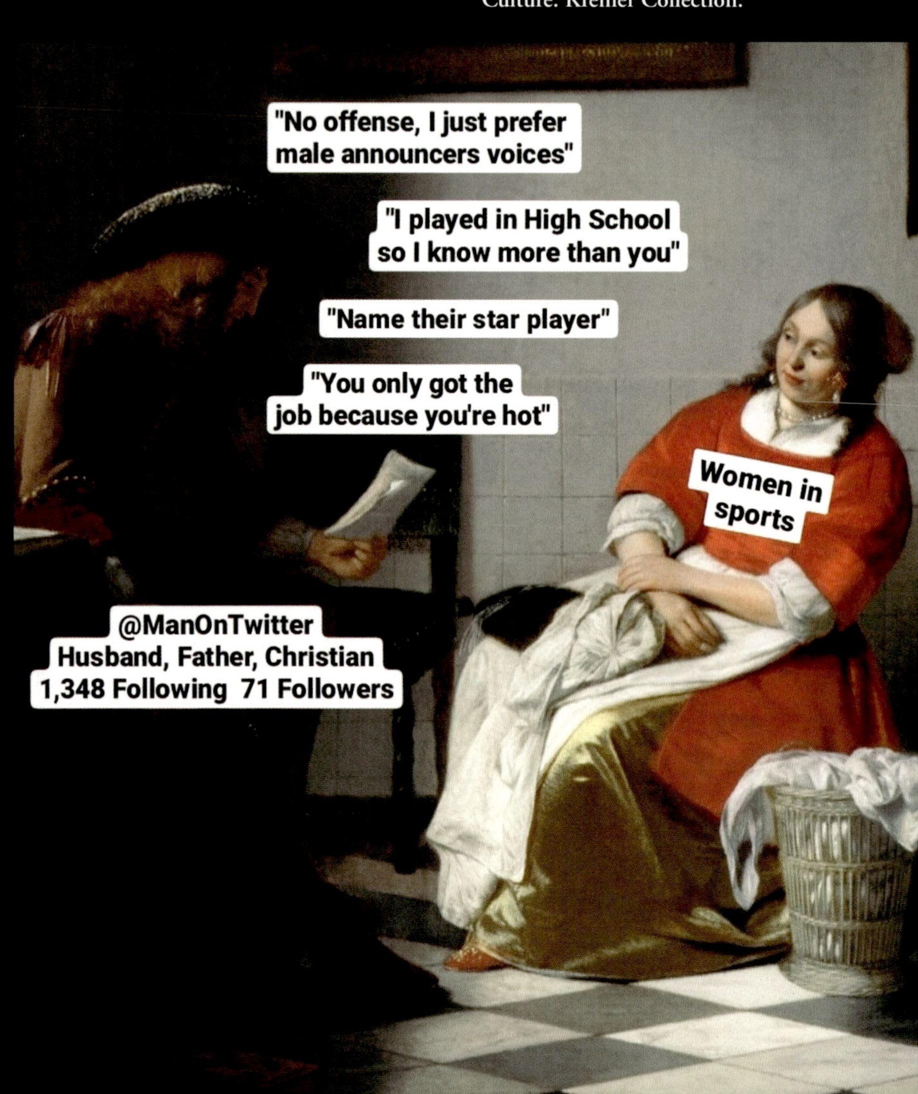

Once I settle on the sports image, it's a matter of coming up with the art comparison. That usually breaks down in one of three ways:

- I see a sports image and immediately match it with a work of art I have saved in Meme Fuel, or with a famous piece I've seen online or in a book but haven't had the chance to see in person.
- The sports image clearly resembles a theme in art history, such as "the Lamentation of Christ," or "Venus mourning Adonis." Then it's just a matter of searching for the version of said theme that matches best.
- The sports image clearly represents an artist's style or a time period in art, like Salvador Dalí or René Magritte (surrealism), leading me to look through their catalog to find exactly the right piece.

Between the three methods, something usually comes together, and I'll post it across the various platforms I manage. For this book, I wanted to showcase a blend of new content and past hits. Social media leaves little room for prose and reflection, so this is a chance to offer nuance and detail and allow you, the reader, to potentially see things from a new vantage point.

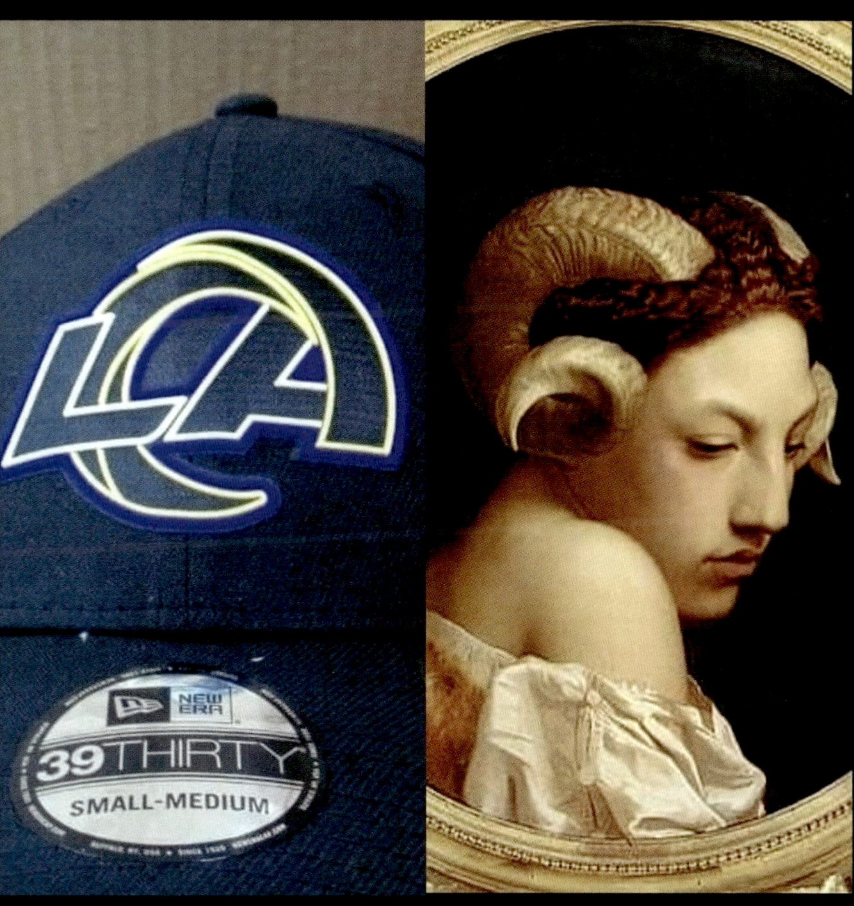

My first ever side-by-side, posted on March 9, 2020, when the LA Rams logo leaked, photo by Charles Robinson.

Woman's head with ram horns (detail), 1853, Jean-Léon Gérôme. Musée des Beaux-Arts de Nantes. Flipped from the original.

BASKETBALL

Basketball is, for my money, the most art-coded sport. An intricate dance between bodies, a basketball game is a 5x5 symphony of movement, drama, comedy, and tragedy, all playing out on a confined canvas. Elements such as the sun and moon, which come up constantly in art history, can double as the ball, and limb placement often matches the various contortions you see on the hardwood.

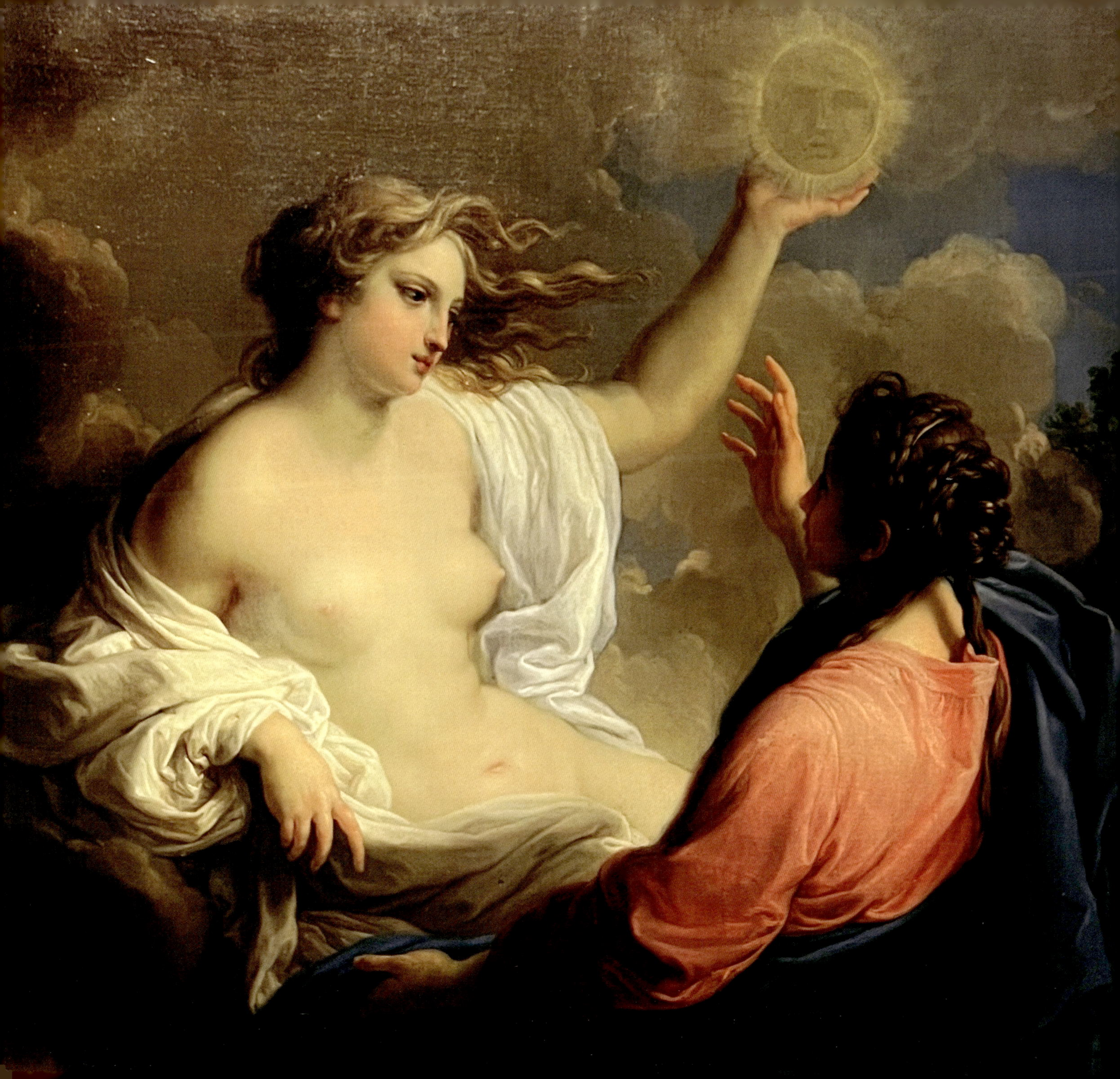

THE REAL AI

Many wrote off Allen Iverson and the Philadelphia 76ers heading into the 2001 Finals. Granted, outside of Iverson the roster was mediocre at best, lending credence to the media's predictions of a four-game sweep by the Lakers. As the *Las Vegas Sun* noted: "At sports books around town, including the Imperial Palace and the Orleans, the Lakers are favored to win the seven-game series against the Philadelphia 76ers at a value of minus 2000." That means you'd need to bet $2,000 to win $100. They further noted, "Not even when Michael Jordan was busy leading the Chicago Bulls to six NBA titles in the 1990s has the line ever been so one-sided."

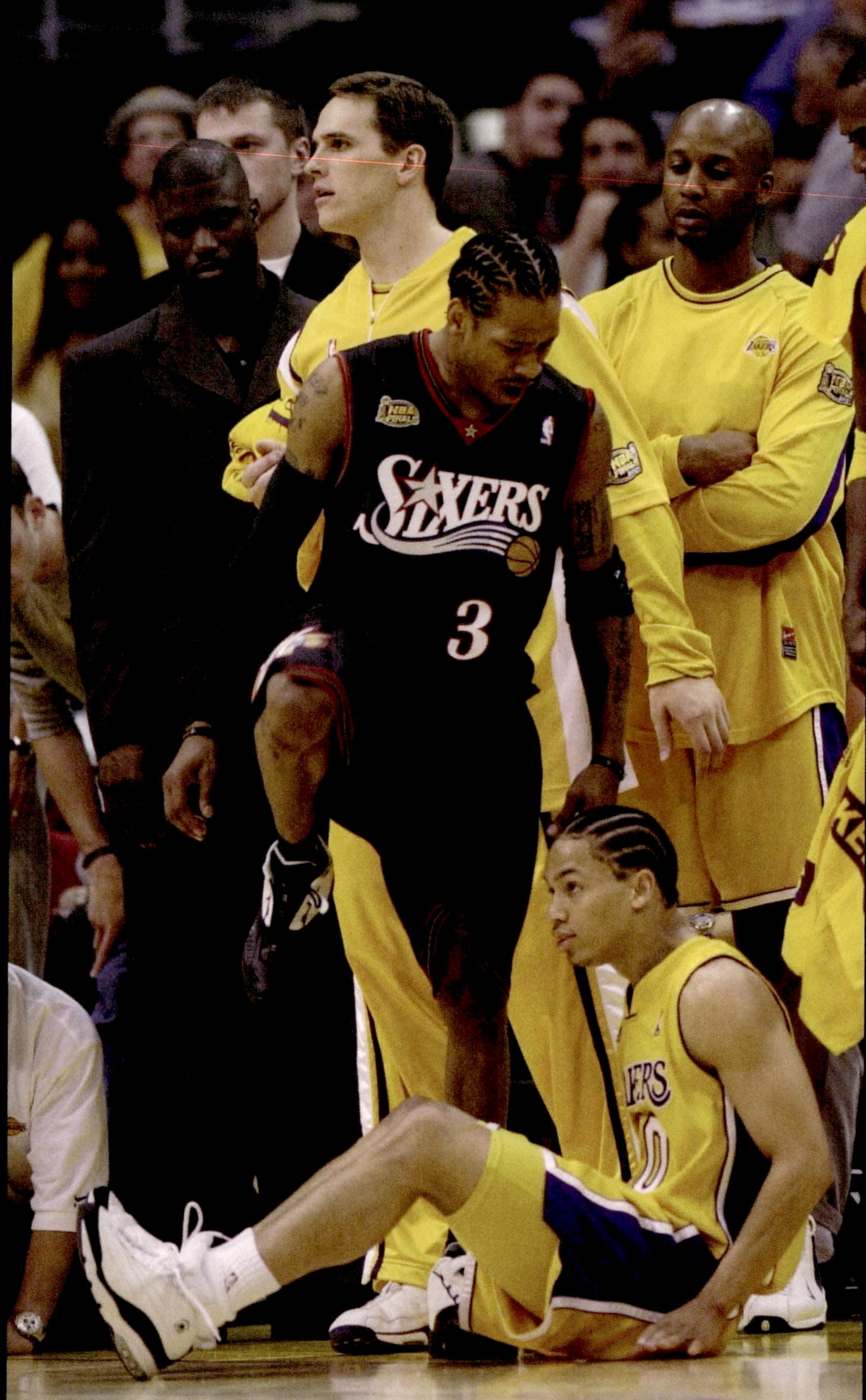

This page: Allen Iverson (#3) of the Philadelphia 76ers steps over Tyronn Lue (#10) of the Los Angeles Lakers in Game 1 of the NBA Finals at Staples Center on June 6, 2001, in Los Angeles, California. The 76ers won 107–101. Photo by Otto Greule/ALLSPORT.

Opposite page, left: *The Resurrection* (detail), circa 1450–90, unknown artist. Walters Art Museum. Flipped from the original.

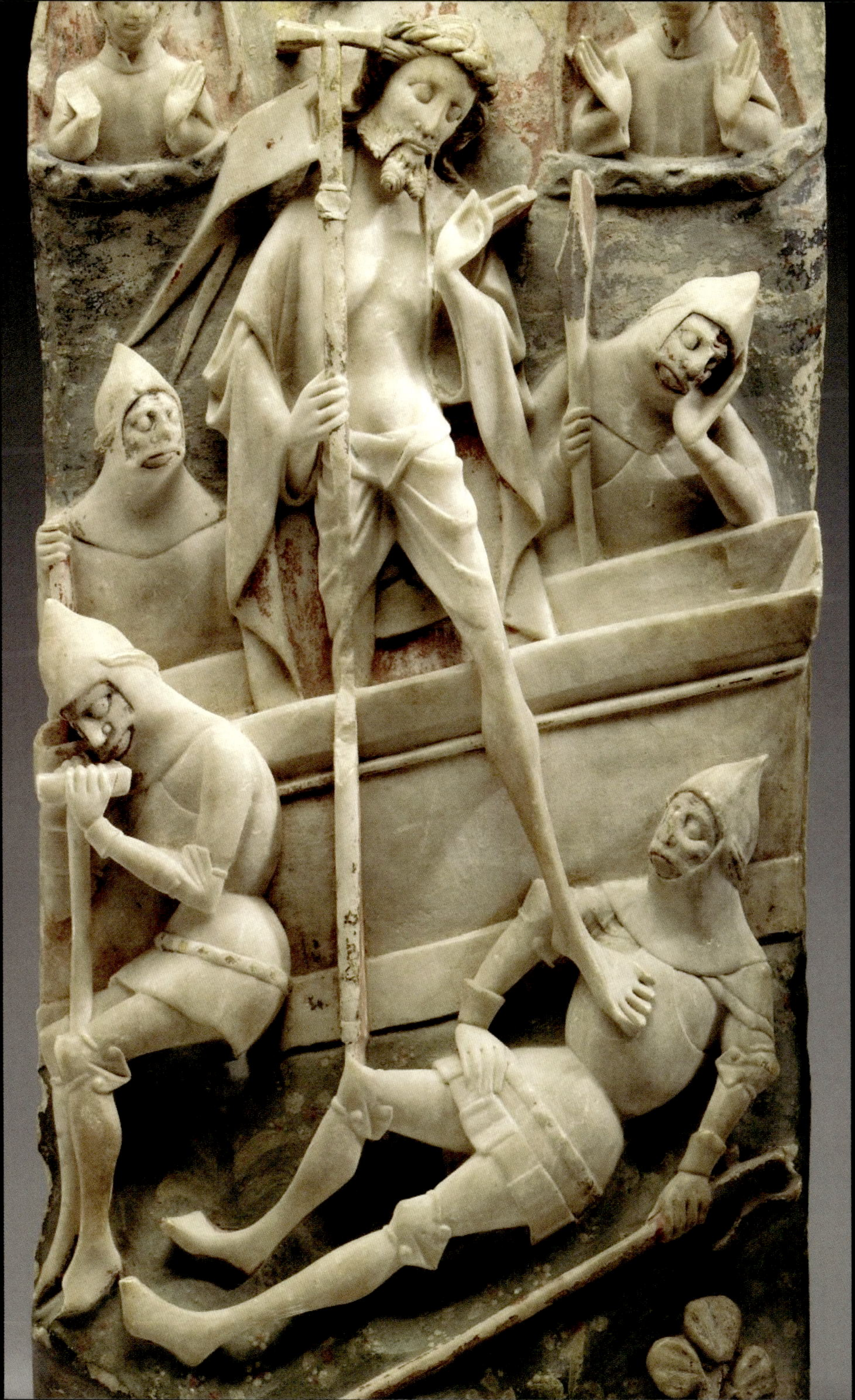

Though Iverson had a campaign that would see him land All-Star Game MVP and MVP of the league, the 76ers remained major underdogs; so their Game 1 win—highlighted by Iverson stepping over Ty Lue—after so many pegged them to lose could be seen as a resurrection of sorts. And it certainly left us with an image just as iconic as the biblical one, even though the 76ers would go on to lose in five. The series clincher left us with another lasting photo, with Kobe Bryant cradling the Larry O'Brien Championship Trophy like a baby Jesus.

Bottom left: Kobe Bryant (#8) of the Los Angeles Lakers poses with the Larry O'Brien Championship Trophy after defeating the Philadelphia 76ers in Game 5 of the 2001 NBA Finals at the First Union Center on June 15, 2001, in Philadelphia, Pennsylvania. Copyright © 2001 NBAE. Photo by Jesse D. Garrabrant/NBAE via Getty Images.

Bottom right: *Adoration of the Magi* (detail), seventeenth century, unknown artist (after Nicolas Poussin). Dulwich Picture Gallery.

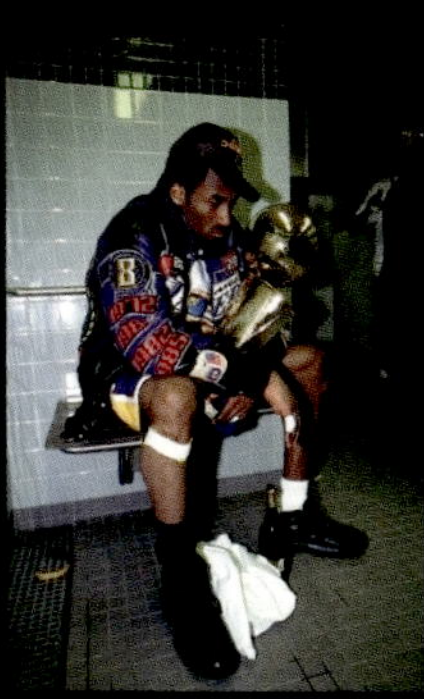

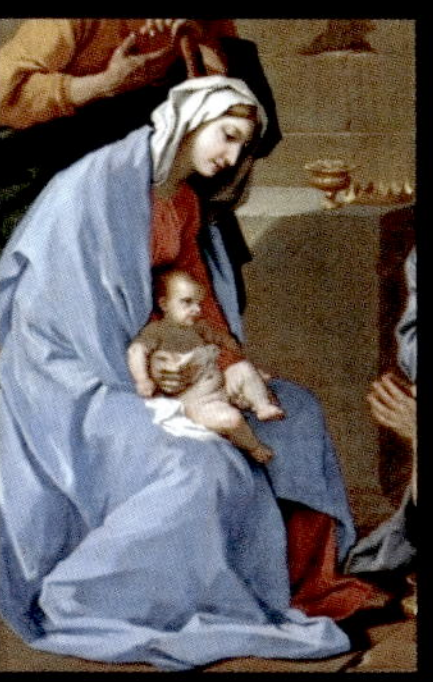

SABRINA LEADING THE LIBERTY

There are multiple layers to this one:

First, the nearly identical placement of each of the figures, as well as Sabrina Ionescu's arm placement. Second, the name of the painting—*Liberty Leading the People*—could also be the title of this moment in sports history, with Sabrina Ionescu leading the New York Liberty to victory. And last—and this is a small one—at the time, one of the Liberty's players was French: Marine Johannès.

I spent some time questioning whether the nudity component of the artwork was appropriate, as it's always important to take into account to avoid any distasteful comparisons. It can sometimes be the central focus of a match, for example, when Mike Tyson's exposed butt flashed prior to his fight against Jake Paul and I compared it to the naked behind of a statue. In this case, it's much more of a background ingredient, and one which some have argued symbolizes strength and inspiration far more than sexualization. For that reason, I decided to roll with it.

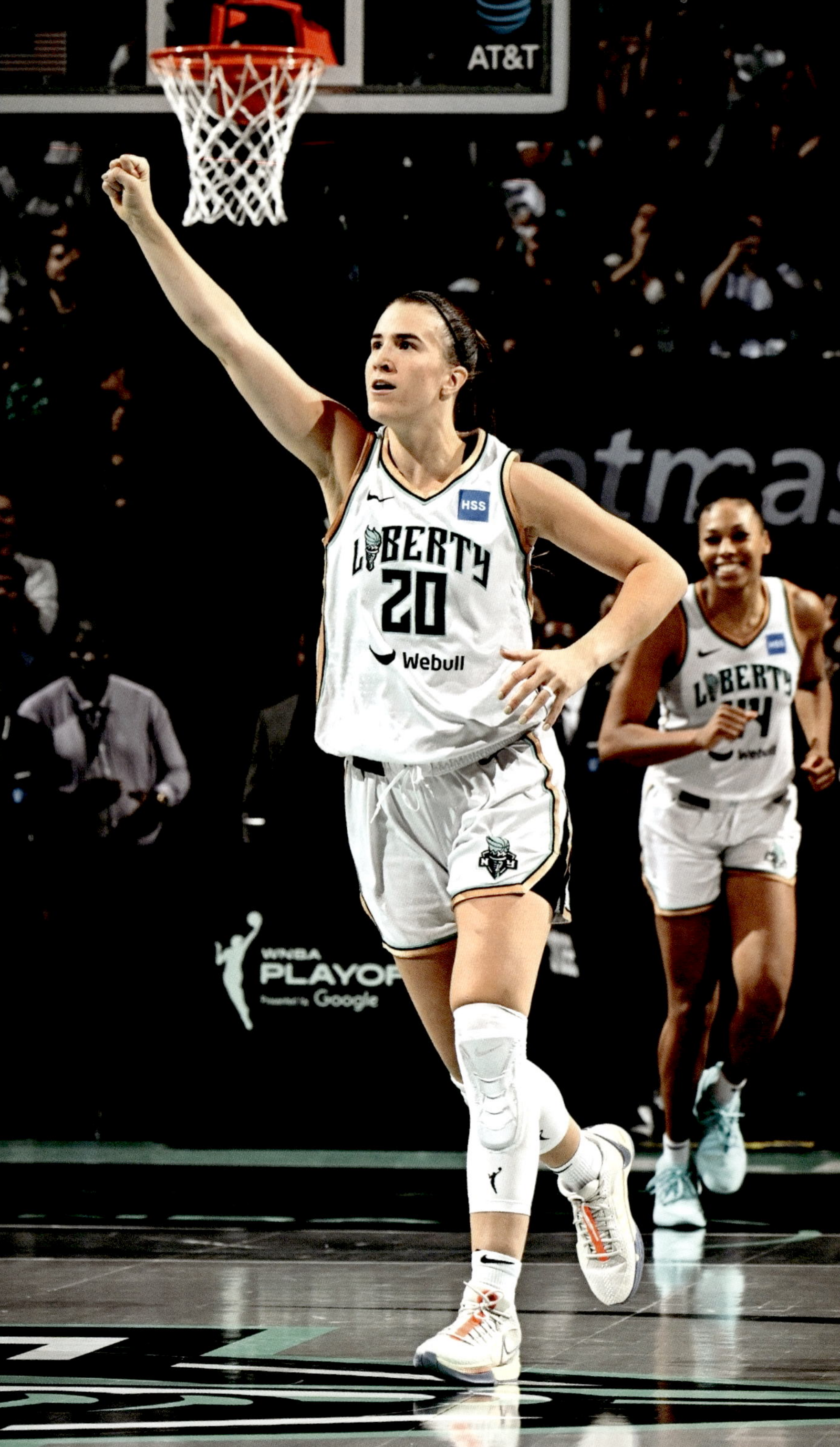

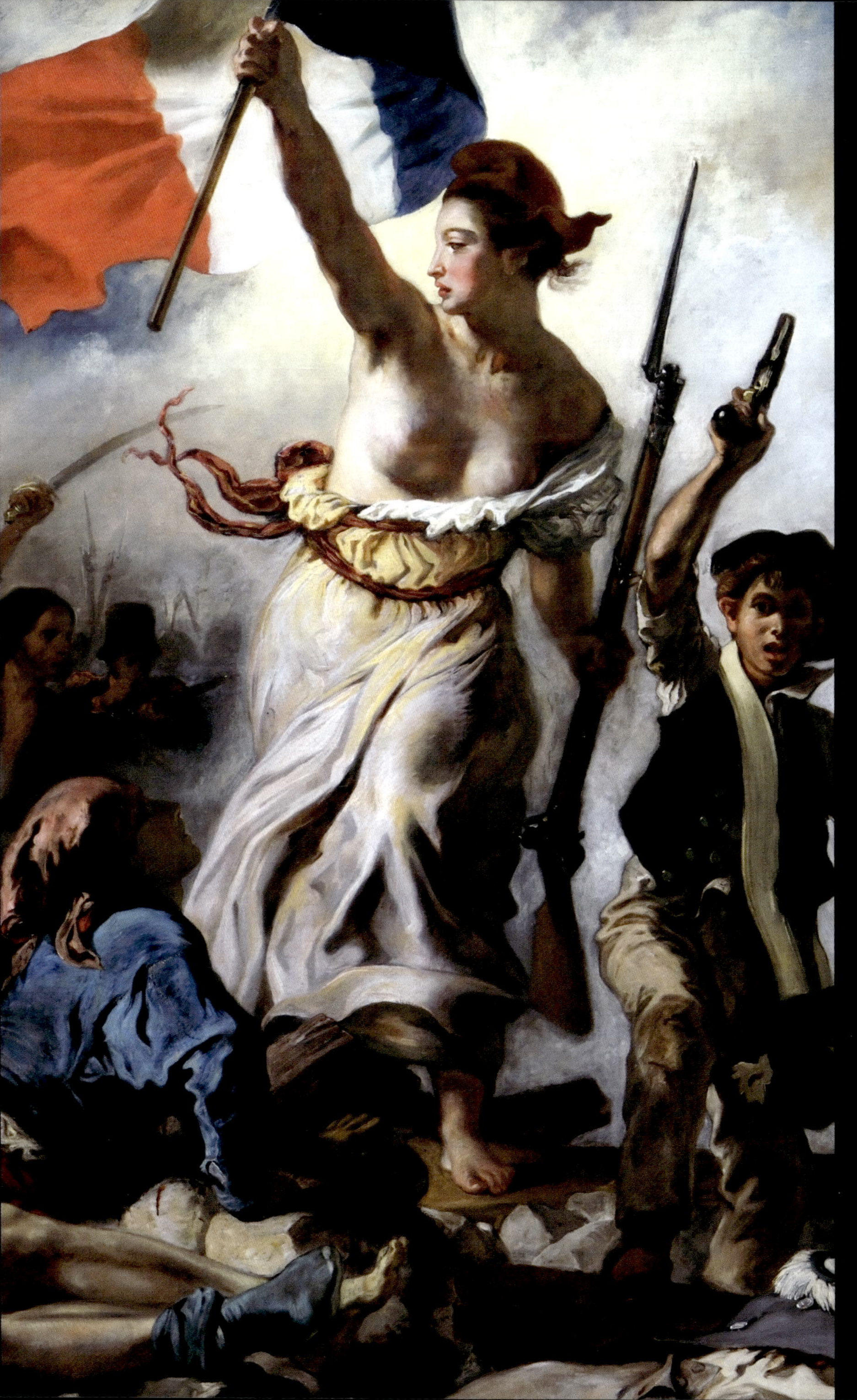

Opposite page: Sabrina Ionescu (#20) of the New York Liberty celebrates a win against the Washington Mystics during the 2023 WNBA Playoffs on September 19, 2023, in Brooklyn, New York. Copyright © 2023 NBAE. Photo by David Dow/NBAE via Getty Images.

This page: *Liberty Leading the People* (detail), 1830, Eugène Delacroix. Digital image by Shonagon. Louvre Museum.

2023 NBA SHOT OF THE SEASON

This shot of Russell Westbrook by Joe Murphy won the 2022/23 NBA Fan Favorite award for Photo of the Year, and this comparison ended up being one of my most popular for that NBA season.

The photo itself is pure art. It manages to capture the emotion on Russell Westbrook's face while also perfectly framing the action of the scene with the star guard flanked by two defenders, all set against a vibrant blue background.

From the photographer himself, Joe Murphy: "The remote camera is called my 'overhead,' set up over the basket on the catwalk hours before the game. All the cameras are synced to the arena flash strobes that take over two

Russell Westbrook (#0) of the Los Angeles Clippers celebrates during a game against the Memphis Grizzlies on March 29, 2023, at FedExForum in Memphis, Tennessee. Copyright © 2023 NBAE. Photo by Joe Murphy/NBAE via Getty Images.

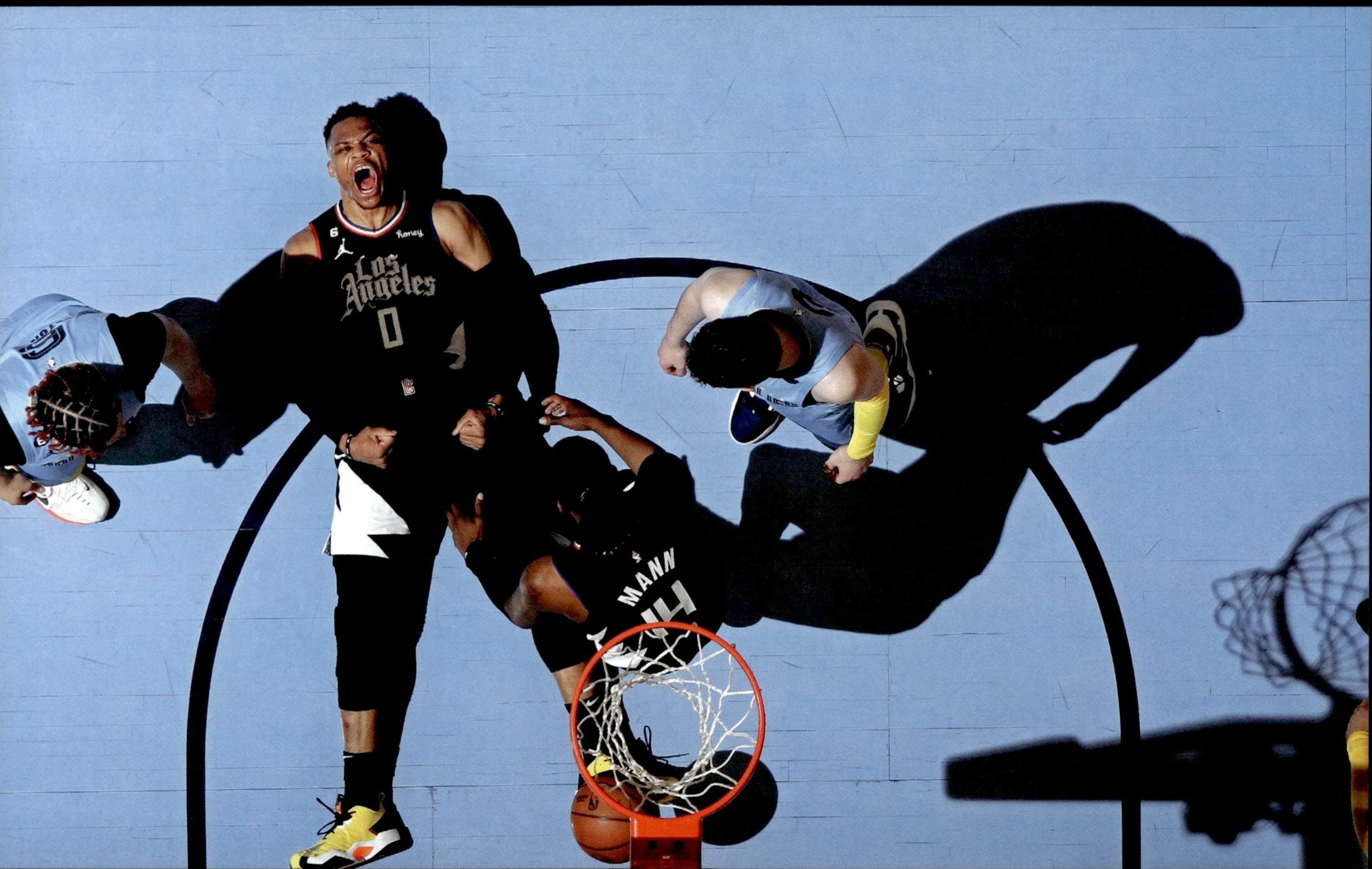

seconds to recycle, so you only get one photo." He goes on to break down the moment: "I was sitting at the opposite end of the court with my long lens downcourt camera. I have a separate trigger taped to my camera that fires the remote cameras at the same time. Russ went to the basket and then fell backwards to the ground, watching the ball go through the hoop while on the ground. When I saw him flex to celebrate, I could tell he was screaming, so I hit the remote button hoping he was looking straight up. It was a quick moment, but I am happy I captured it from the best angle!"

The Murphy shot is reminiscent of a classic Kandinsky composition, with lines, curves, and shapes layered on the same canvas, and visually and spiritually, it matches well.

Pointed and Round (Spitz und Rund) (detail), 1925, Wassily Kandinsky. Solomon R. Guggenheim Museum. Rotated from the original.

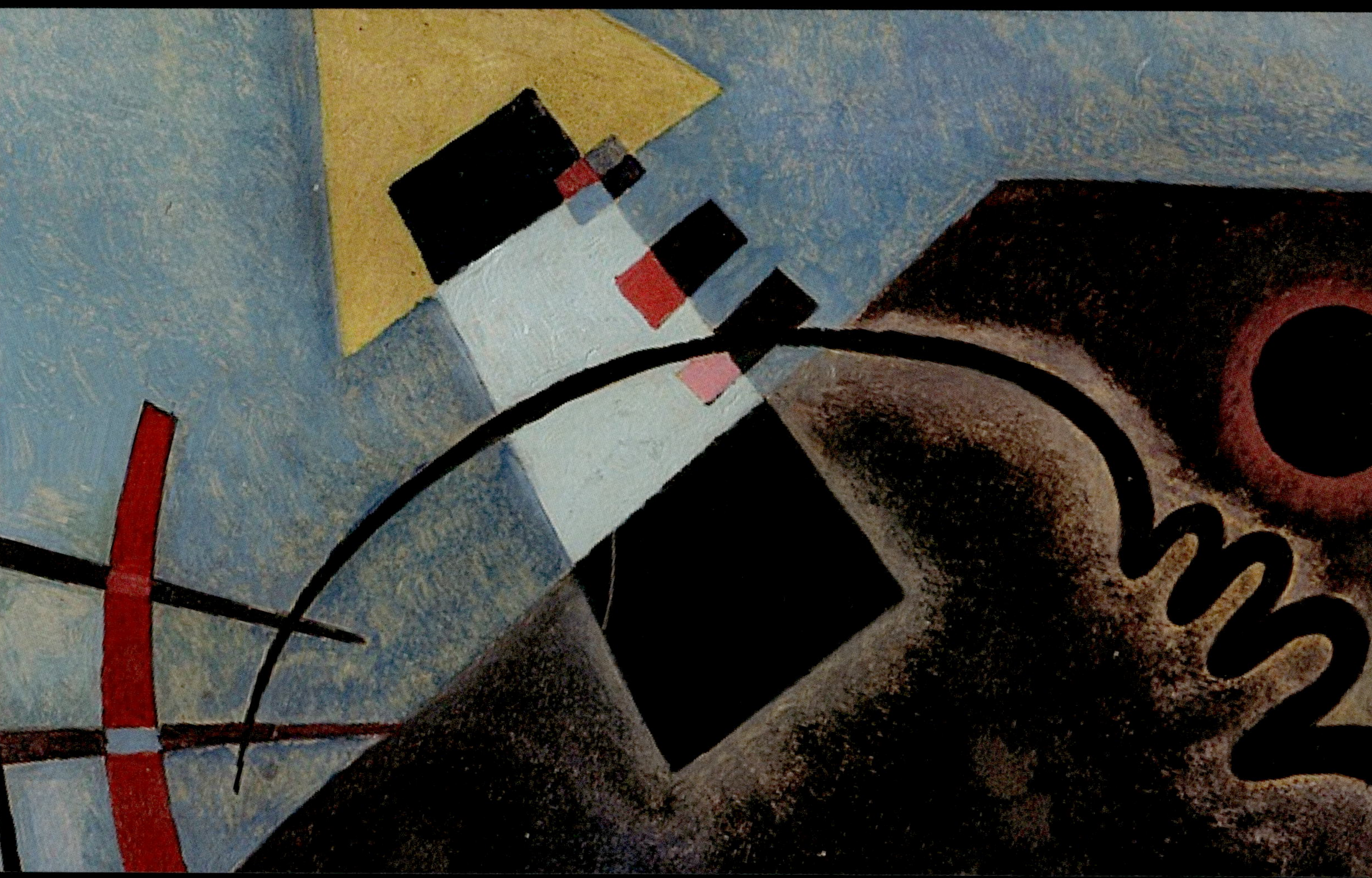

THE CAITLIN CLARK EFFECT

Caitlin Clark of the Indiana Fever is unequivocally the highest-profile athlete to follow ArtButMakeItSports. That, coupled with her athletic achievements, makes her a favorite to feature. The photo dropped during Media Day prior to the start of the 2024 WNBA season, with people online remarking that it reminded them of something artistic that they couldn't quite put their finger on.

I figured the theme of Judith with the Head of Holofernes would work perfectly. As the story goes, Holofernes—an Assyrian general—was on the verge of destroying the city of Bethulia, where Judith lived. The widow Judith was allowed to enter Holofernes's tent in the middle of the night because of his lust. However, he passed out, and was beheaded by Judith.

There are depictions of the story that focus on the act (see, *Judith Slaying Holofernes* by Artemisia Gentileschi, opposite), but I wanted an image showing the aftermath, of which there are many. After a bit of digging, I decided on this piece once attributed to Charles Mellin, for the almost identical arm placement, as well as the matching facial expression.

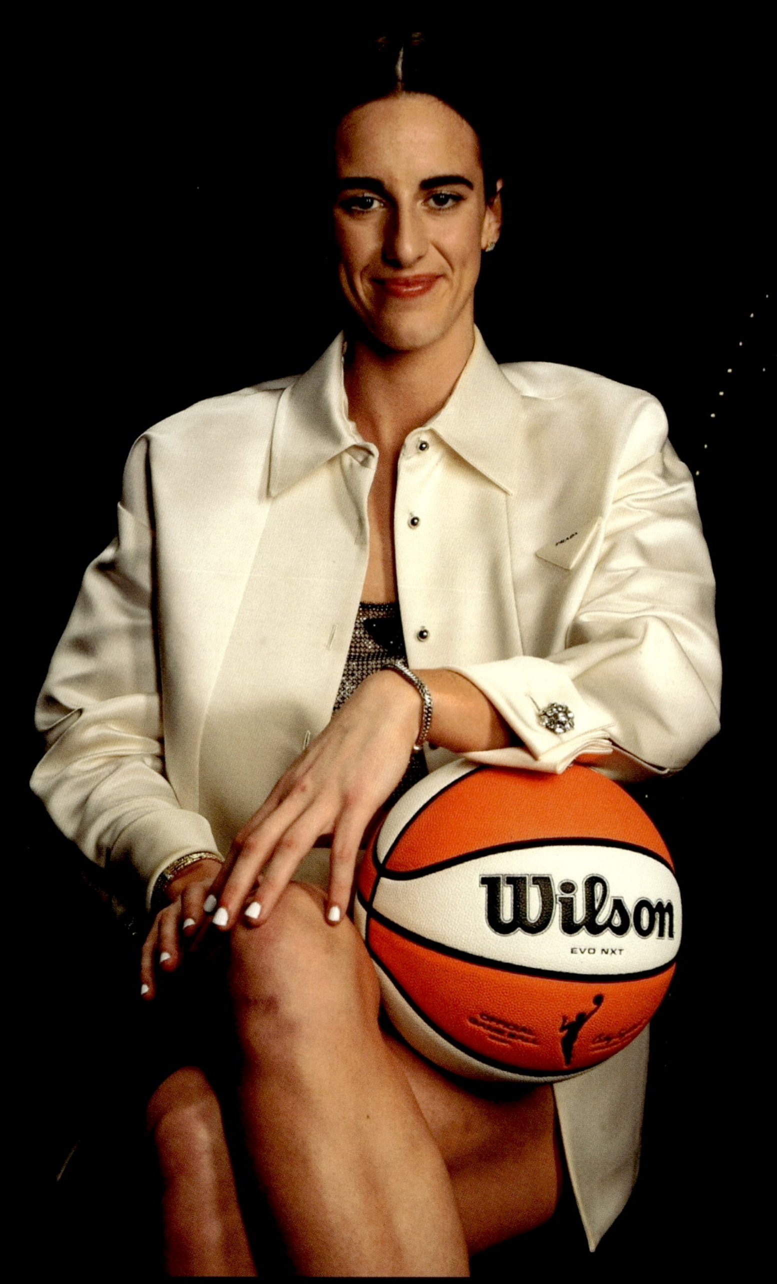

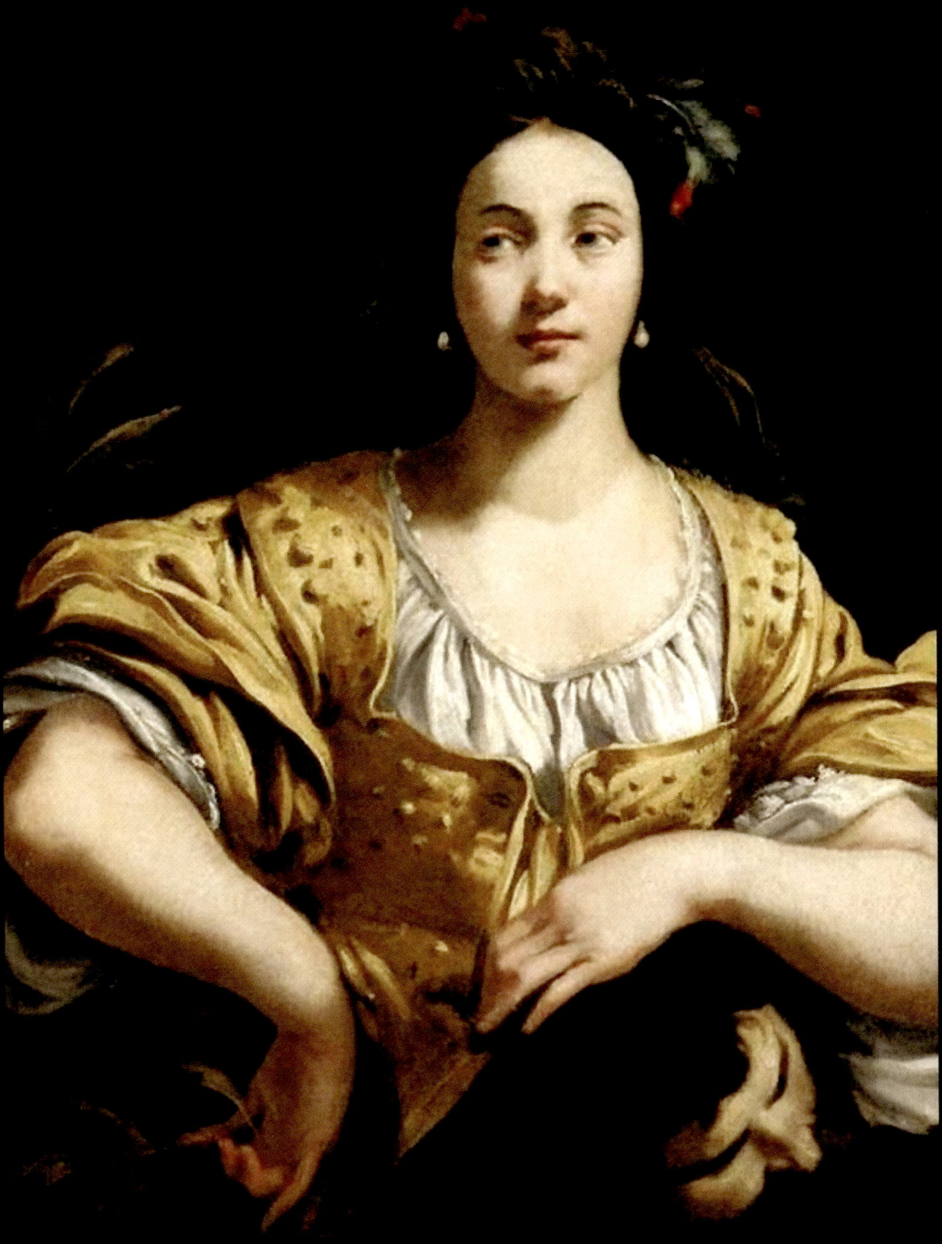

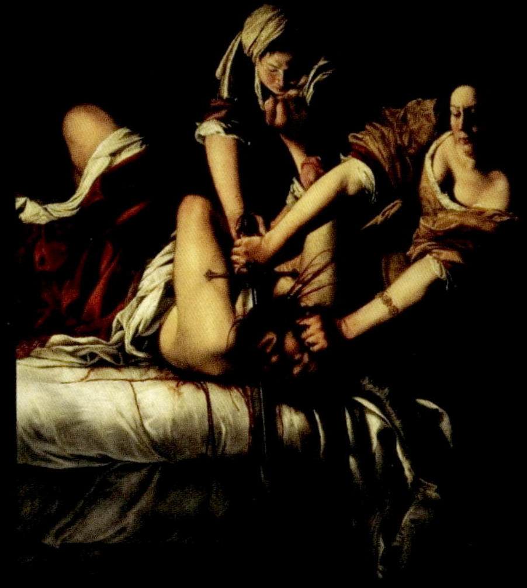

This page, top: *Judith Beheading Holofernes*, 1614–20, Artemisia Gentileschi. Digital image by Google Cultural Institute. Uffizi Gallery.

Opposite page: Caitlin Clark poses for a portrait after being selected first overall by the Indiana Fever during the 2024 WNBA Draft on April 14, 2025, at the Brooklyn Academy of Music in Brooklyn, New York. Copyright © 2024 NBAE. Photo by Brian Babineau/NBAE via Getty Images.

This page, left: *Judith with the Head of Holofernes*, circa 1630, formerly attributed to Charles Mellin. Digital image by Web Gallery of Art. Private collection. Flipped from the original.

DAWN WITH THE HEAD OF EVERYONE

Another page, another decapitation, this time Perseus showing off the head of the slain Gorgon Medusa. I picked this comparison for two more elementary reasons. First, the vanquishing of an opponent, as UConn entered the championship game having won 15 straight but fell 64–49 to a dominant South Carolina squad.

And second, the matching of Medusa's head and guts to the net. The "guts" were the most important factor in picking which version of Perseus and Medusa I went with. My local version, Antonio Canova's at the nearby Metropolitan Museum of Art, is stunning in its own right, but it doesn't have the entrails and is at a slightly different angle.

It's a fitting moment for the best coach in the women's game, as Staley continues to vanquish the opposition with each subsequent season.

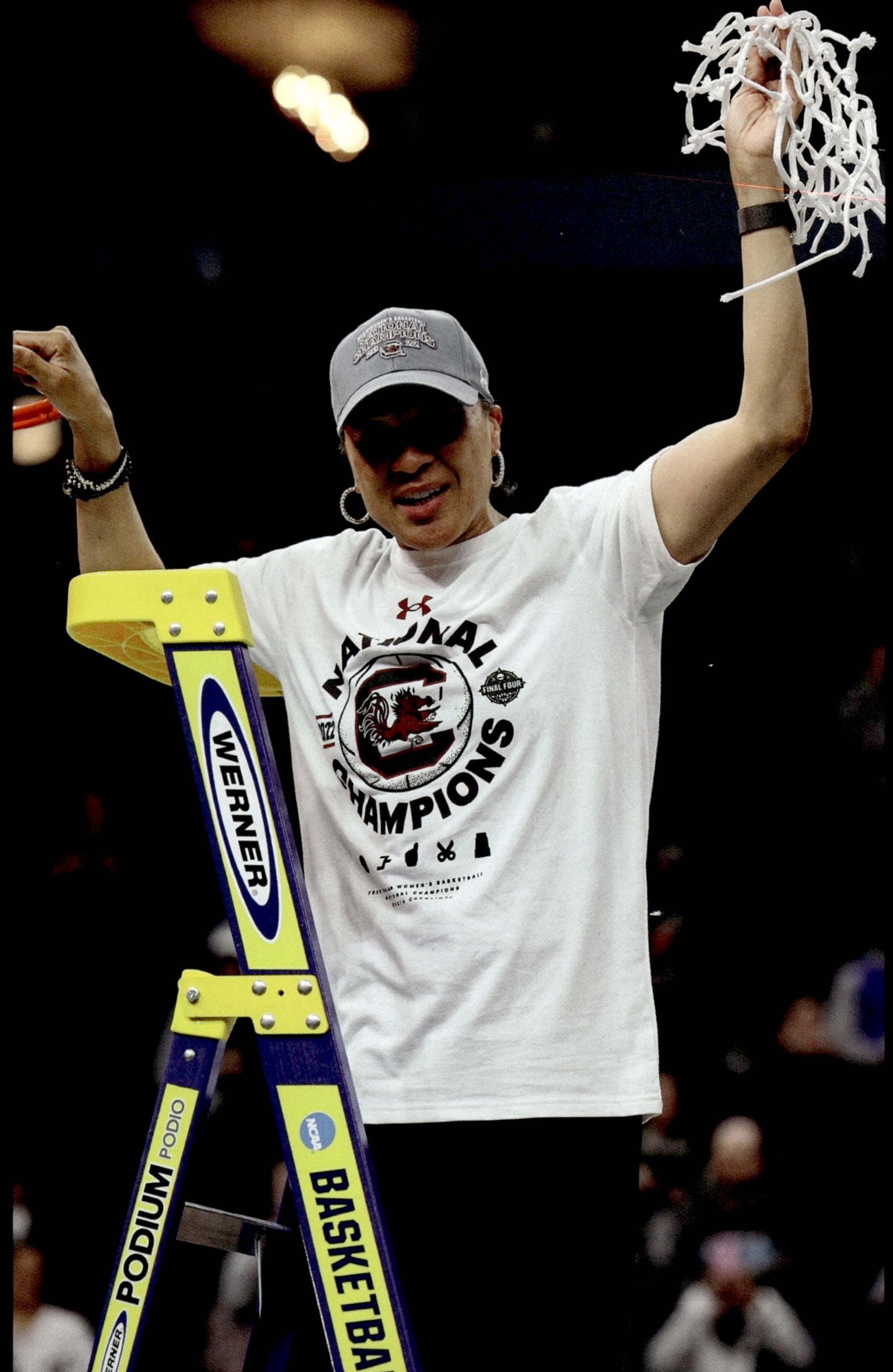

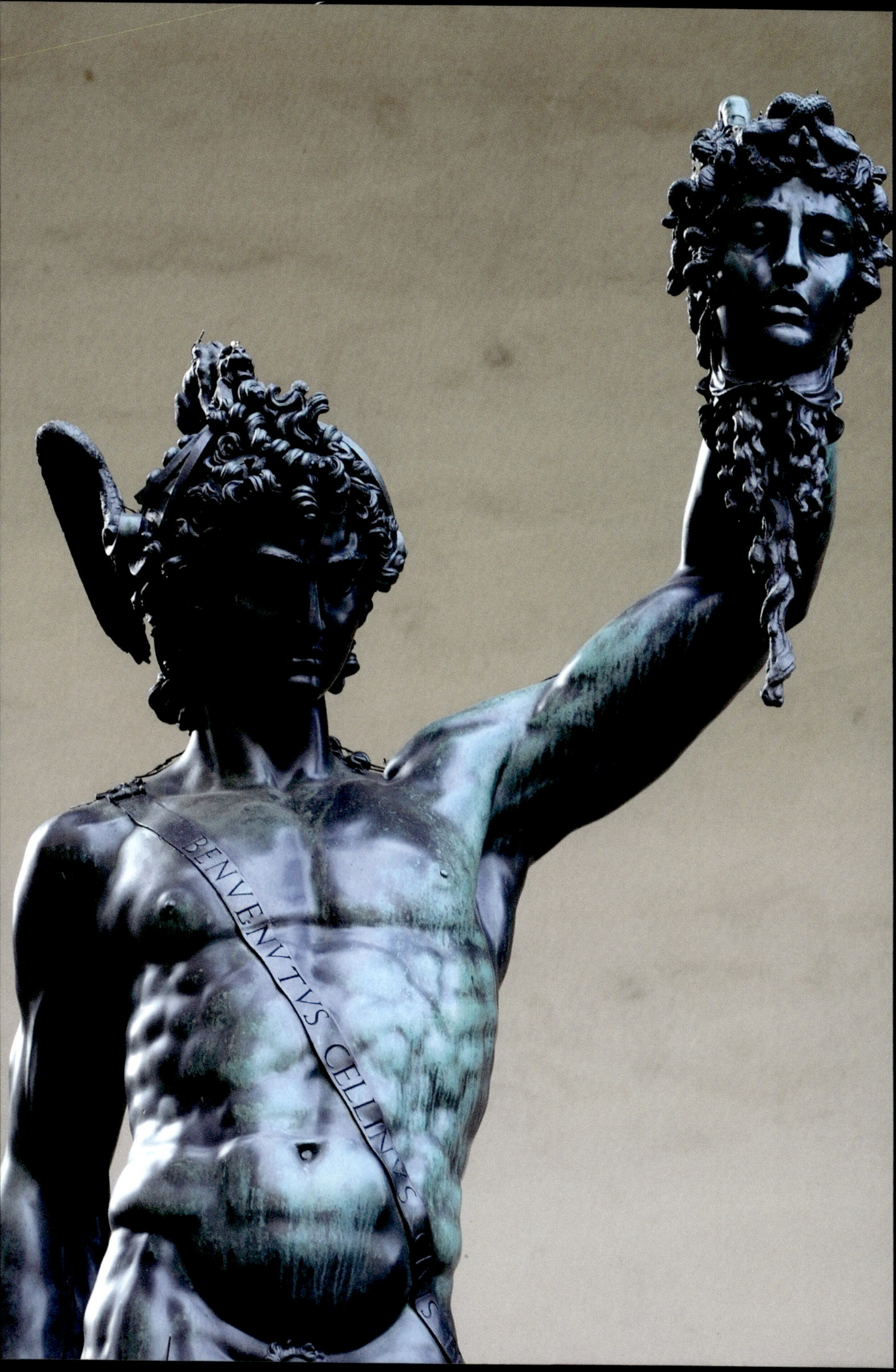

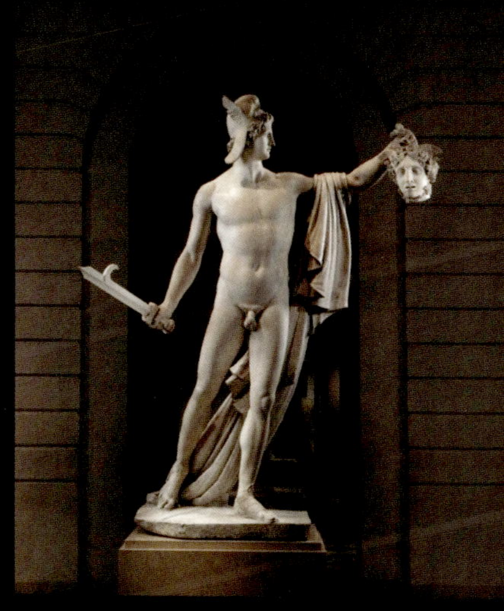

Opposite page: Head coach Dawn Staley of the South Carolina Gamecocks cuts down the net after her team defeats the UConn Huskies 64–49 during the 2022 Division I NCAA Women's Basketball National Championship game at Target Center on April 3, 2022, in Minneapolis, Minnesota. Photo by Andy Lyons/Getty Images.

This page, left: *Perseus with the Head of Medusa* (detail), 1545–54, Benvenuto Cellini. Digital image by Livioandronico. Loggia dei Lanzi.

This page, top: *Perseus with the Head of Medusa*, 1804–6, Antonio Canova. Metropolitan Museum of Art.

PAIGE PAINTS A PICTURE

Paige Bueckers, an artist on and off the court.

Left: Paige Bueckers (#5) of the UConn Huskies looks on prior to a game between the Huskies and the USC Trojans in the Elite Eight round of the NCAA Women's Basketball Tournament at Moda Center on April 1, 2024, in Portland, Oregon. Photo by Soobum Im/Getty Images.

Right: *Self Portrait*, circa 1532–1625, attributed to Sofonisba Anguissola. Digital image by Artvee. Private collection.

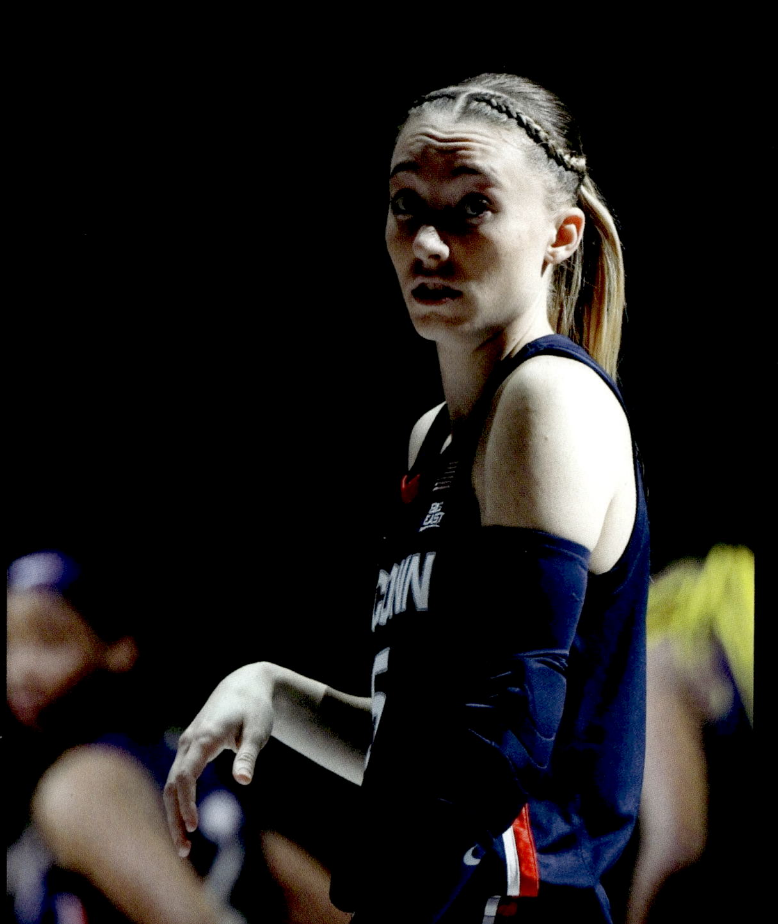

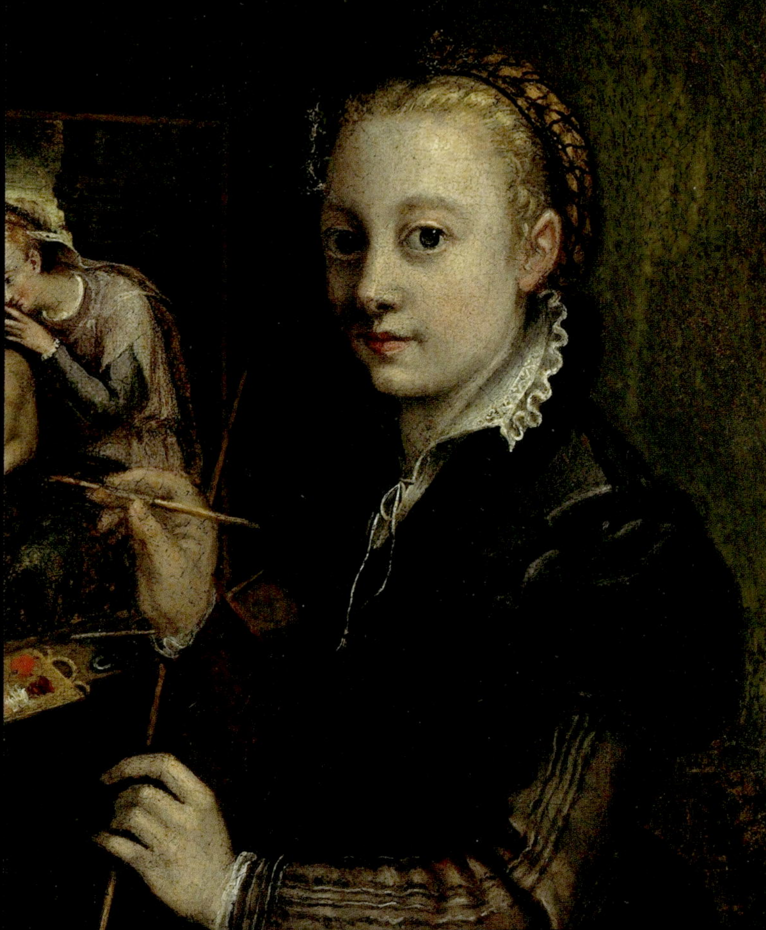

AN ANGEL APPEARS

You could fill a novel with the discourse this moment caused at the time and support a trilogy with the subsequent fallout, but for the sake of time (and sanity), I'll just let the image do the talking (but also point out that Angel is represented by an angel!).

Left: LSU's Angel Reese (#10) taunting Iowa's Caitlin Clark (#22) and pointing to her ring finger after winning the championship game vs. Iowa at American Airlines Arena Dallas, Texas, April 2, 2023. Photo by Greg Nelson/Sports Illustrated via Getty Images.

Right: *The Inspiration of Saint Matthew* (detail), circa 1602, Caravaggio. San Luigi dei Francesi. Image rotated from the original.

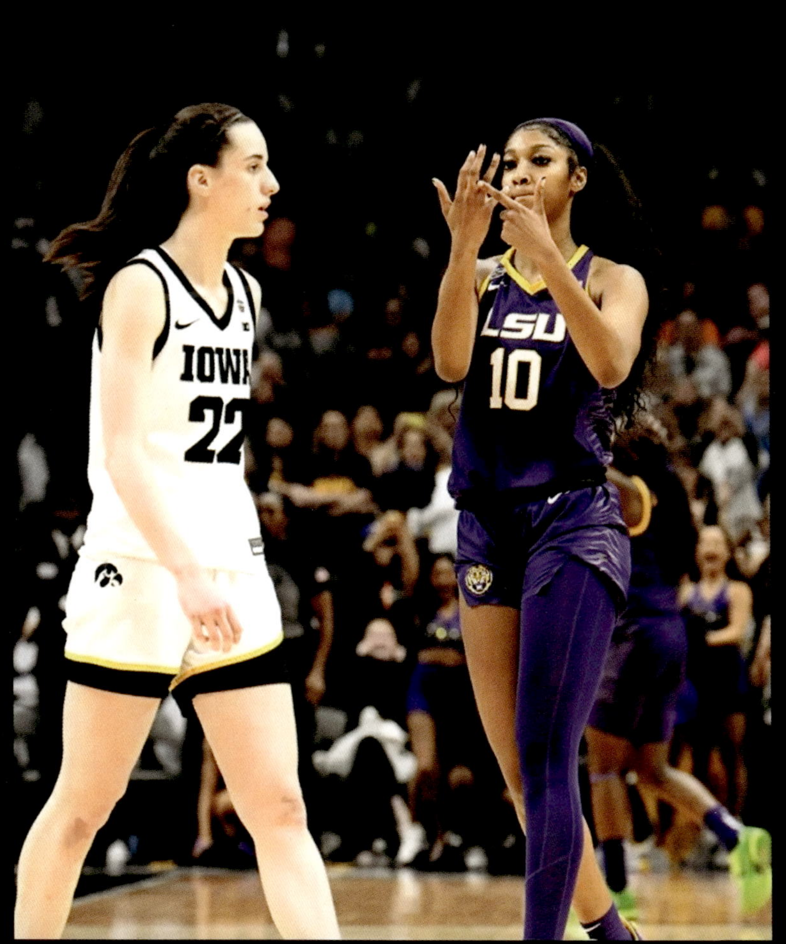

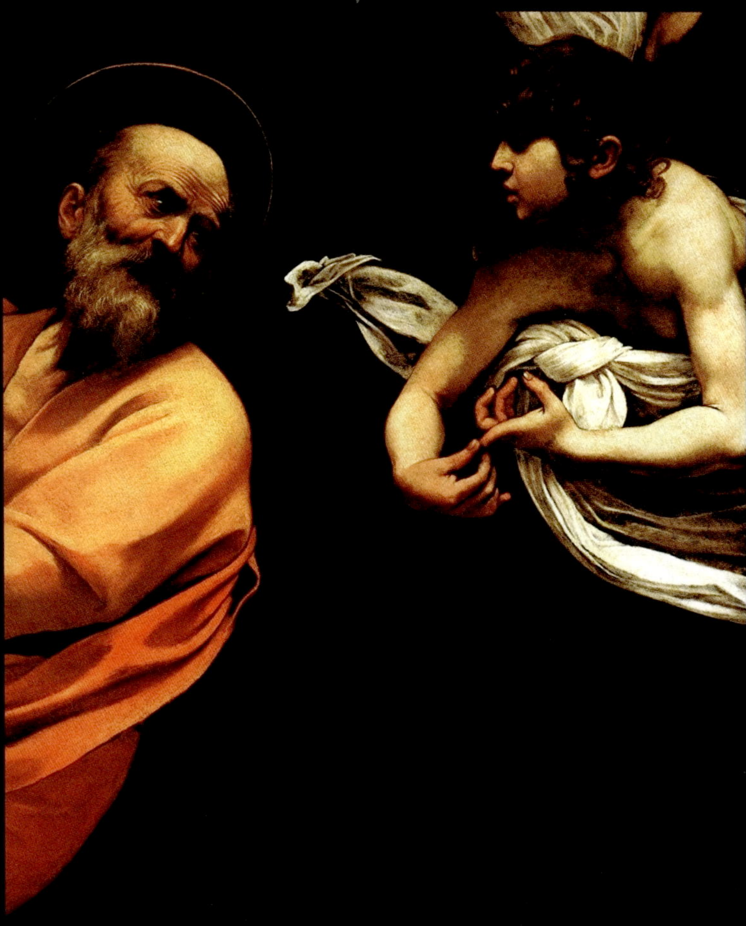

GOOD TO THE LAST DROP

Though I've been able to feature my teams (Knicks, Liberty, Giants, Yankees, Predators, Tottenham, Gotham FC, and Vandy Sports) and their various—albeit sparser than I'd hope for—successes over the years, this is the first time I was able to use a photo from a championship I was able to witness live (thanks for taking me, Lauren Dwyer!). I felt this amazing snap by Russ Steinberg perfectly captured my emotions in the moment: The oversized bottle represents the massive release of pent-up frustration, of which there has been much over the years for the Liberty. The skeleton as the trophy shows that we should cherish every last drop, lest we never experience success

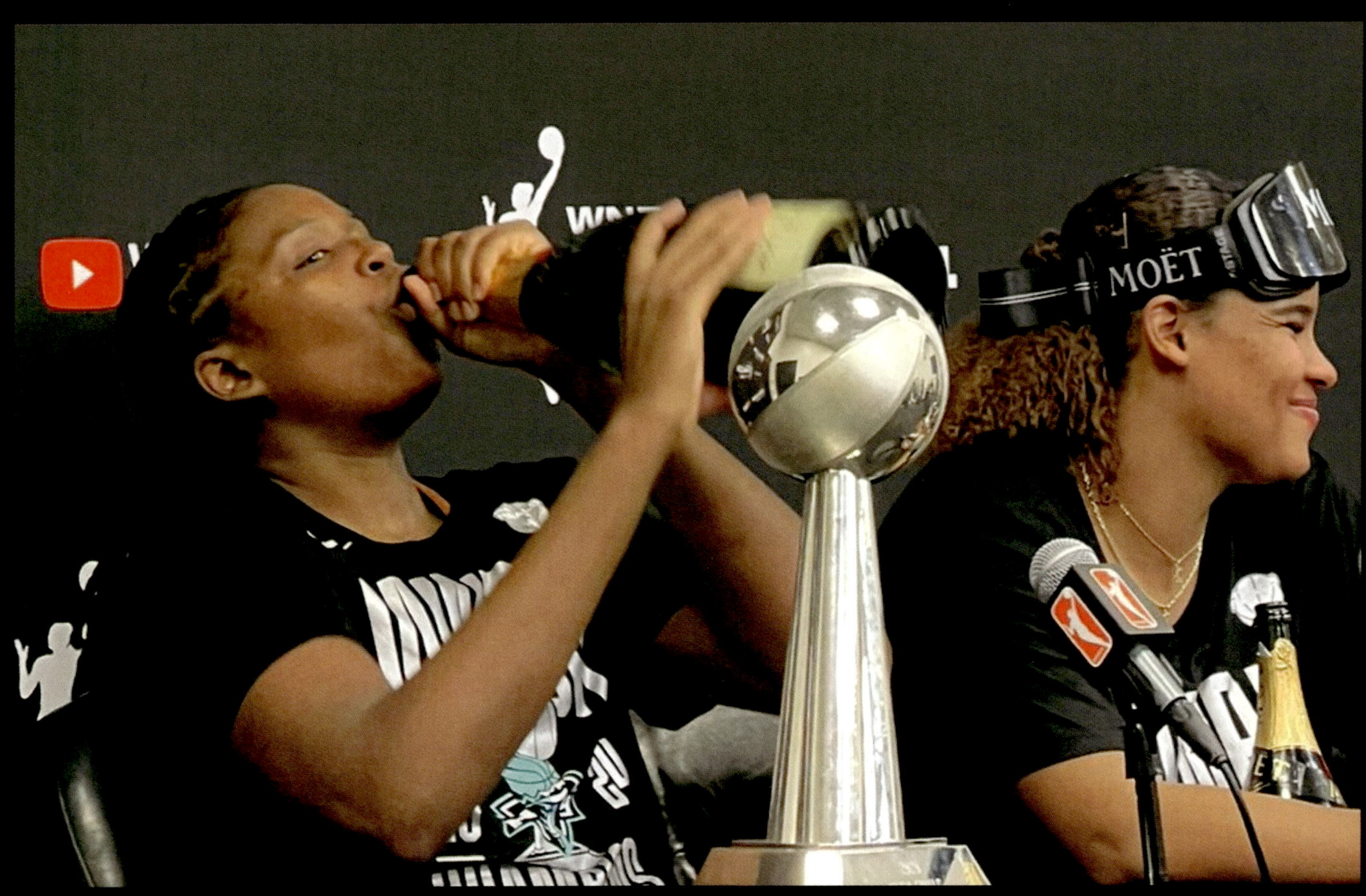

again, as death is always lurking. Given how fleeting postseason success has been across my fandom, it's probably advice I should heed.

Opposite page: Jonquel Jones celebrating the New York Liberty's 2024 WNBA championship win. Photo by Russ Steinberg (@Russ_Steinberg).

This page: *The Last Drop* (detail), circa 1639, Judith Leyster. Digital image by Google Arts & Culture. Philadelphia Museum of Art.

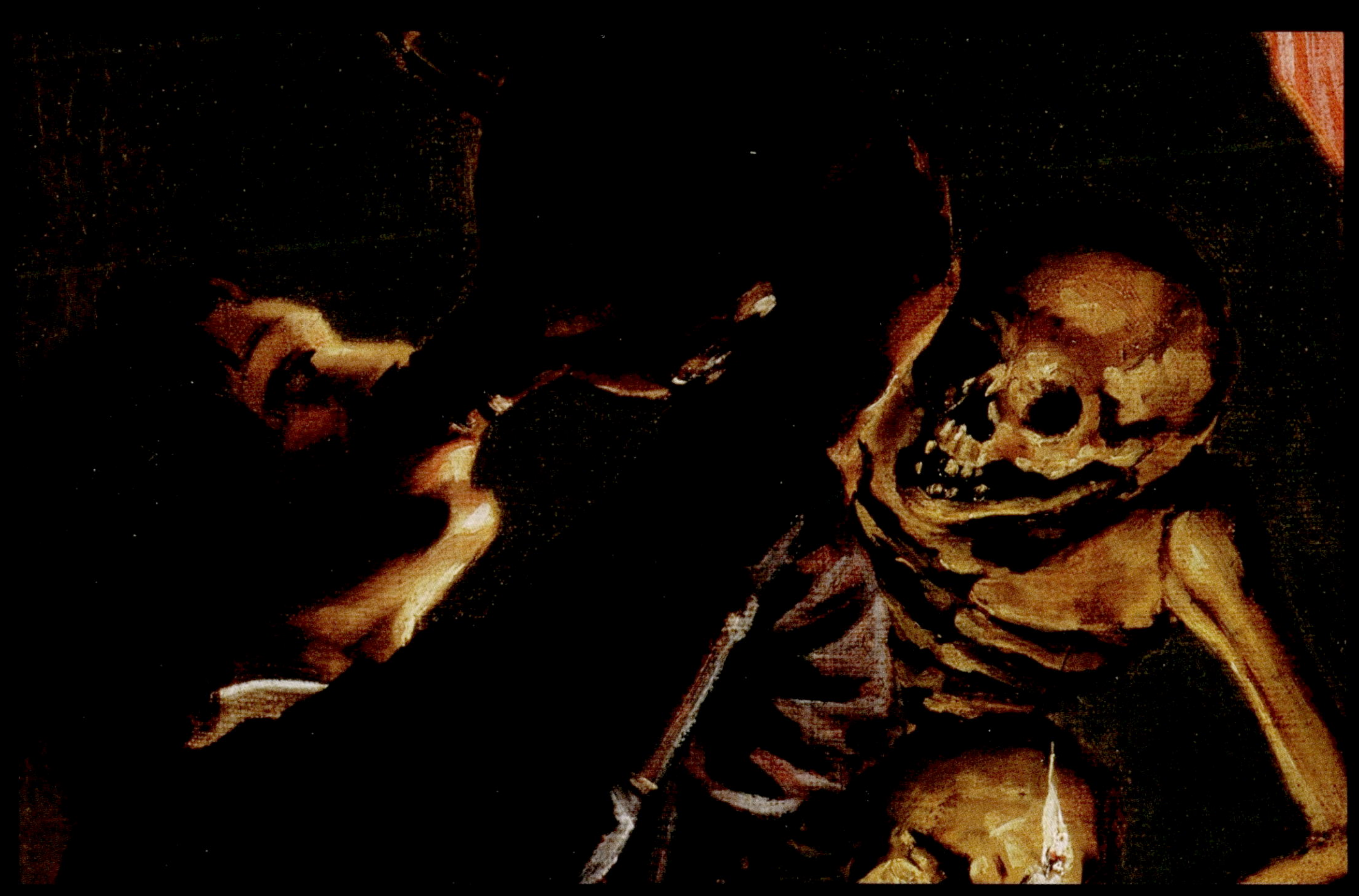

WINGED VICTORY

Niké of Samothrace, or *Winged Victory,* is one of the more recognizable sculptures in the world and is often included in Art History 101 textbooks. Originally a votive offering discovered in 1863 on the island of Samothrace, it has sat prominently at the top of the main staircase in the Louvre since 1884. Overpowering and sweeping with grace, the sculpture depicts the goddess Niké atop a ship, likely at sea, in a similar pose as that of Dee Brown as he flew past an ocean of onlookers at the 1990 Slam Dunk Contest. It's an iconic Nat Butler shot, from the only angle to truly capture Brown steering his ship without a head, and with only a wing as his sail. A museum of dunks would have the Dee Brown no-look atop its main staircase, and while I've deployed Niké of Samothrace for other instances, it feels most fitting when alongside its headless brethren.

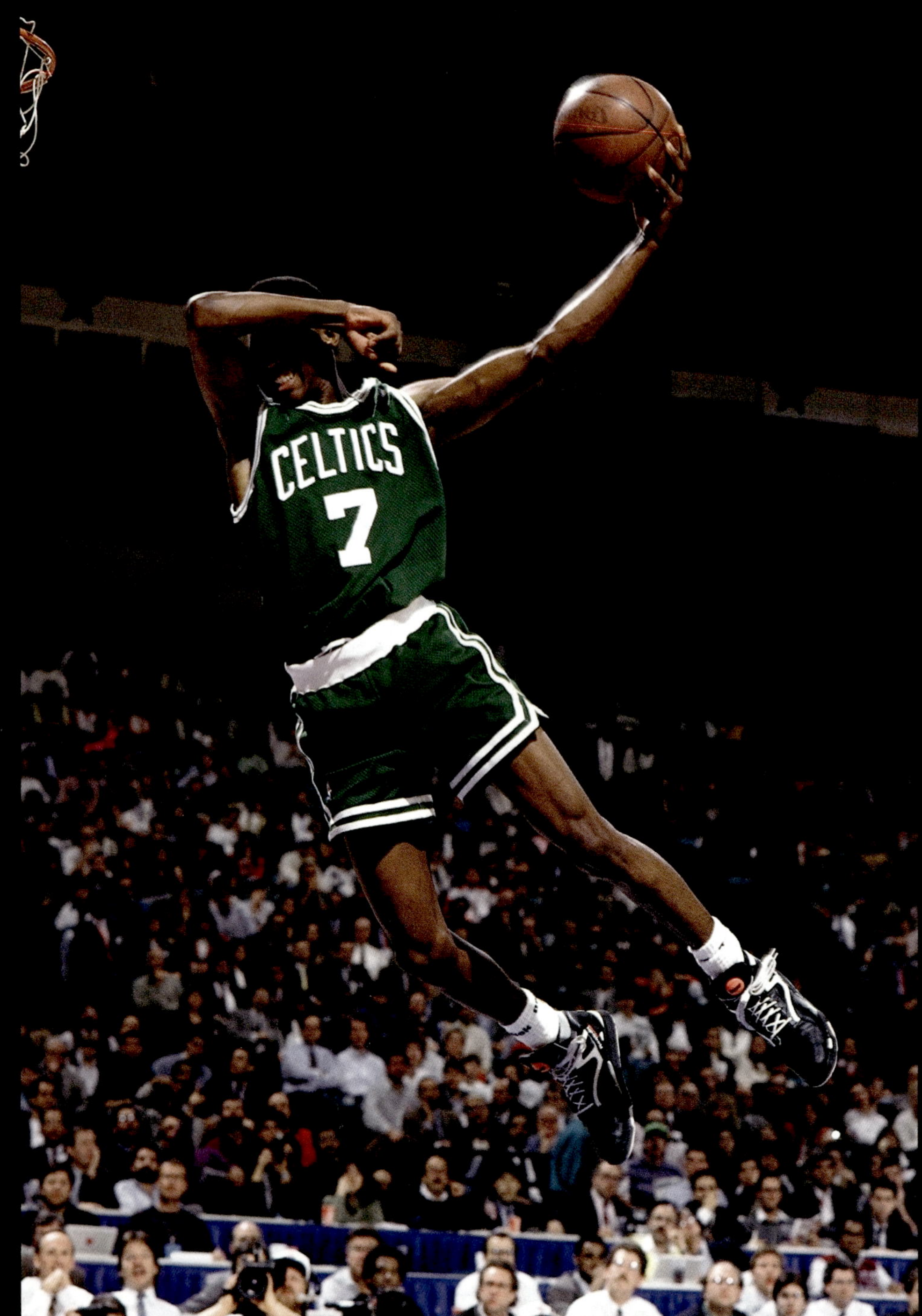

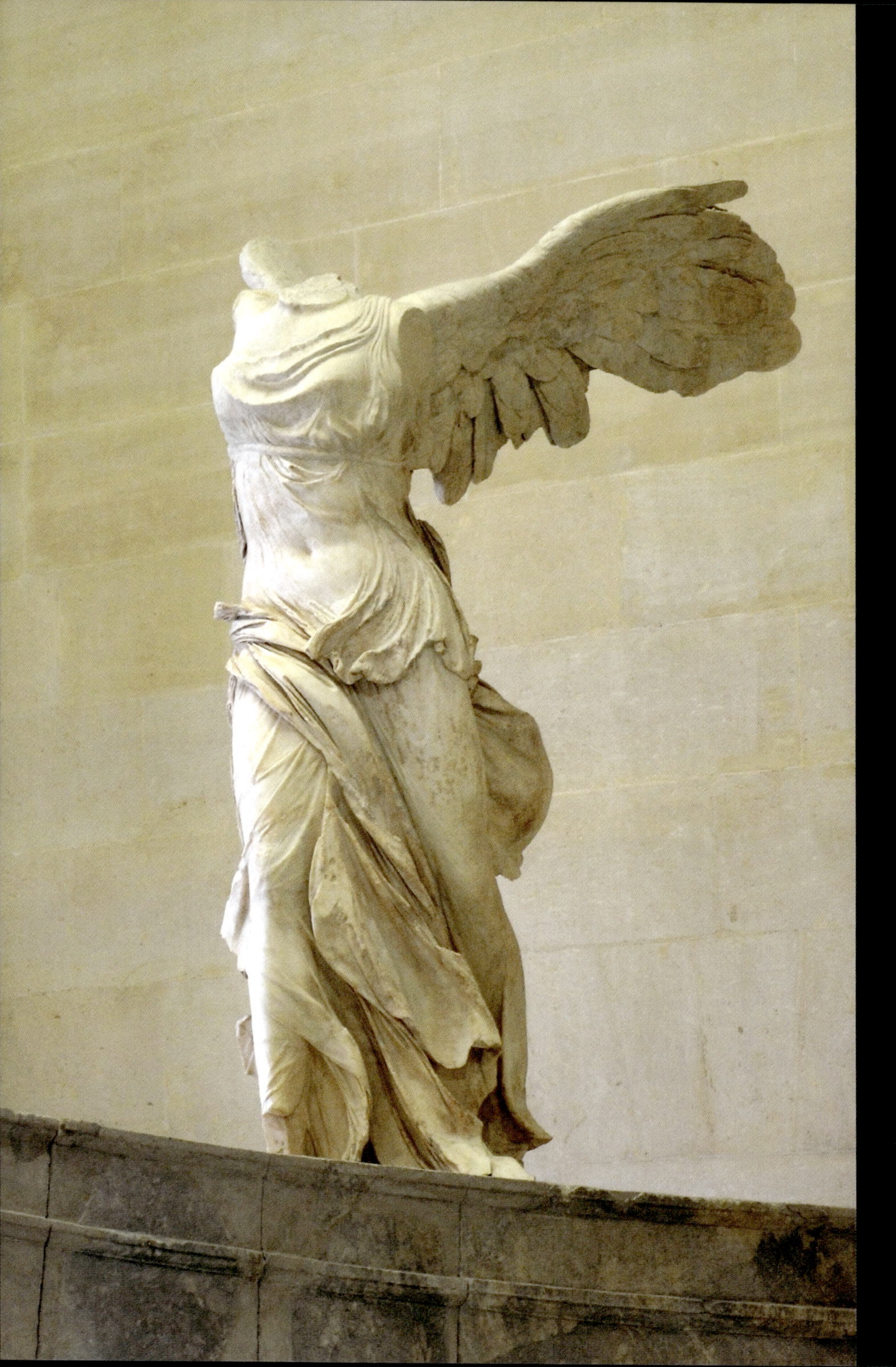

Opposite page: Dee Brown (#7) of the Boston Celtics goes up for a no-look slam dunk in the Slam Dunk Contest during the 1990 NBA All-Star Weekend at the Miami Arena in Miami, Florida. Copyright © 1990 NBAE. Photo by Nathaniel S. Butler/NBAE/Getty Images.

This page: *Winged Victory of Samothrace*, 200–175 BC, unknown artist. Digital image by Shonagon. Louvre Museum.

BRON IN-SEASON TOURNEY

Maybe by the time this book is out, the NBA Cup will have some prestige surrounding it. But it was very much lacking in its first iteration, especially because it was conquered by a franchise that's had more MVPs than anyone else and (at least at the time of writing) the second most championships to only the Celtics. We're knocking everything down a few pegs only to build it fully back up, as I absolutely adore this painting, and I think this LeBron moment matches perfectly.

The figurehead of surrealism, Dalí painted some truly out-there pieces, many of which are known for distortion. Though this painting isn't an everyday scene and has an interesting title, you'd never in a million years guess it's from his catalog. But here it is, in all its basic glory, just like the NBA Cup championship in LeBron and the Lakers' trophy case.

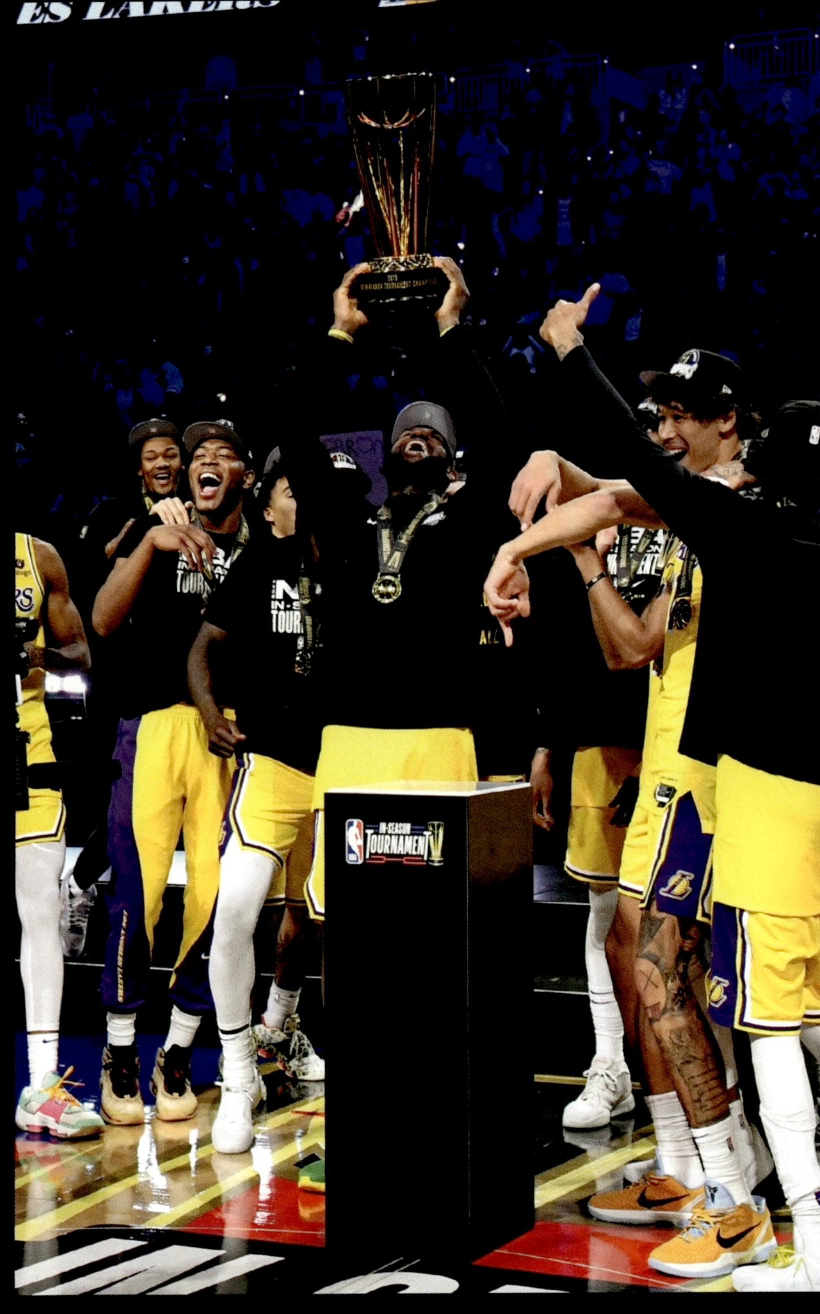

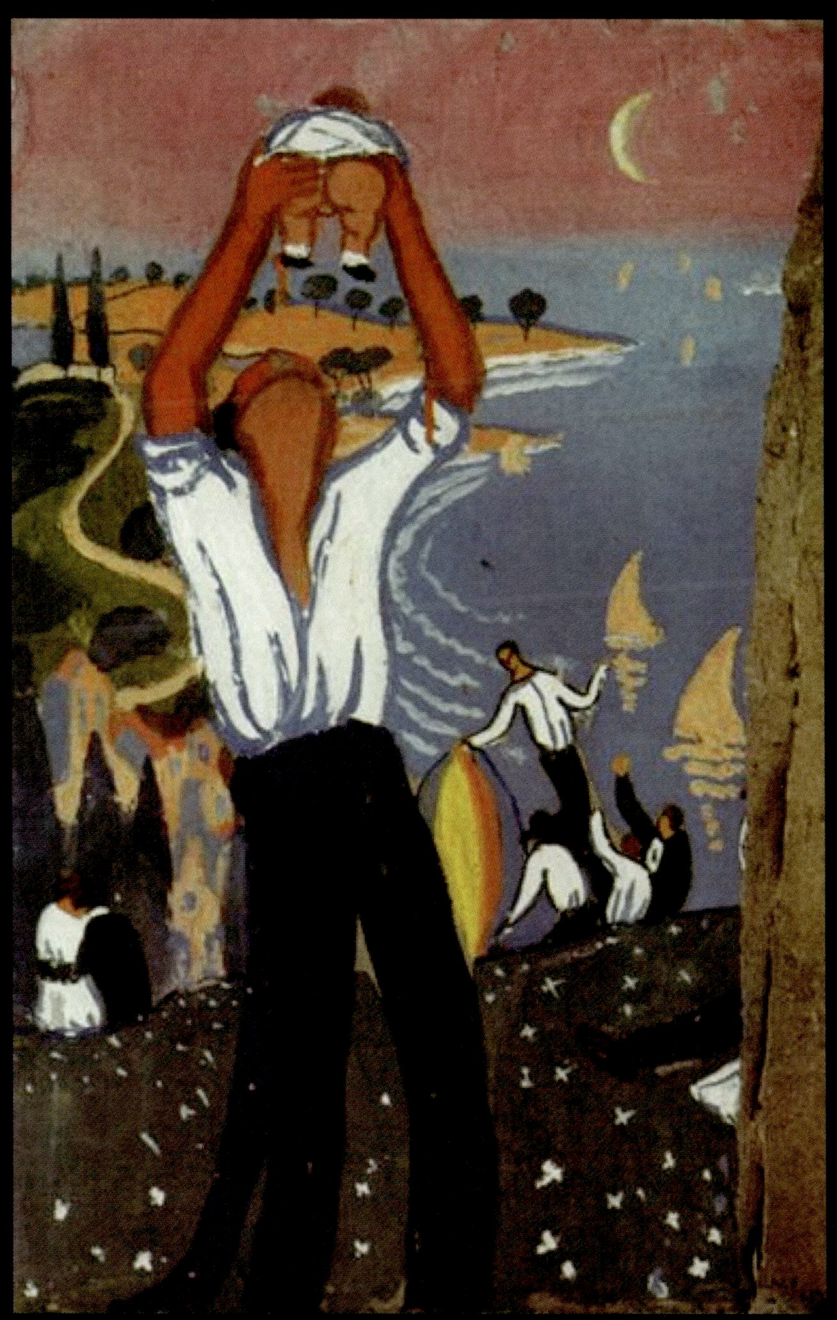

Opposite page: LeBron James (#23) of the Los Angeles Lakers holds the NBA Cup after the In-Season Tournament championship game on December 9, 2023, at T-Mobile Arena in Las Vegas, Nevada. Copyright © 2023 NBAE. Photo by Andrew D. Bernstein/NBAE via Getty Images.

This page: *Man Holding Up a Baby as Though He Were Drinking from a Bottle*, 1921, Salvador Dalí. WikiArt.

SUNSET

As a fellow Jew with ties to Long Island, I've always had Sue Bird atop my list of athletes I root for. After an illustrious career, Bird cemented her legacy as an all-time final—championship trophy. The comparison to the van Gogh here felt fitting, as Bird's ambassadorship for the WNBA and women's sports sowed the landscape for future success, a labor of love we're already reaping the rewards of just a handful of years later.

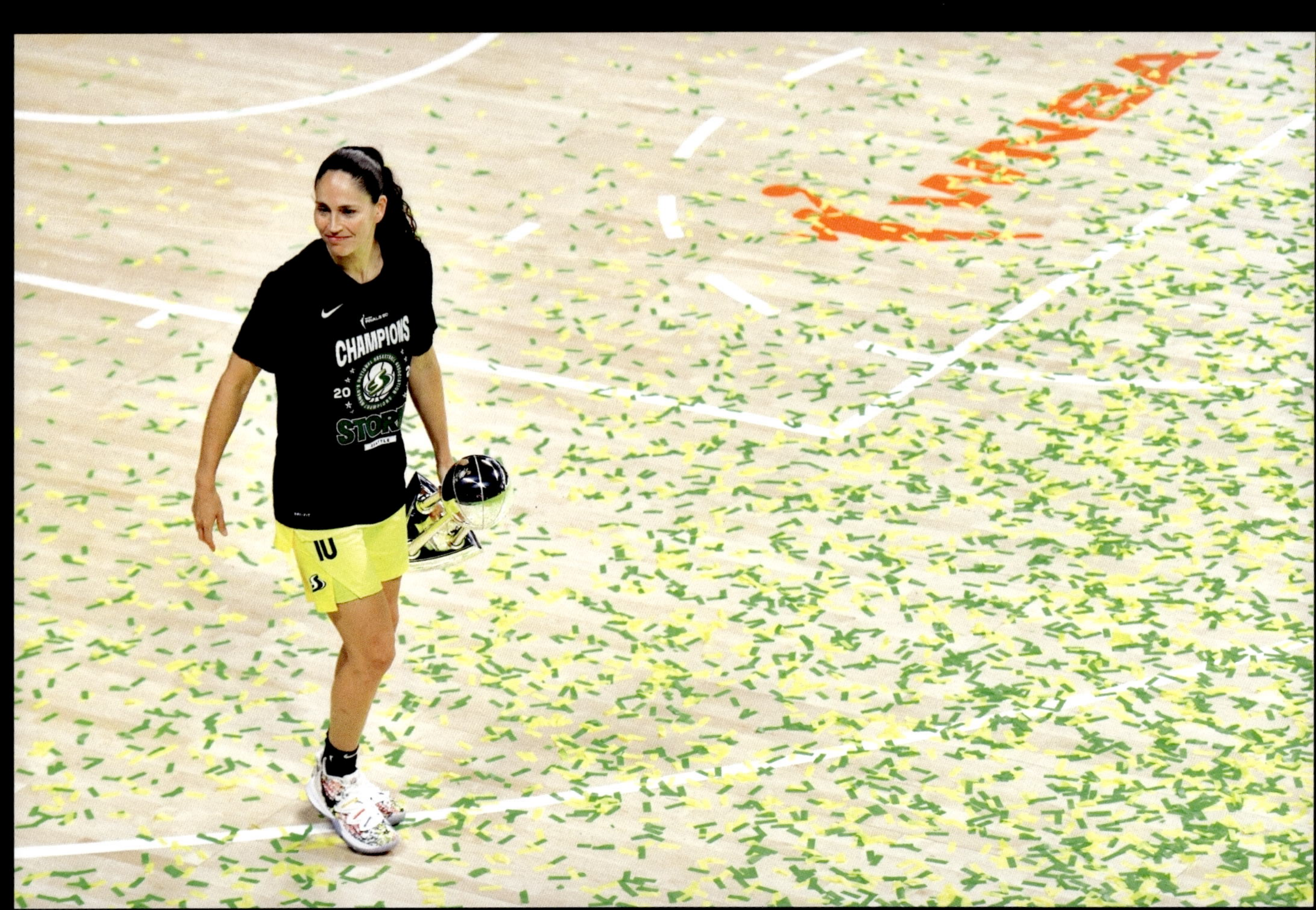

Opposite page: Sue Bird (#10) of the Seattle Storm walks across the court after winning the WNBA Championship following Game 3 of the WNBA Finals against the Las Vegas Aces at Feld Entertainment Center on October 6, 2020, in Palmetto, Florida. Photo by Julio Aguilar/Getty Images.

This page: *The Sower (Sower at Sunset)* (detail), 1888, Vincent van Gogh. Kröller-Müller Museum.

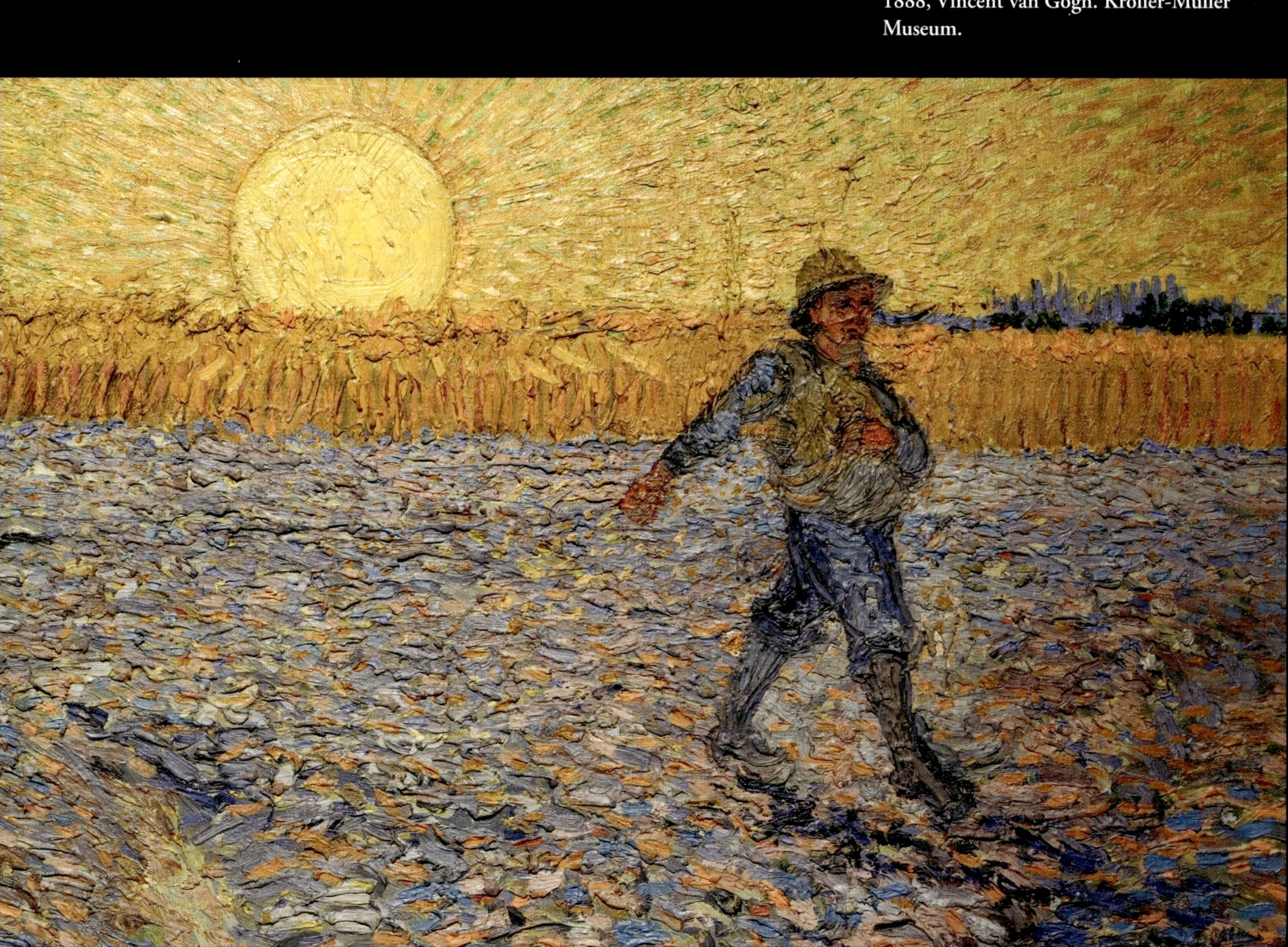

THE A'NNUNCIATION

Some of my favorite matchups have zero connections other than what's present visually. That's the case here, with an added Easter egg that A'ja Wilson and her South Carolina Gamecocks beat the Stanford Cardinal days earlier in the 2017 Women's Final Four. Their unofficial mascot? A tree, represented in Botticelli's *Cestello Annunciation*.

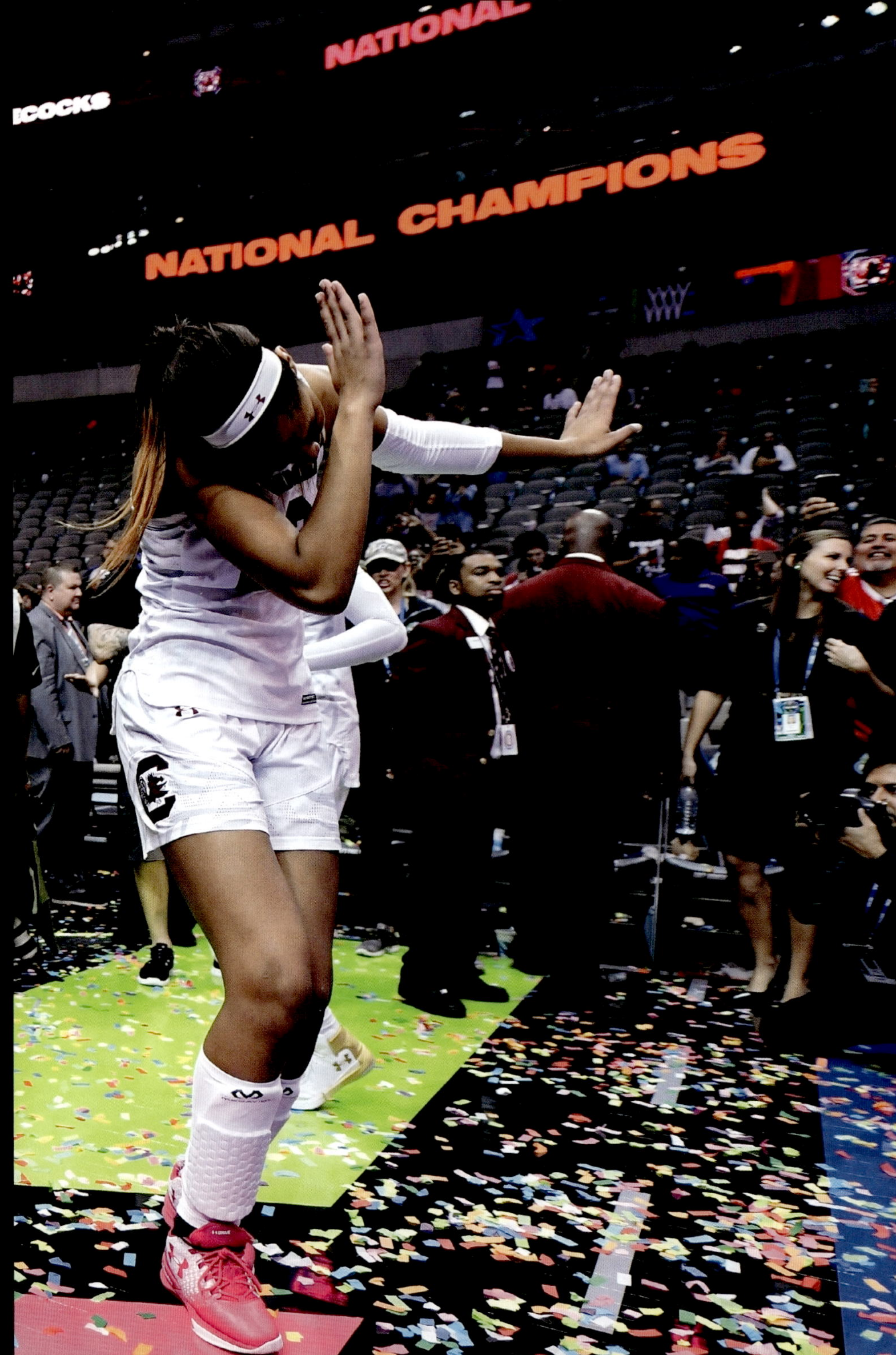

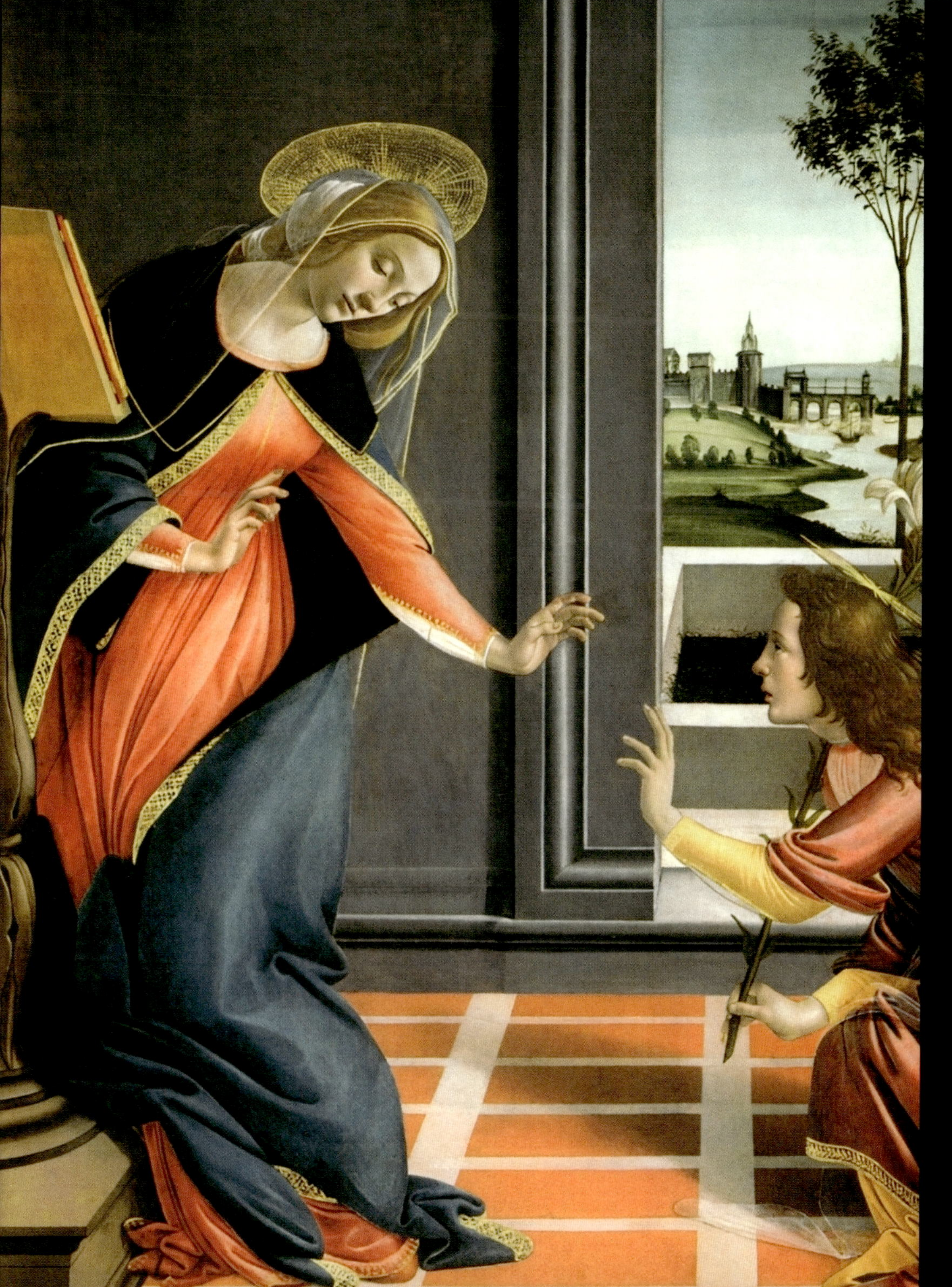

Opposite page: A'ja Wilson (#22) of the South Carolina Gamecocks dabs during the 2017 Women's Final Four at American Airlines Center on April 2, 2017, in Dallas, Texas. Photo by Ben Solomon/ NCAA Photos via Getty Images.

This page: *Cestello Annunciation* (detail), 1489, Sandro Botticelli. Uffizi Gallery. Flipped from the original.

HARDEN FASHION

The NBA's biggest enigma, you could write a novel on James Harden alone. Mercurial, constantly in the news cycle, and toeing the line between fashionable and farcical, he's positioned himself as must-meme TV, and the only one worthy of a page dedicated specifically to fashion.

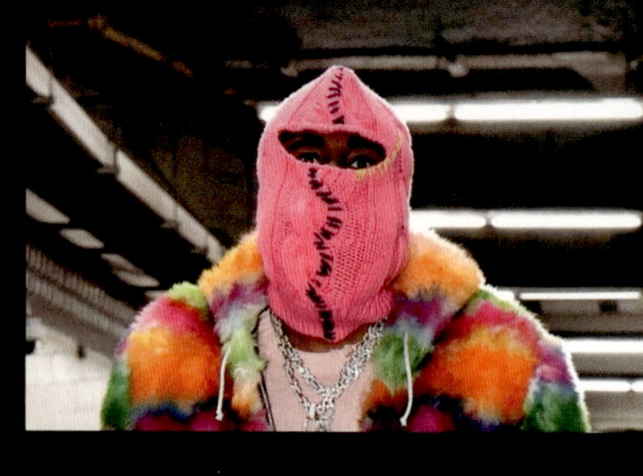

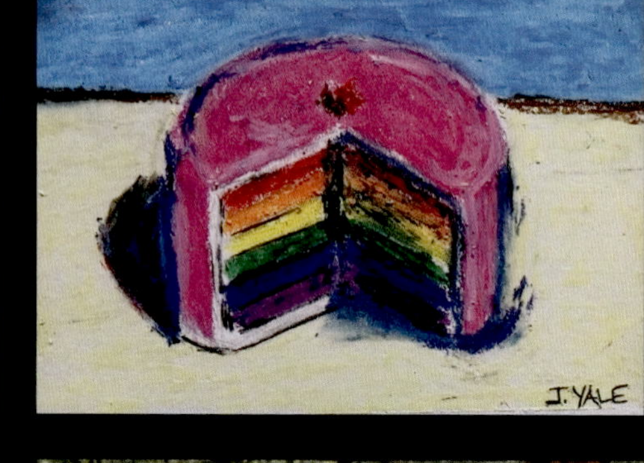

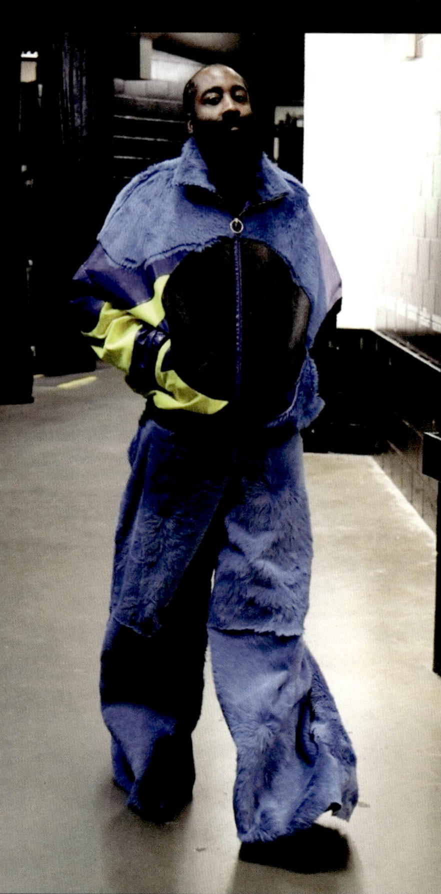

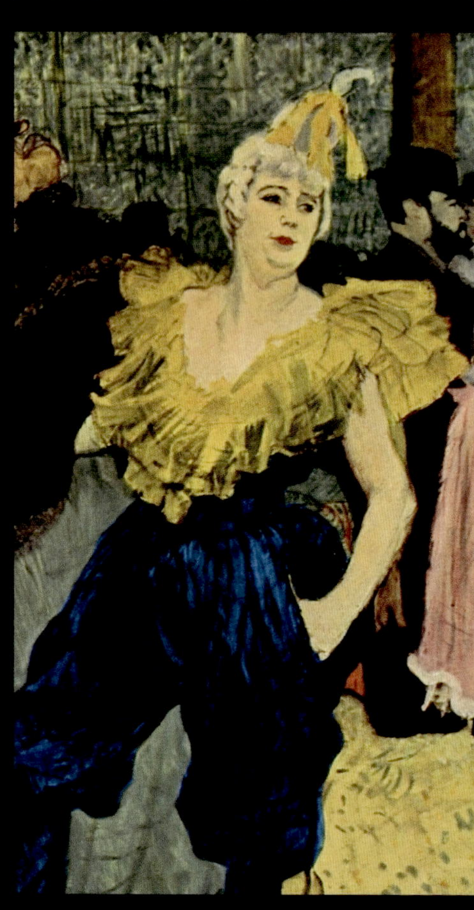

Top left: James Harden (#1) of the Philadelphia 76ers arrives at the arena before the game against the New York Knicks on December 25, 2022, at Madison Square Garden in New York, New York. Copyright © 2022 NBAE. Photo by Nathaniel S. Butler/NBAE via Getty Images.

Top right: *Hommage à Wayne Thiebaud* 2020, Jim Yale, with a special shout-out to Ms. Foran who inspired the piece. Reproduced with permission.

Bottom left: James Harden (#1) of the Philadelphia 76ers arrives at the arena before Round Two, Game 1 of the 2023 NBA Playoffs on May 1, 2023, at TD Garden in Boston, Massachusetts. Copyright © 2023 NBAE. Photo by Brian Babineau/NBAE via Getty Images.

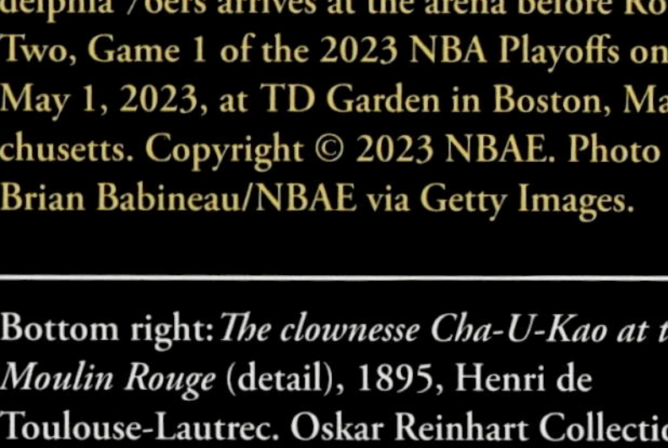

Bottom right: *The clownesse Cha-U-Kao at the Moulin Rouge* (detail), 1895, Henri de Toulouse-Lautrec. Oskar Reinhart Collection.

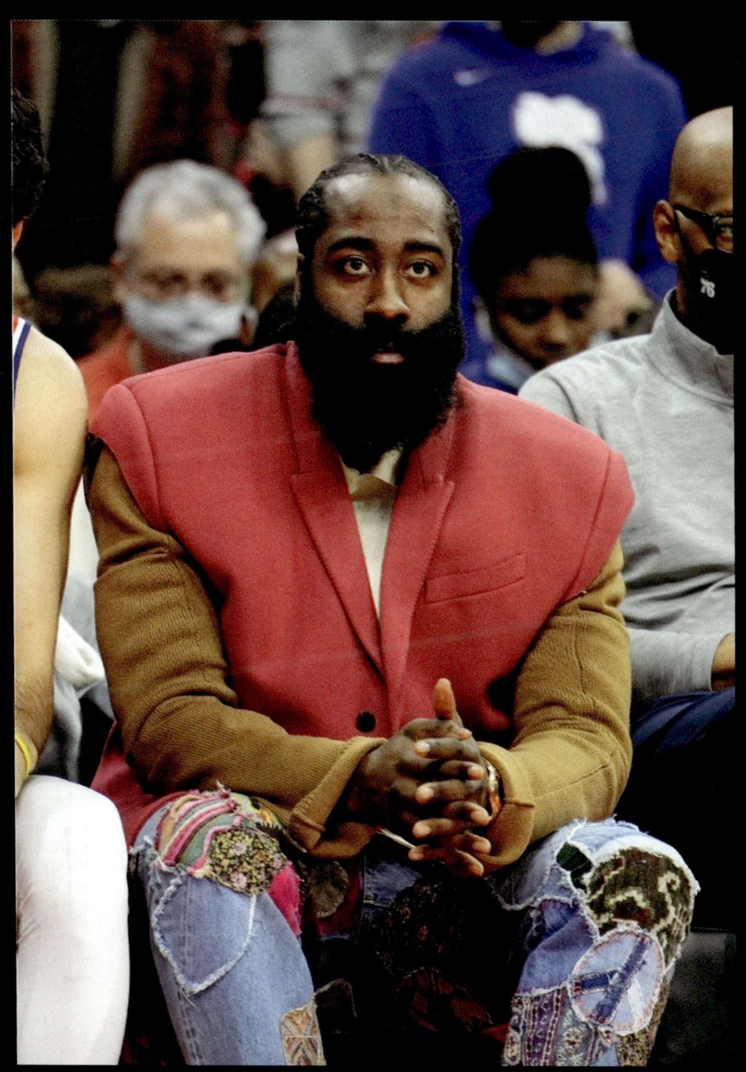

James Harden (#1) of the Philadelphia 76ers looks on during a game against the Boston Celtics on February 15, 2022, at Wells Fargo Center in Philadelphia, Pennsylvania. Copyright © 2022 NBAE. Photo by Jesse D. Garrabrant/NBAE via Getty Images.

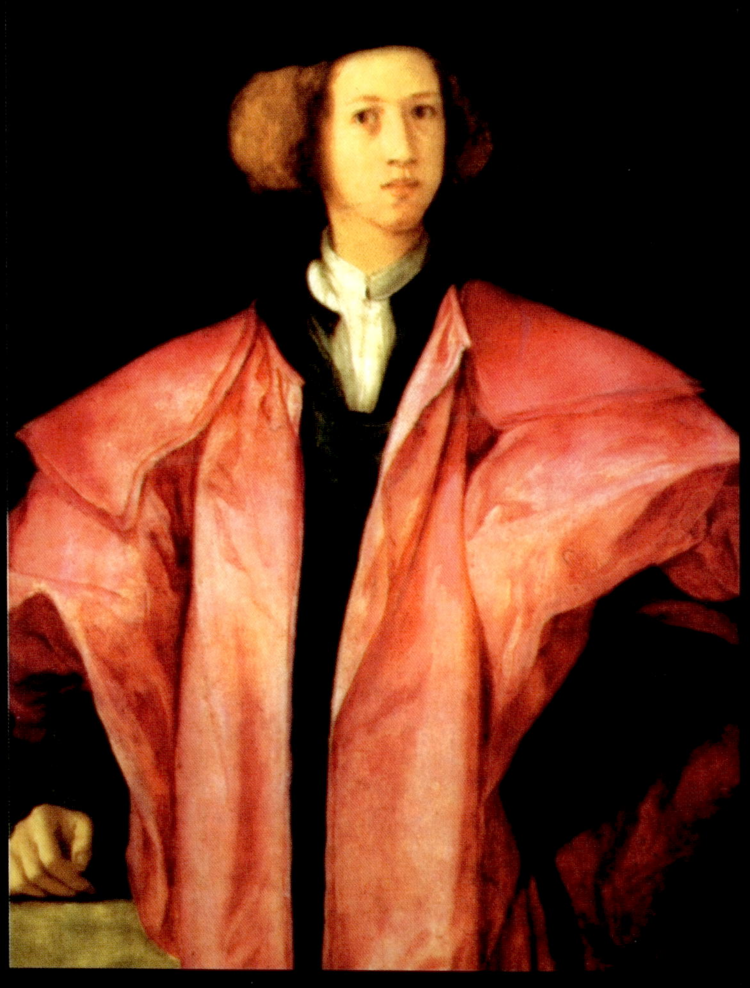

Portrait of a Young Man, 1525–26, Jacopo Pontormo. Digital image by the Yorck Project. Lucca Pinacoteca Civica collection.

AENEAS, ANCHISES, AND ASCANIUS

As the story in the epic poem *The Aeneid* goes, the hero Aeneas leads his family from burning Troy. In Bernini's masterpiece, Aeneas carries his father, Anchises, on his shoulder, with his son, Ascanius, in tow. Anchises holds up a statuette of the Penates, a small sculpture of the gods tasked with protecting the Roman home.

Dirk Nowitzki did all the heavy lifting for the 2011 Mavericks, and the physical resemblance to Anchises is uncanny. You can also perfectly tie the Penates to the Bill Russell NBA Finals MVP trophy.

Dirk also ushered in a new era of extremely versatile big men, so it feels fitting to use a sculpture that, depending on how you crop it, can tell a variety of stories. Another angle proved to have the perfect optical alignment to this viral photo by Benn Sieu of Giannis Antetokounmpo being held back by a coach while his brother Thanasis looks on (building in an additional layer of family—Dom Toretto would be proud).

I've yet to use a version that shows the youngster Ascanius, but rest assured that his time will come, as I love celebrating this Bernini sculpture and all its storytelling abilities.

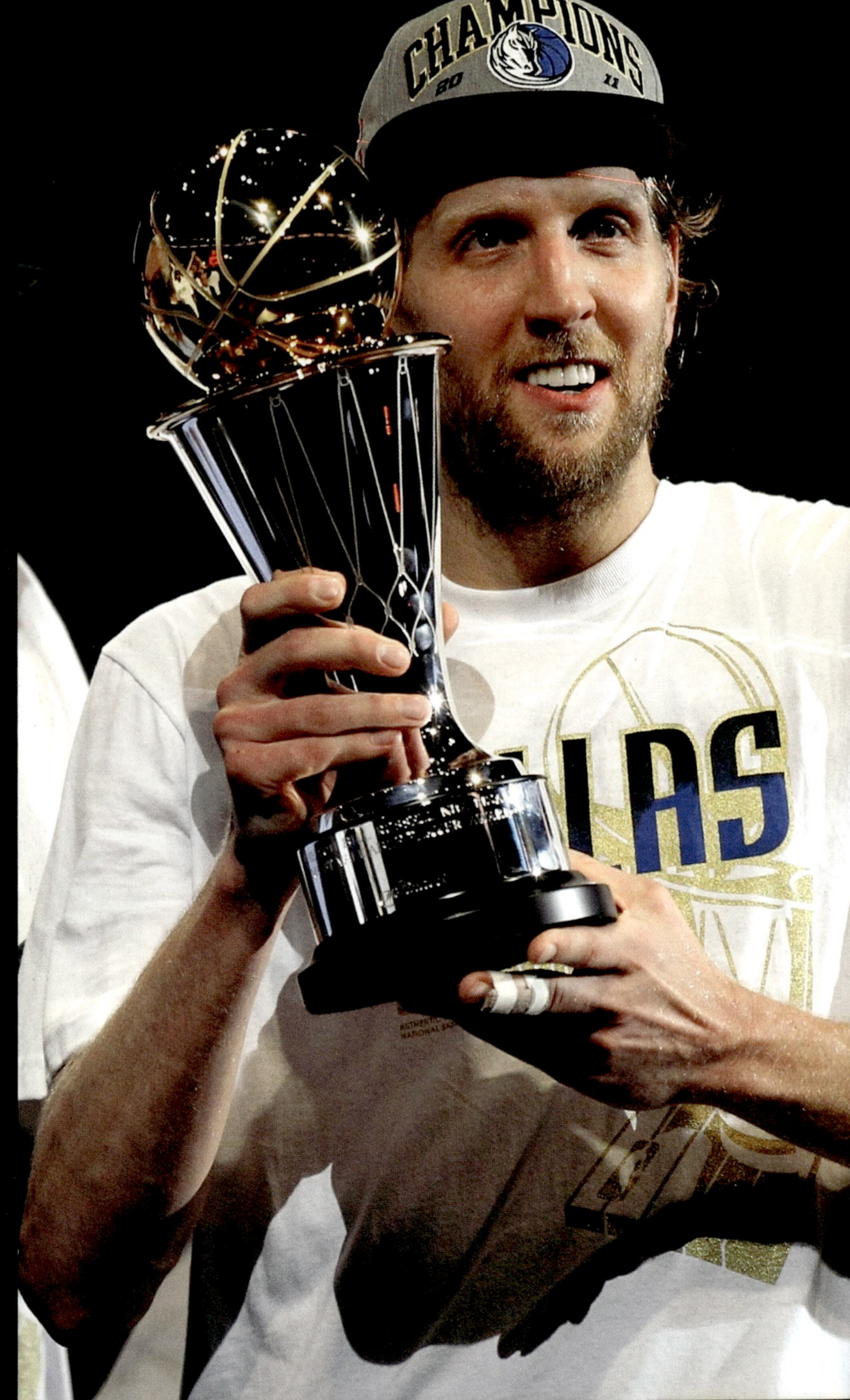

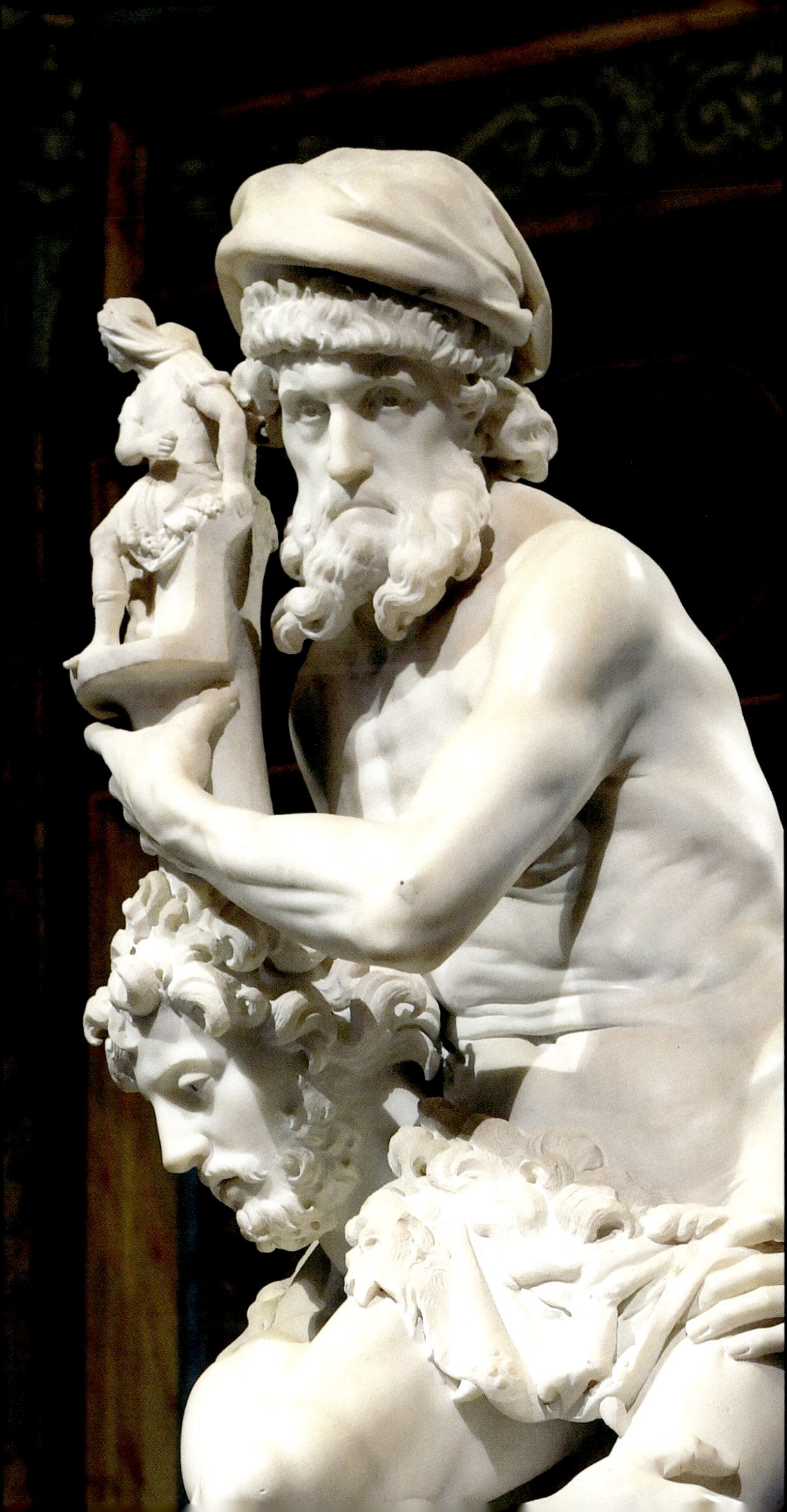

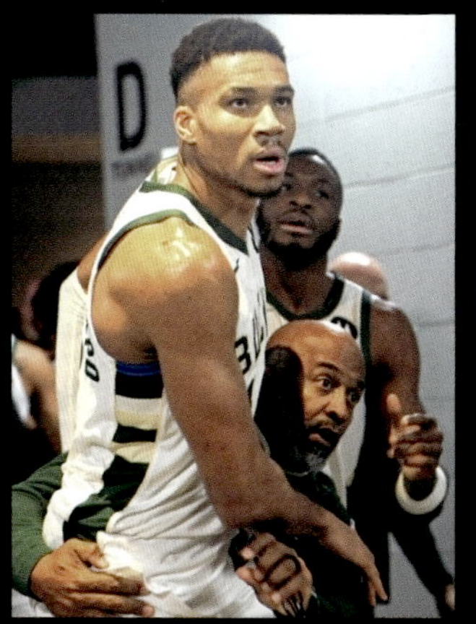

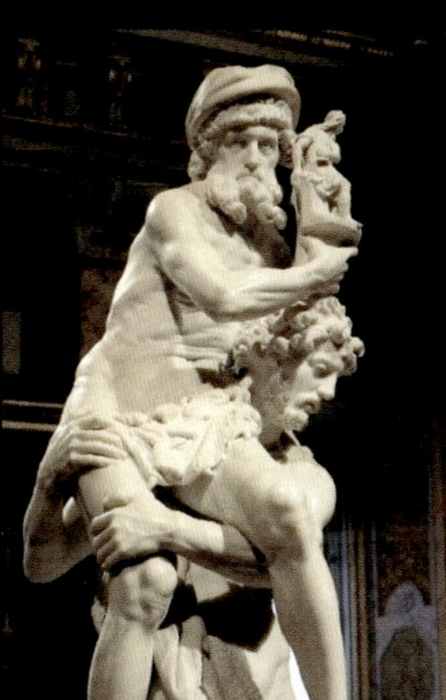

Opposite page: Dirk Nowitzki (#41) of the Dallas Mavericks holds up the Bill Russell NBA Finals MVP trophy after Bill Russell presented it to him following the Mavericks' 105–95 win against the Miami Heat in Game 6 of the 2011 NBA Finals at American Airlines Arena on June 12, 2011, in Miami, Florida. Photo by Ronald Martinez/Getty Images.

Above, left: Milwaukee Bucks forward Giannis Antetokounmpo (#34) is restrained by a coach outside the Indiana Pacers locker room after the game at Fiserv Forum on December 13, 2023, in Milwaukee, Wisconsin. Copyright © Benny-Sieu-Imagn Images. Photo by Benny Sieu-Imagn Images.

This page: *Aeneas, Anchises and Ascanius*, 1618, Gian Lorenzo Bernini. Galleria Borghese. Flipped from the original in above, right.

THE EN POINTE GOD

Here we see a classic example of what the people truly want: ArtButtMakeItSports.

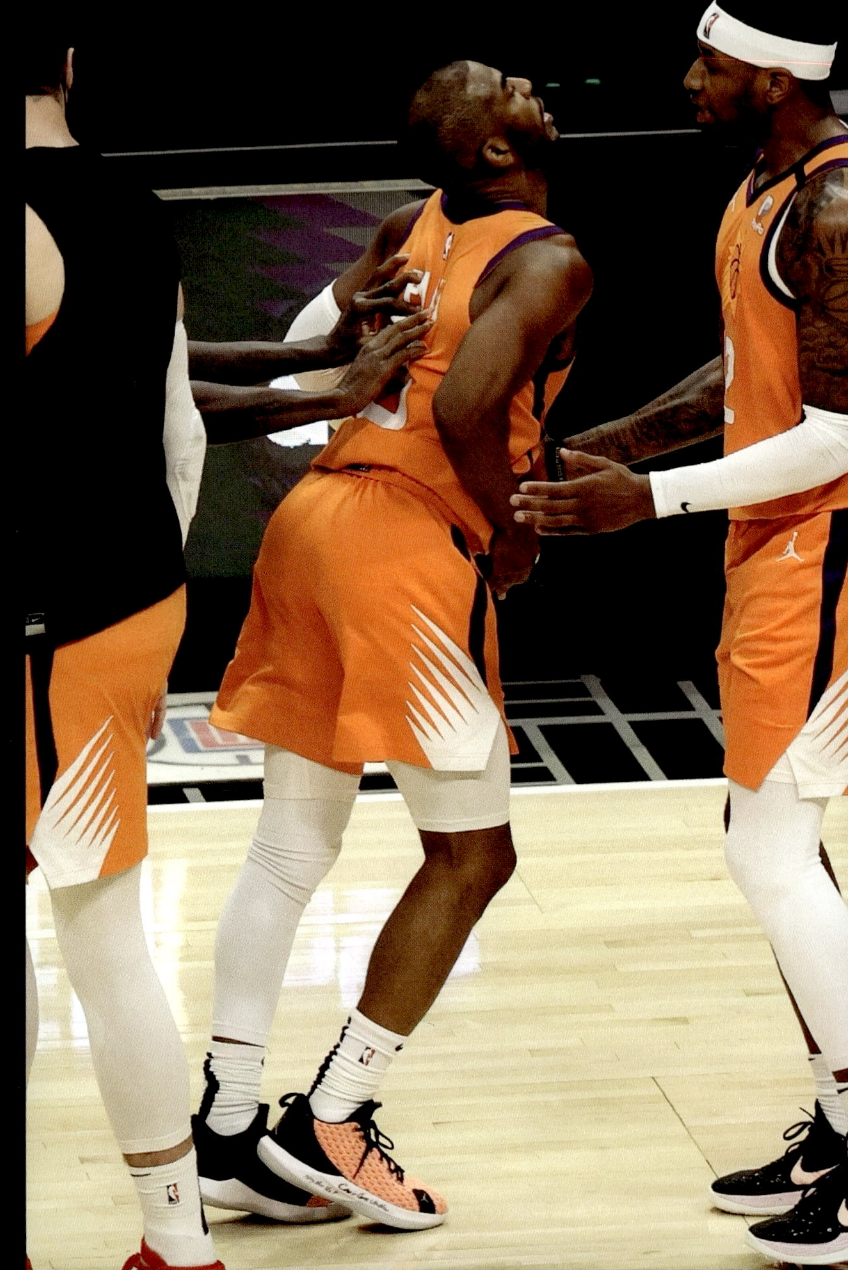

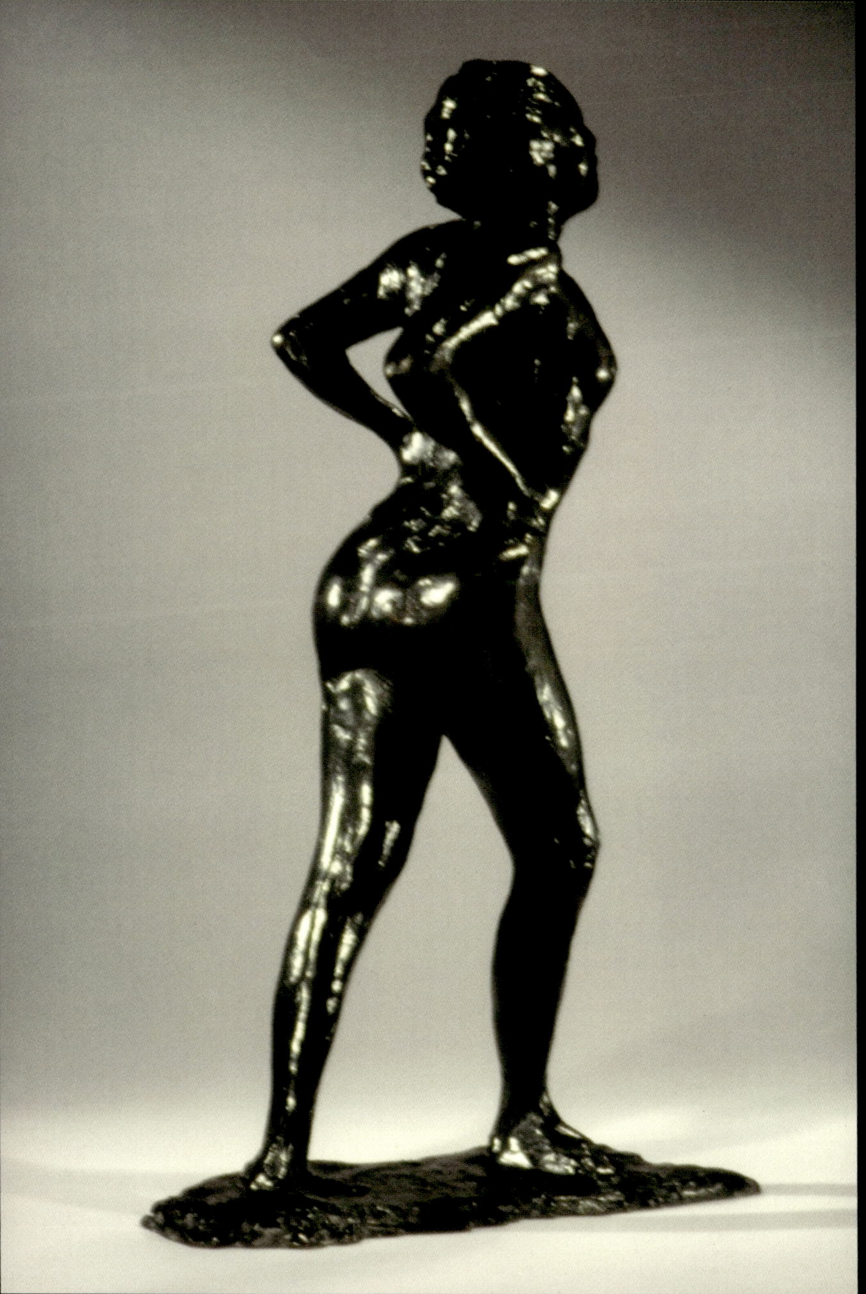

Opposite page: Patrick Beverley (#21) of the LA Clippers pushes Chris Paul (#3) of the Phoenix Suns during the second half of Game 6 of the Western Conference Finals at the Staples Center on June 30, 2021, in Los Angeles, California. Photo by Ronald Martinez/Getty Images.

This page: *Dancer at Rest, Hands Behind Her Back, Right Leg Forward*, modeled circa 1895, cast 1920, Edgar Degas. Metropolitan Museum of Art.

BASEBALL AND SOFTBALL

Baseball is by far my favorite sport, which might surprise you if you follow the account, given the dearth of posts compared to those of basketball, football, and even soccer. There are a few factors behind this:

1. Baseball is spread out, and often the best posts happen when multiple people are clustered. A majority of television angles and photos concentrate on a single player, which rarely leads to something meme-able.
2. Movements aren't nearly as dynamic as in other sports. Outside of the occasional diving play, most of baseball takes place on two feet, whereas folks are flying on any given play in football and are often airborne in basketball.
3. I don't get tagged in nearly as many baseball photos as I do other sports. The NFL will always be no. 1, 2, and 3 when it comes to my audience. Additionally, basketball and soccer are both global. MLB is—with the exception of a few international pockets like Japan—pretty strictly American.

It's not all negative, though, as I'm sitting on a handful of great paintings just begging to be turned into baseball pairings, including this classic Bronzino from the National Gallery in London. And when a baseball post does drop, it tends to be higher quality, because of the built-in limitations.

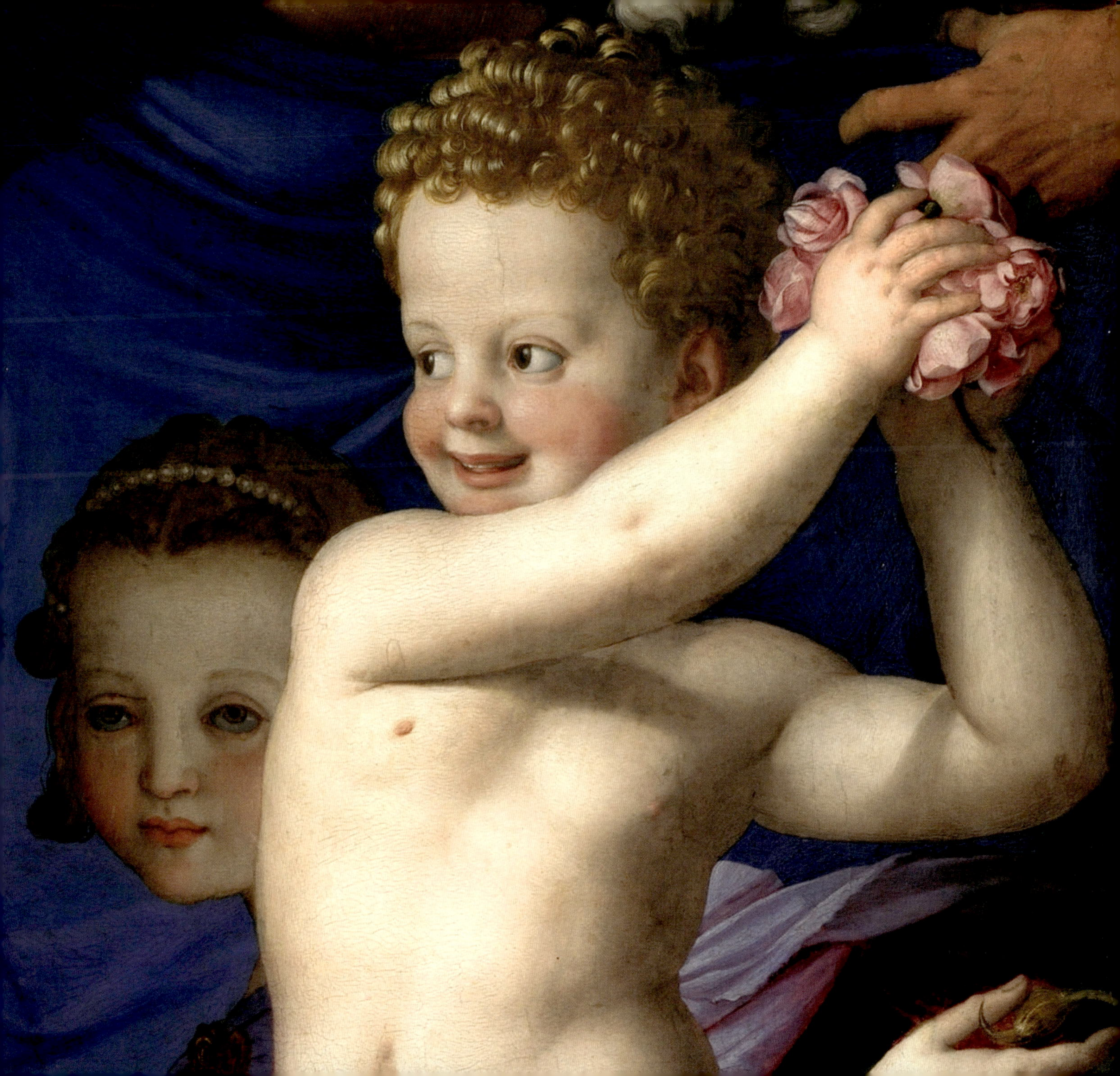

THE CATCH

“The Catch” is the signature play from arguably baseball’s brightest star: Willie Mays. With the score knotted up 2–2 in the top of the eighth inning of Game 1 of the 1954 World Series, Cleveland Indians (now the Guardians) first baseman Vic Wertz hit a towering shot to dead center (425 feet—a distance that in today’s stadiums would be a certain home run). Willie Mays, playing center field for the New York Giants, tracked the ball down, made an over-the-shoulder catch, and fired the ball back into the infield, preventing the runners on base from scoring. His Giants would go on to win the game 5–2 in extra innings (and take the series 4–0), solidifying the moment in MLB history.

Here, “The Catch” is matched with one of the most recognizable motifs in art history: The Ascension. The pairing felt fitting not only for the visual alignment but also for its parallel to the gravity of the play itself, as it came to represent the Giants’ comeback and secured Mays’s iconic place in baseball lore.

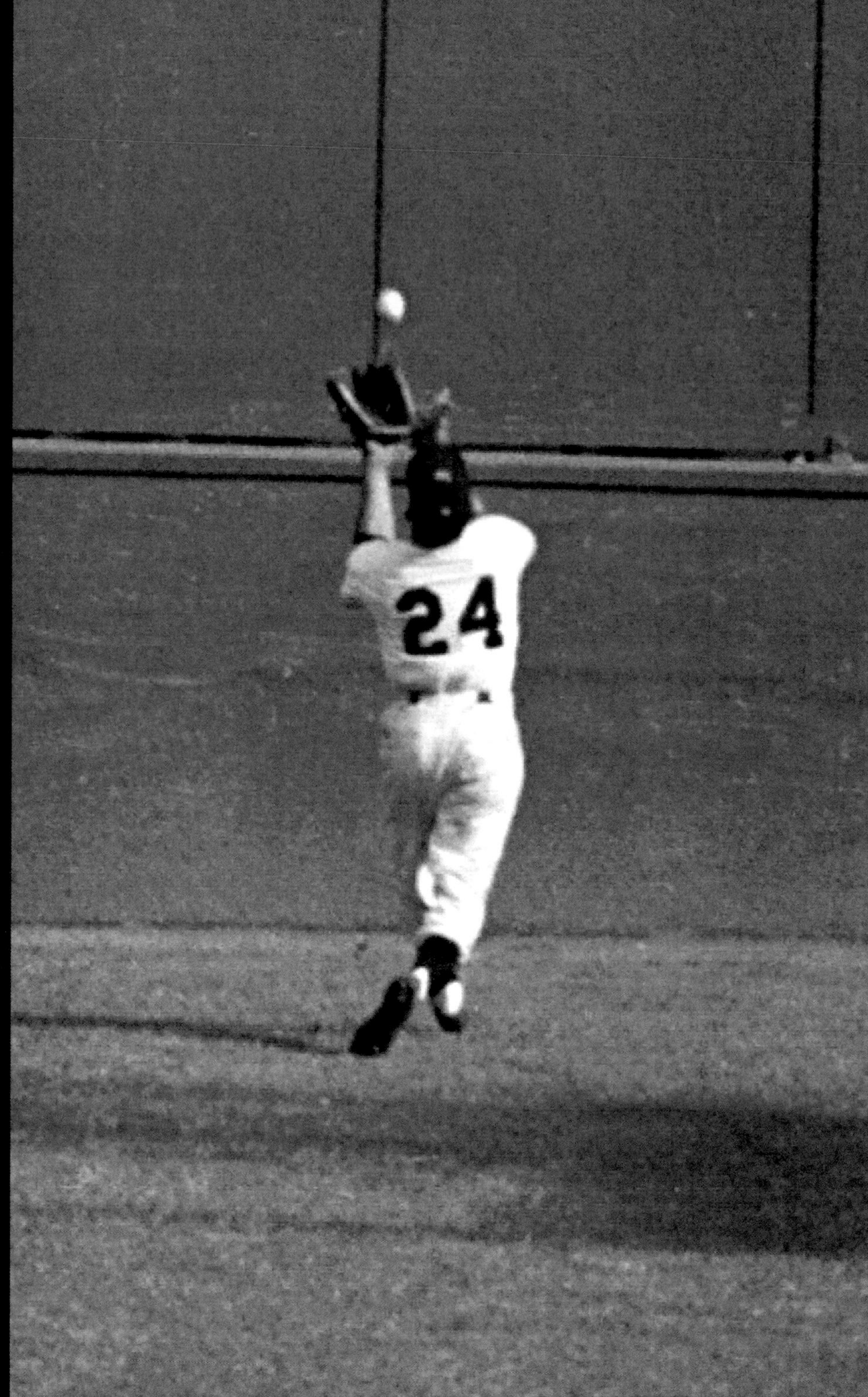

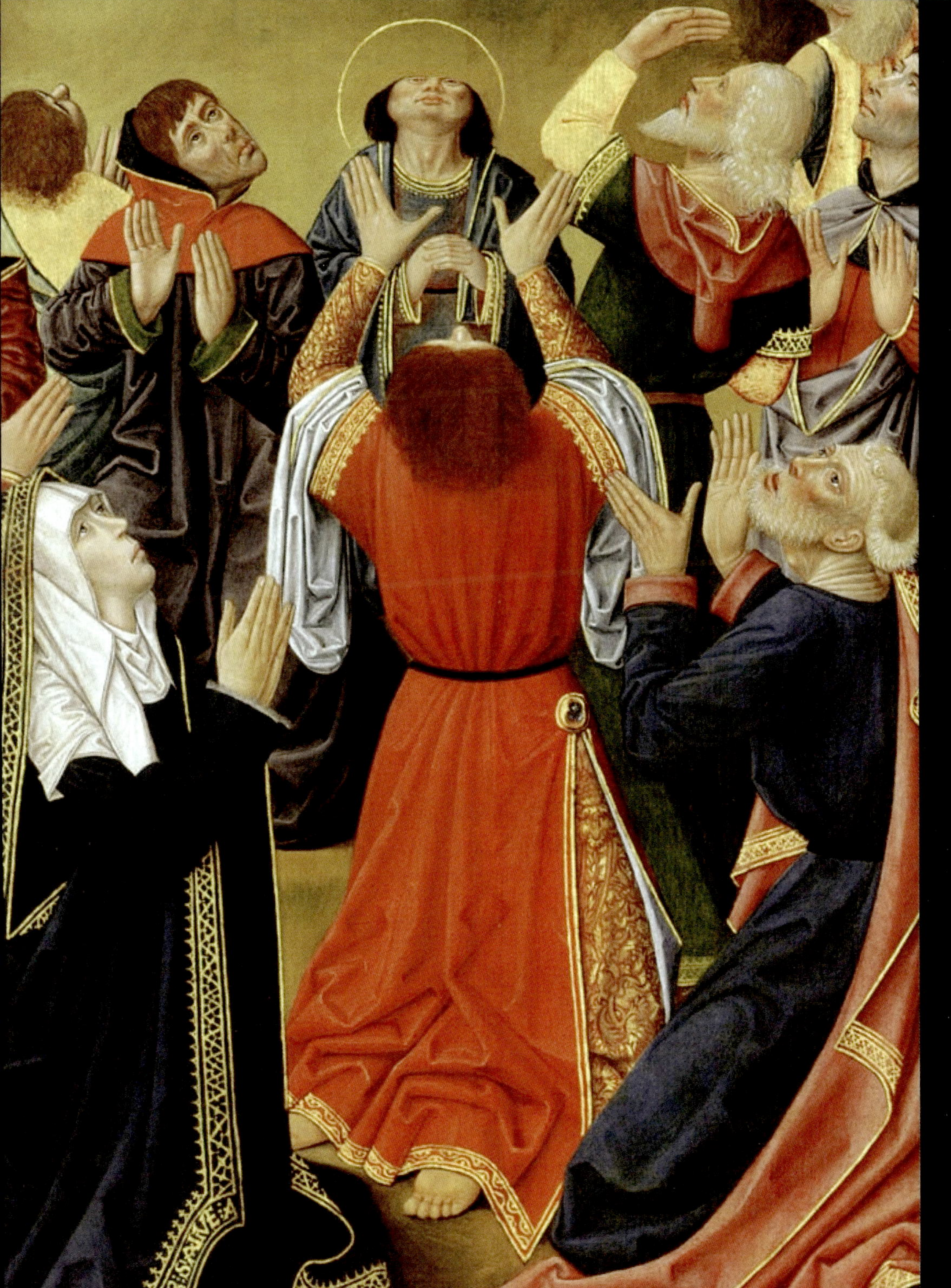

Opposite page: Willie Mays (#24) makes his famous catch off the bat of Vic Wertz in the 1954 World Series on September 29 at the Polo Grounds in New York City. Photo by NY Daily News Archive via Getty Images.

This page: *Altarpiece from Thuison-les-Abbeville: The Ascension* (detail), circa 1495, unknown French artist. Art Institute of Chicago.

THE NEEDLE IN EVERY HAYSTACK

The University of Oklahoma's softball program under coach Patty Gasso has become a dynasty, with the Sooners winning the National Championship eight times since 2000. It's the reason why this image of the Sooners holding up the winner's trophy in celebration has become *the* image to define the Women's College World Series.

There are a few things at play here. First, the visual buildup; a group of players all reaching, creating a single, freestanding unit—much like a haystack. When considering Monet's *A Haystack in the Evening Sun*, we see that no matter how the environment around us might change, the core of who we are and what we know

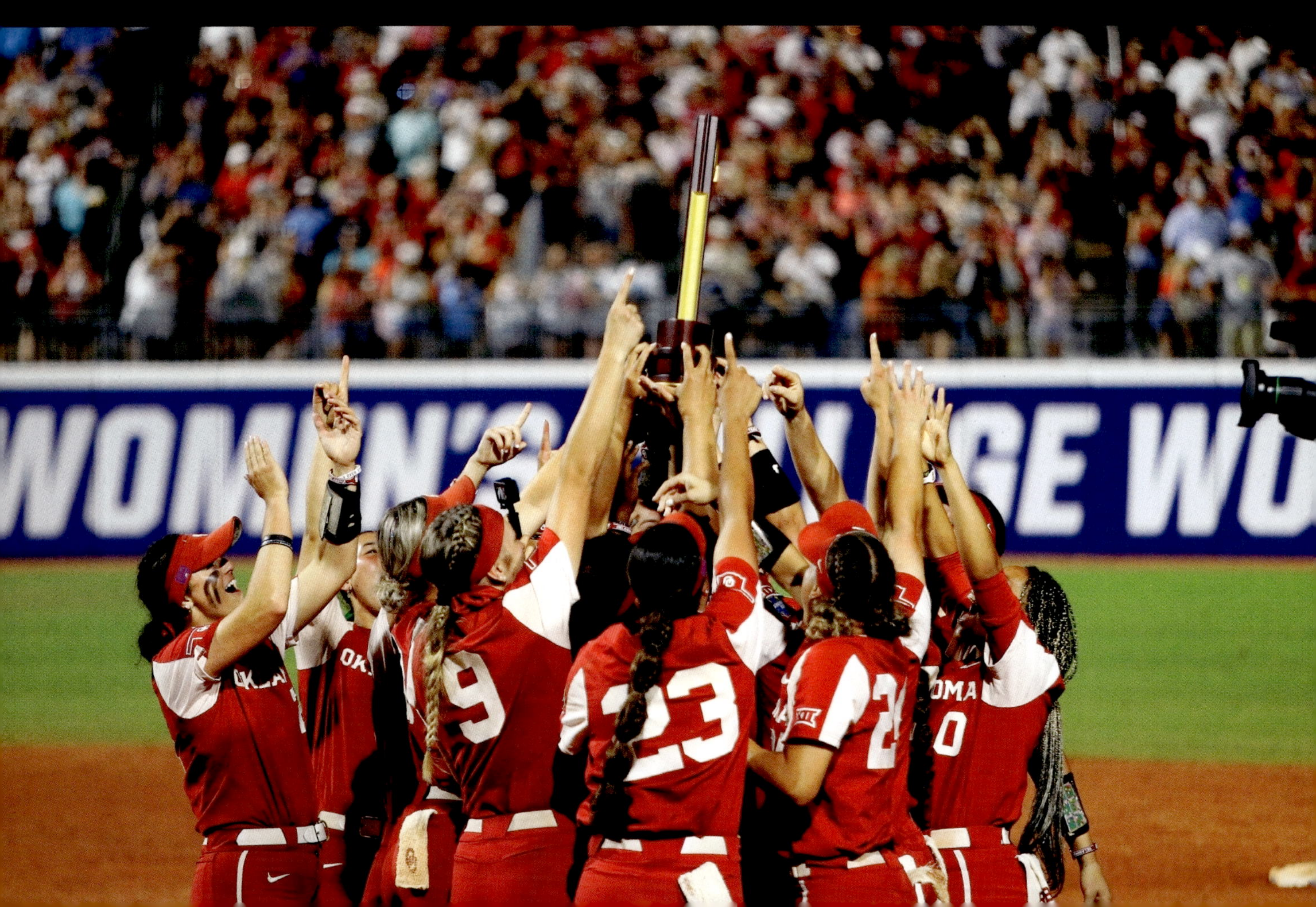

as truth remains the same. This isn't the only haystack work from him. He painted haystacks repeatedly, year after year. Just as these images repeated over time, so does Oklahoma's World Series dominance. There are roughly twenty-five haystacks in the series, so if the prophecy continues to play out, there's a good chance that the Sooners will be hoisting another trophy soon.

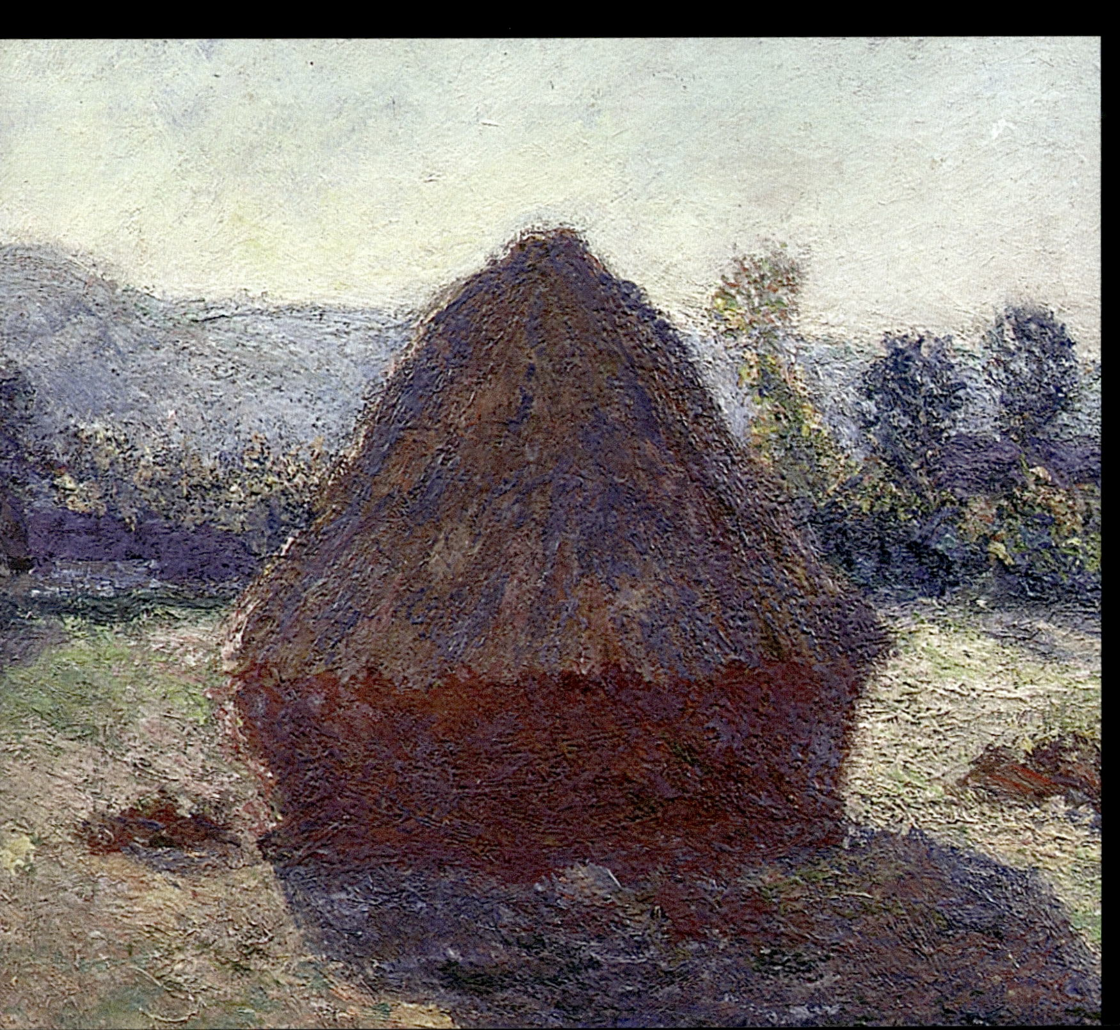

Opposite page: The Oklahoma Sooners lift up the NCAA trophy as they celebrate their championship win over the Texas Longhorns during the NCAA Women's College World Series finals at the USA Softball Hall of Fame Complex (now Devon Park) on June 9, 2022, in Oklahoma City, Oklahoma. The Sooners won the NCAA Championship with the 10–5 victory. Photo by Brian Bahr/Getty Images.

This page: *Wheatstack at Sunset* (detail), 1891, Claude Monet. Wikimedia.

The 162-game baseball season is a grind, where even a regular-season rivalry between the Red Sox and Yankees can feel like a chore. But back in 2004, these matchups were appointment television. The teams were less than a year removed from Game 3 of the 2003 ALCS, where Red Sox ace Pedro

The rivalry entered 2004 as a powder keg, and on July 24, it exploded when Red Sox pitcher Bronson Arroyo beaned Yankees slugger Alex Rodriguez on the left arm. Rodriguez exchanged words with Sox catcher Jason Varitek, which quickly escalated into the latter attacking the

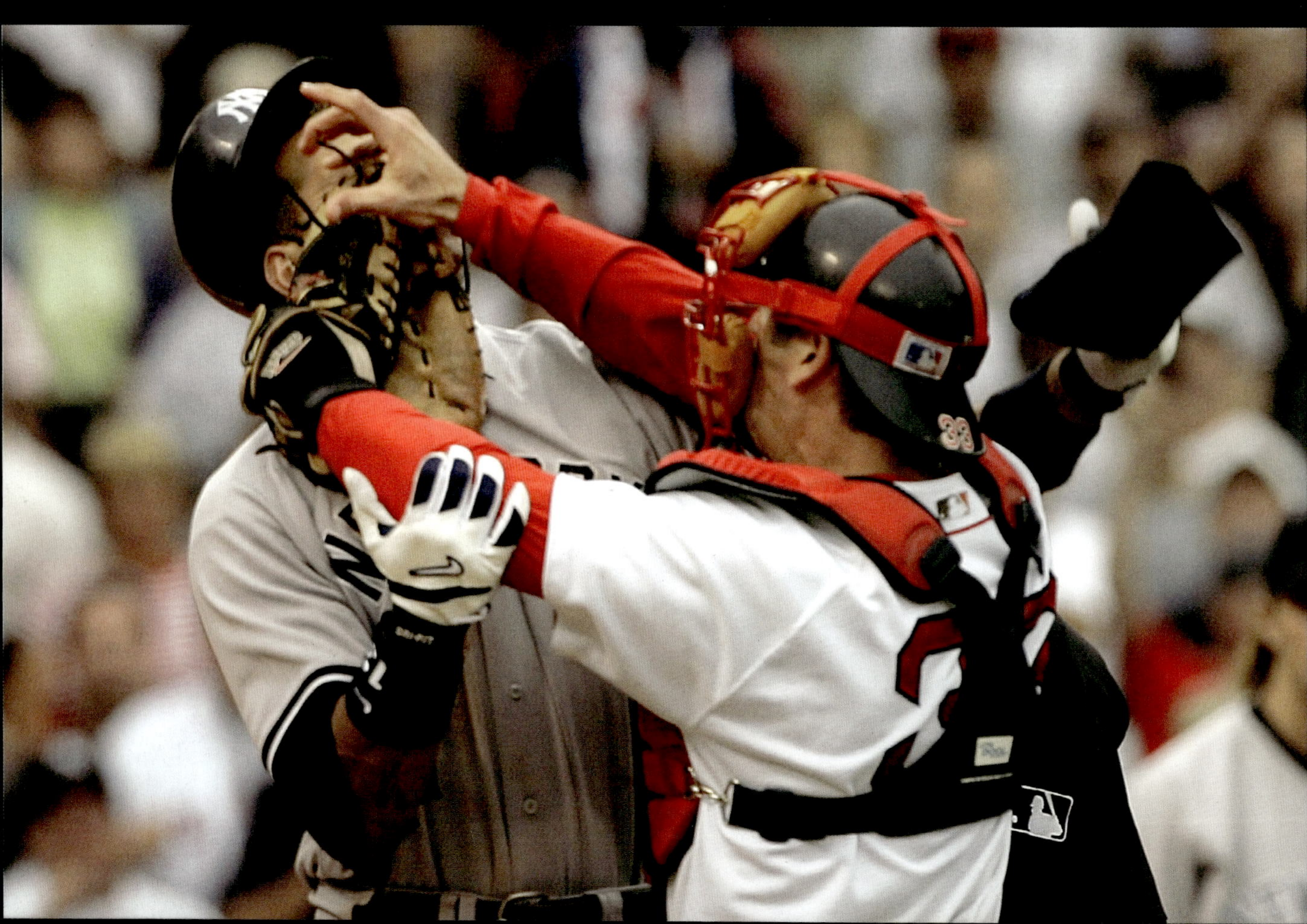

former, leading to this epic photo of hand embedded in leather and flesh.

The vibes are a complete 180 from *Christ Healing the Blind*, but that's partly why I picked it, as it allows the viewer to absolve themselves completely and reimagine the photo as Varitek simply alleviating Rodriguez of his astigmatism.

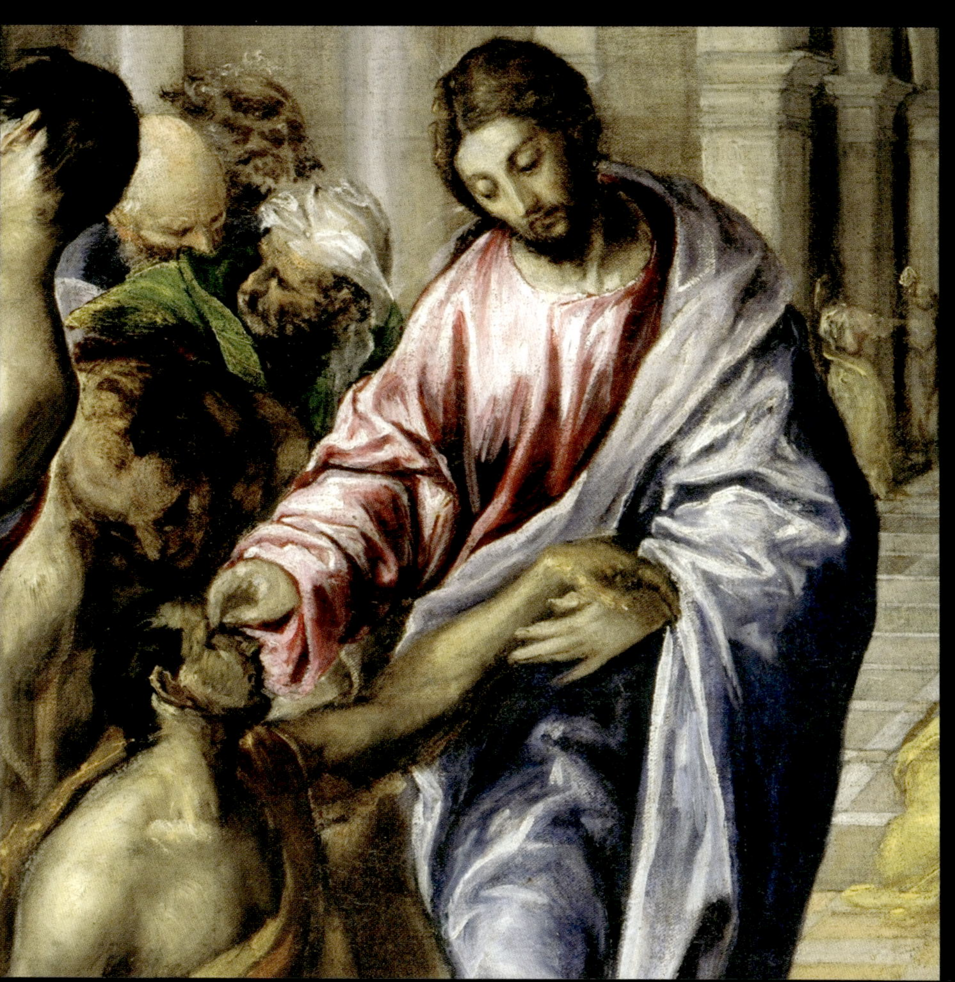

Opposite page: Boston Red Sox catcher Jason Varitek strikes New York Yankees batter Alex Rodriguez at Fenway Park in Boston on July 24, 2004. The two fought after Rodriguez was hit by a pitch thrown by Red Sox pitcher Bronson Arroyo. The Red Sox won, 11–10, with a ninth-inning game-winning home run by Bill Mueller. Photo by Jim Rogash/WireImage.

This page: *Christ Healing the Blind* (detail), circa 1570, El Greco. Metropolitan Museum of Art.

FREEZE

In Munich the art flows just as freely as the beer, something this uncultured American was unaware of until I visited the city on a business trip. I was lucky enough to swing an extra day and managed to blitz through seven museums in twenty-four hours, the highlight of which was the Alte Pinakothek, home to one of the world's finest collections of fifteenth-century art, including this gem by the legend Fra Angelico, an Early Renaissance leader who strictly depicted religious subjects.

In *Saint Cosmas and Saint Damian Salvaged,* we see destruction and salvation—a parallel to the relationship between beer and art, perhaps—as we move throughout the canvas. It's also a link we can make to an inter-inning promotion/game by the Atlanta Braves, in which a fan runs the outfield warning track with a head start, only to eventually be chased down by "the

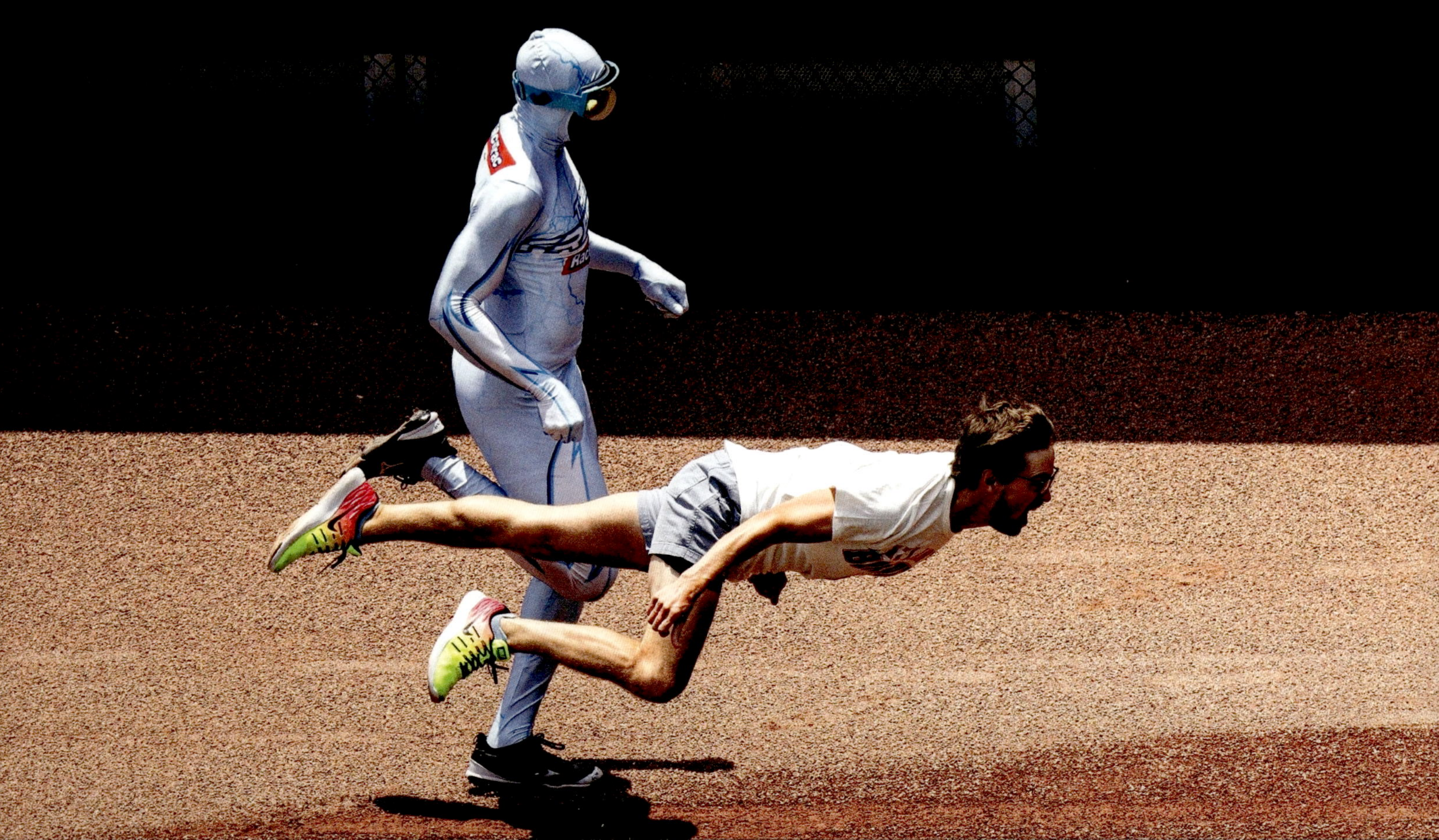

Freeze," an anonymous track star dressed in a bodysuit. On rare occasions, our plebeian representative manages to outmaneuver the professional; but in this scene captured by Kevin Liles, we see an all-too-familiar moment for the proletariat unfolding. Pain, suffering, and redemption—familiar themes in artwork, but also in viral seventh-inning-stretch advertising campaigns. No matter how much of a head start we have, it's always important to note that the proverbial Freeze may be just over your shoulder.

Opposite page: A contestant goes airborne and falls while racing the Freeze during the Atlanta Braves' game against the Arizona Diamondbacks at Truist Park on July 20, 2023, in Atlanta, Georgia. Photo by Kevin D. Liles/ Atlanta Braves/Getty Images.

This page: *Saint Cosmas and Saint Damian Salvaged* (detail), 1438–43, Fra Angelico. Digital image by LJ Rader. Convent San Marco. Flipped from the original.

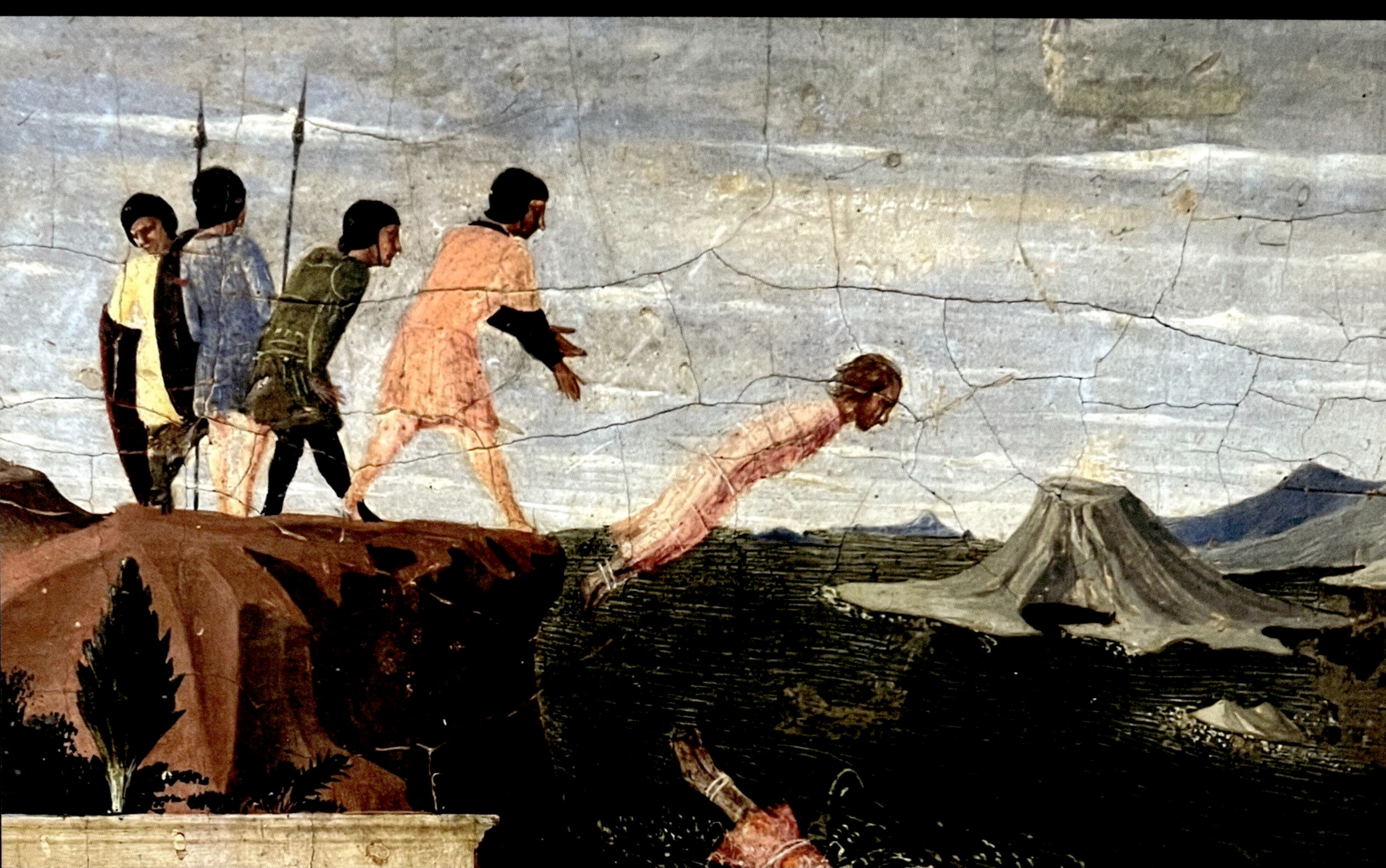

SLIDING SUPREMATISM

The pinnacle of sports photography is reached when an everyday moment in an ordinary game is so perfectly framed that it becomes worthy of elevation. Malevich is then especially appropriate here, as the movement he founded, suprematism, aimed to communicate pure feeling, freed from the things that predetermined the structure of life and art. So long as the essence is on display, the factors and construct are no longer necessary. Art for art's sake, regardless of the "rules." Here we see photographer Meg McLaughlin painting a masterpiece with the same principles: the colors, shapes, and position tell the story, not any complicated preconceived narrative.

Left: Fernando Tatis Jr. (#23) of the San Diego Padres contorts to avoid a tag at home plate in a game vs. the San Francisco Giants on March 28, 2024. Photo by Meghan McLaughlin/San Diego Union-Tribune/ZUMA Press.

Right: *Suprematist Composition: Airplane Flying*, 1915, Kazimir Malevich. Museum of Modern Art.

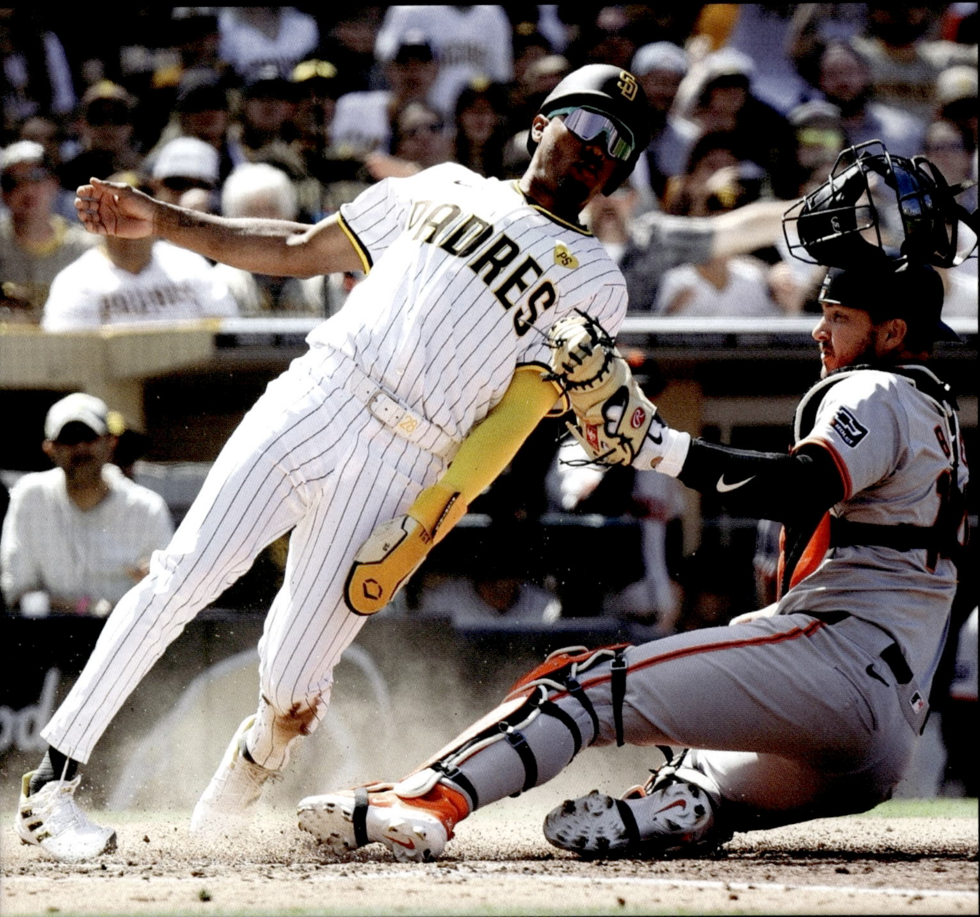

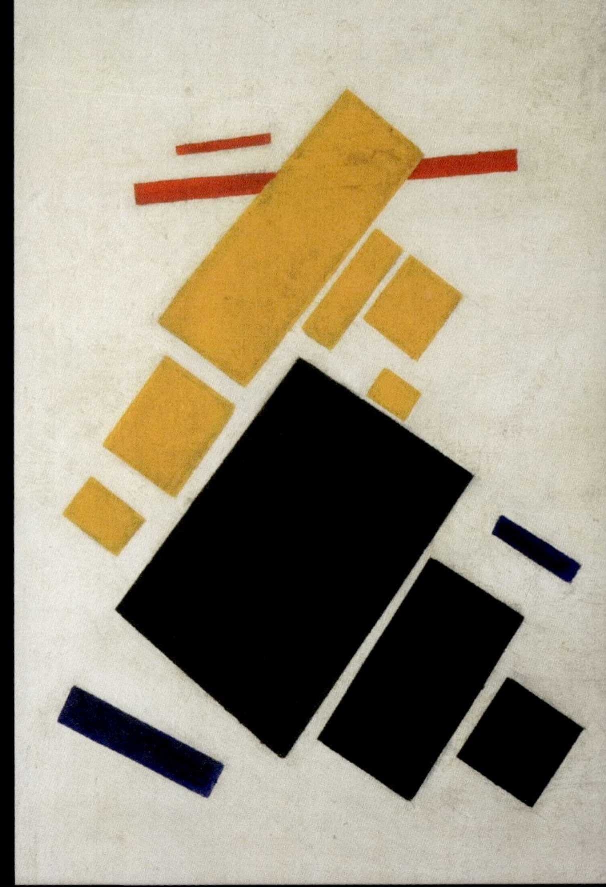

Here's another play-at-the-plate as Russian suprematism, this one via Kelsey Grant and Vera Ermolaeva. There's something so aesthetically pleasing about seeing nearly perfect corresponding components, both in look, weight, and feel. In the case of this moment, the reach of the player's yellow glove onto the base before the tag is the crucial part to capture, as it represents the winning run of the game. I was pumped to capture both parts, as well as his diving body (and the chalk of the batter's box and foul line!), with one painting.

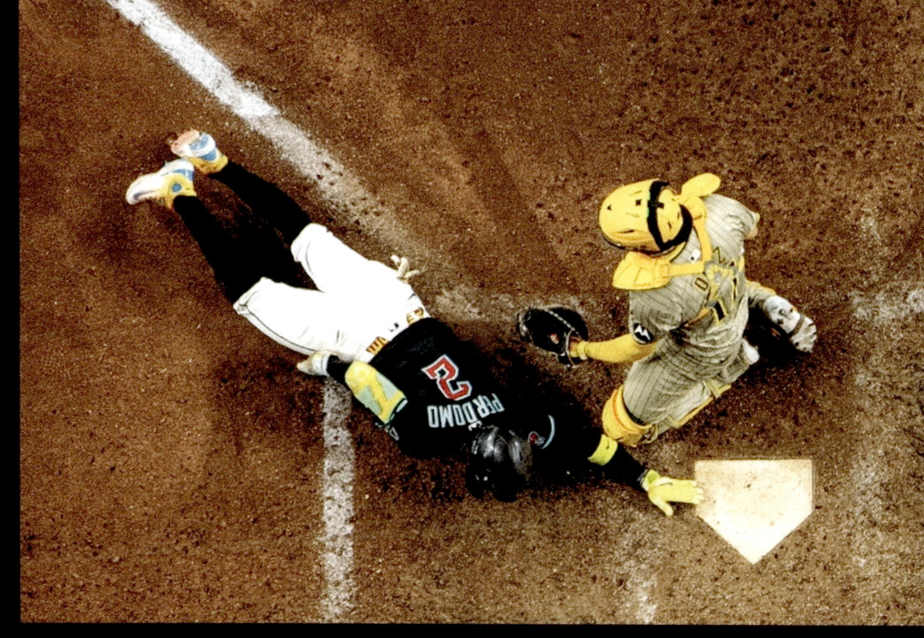

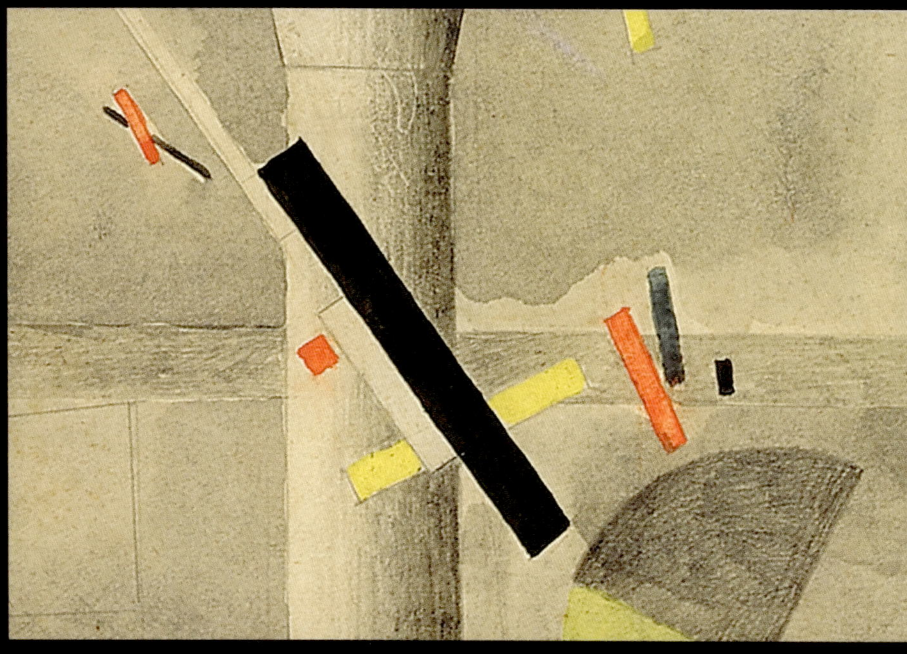

Top: Geraldo Perdomo (#2) of the Arizona Diamondbacks scores the game-winning run past catcher Elias Díaz (#17) of the San Diego Padres during the ninth inning of the MLB game at Chase Field on June 14, 2025, in Phoenix, Arizona. Photo by Kelsey Grant/Arizona Diamondbacks/ Getty Images.

Bottom: *Suprematist Design for a Façade* (detail), 1920, Vera Ermolaeva. Photograph courtesy of Sotheby's, Inc. © 2025.

PITCHCRAFT

NiJaree Canady truly practices witchcraft on the mound, befuddling hitters with a potion brewed mixing strength, creativity, and sorcery. The first $1M NIL player in college softball (she transferred from Stanford to Texas Tech), Canady is helping usher the sport into the upper echelon of the public consciousness.

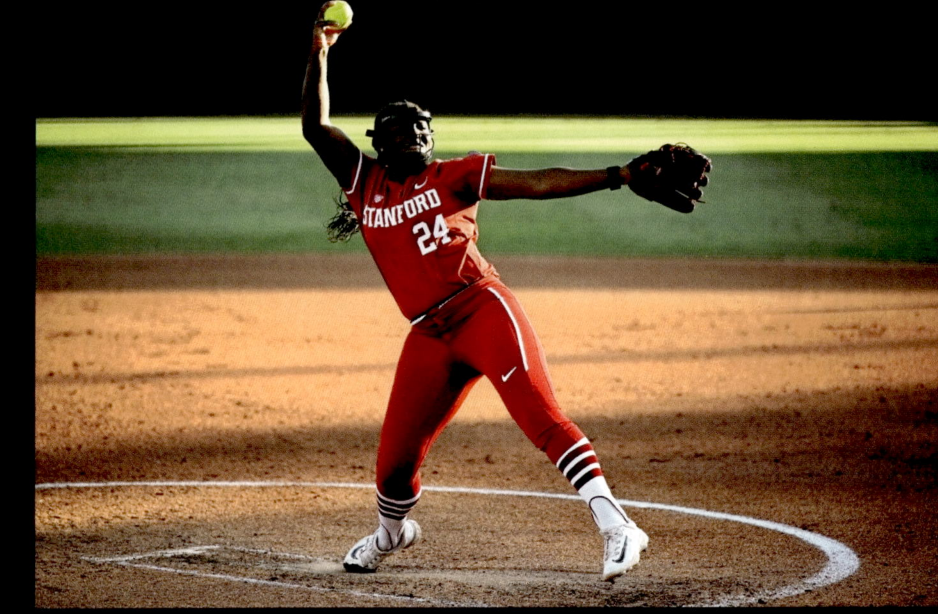

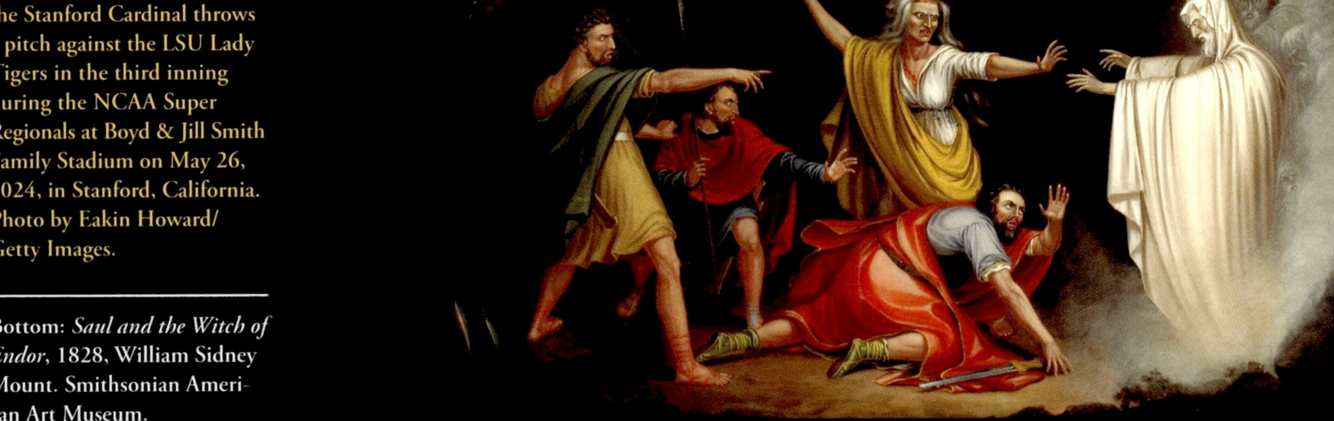

Top: NiJaree Canady (#24) of the Stanford Cardinal throws a pitch against the LSU Lady Tigers in the third inning during the NCAA Super Regionals at Boyd & Jill Smith Family Stadium on May 26, 2024, in Stanford, California. Photo by Eakin Howard/ Getty Images.

Bottom: *Saul and the Witch of Endor*, 1828, William Sidney Mount. Smithsonian American Art Museum.

Smith, aka the Wizard. For this frame of Smith's signature backflip, I went with a background acrobat in Stettheimer's *Asbury Park South.*

October 20, 1987. Photo by Rich Pilling/Sporting News via Getty Images.

Right: *Asbury Park South* (detail), 1920, Florine Stettheimer. Digital image by NY Books.

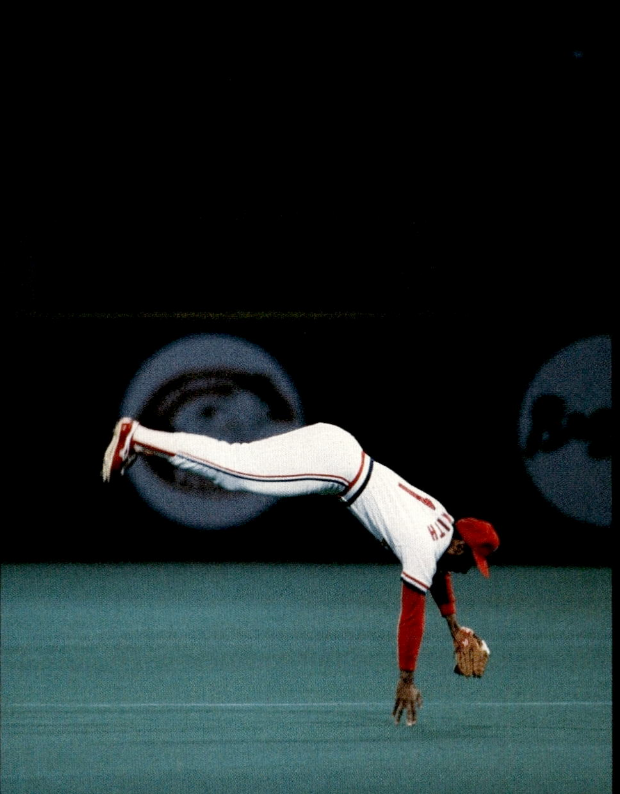

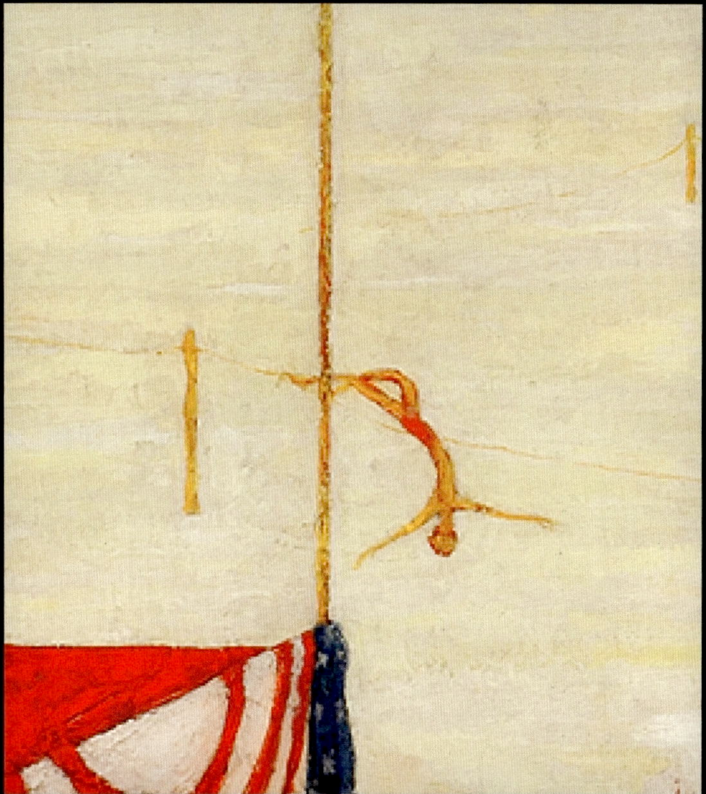

SHEPHERDING A NEW GAME

There are parallels between Jackie Robinson and both the figure in the painting, David, and the artist, Elizabeth Jane Gardner Bouguereau. As many know, the former broke the color barrier, debuting for the Dodgers on April 15, 1947. Gardner Bouguereau was similarly a pioneer, moving to Paris despite the fact that the leading institution, the École des Beaux-Arts, did not admit women—she'd go on to take private classes and become one of the first American women to exhibit her work at the Paris Salon. As for David, he's legendary for taking on the larger-than-life Goliath, comparable to how Robinson took on the institution of MLB.

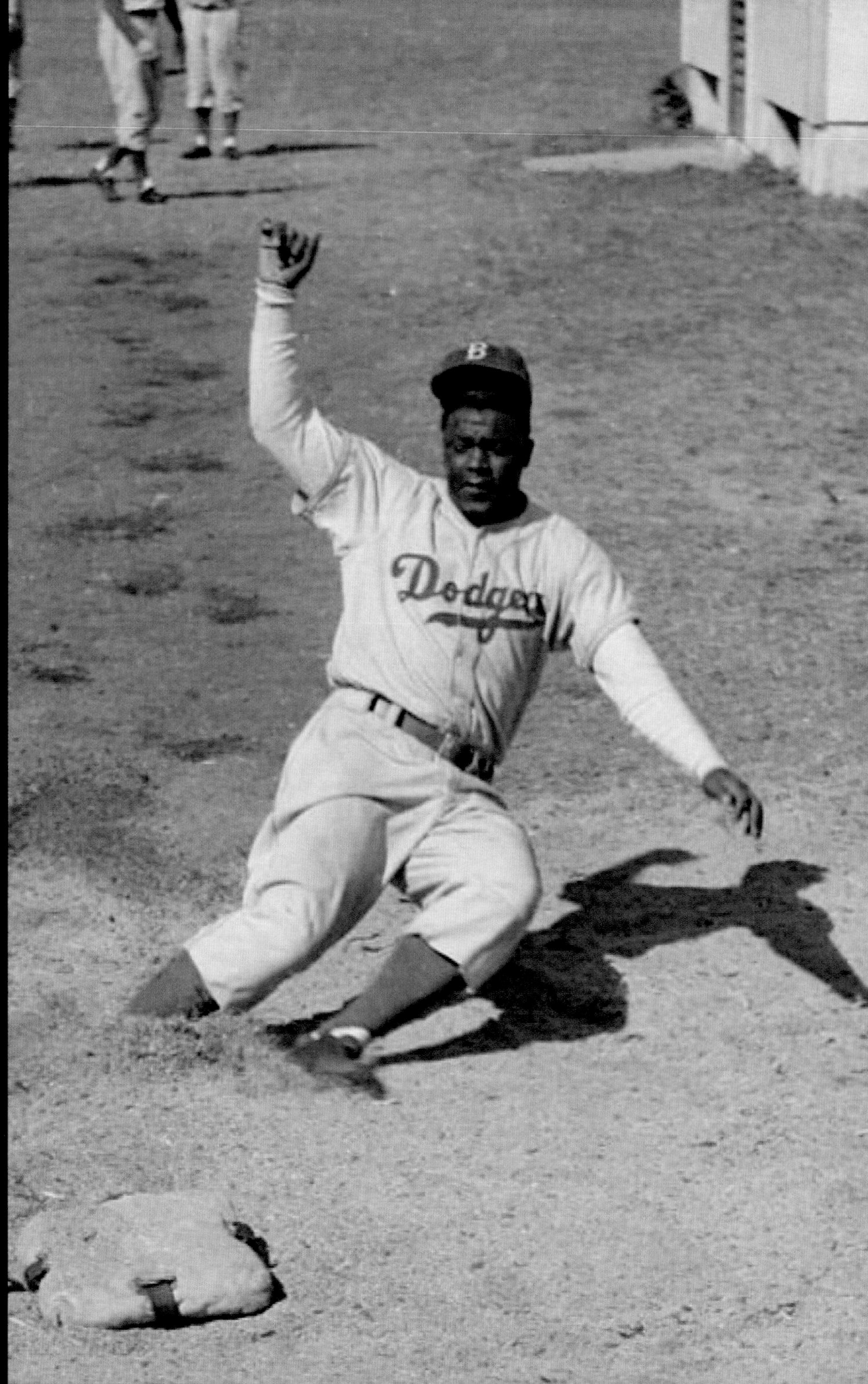

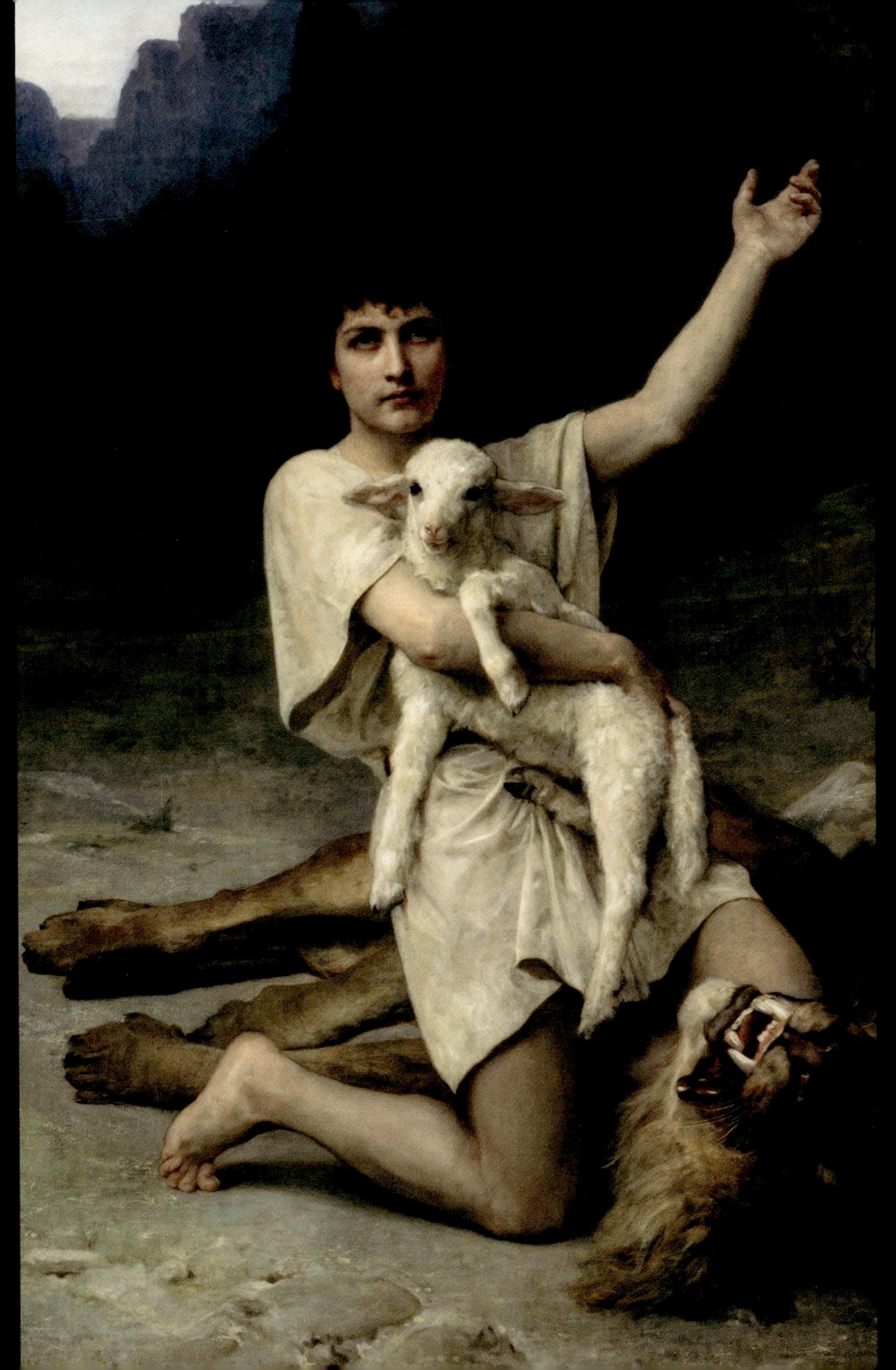

Opposite page: Jackie Robinson, the bright star of the Brooklyn Dodgers, shows off his sliding technique in March of 1950. Photo by Bettmann via Getty Images.

This page: *The Shepherd David*, circa 1895, Elizabeth Jane Gardner Bouguereau. National Museum of Women in the Arts.

JUMPING FOR GOYA

As the Museo Nacional del Prado writes, "Four young women laugh and play at blanket-tossing a doll or manikin in the air. The latter's movement is the result of their caprice. Its carnival origins are visible in the use of masks and joking, but the blanket-tossing of a doll is used here by Goya as a clear allegory of women's domination of men."

I think it's an apt comparison for softball. Baseball will always be my favorite sport to follow, but something about softball's fast-paced, seat-of-your-pants nature makes it a much more fun watch.

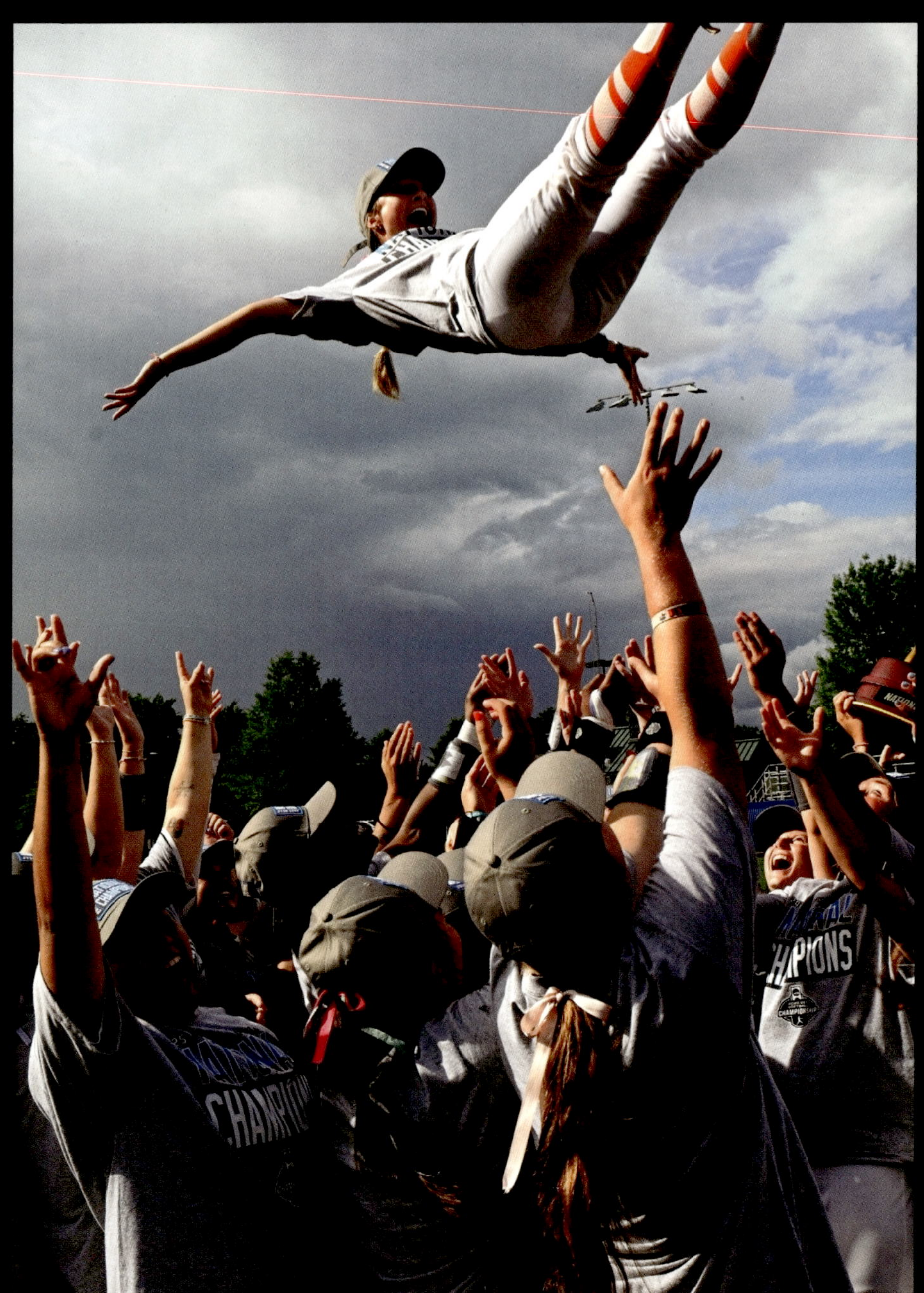

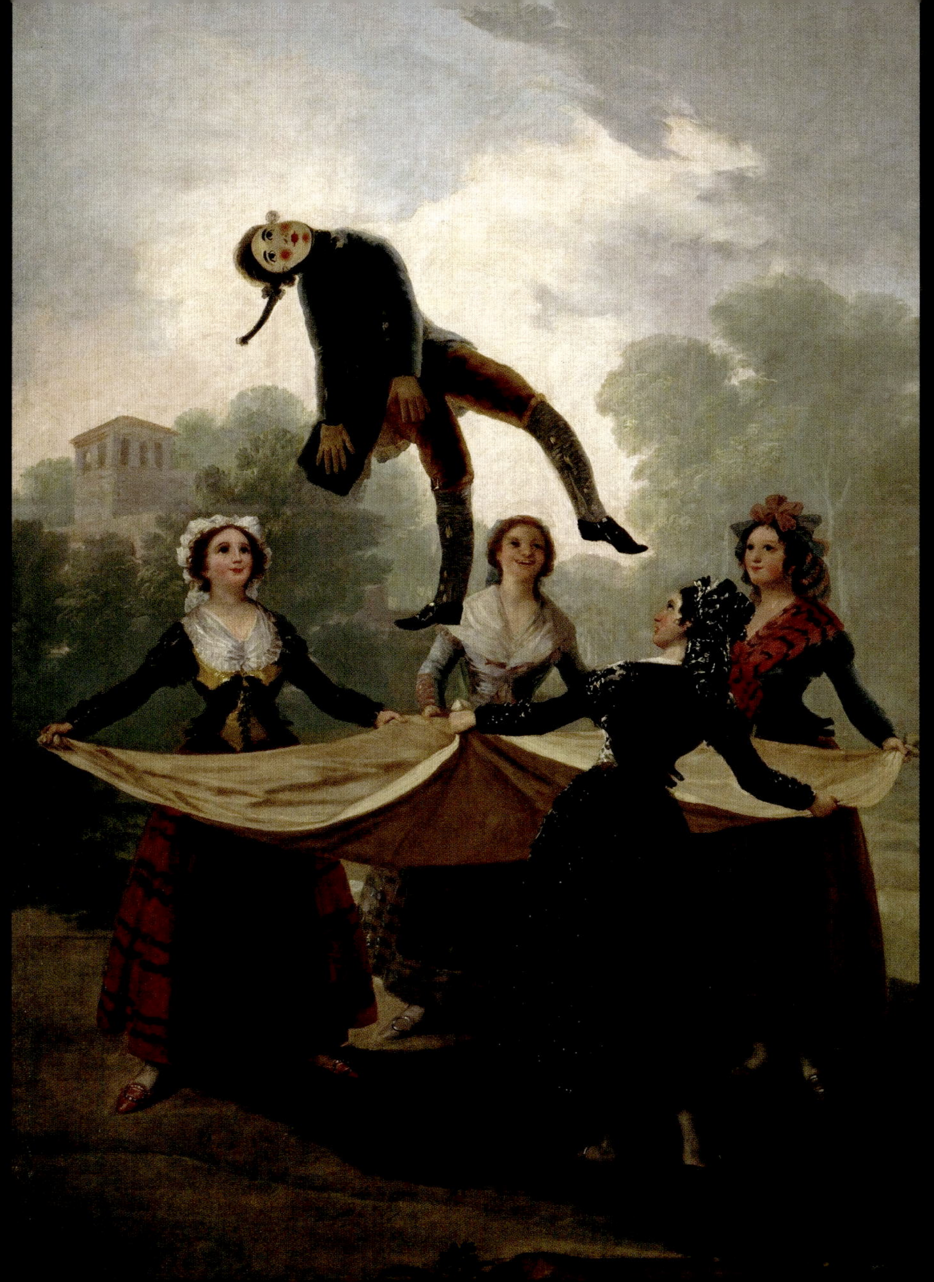

Opposite page: The UT Tyler Patriots celebrate winning their second straight championship during the Division II Women's Softball Championship held at Frost Stadium at Warner Park on May 28, 2025, in Chattanooga, Tennessee. Photo by Marshall Stephens/NCAA Photos via Getty Images.

This page: *El pelele*, 1791, Francisco de Goya. Museo del Prado.

AMERICAN FOOTBALL

While I'm admittedly much more interested in college football than I am in the NFL, it's impossible to ignore the pull "The Shield" has on America's consciousness. It makes for great art comparisons too, as the NFL isn't short on violence, chaos, and tension, all of which can be found in great art across time.

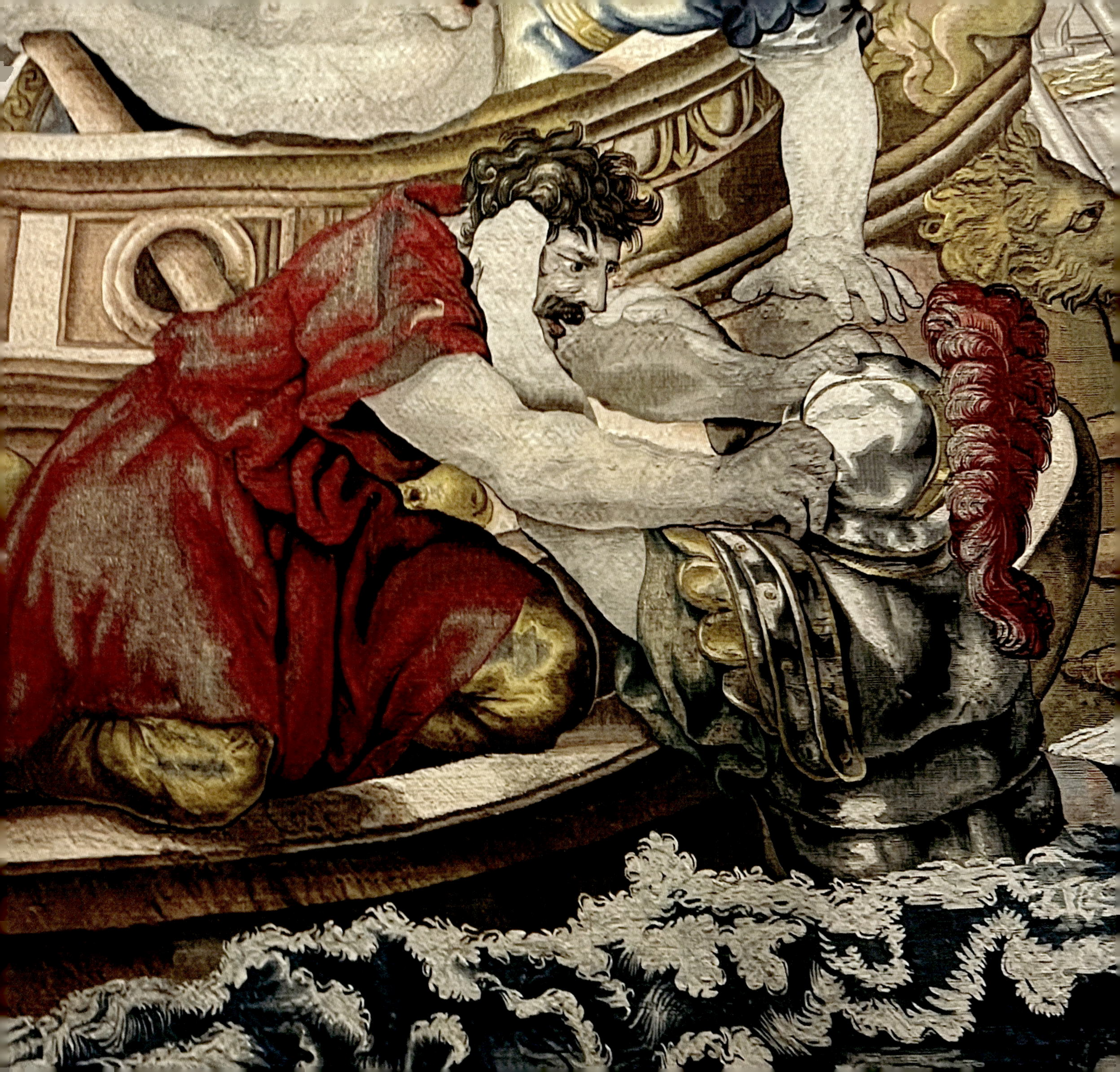

THE CATCH (FOOTBALL)

Dwight Clark's grab capped a 14-play, 83-yard, game-winning drive to propel the eventual Super Bowl XVI champion San Francisco 49ers past the Dallas Cowboys in the 1982 NFC Championship Game, a moment that became the NFL's own "The Catch" (see page 44). Part of what solidified the event in the annals of history is the photograph, framing the play as art in and of itself. For the fine art comparison, I wanted something that captured not just the colors, but also the movement, as the poetic motion of both figures is what makes the composition lasting. Popova's piece gets the red figure with outstretched arms and the ball sitting just above, with the defender reaching to no avail.

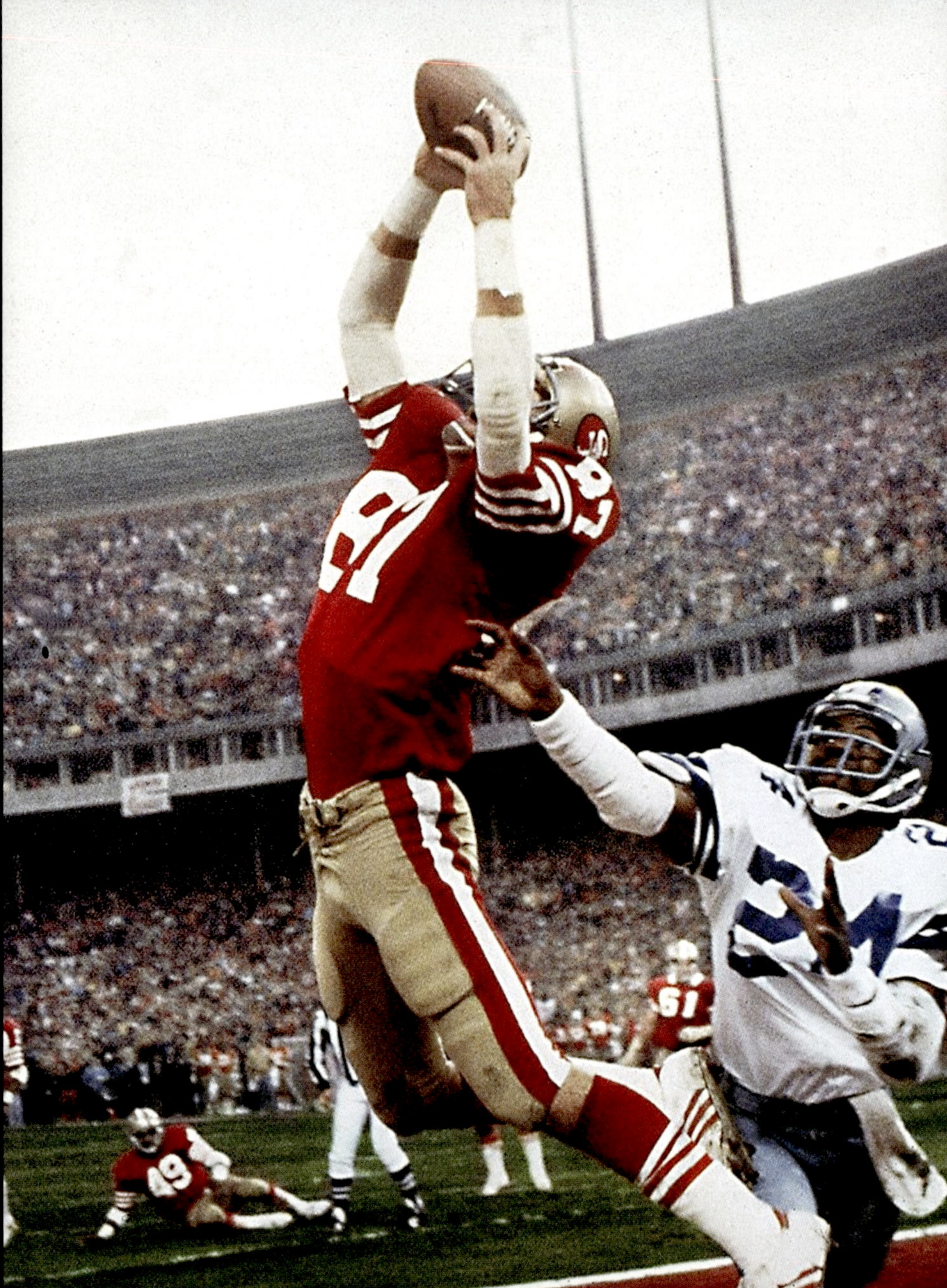

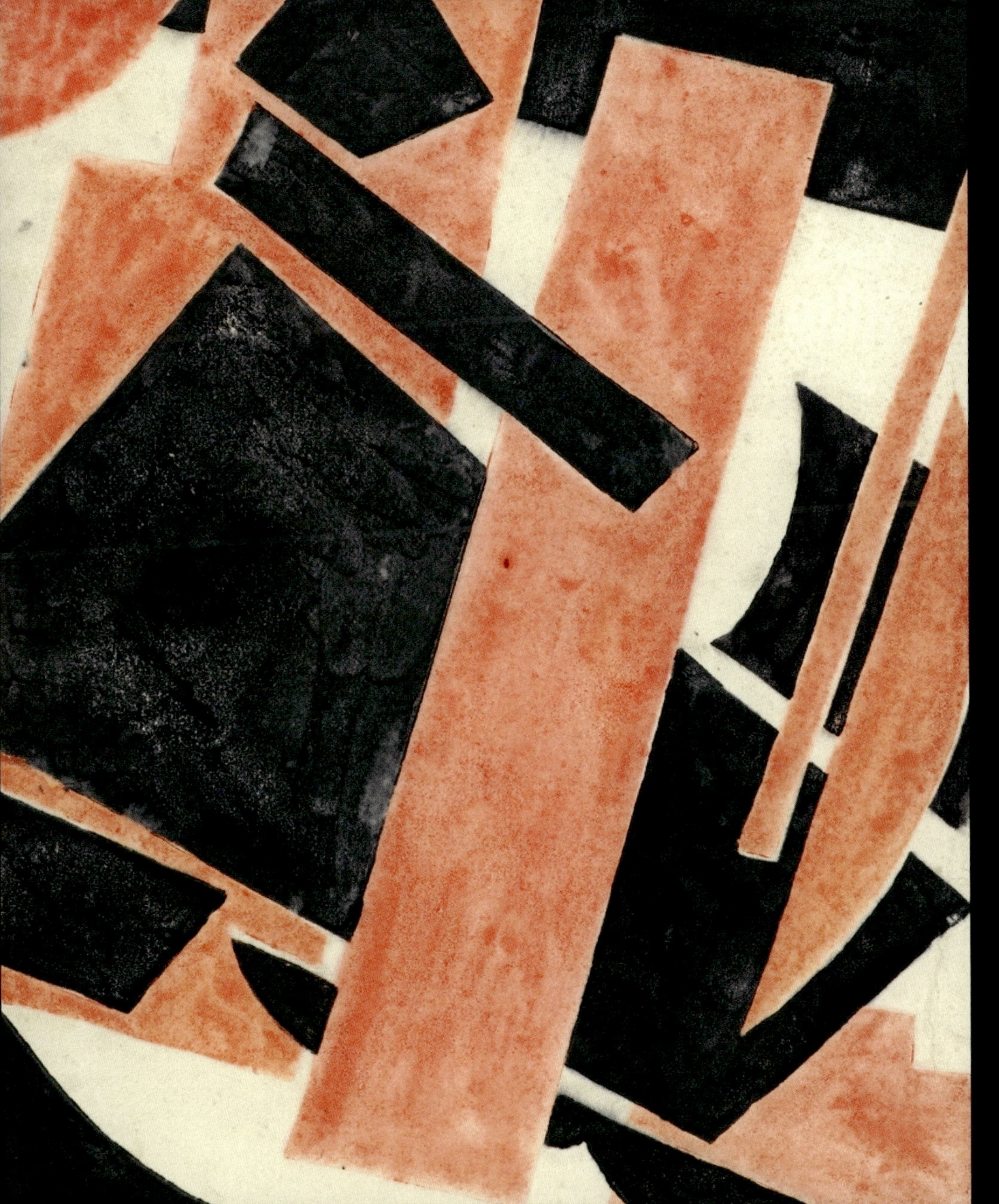

Opposite page: San Francisco 49ers Dwight Clark (#87) makes “The Catch” and game-winning touchdown against Dallas Cowboy Everson Walls (#24) in the 1982 NFC Championship Game on January 10, 1982, in San Francisco, California. Photo by Walter Iooss Jr./Sports Illustrated via Getty Images/ Getty Images.

This page: *Six Prints: one print*, 1917–19, Liubov Popova. The Peggy and David Rockefeller Collection. Rotated from the original.

RISE OF THE REBEL ANGELS

Seemingly weekly I get tagged in an image of a player leaping over defenders. Because of the frequency, my default is to ignore these photos unless there's something truly spectacular and unique—because almost always the go-to counterpart is some version of Fall of the Rebel Angels, and eventually it becomes repetitive. The first time I deployed the theme was with Josh Allen's signature hurdle, pairing it with Luca Giordano's 1666 version.

A photo of Saquon Barkley leapfrogging provided the rare opportunity to make a post with something outside of the genre, as the emphasis was on him turned backward.

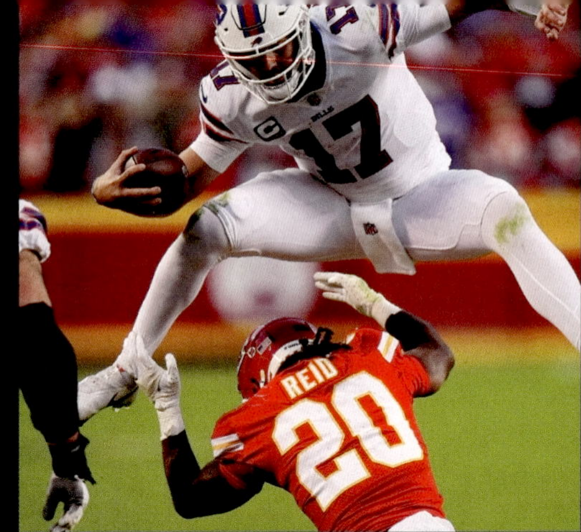

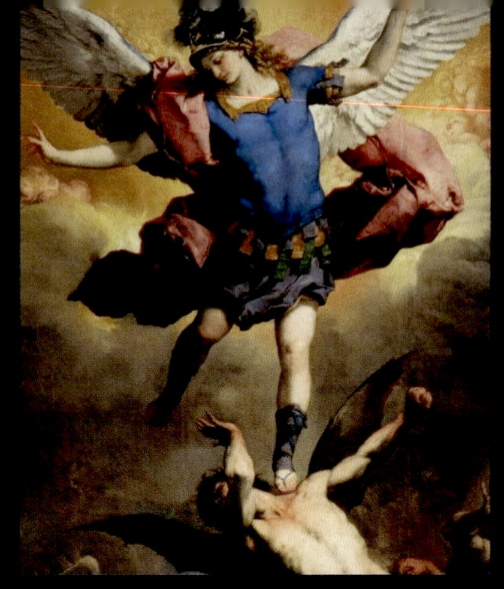

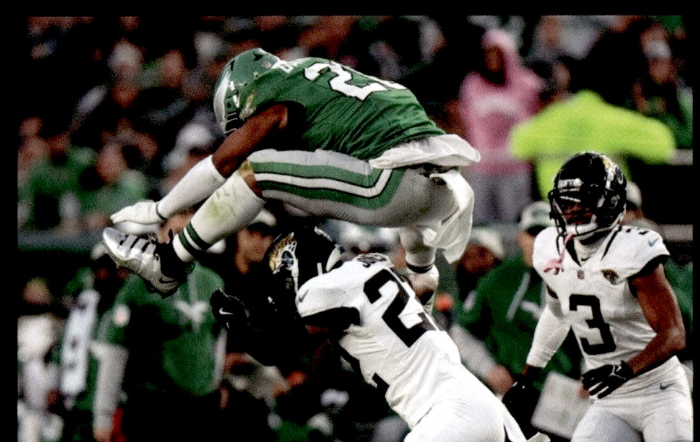

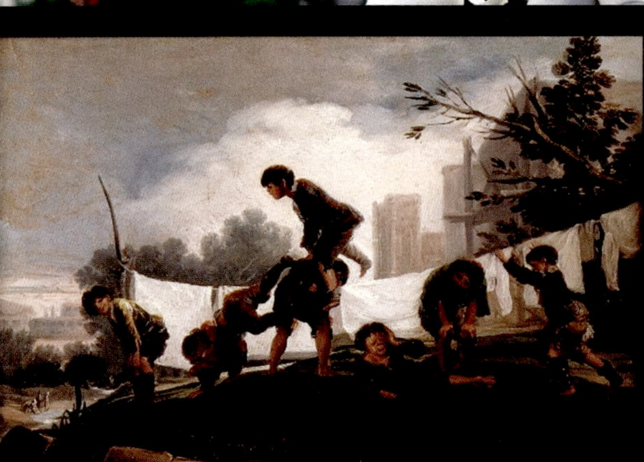

Top Left: Josh Allen (#17) of the Buffalo Bills hurdles over Justin Reid (#20) of the Kansas City Chiefs during the fourth quarter at Arrowhead Stadium on October 16, 2022, in Kansas City, Missouri. Photo by Jason Hanna/ Getty Images.

Top right: *The Fall of the Rebel Angels* (detail), 1666, Luca Giordano. Digital image by Google Cultural Institute. Kunsthistorisches Museum. Flipped from the original.

Middle: Saquon Barkley (#26) of the Philadelphia Eagles hurdles Jarrian Jones (#22) of the Jacksonville Jaguars in the second quarter of a game at Lincoln Financial Field on November 3, 2024, in Philadelphia, Pennsylvania. Photo by Elsa/Getty Images.

Bottom: *Juego de niños*, 1777–85, Francisco Goya. Museu de Belles Arts de València. Flipped from the original.

Yet my favorite pairing of the genre was Sebastiano Ricci's version with this truly magical shot by Nicolas Stempien-lauff from a Paris Musketeers game. It's such a perfect match that we made it the cover!

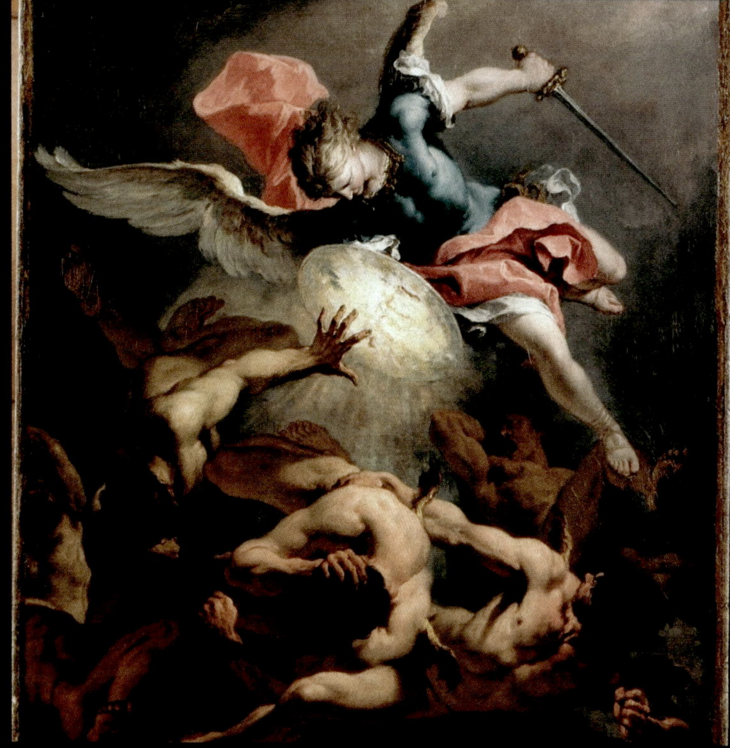

Bottom: Running back Chris Voumbo (#45) of the Paris Musketeers goes airborne in a 2024 game against the Munich Ravens in the European League of Football. Photo by Nicolas Stempien-lauff.

Top: *The Fall of the Rebel Angels*, circa 1720, Sebastiano Ricci. Digital image by Google Arts & Culture. Dulwich Picture Gallery. Flipped from the original.

THE REARRANGING OF LAWRENCE

Football players are gladiators, and the public (me included) are often desensitized to just how violent the game can be. We see action stopped for injuries, players being carted off, et cetera, but every single play contains numerous mini-encounters that would incapacitate even the strongest fan.

I'm sure there's art out there that captures the same facial disorientation that comes from a blow to the head, but I felt like this photo needs the treatment of something abstract that still retains portions of realism. That points to cubism, and potentially Picasso. But because the pairing calls for such exaggerated distortion and facial movement, I thought of a contemporary of Picasso, Juan Gris, whose style hedges more toward the surreal. I settled on Gris's 1912 portrait of Picasso, which has the perfect blend of realism, fantasy, and action, and completes the full-circle loop in having both artists in the comparison.

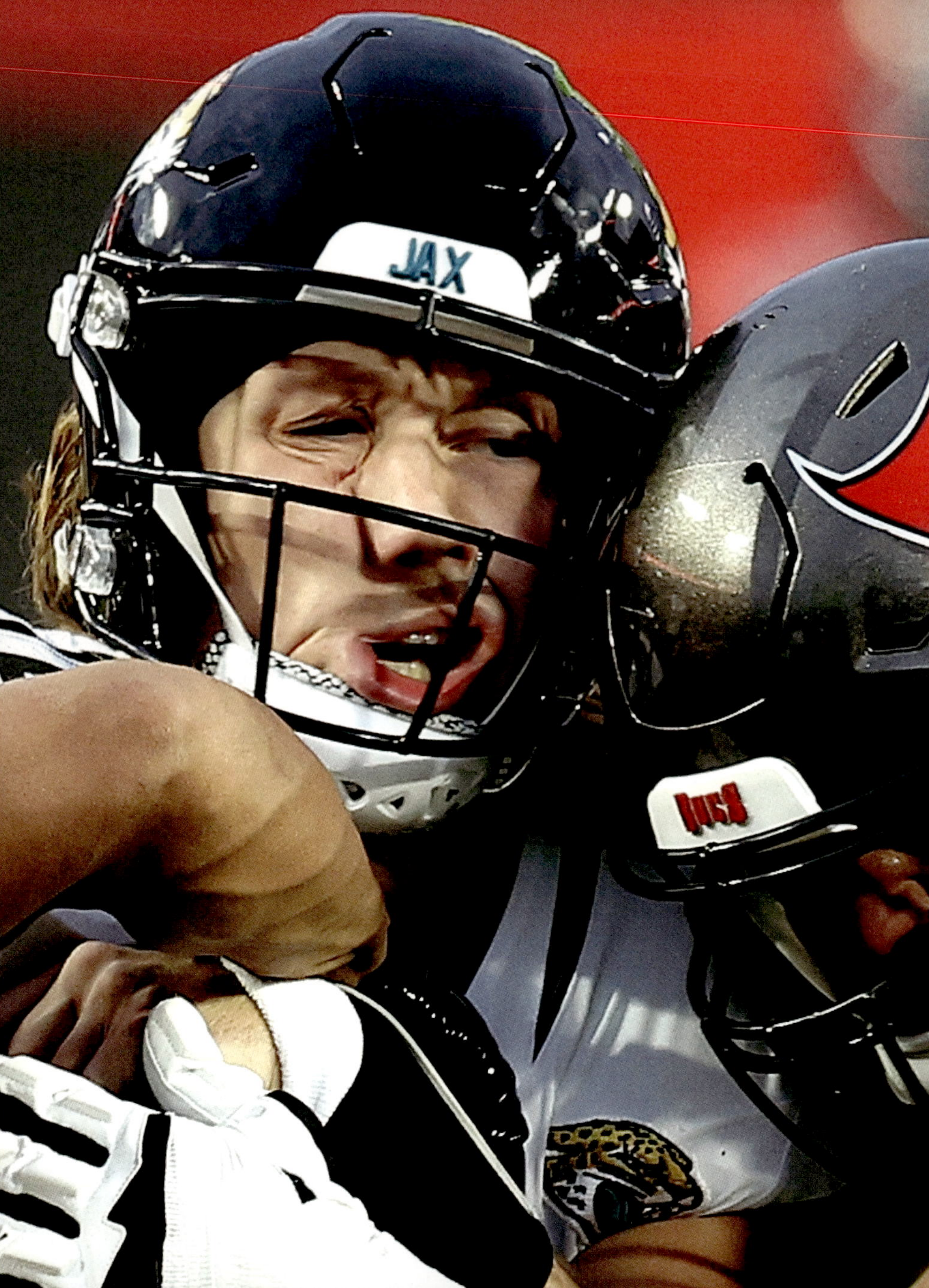

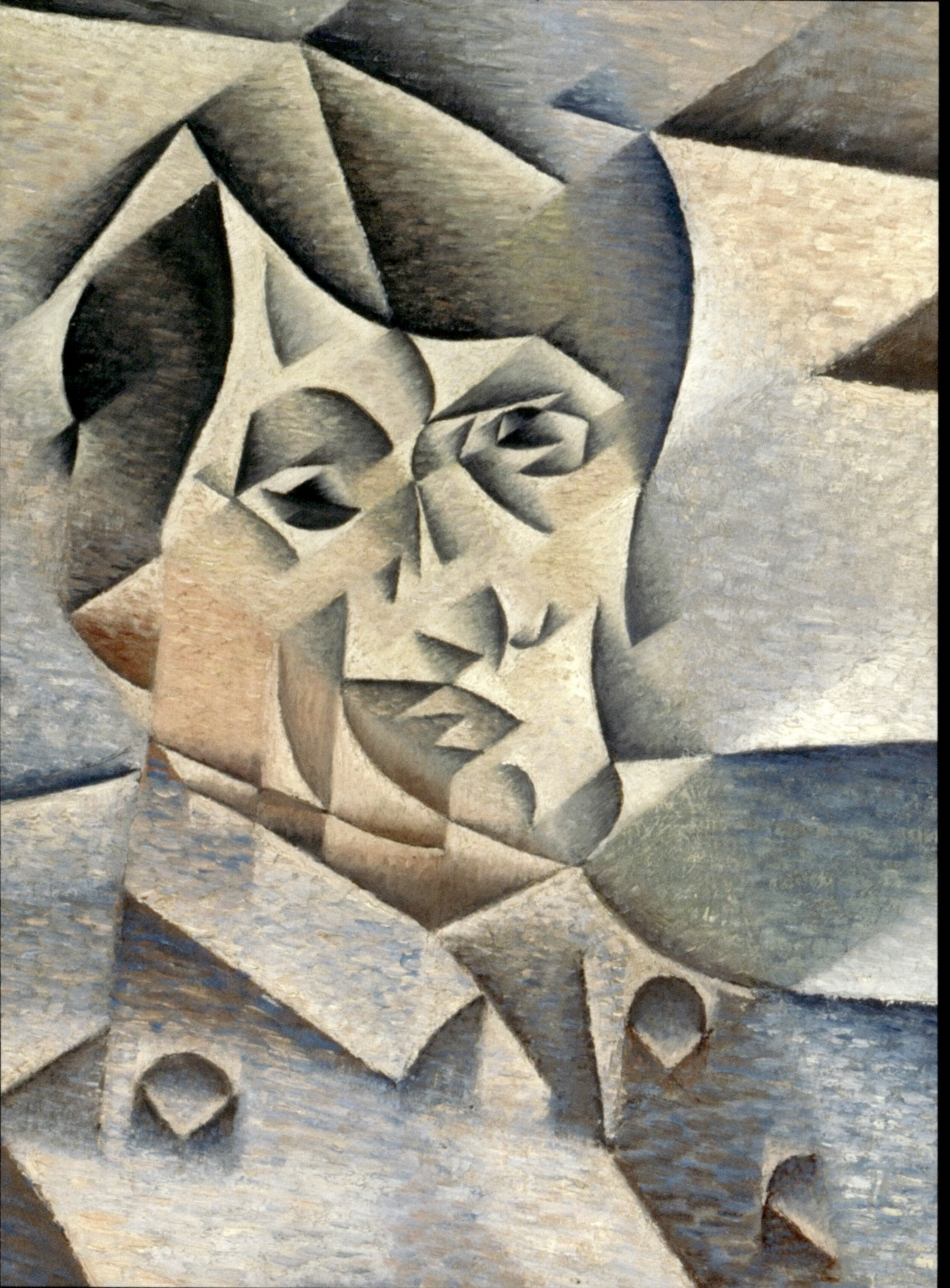

Opposite page: Trevor Lawrence (#16) of the Jacksonville Jaguars is hit by Logan Hall (#90) of the Tampa Bay Buccaneers during the second quarter at Raymond James Stadium on December 24, 2023, in Tampa, Florida. Photo by Mike Carlson/Getty Images.

This page: *Portrait of Pablo Picasso* (detail), 1912, Juan Gris. Digital image by Google Arts & Culture. Art Institute of Chicago.

JUSTIN JEFFERSON'S GRIDDY

The Griddy, apparently around since 1305.

Left: Minnesota Vikings wide receiver Justin Jefferson (#18) celebrates his first-quarter, 5-yard touchdown reception by doing "the Griddy" during an NFL game between the Minnesota Vikings and Green Bay Packers on September 11, 2022, at U.S. Bank Stadium in Minneapolis, Minnesota. Photo by Nick Wosika/Icon Sportswire via Getty Images.

Right: *Lamentation* (detail), 1305, Giotto. Digital image by Gennadii Saus i Segura. Scrovegni Chapel.

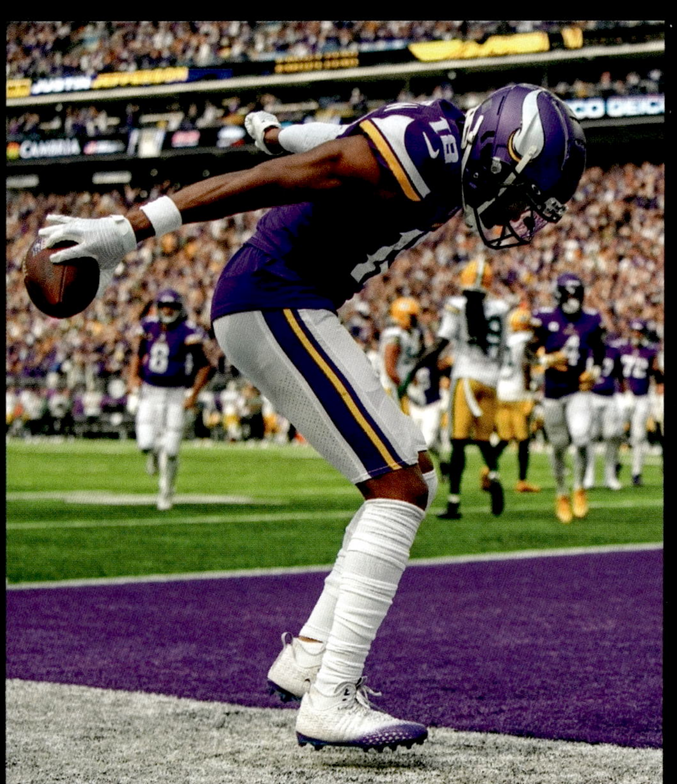

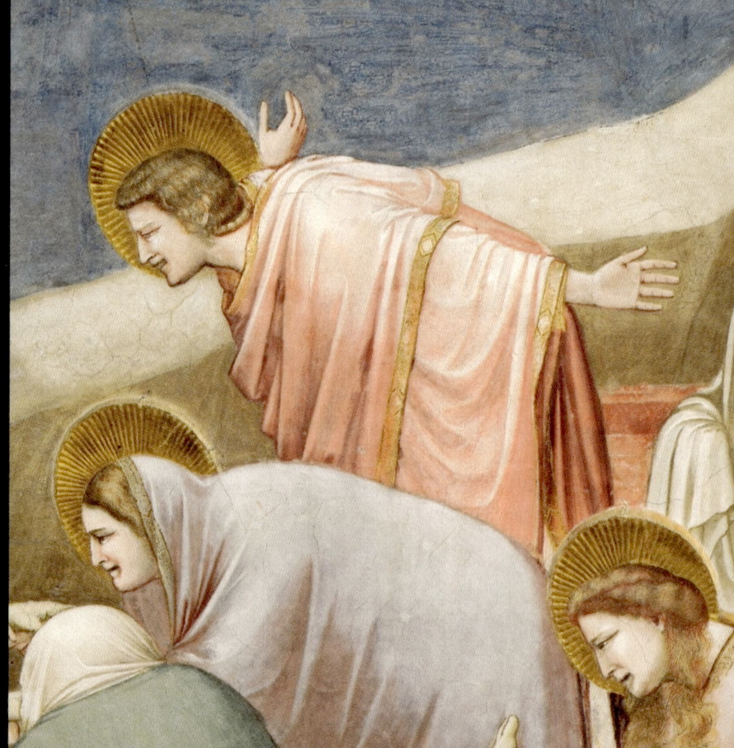

LEFT SHARK

I love myself a good interlude during a game, and nothing ever manages to eclipse the Super Bowl halftime show. Each year I repost matchups of past favorites, and the one that inevitably gets the most attention is Katy Perry from Super Bowl XLIX and John Singleton Copley's *Watson and the Shark* for obvious reasons.

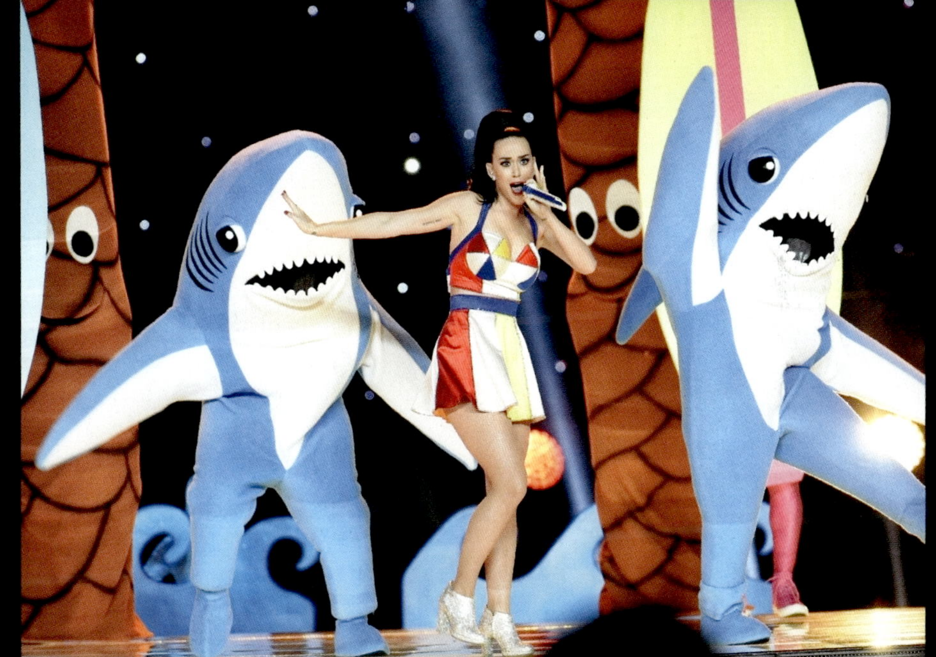

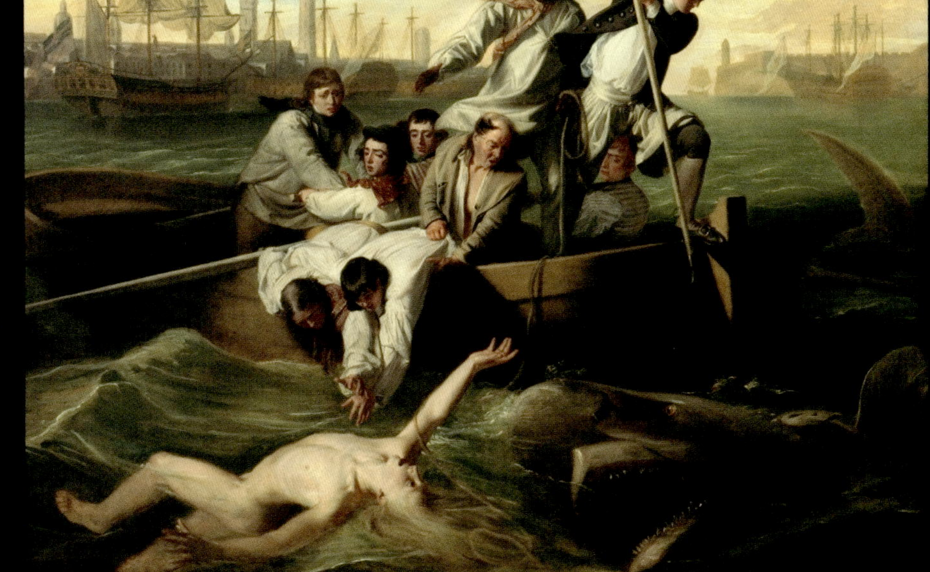

Top: Recording artist Katy Perry performs onstage during the Pepsi Super Bowl XLIX halftime show at University of Phoenix Stadium on February 1, 2015, in Glendale, Arizona. Photo by Kevin Mazur/WireImage.

Bottom: *Watson and the Shark* (detail), 1778, John Singleton Copley. National Gallery of Art.

LONDON FALLING

This photo earned Kevin Sabitus the gold in the American Football category at the World Sports Photography Awards, his second of three consecutive wins, and rightfully so, as it's the perfect example of how luck is just preparation meeting opportunity.

You could say the opposite was the case for Saint Peter. Pope Clement I in his letter to the Corinthians, chapter 5, in referencing Peter's crucifixion, noted, "Peter, through unjust envy, endured not one or two but many labours." Alas, while the sinew between these two images isn't there on a spiritual level, the visual interrelation is undeniable, as Saint Peter met his ultimate end with his head pointed downward, just as Drake London is positioned heading into the end zone. There are numerous options to pick from, but de Crayer's depiction seems to get the angle just right.

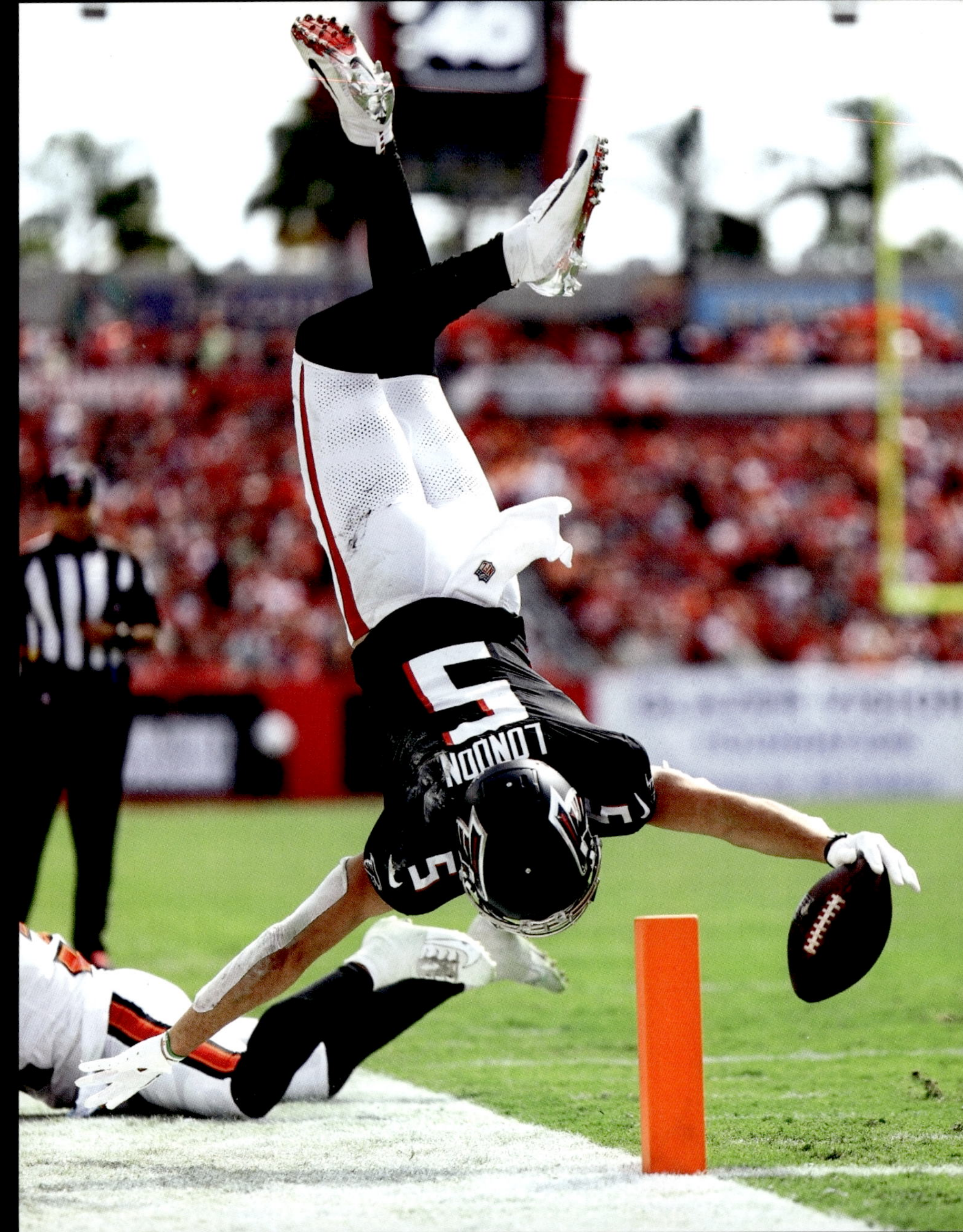

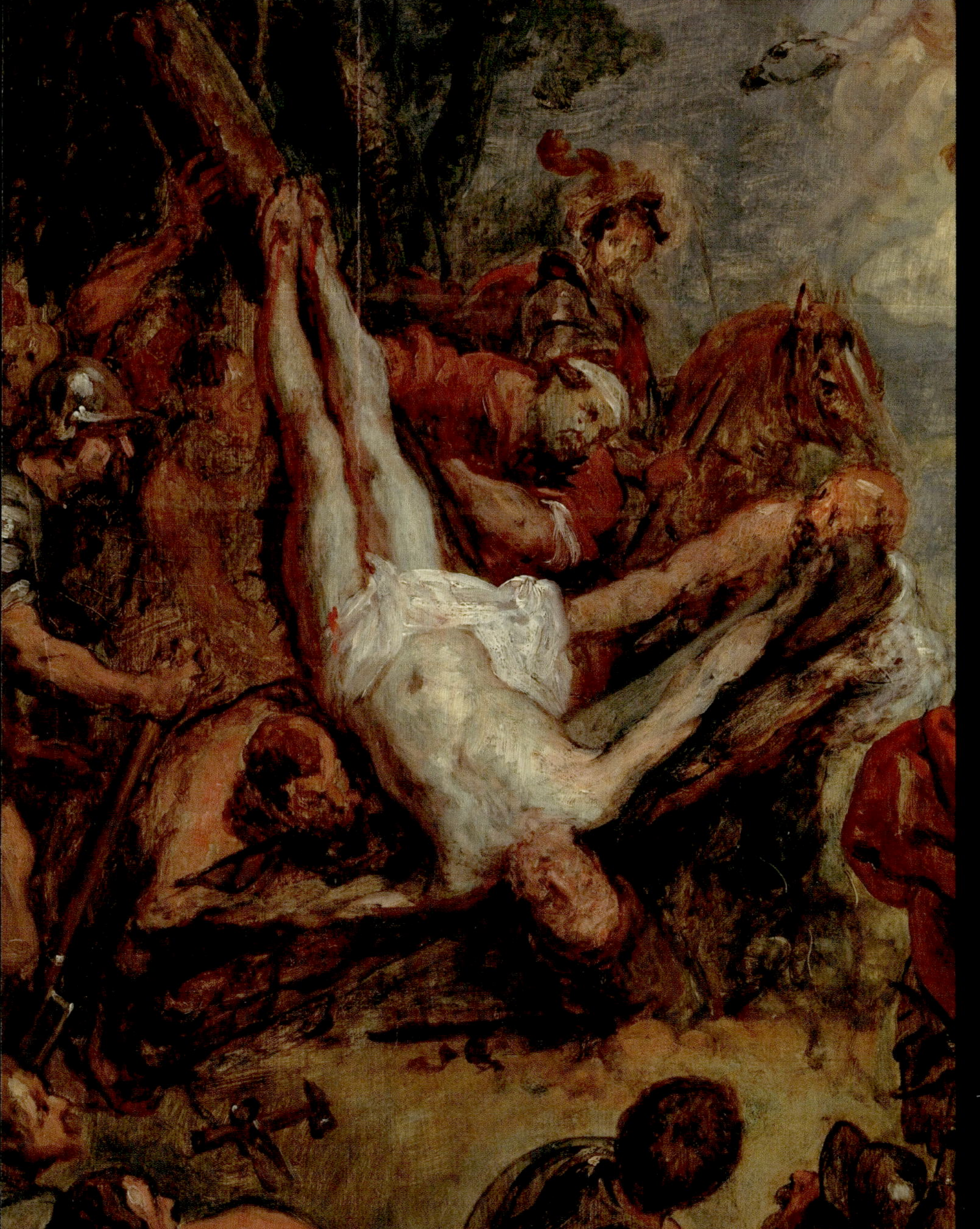

Opposite page: Drake London (#5) of the Atlanta Falcons dives and is stopped short of the goal line by Antoine Winfield Jr. (#31) of the Tampa Bay Buccaneers in the third quarter of the game at Raymond James Stadium on October 22, 2023, in Tampa, Florida. Photo by Kevin Sabitus/Getty Images.

This page: *The Martyrdom of Saint Peter* (detail), 1664–69, Gaspar de Crayer. Museum Boijmans Van Beuningen.

THE FEAST OF KELCE

For me, missing an NFL playoff game is sacrilege, let alone one as hyped as the 2024 AFC divisional playoff tilt between the Chiefs and the Bills. And yet, sometimes duty calls, and in the case of January 21, 2024, it took the form of my mother-in-law's birthday dinner. I love her to death, but I had an inkling that FOMO would turn material, and I'd miss the meme-able moment of the century, to the extent that I posted this message at 6:16 p.m. ET: *programming note—have a dinner that I can't get out of with no phones allowed so will be out of commission until roughly 8:30. But tag away and I'll pick up anything worthwhile that I miss when I'm back online.*

My worst fears were proven, as at 7:57 p.m. the NFL tagged me in a Tweet with the now iconic photo of Jason Kelce shirtless, asking, "what say you, @ArtButSports?"

Jason Kelce (#62) of the Philadelphia Eagles celebrates after the Kansas City Chiefs score a touchdown during the first half of the AFC divisional playoff game against the Buffalo Bills at Highmark Stadium on January 21, 2024, in Orchard Park, New York. Photo by Kathryn Riley/Getty Images.

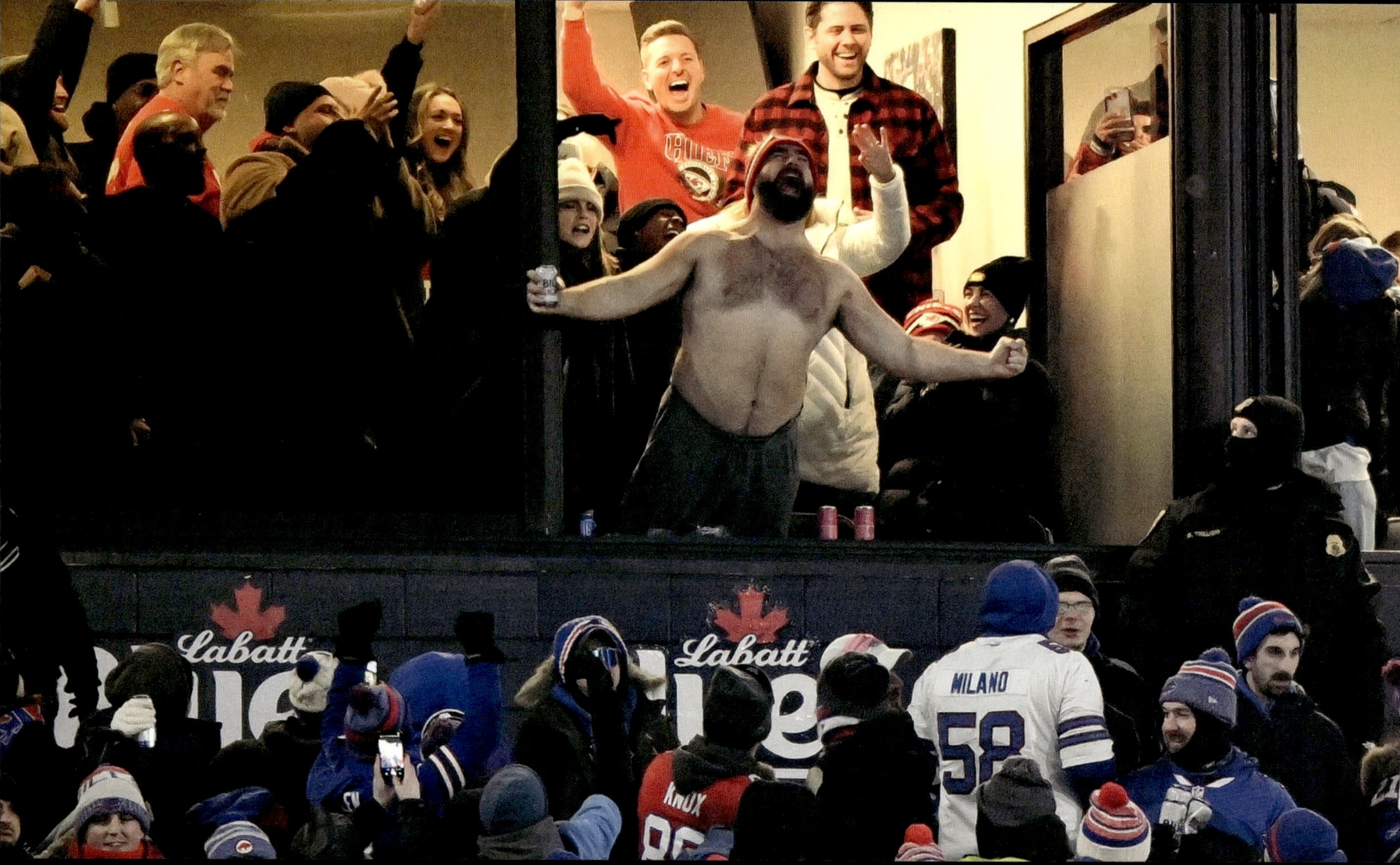

It was the first time the NFL Twitter (now X) admin had acknowledged my existence, by far the highest-profile moment the account has experienced to date. Luckily, dinner ended early, and I saw the tweet a handful of minutes later in the cab home. I quickly asked who the photographer was, got an answer (shout-out to Kathryn Riley, who crushes it week in and week out), and had this post fired into the ether by 8:13 p.m. As soon as it hit the timeline, my phone, which was on its last legs, started overheating from all the notifications that were pouring in. It ended up being my most-shared post, and most importantly, it got mentioned on the *New Heights* podcast (run by Travis and Jason Kelce)!

The Feast of Bacchus, 1654, Philips de Koninck. Museum Bredius.

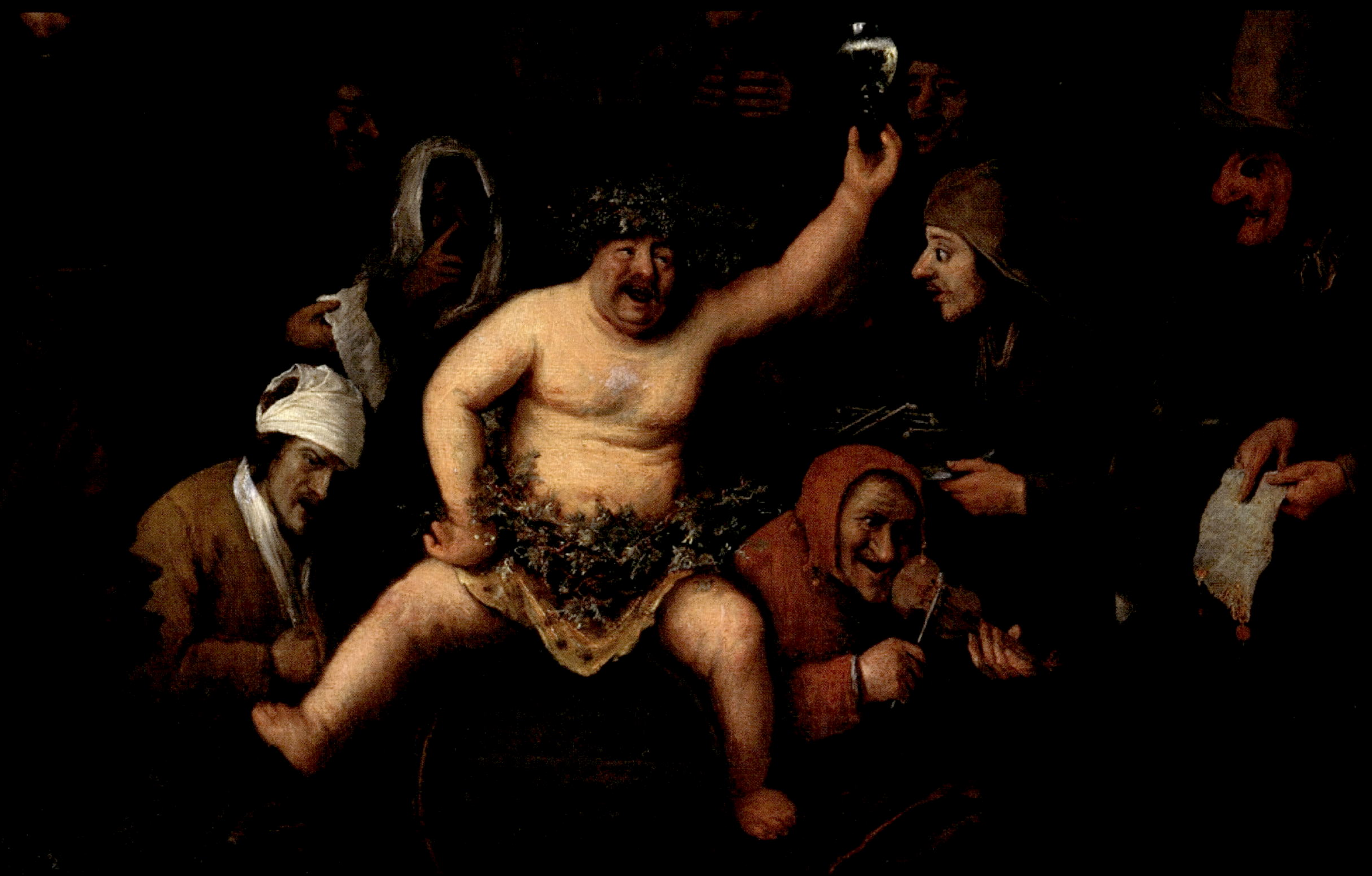

90-WATT ASCENT

Hieronymus Bosch is most famous for his iconic painting *The Garden of Earthly Delights*. His lesser-recognized work, however, is just as breathtaking. *Ascent of the Blessed* fits in that category, and this particular figure within it matches well for T. J. Watt's signature running-out-of-the-tunnel pregame leap.

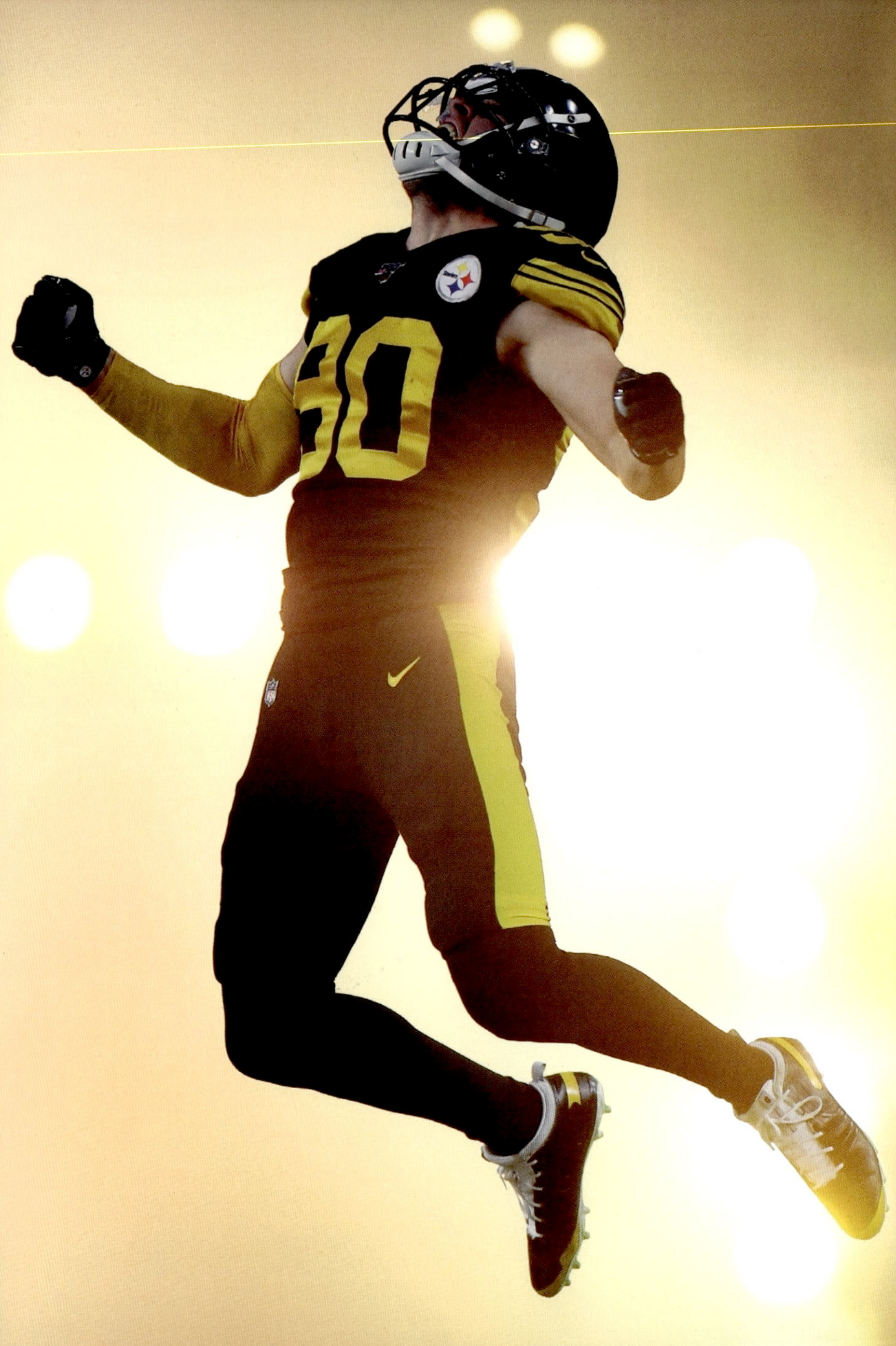

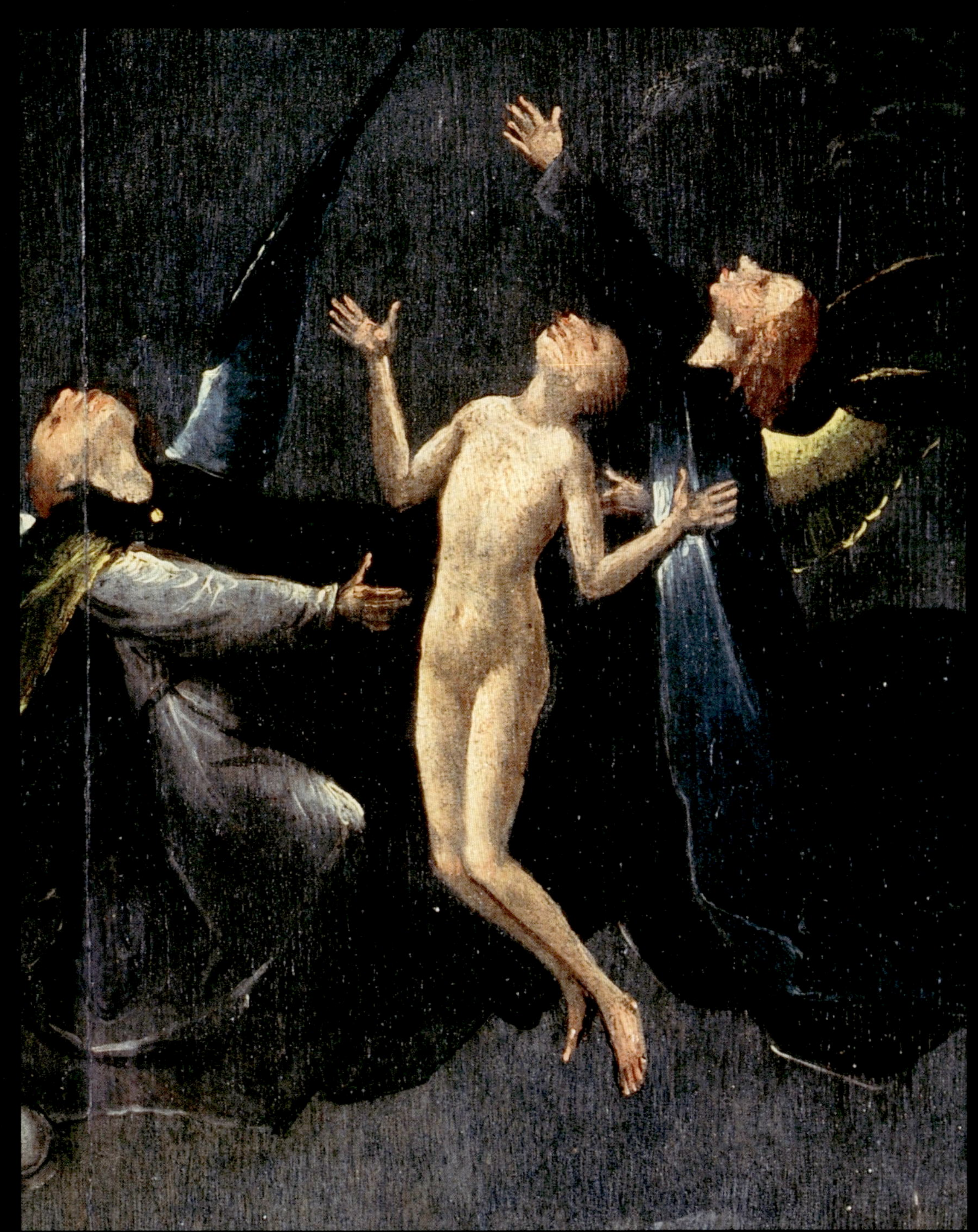

Opposite page: T. J. Watt (#90) of the Pittsburgh Steelers jumps in the air as he runs onto the field before the game against the Buffalo Bills at Heinz Field on December 15, 2019, in Pittsburgh, Pennsylvania. Photo by Joe Sargent/Getty Images.

This page: *Ascent of the Blessed* (detail), circa 1500–04, Hieronymus Bosch. Doge's Palace.

SOCCER/ FOOTBALL

There is no sport more global than footy—a universal language without the need for translation. A "Tobin Heath nutmeg" and "Johan Cruyff turn" are understood in all corners of the world, just like fine art. Occasionally, football and art even intentionally intersect, as in the case of Boccioni's *Dynamism of a Soccer Player*

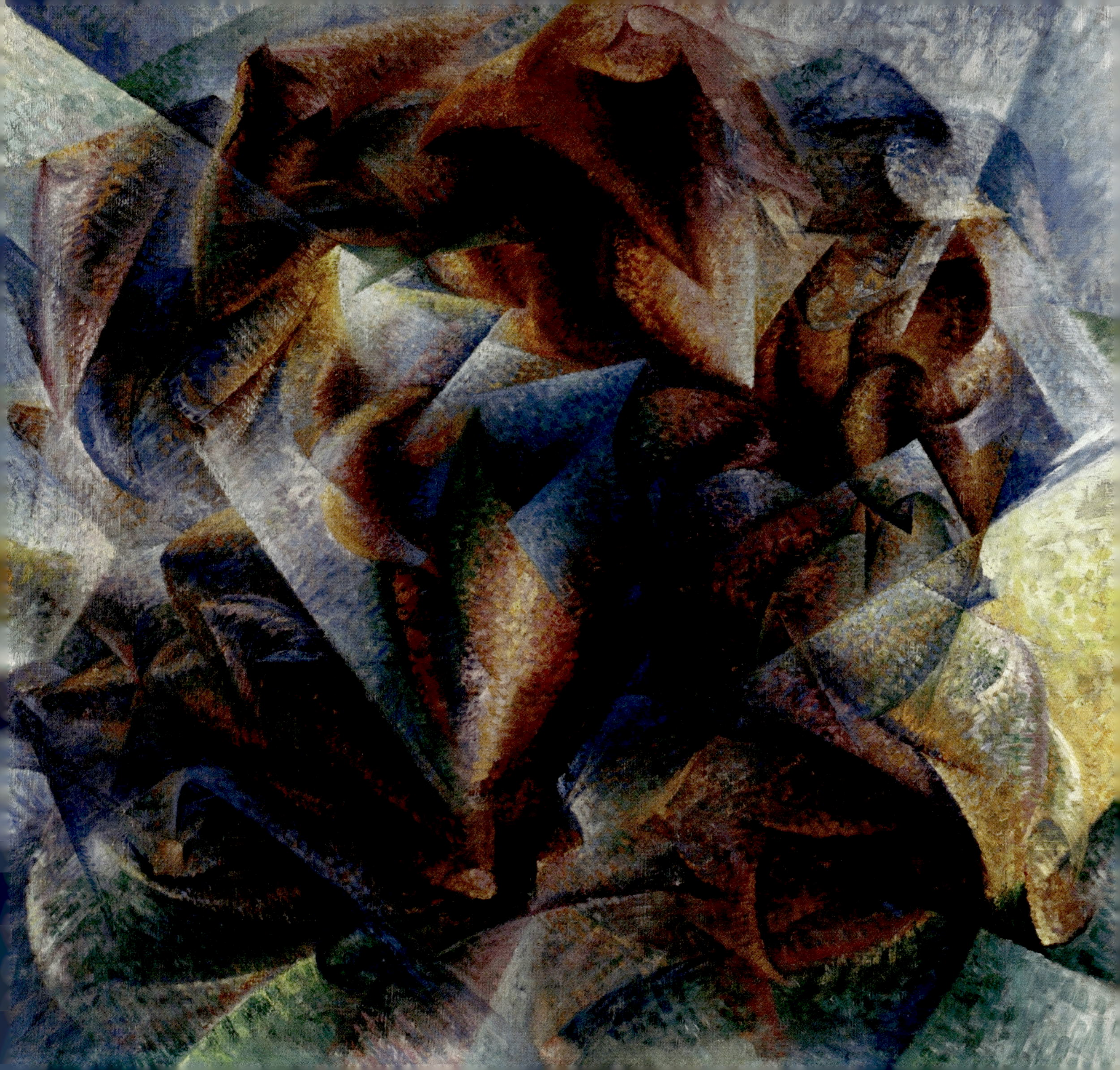

THE CARRYING OF THE MESSI-AH

In artwork, Saint Christopher is often shown carrying a baby across a river. Throughout the journey, the infant becomes heavier and heavier—when they finally arrive at the shore, the child reveals his true identity as the Son of God, and in turn Christopher gains the unofficial title of "Christ-bearer." As the story goes, the infants tell Saint Christopher that he has just carried the weight of the world.

When Lionel Messi scored his first goal for Barcelona on May 1, 2025, it was Ronaldinho, the reigning FIFA World Player of the Year, who provided the assist. In celebration, the Brazilian superstar hoisted the Argentinian prodigy on his shoulders, and a legendary photo was born. As we look back at the career Messi has had, it's easy to see the parallels to the story of Saint Christopher and the infant Christ, as—regardless of which team you root for—Messi represents a central figure of religious proportions.

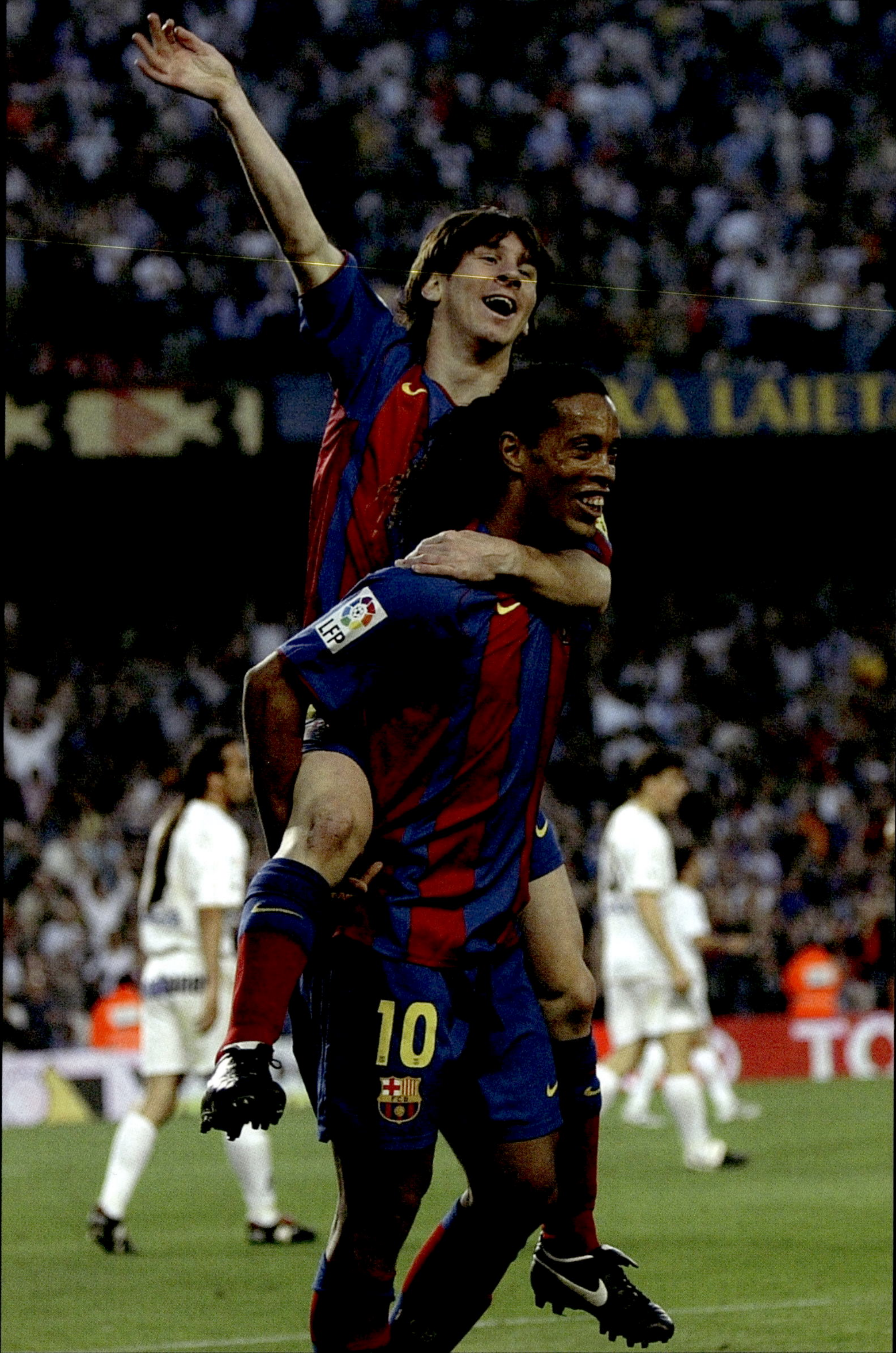

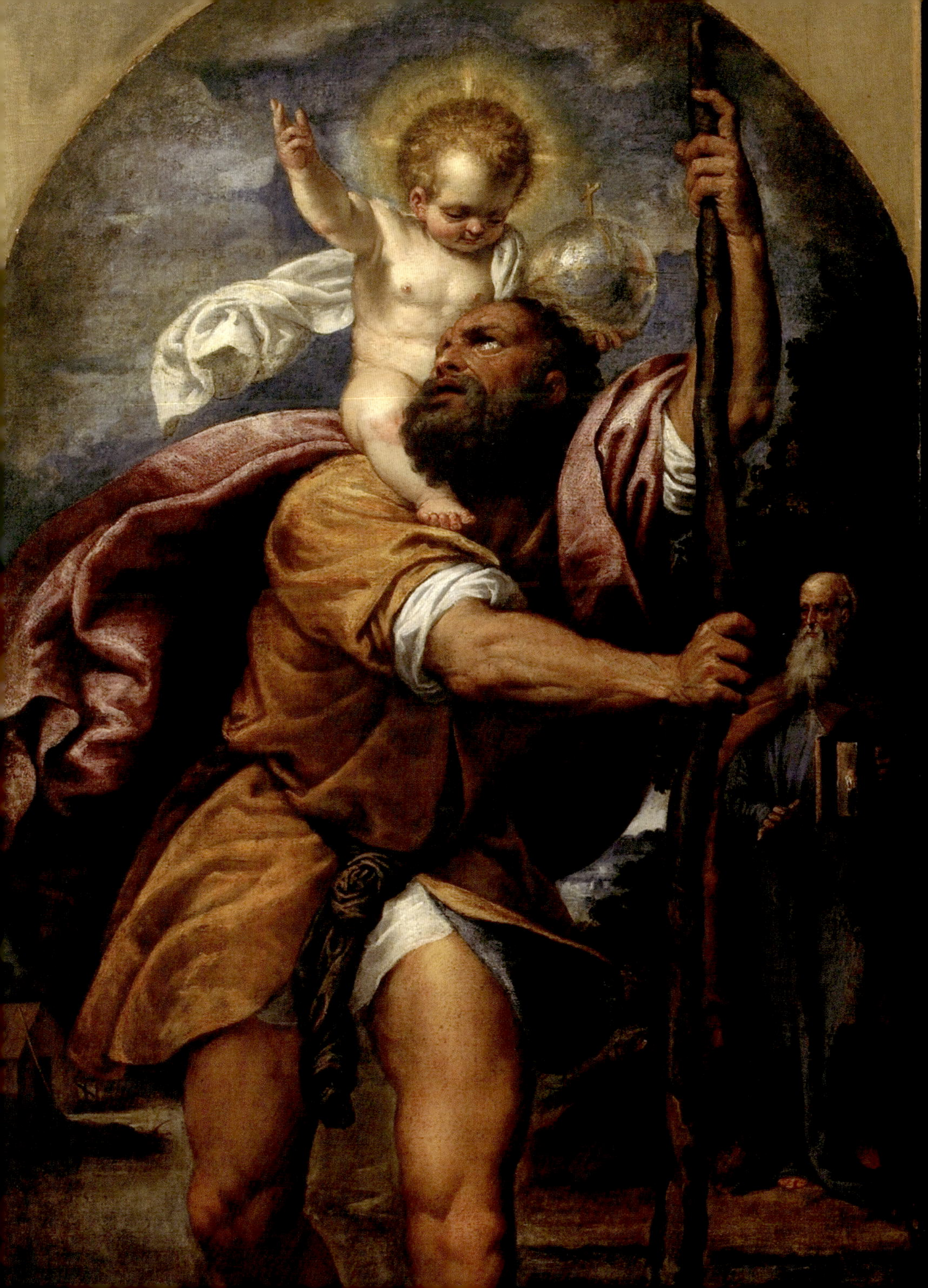

Opposite page: FC Barcelona's Argentinian Lionel Messi (waving) and Brazilian Ronaldinho celebrate their second goal against Albacete during their Spanish league football match at the Camp Nou stadium in Barcelona, May 1, 2005. FC Barcelona won 2–0. Photo by Lluis Gene/AFP via Getty Images.

This page: *St. Christopher and the Christ Child* (detail), late sixteenth century, unknown Venetian artist. The Walters Art Museum.

MILAN DERBY

There's a massive discrepancy between the number of sports images featuring athletes photographed from behind and the number of paintings available to match. It's a shame, both because ideally, I'd have more supply to meet demand, and *rückenfigur* as a genre, when executed properly, is haunting and beautiful and arguably my favorite type of painting. Translating to "back-figure," rückenfigur is originally tied to the late-eighteenth- and early-nineteenth-century movement of German Romanticism, which dominated the cultural fabric of German-speaking countries at the time.

When thinking through rückenfigur options, there are two artists who inevitably bubble to the surface: Caspar David Friedrich and Johan Christian Dahl. The two were contemporaries and even depicted each other in their work (Dahl's *Two Men before a Waterfall at Sunset* shows

Marco Materazzi of Inter Milan and Rui Costa of AC Milan look on as Inter fans shower the pitch with flares during the UEFA Champions League quarter-final second leg at the San Siro Stadium on April 12, 2005, in Milan, Italy. Photo by Mike Hewitt/Getty Images.

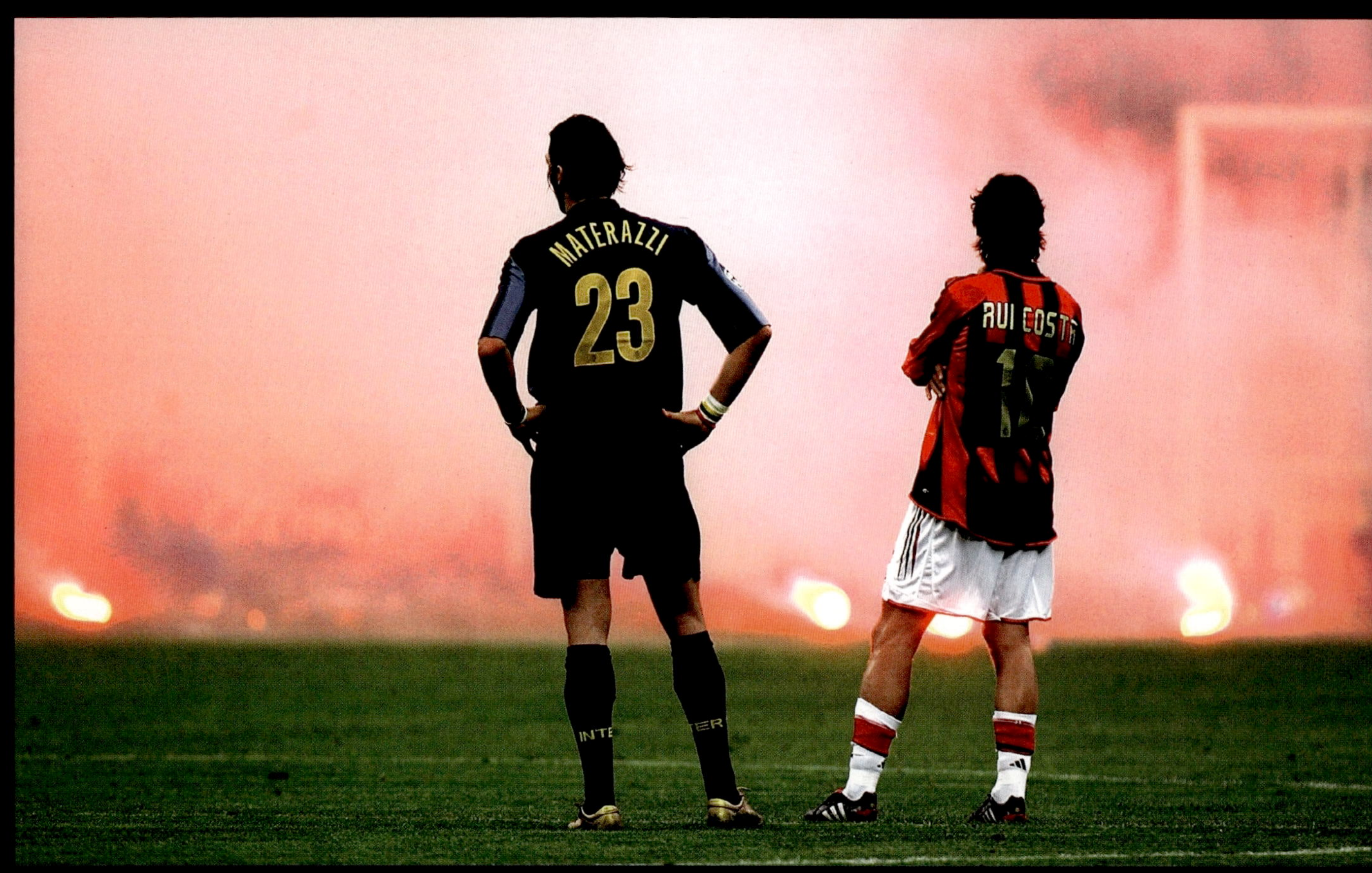

the two side by side). Given their status in the pantheon of rückenfigur, it felt right to feature them for one of the most famous soccer photos taken from this angle. Rui Costa and Marco Materazzi pause together at the 2005 Champions League meeting—that doubled as the Milan Derby—which was interrupted by fans throwing flares onto the pitch. It's a glimpse into the humanity between two athletes, and proof that even if you're operating in the same competitive sphere, there's no reason to not reflect and take in the moment, just like Chrisitan Dahl and David Friedrich. It doesn't matter that they're on different teams (and not dressed in the same colors like the figures in the rückenfigur paintings). In this moment, they are one—an allegory of soccer kinship under the blanket of competition.

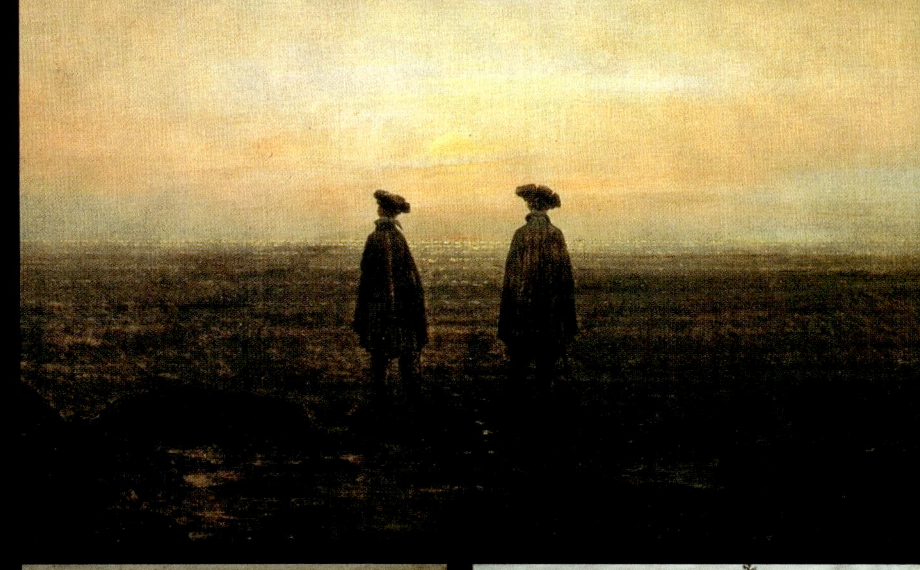

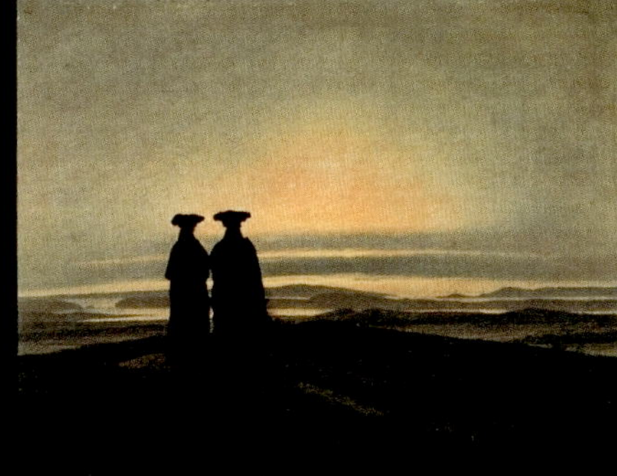

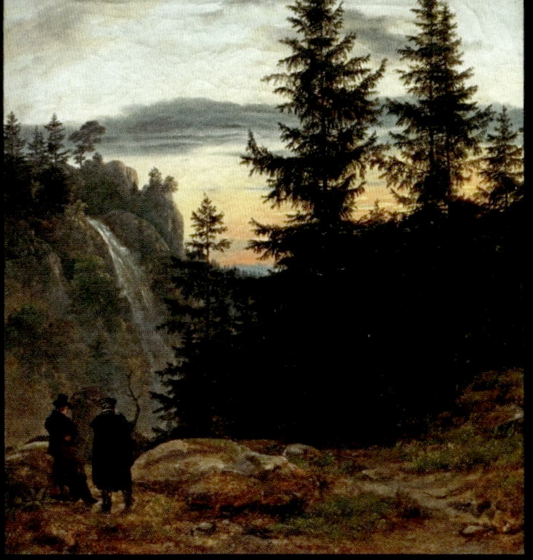

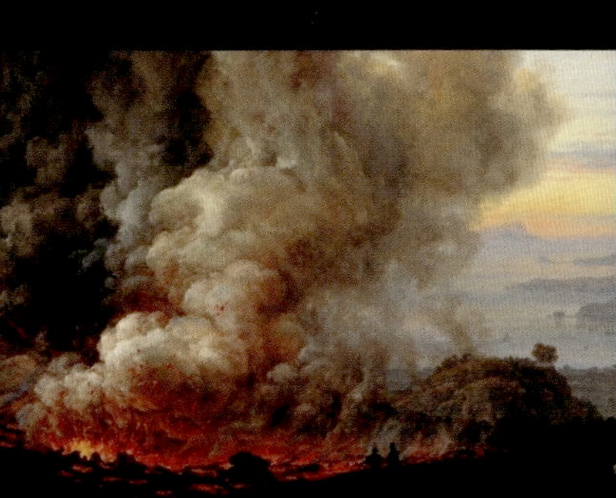

Top: *Two Men by the Sea* (detail), 1817, Caspar David Friedrich. Digital image by Zeno.org. Alte Nationalgalerie.

Middle left: *Evening Landscape with Two Men*, 1837, Caspar David Friedrich. Digital image by Web Gallery of Art. Hermitage Museum.

Middle right: *Two Men before a Waterfall at Sunset* (detail), 1823, Johan Christian Dahl. Digital image by Sotheby's London. National Gallery of Norway.

Bottom: *An Eruption of Vesuvius* (detail), 1824, Johan Christian Dahl. The Metropolitan Museum of Art.

THE MOST FAMOUS SHOT OF THEM ALL

Squarely on the Mount Rushmore of American sports moments is Brandi Chastain's World Cup–winning penalty kick in 1999. It served as a seminal event for women's sports in the United States and helped catapult a movement that continues to see growth in the sport and unleash greatness in its path.

A shot of this magnitude requires art of equal weight, which is why I think an image of a kneeling deity does it justice.

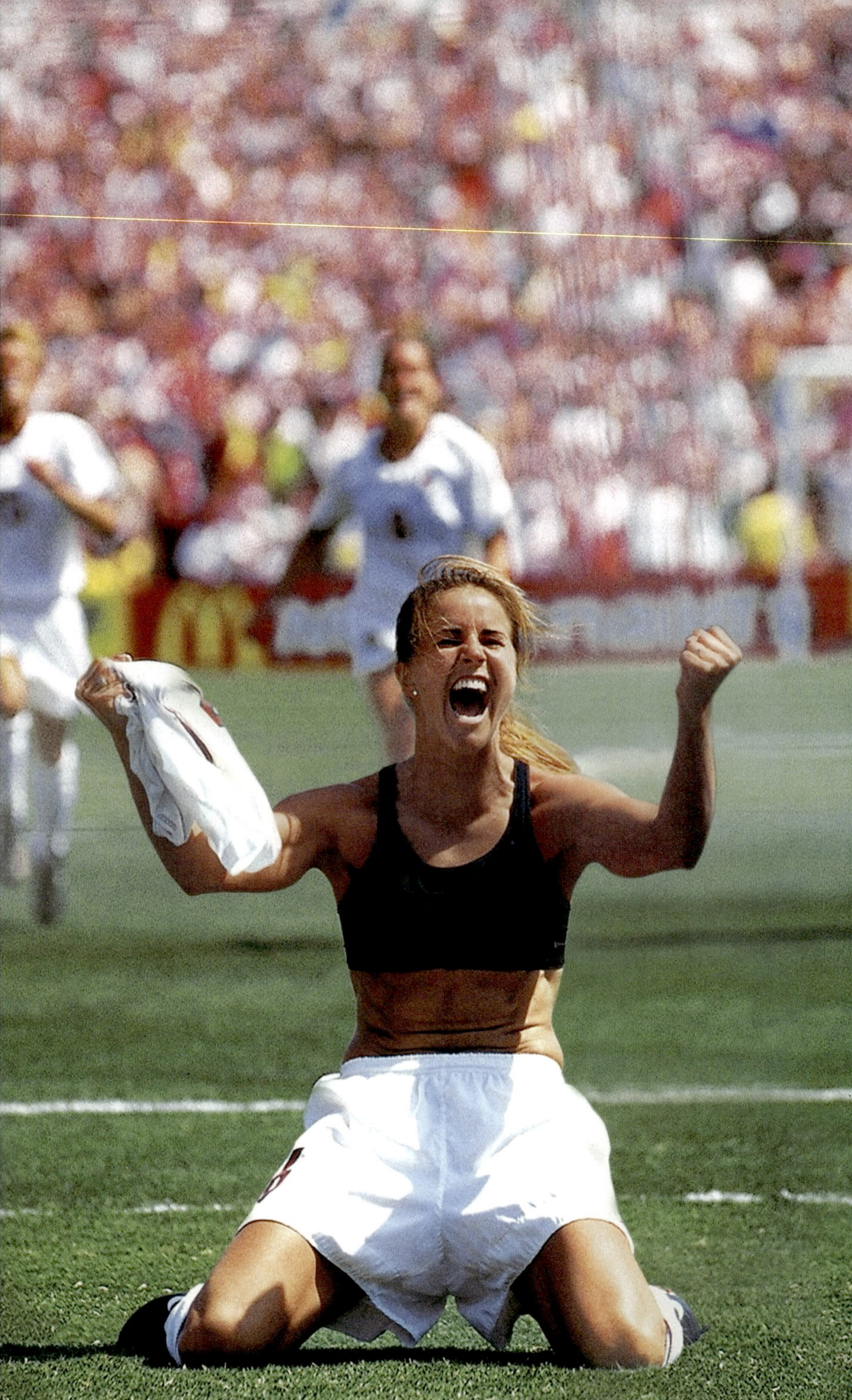

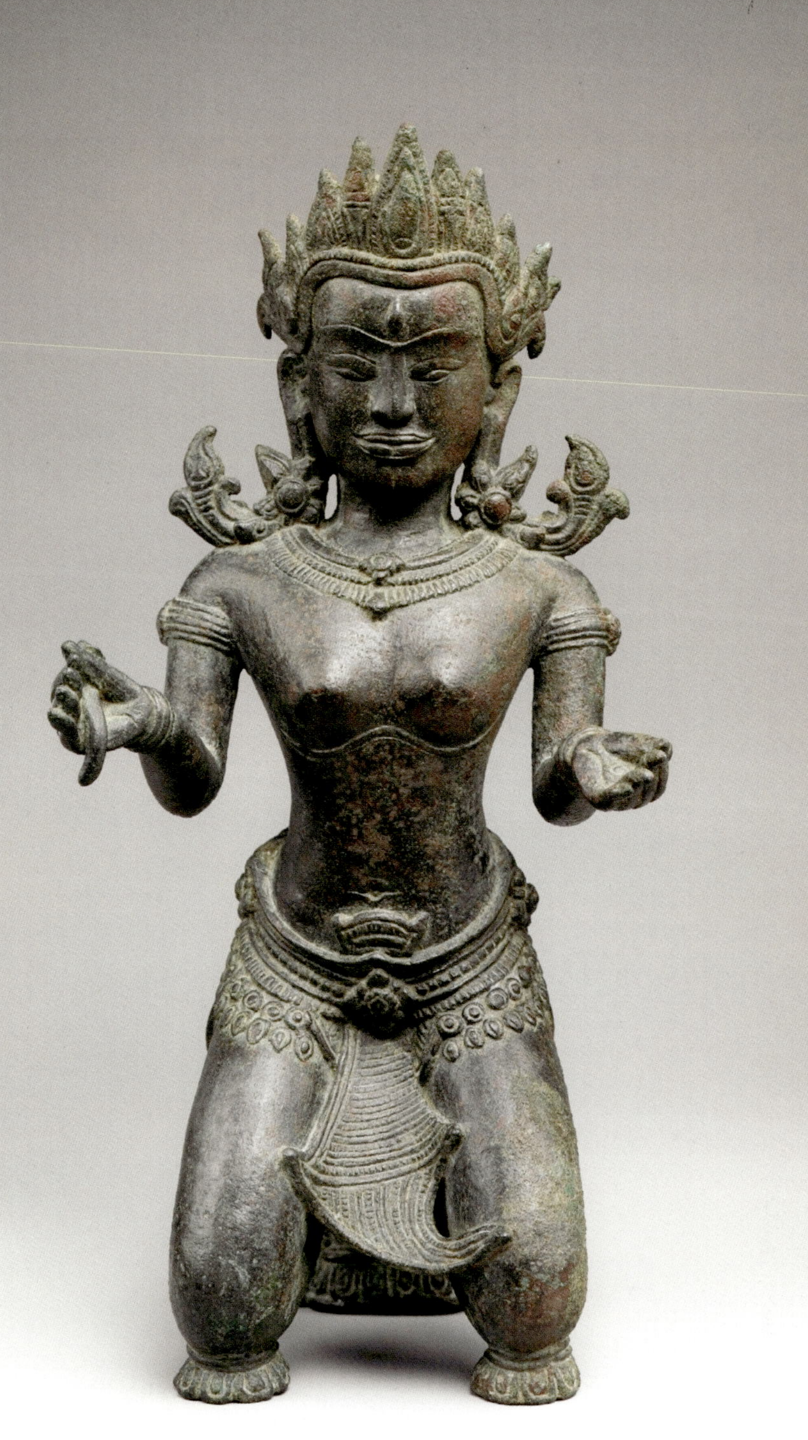

Opposite page: Team USA's Brandi Chastain celebrates after scoring the winning penalty kick in the World Cup final vs. China on July 10, 1999, in Pasadena, California. Photo by Robert Beck/Sports Illustrated via Getty Images/ Getty Images.

This page: *Kneeling Female Deity*, late twelfth century, unknown artist, Cambodia or Thailand. The Metropolitan Museum of Art.

FOOTY EXTENSIONS

Though the side-by-sides have come to dominate the grid, on occasion I see an image that I think is best treated with what I call a "blend," as in, the sports image becomes an extension of the artwork itself. These feel a bit like cheating, because they're a bit easier to make, so I'm picky about deploying them.

With the Erik ten Hag photo, I knew I wasn't going to find corresponding artwork showing a bubble on a man's head, so the blend was partly born from necessity. But it also gave me an excuse to use one of my favorite pieces, a mainstay at the Metropolitan Museum of Art and a personal favorite because it captures the true core value of the account: that art can be playful.

Another William Blake image, the on-the-nose hand of God image, blends with the "Hand of God," Diego Maradona's famous opening goal in the Argentina vs. England 1986 World Cup quarterfinals, where the ball deflected off his hand but was not called by the match official. (Argentina would win the match 2–1 and ultimately take home the trophy.) Blake also felt appropriate because like Maradona, he was multifaceted. The former was an accomplished (though almost exclusively posthumously recognized) poet, painter, and printmaker. The latter won at all stages and stops, for club and country, and possessed a playing style that cemented his legacy as a dynamic figure who could score, pass, dribble—and everything in between.

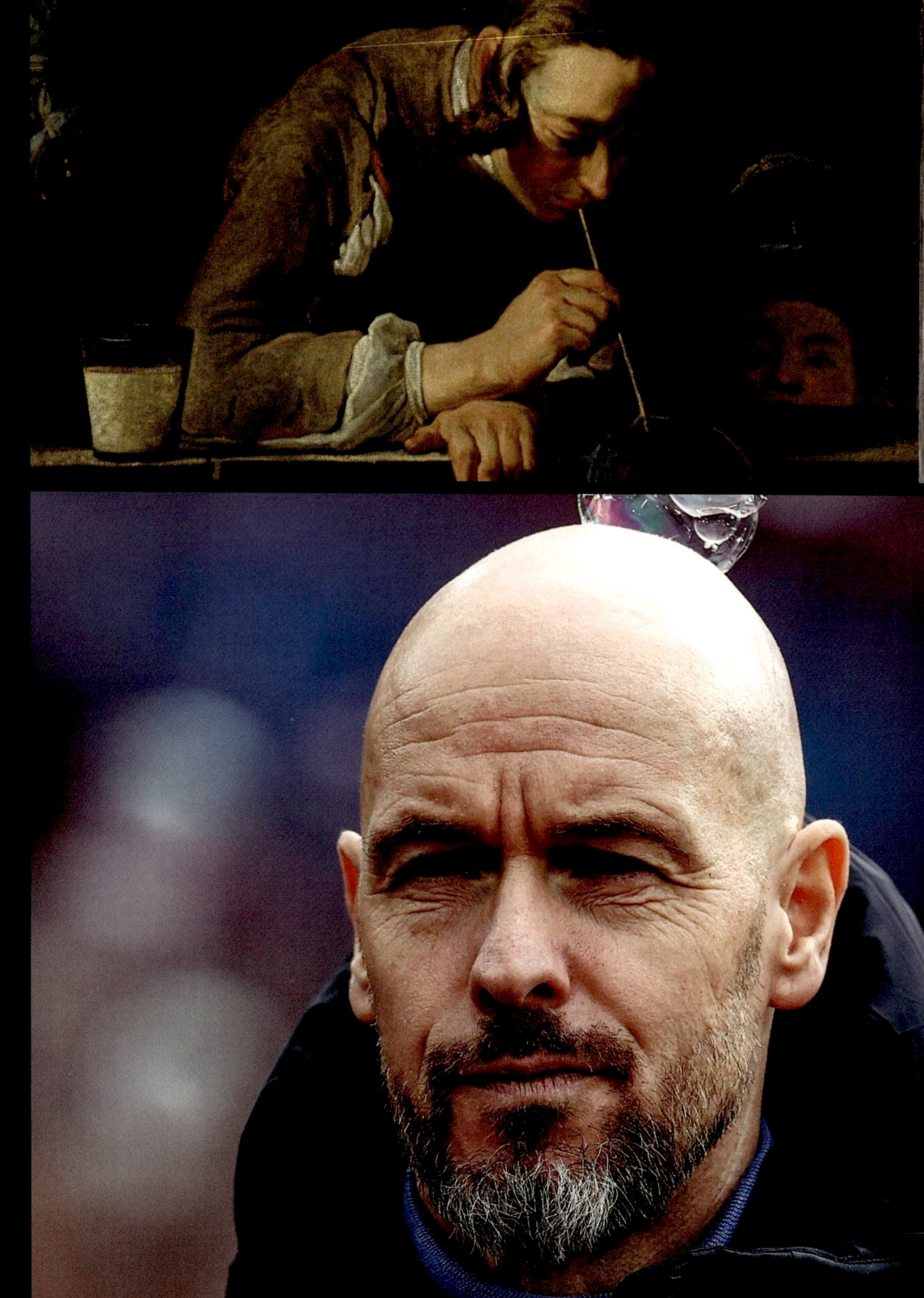

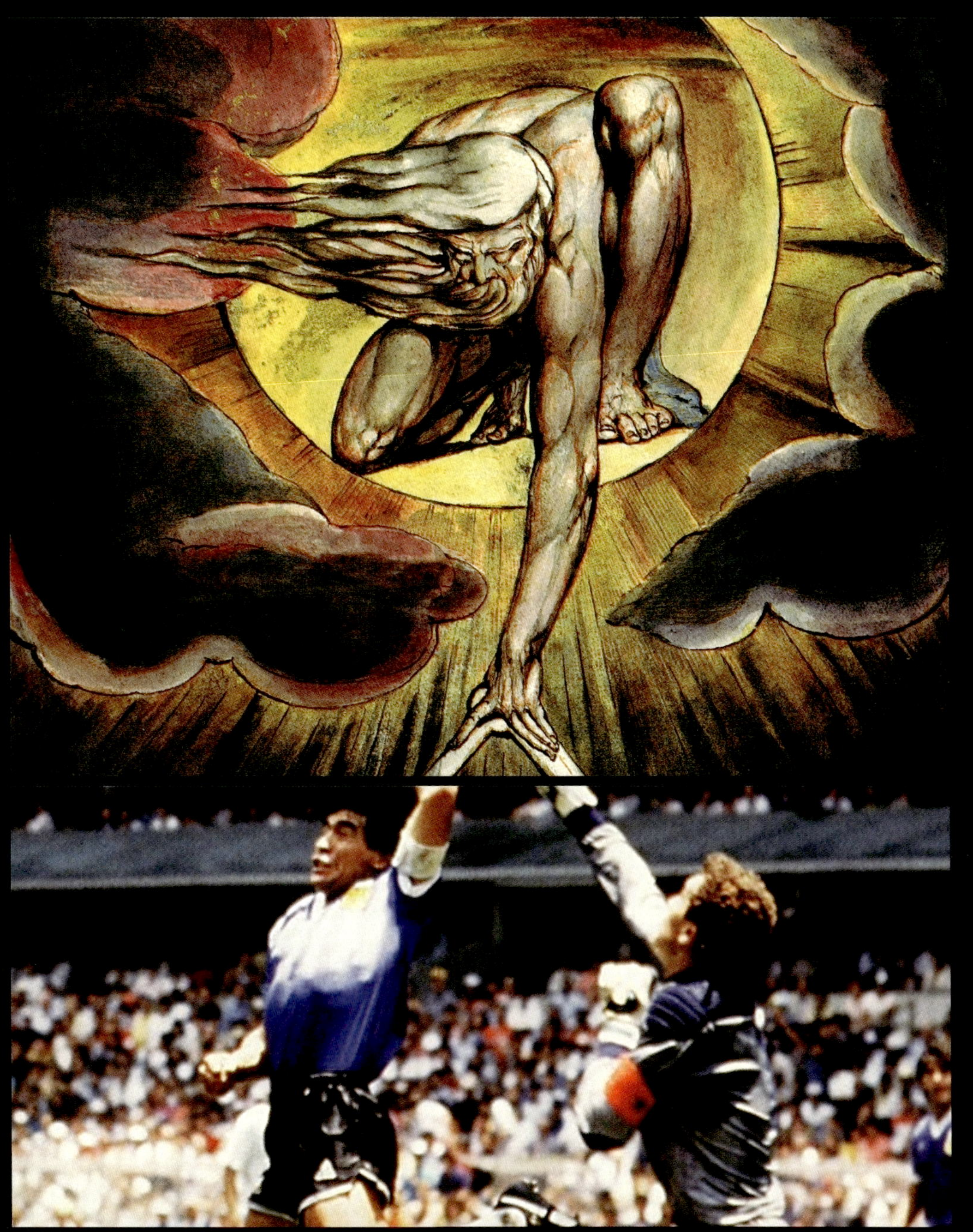

Opposite page, bottom: A bubble pops on the head of Manchester United manager Erik ten Hag during the Premier League match between West Ham United and Manchester United at London Stadium on December 23, 2023, in London, England. Photo by Charlotte Wilson/Offside via Getty Images.

Opposite page, top: *Soap Bubbles* (detail), circa 1733–34, Jean-Baptiste-Siméon Chardin. The Metropolitan Museum of Art.

This page, bottom: Diego Maradona of Argentina handles the ball past Peter Shilton of England to score the opening goal of the World Cup quarterfinals on June 22, 1986, at the Azteca Stadium in Mexico City, Mexico. Argentina won 2–1. Photo by Bongarts/Staff.

This page, top: "*Europe" Plate i: Frontispiece,* "*The Ancient of Days*" (detail), 1827, William Blake. Digital image by The William Blake Museum. Fitzwilliam Museum.

SOPHIA RAISED

Like the Jonquel Jones moment on page 26, I was lucky enough to be in attendance for another deciding finals games, this time at the 2022 NWSL Championship between the Kansas City Current and Portland Thorns in Washington, DC. We had barely settled into our seats when Thorns star Sophia Wilson took advantage of a KC miscue and slotted home the first and ultimately game-winning goal.

When there's a championship on the line and you're fortunate enough to be in the building, you keep your phone in your pocket until after the game, but as soon as I saw Wilson hit the "Sophia Shrug," I knew it'd make for a solid post. I wanted something that captured the arm placement, but also wanted to incorporate teammate Morgan Weaver and the weightlessness

Sophia Wilson (#9, née Smith) of the Portland Thorns celebrates her goal with Morgan Weaver (#22) during the NWSL Challenge Cup final game between the Kansas City Current and the Portland Thorns at Audi Field on October 29, 2022, in Washington, DC. Photo by Photo by Nikita Taparia (@kryptobanana)/NWSL.

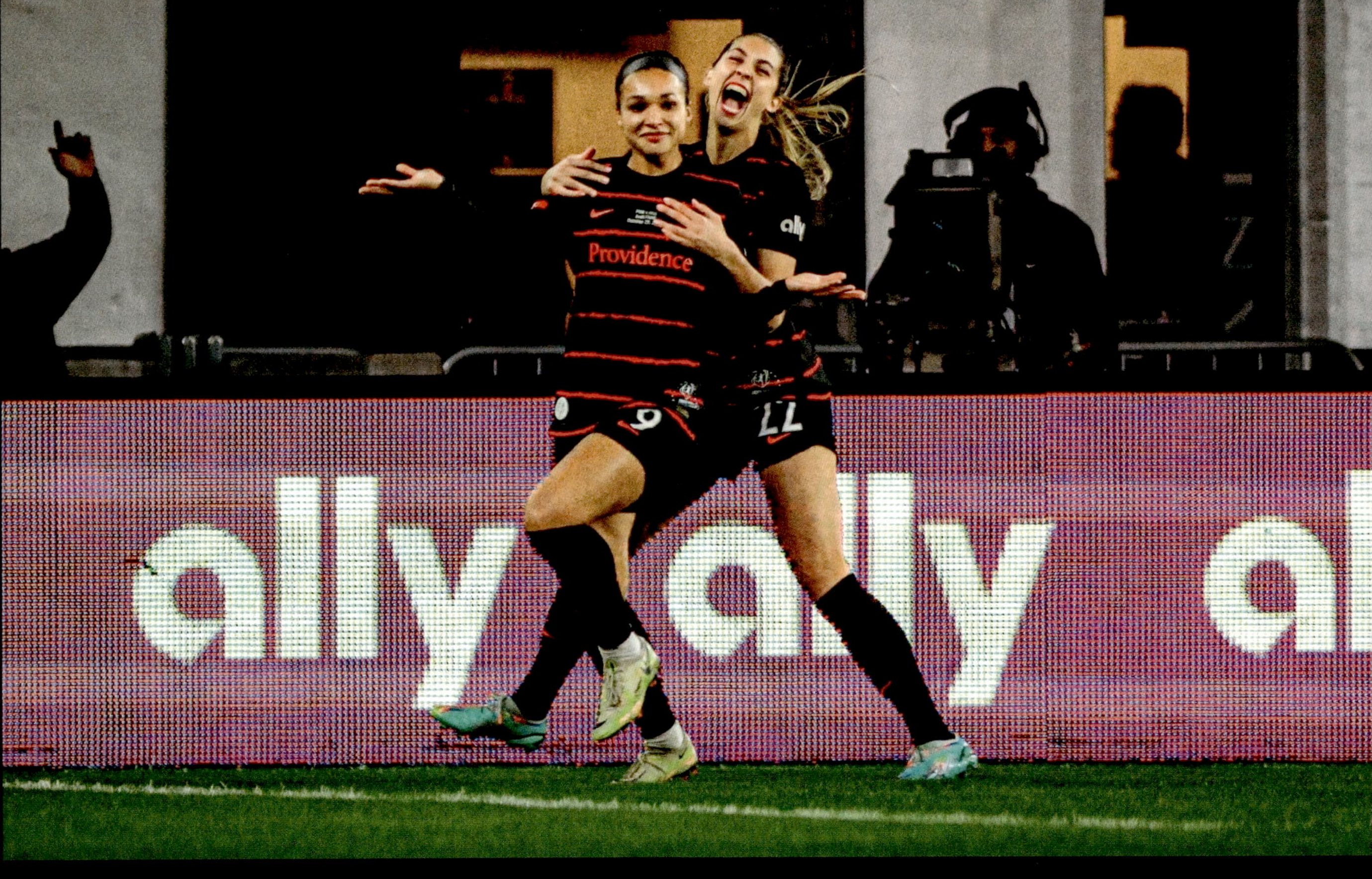

of their concurrent gesticulations. The Assumption of Mary hits on the latter, as a central figure is hovering, propped up by angels, and has something close to the former, as her arms are often depicted as extended. I had previously stumbled upon Giovanni Lanfranco's version, *Mary Magdalen Raised by Angels*, when perusing through images of the Assumption of Mary, and I banked it for the very reason that she looked to be shrugging.

Mary Magdalen Raised by Angels (detail), circa 1616, Giovanni Lanfranco. Digital image by Web Gallery of Art. Museo di Capodimonte.

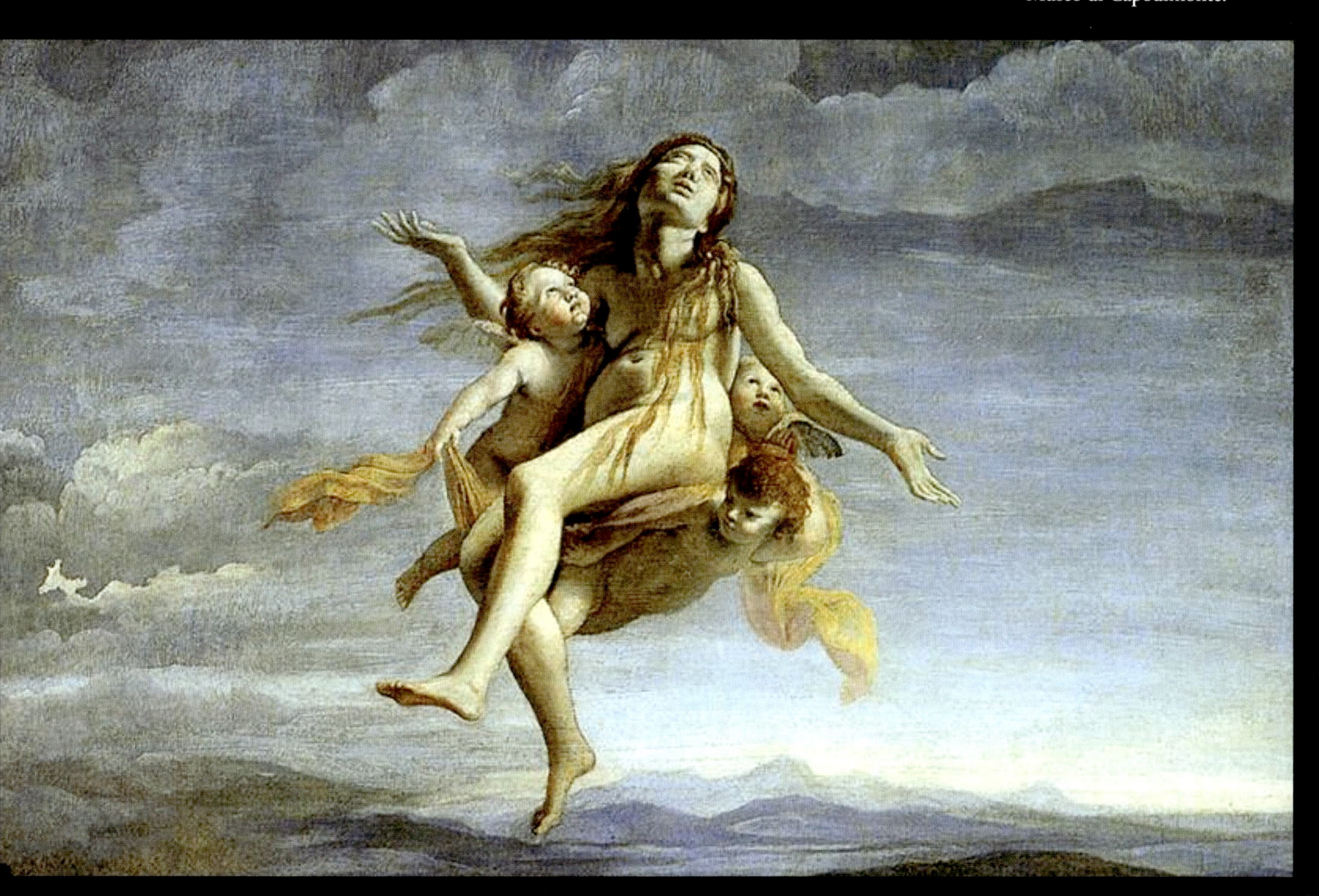

THE INCREDULITY OF THE USWNT

One of my all-time favorites, mostly because there's no caption necessary.

Kelley O'Hara (#5) of the United States shows the bruising she received from a foul by Roselord Borgella (#22) of Haiti during the United States vs. Haiti match during the 2022 CONCACAF W Championship at Estadio Universitario on July 4, 2022, in Monterrey, Mexico. Photo by Brad Smith ISI/ISI Photos/ Getty Images.

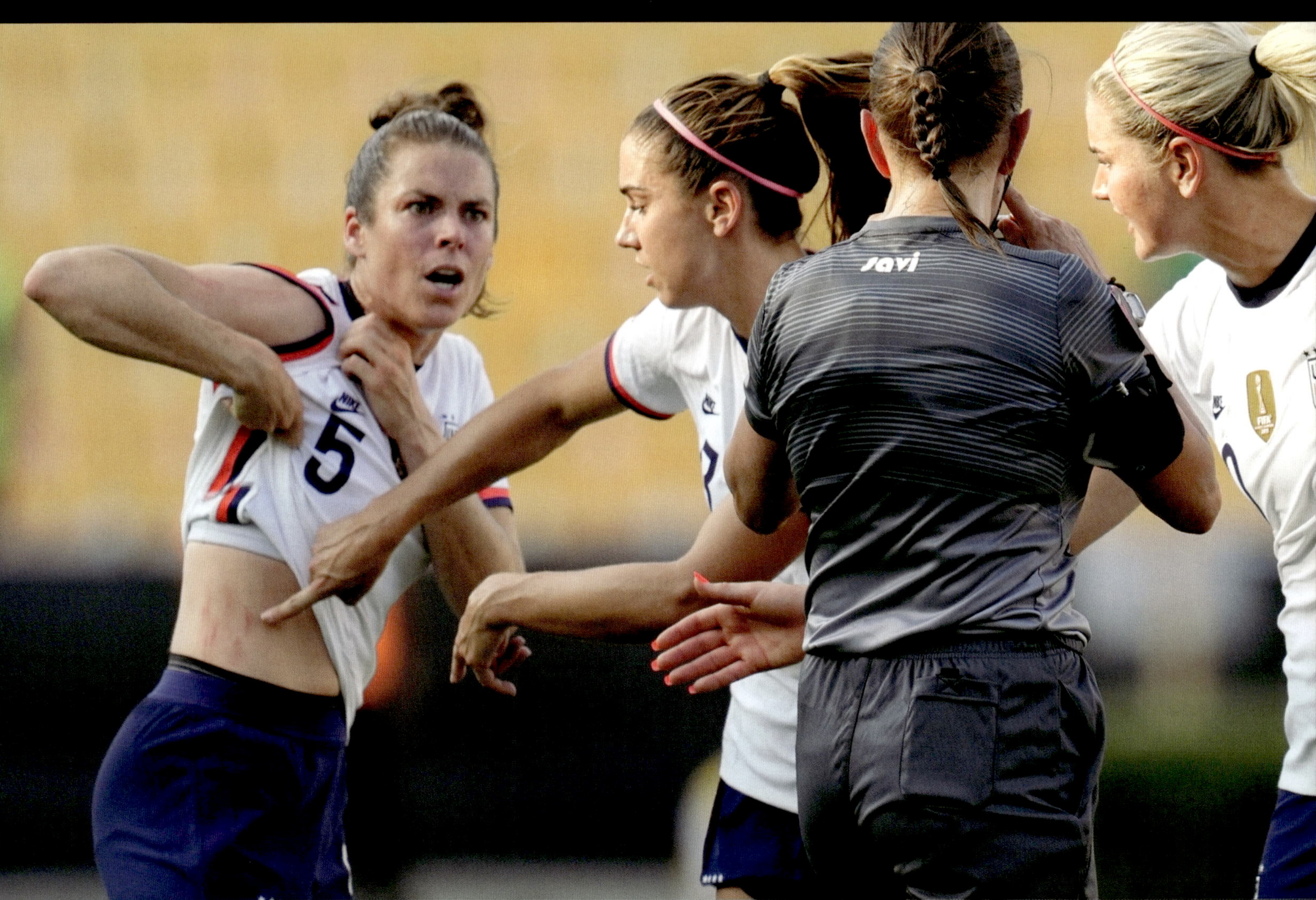

The Incredulity of Saint Thomas (detail), 1675,
Mattia Preti. MUŻA museum.

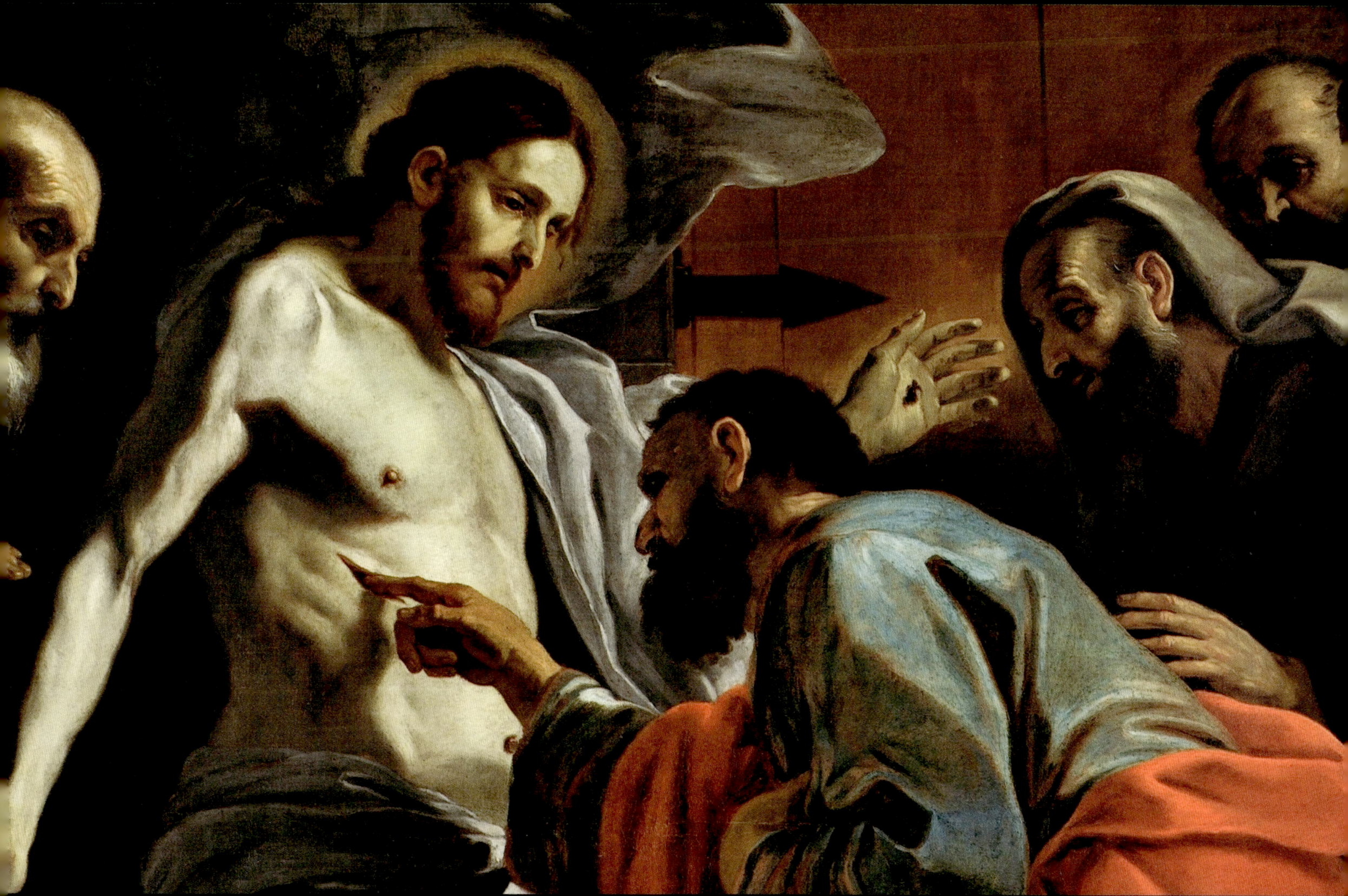

FOOTY FIGHT

We love soccer just as much for the post-play drama as we do for the on-field action. Here's a prime example of the theater playing out in a World Cup match between Nigeria and Canada, a performance with multiple acts stitched into one scene.

Christine Sinclair reacts on the ground after missing a penalty during the 2023 FIFA Women's World Cup Group B football match between Nigeria and Canada on July 21, 2023, at Melbourne Rectangular Stadium, also known as AAMI Park, in Melbourne, Australia. Photo by William West/AFP via Getty Images.

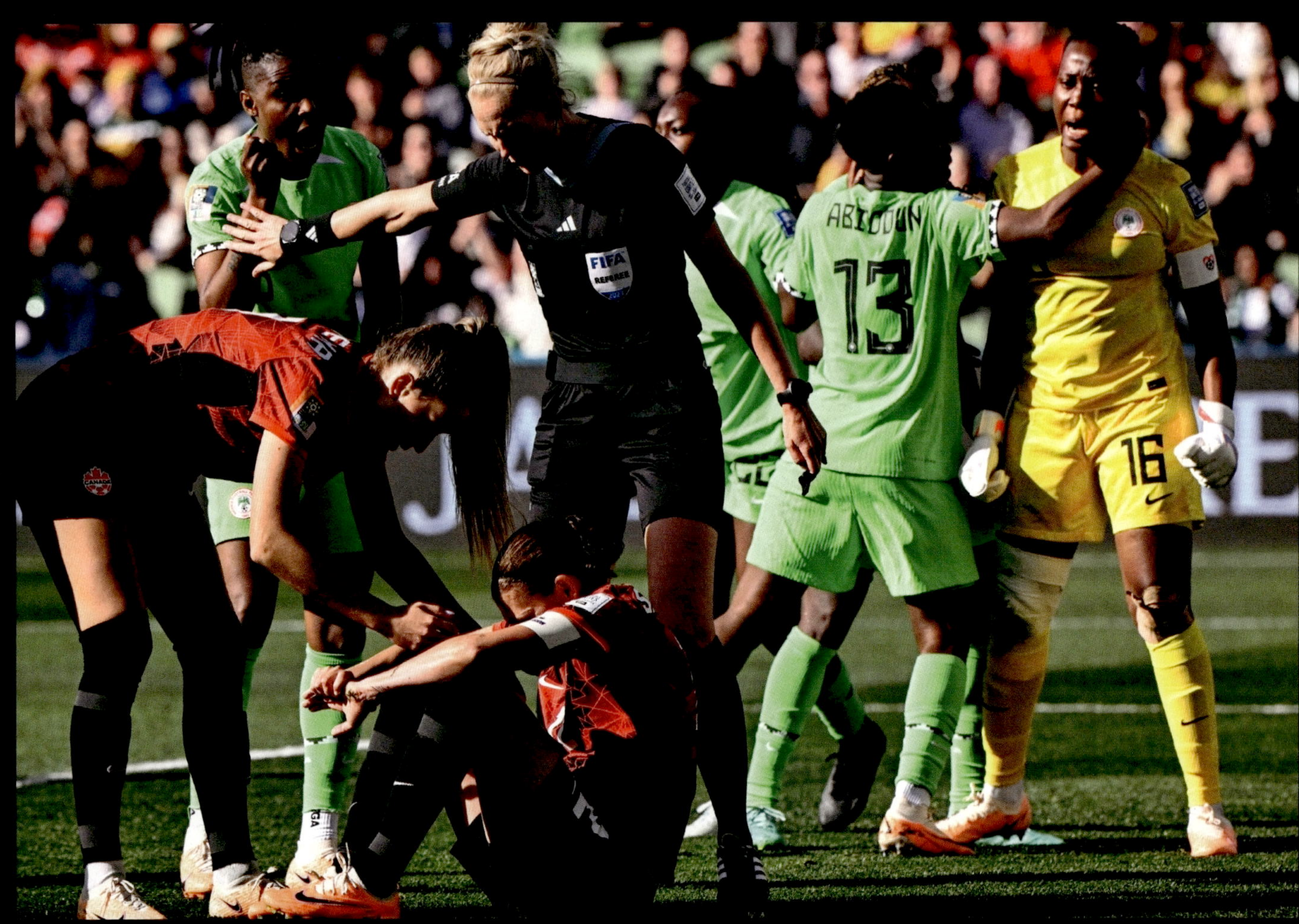

The Death of Sapphira (detail), circa 1652, Nicolas Poussin. Digital image by Cécile Briard. Louvre Museum. Flipped from the original.

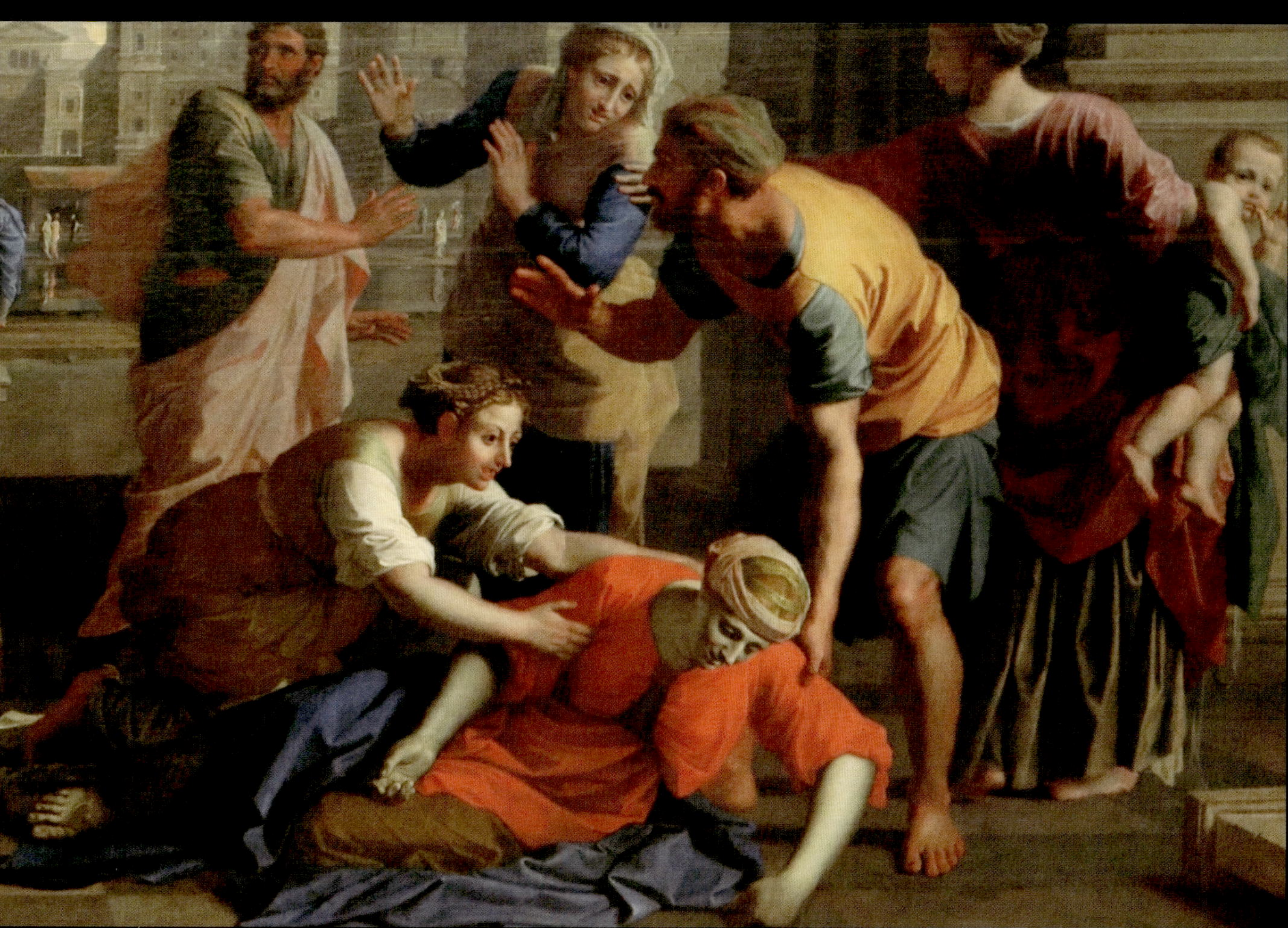

A CALL TO ARMS

A call to arms? In soccer??

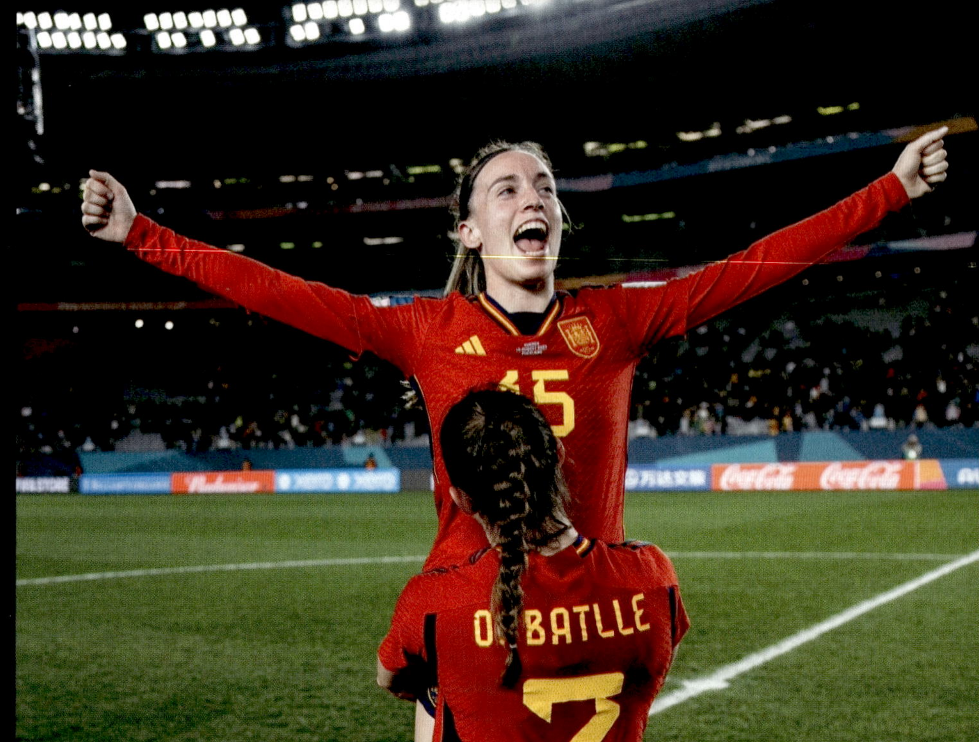

Top: Eva Navarro and Ona Batlle of Spain celebrate the team's 2–1 victory and advance to the final following the FIFA Women's World Cup Australia & New Zealand 2023 Semi Final match between Spain and Sweden at Eden Park on August 15, 2023, in Auckland, New Zealand. Photo by Maja Hitij - FIFA/FIFA via Getty Images.

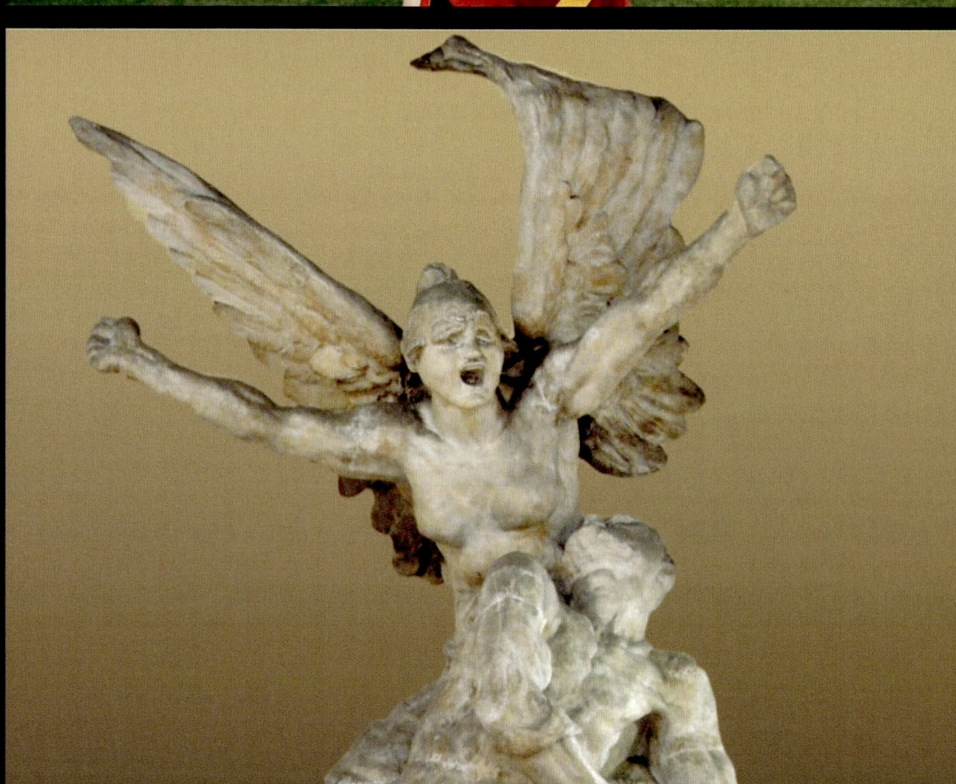

Bottom: *La Defense* (or *The Call to Arms*) (detail), 1917–19, Auguste Rodin. Digital image by Flickr. Musée Rodin.

THE HAIR I LEFT BEHIND ME

A flow so magnificent it deserves its own page.

Left: Erling Haaland of Manchester City lets his hair flow during the UEFA Champions League Group G match between Manchester City and FK Crvena zvezda at Etihad Stadium on September 19, 2023, in Manchester, England. Photo by Simon Stacpoole/Offside/Offside via Getty Images.

Right: *The Girl I Left Behind Me* (detail), circa 1872, Eastman Johnson. Smithsonian American Art Museum.

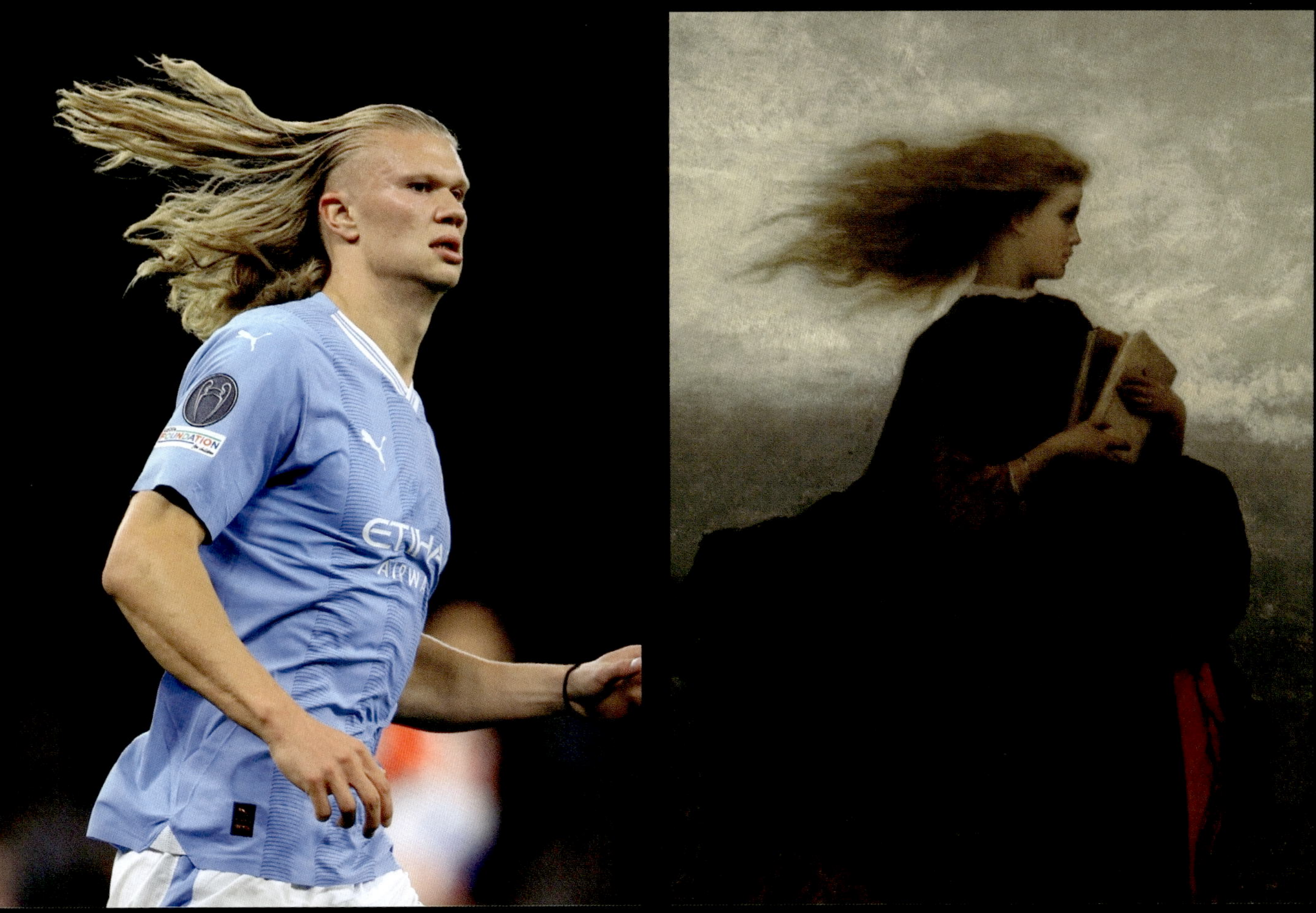

TENNIS

While tennis doesn't often breach the walls of the account's grid, mostly because individual sports are so much harder to capture, it is one of my favorite sports to watch live—I'm convinced the US Open is pound for pound the best sporting event to attend in person, and I try to make it out every year. If you're reading this and ever have an extra ticket, I'm your man.

Tennis Tournament (detail), 1919, George Bellows. Digital image by Botaurus. Metropolitan Museum of Art. Flipped from the original.

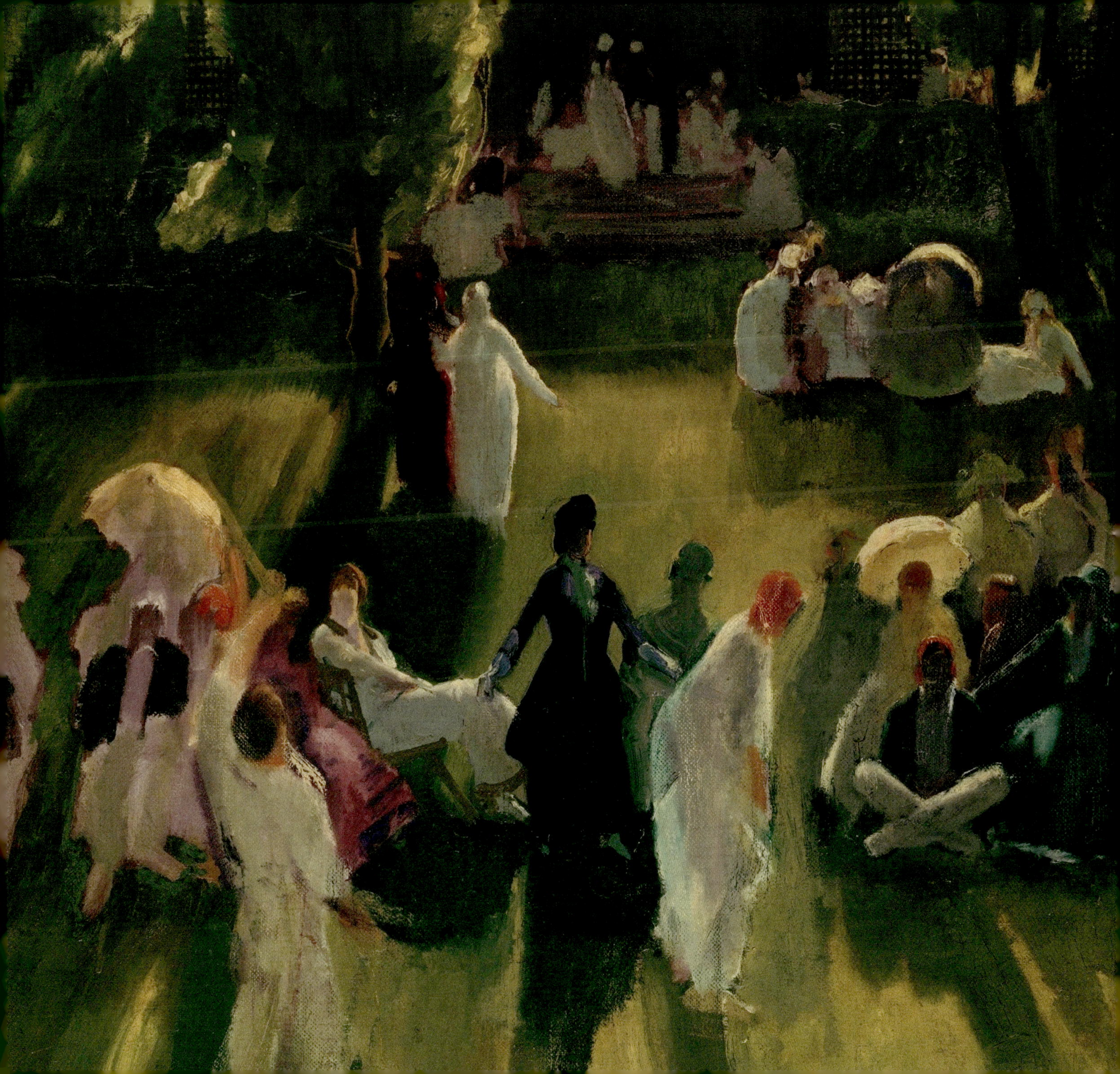

SERENA WILLIAMS

There isn't a single moment that properly captures the significance of Serena Williams. Ultimately, I decided that the best to ever do it deserves more than one image.

I think *Le Ballon* captures the power that Serena held in her hand and unleashed with every shot. And I think Tiepolo's *Immaculate Conception* plays on Serena and her legacy—giving birth to the new age of women's tennis.

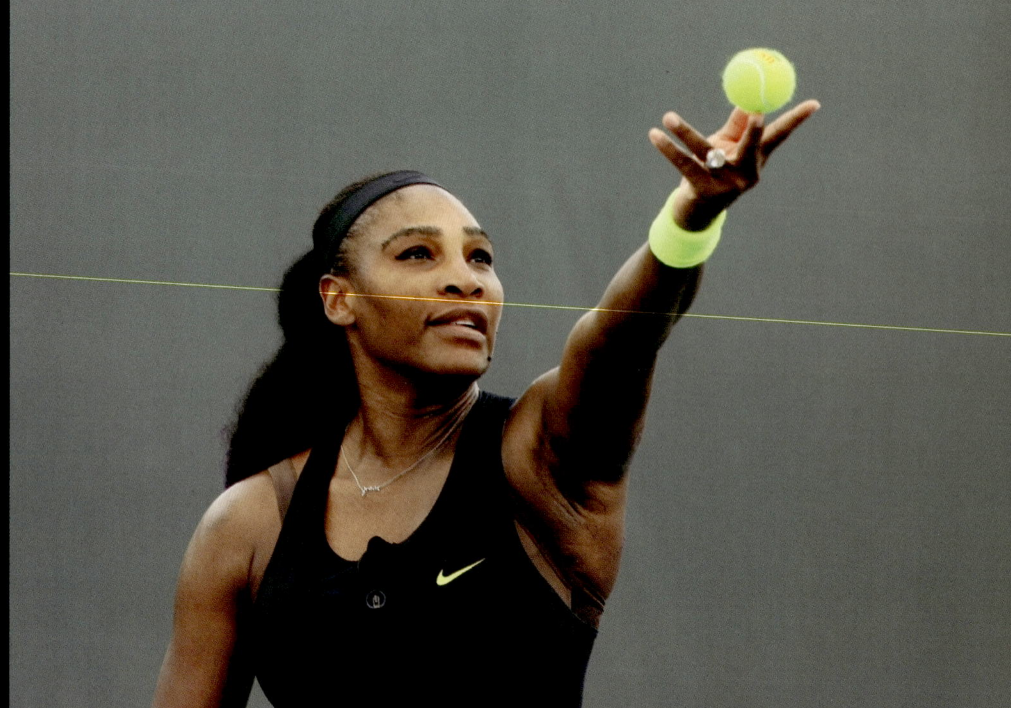

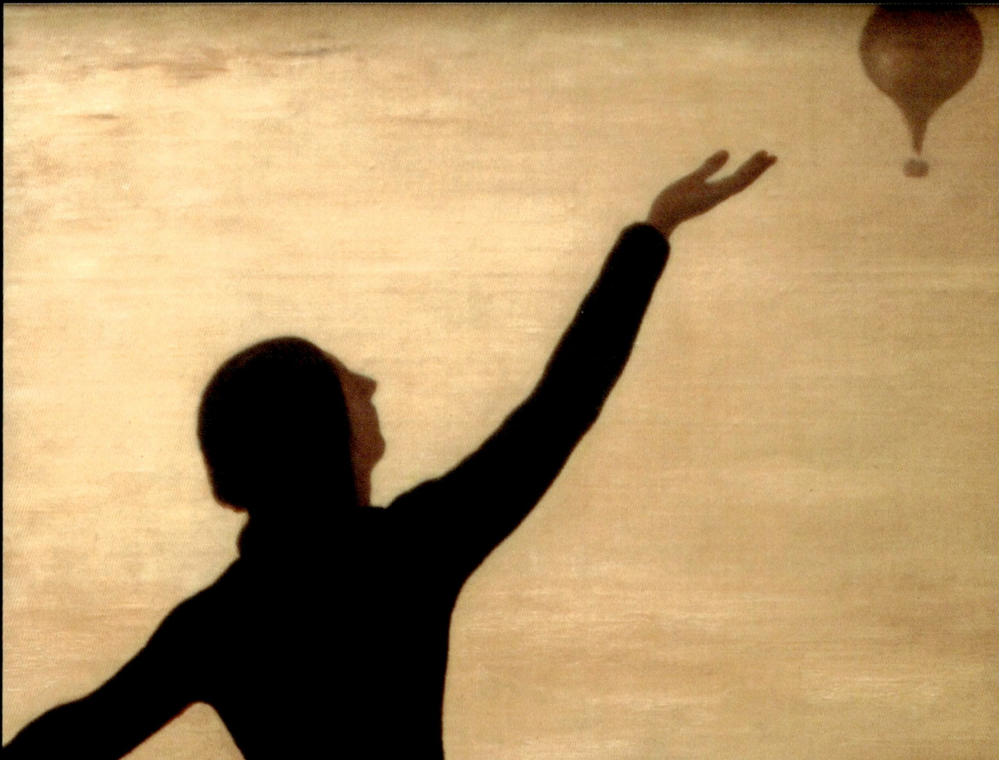

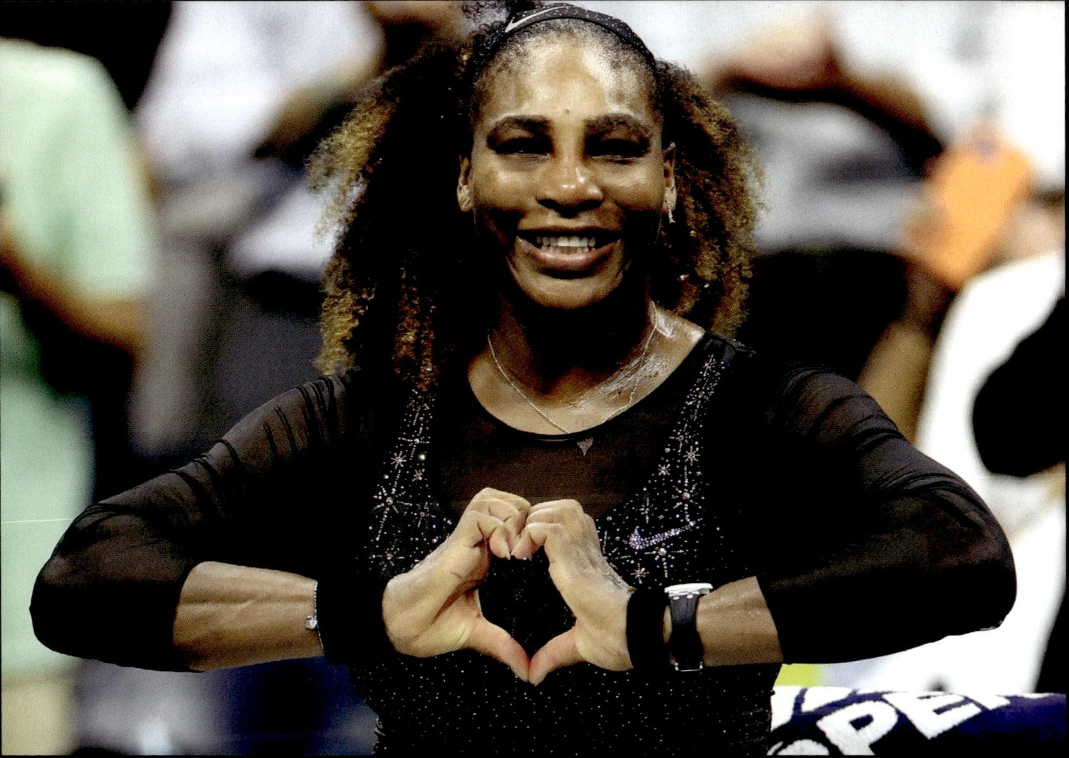

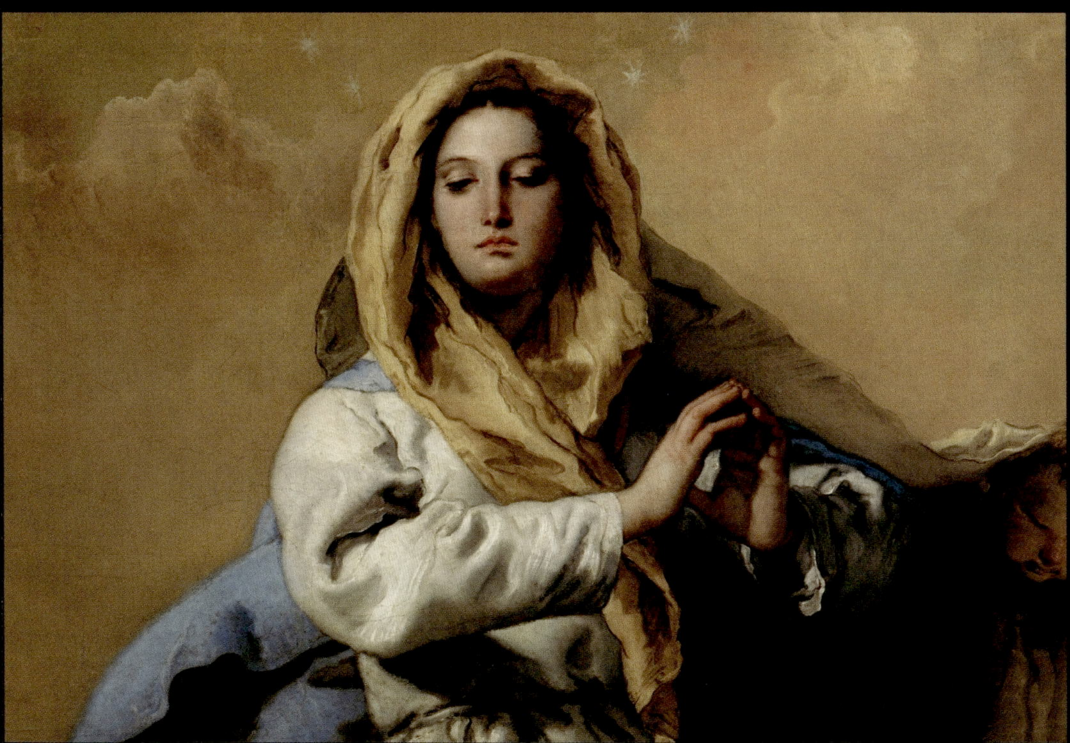

Opposite page, top: Serena Williams serves during her match against Venus Williams during the WTA Top Seed Open Day Four at the Top Seed Tennis Club on August 13, 2020, in Lexington, Kentucky. Photo by Dylan Buell/Getty Images.

Opposite page, bottom: *Le Ballon* (detail), 1870, Pierre Puvis de Chavannes. Musée d'Orsay. Flipped from the original.

This page, top: Serena Williams of the United States celebrates after defeating Danka Kovinić of Montenegro during the Women's Singles First Round on Day One of the 2022 US Open at USTA Billie Jean King National Tennis Center on August 29, 2022, in Flushing, New York. Photo by Al Bello/Getty Images.

This page, bottom: *The Immaculate Conception* (detail), 1767–68, Giovanni Battista Tiepolo. Museo del Prado.

RAFA NADAL

We can't have a tennis section without the king of clay doing his signature fist pump, here matching the famous *Vaison Diadumenos*.

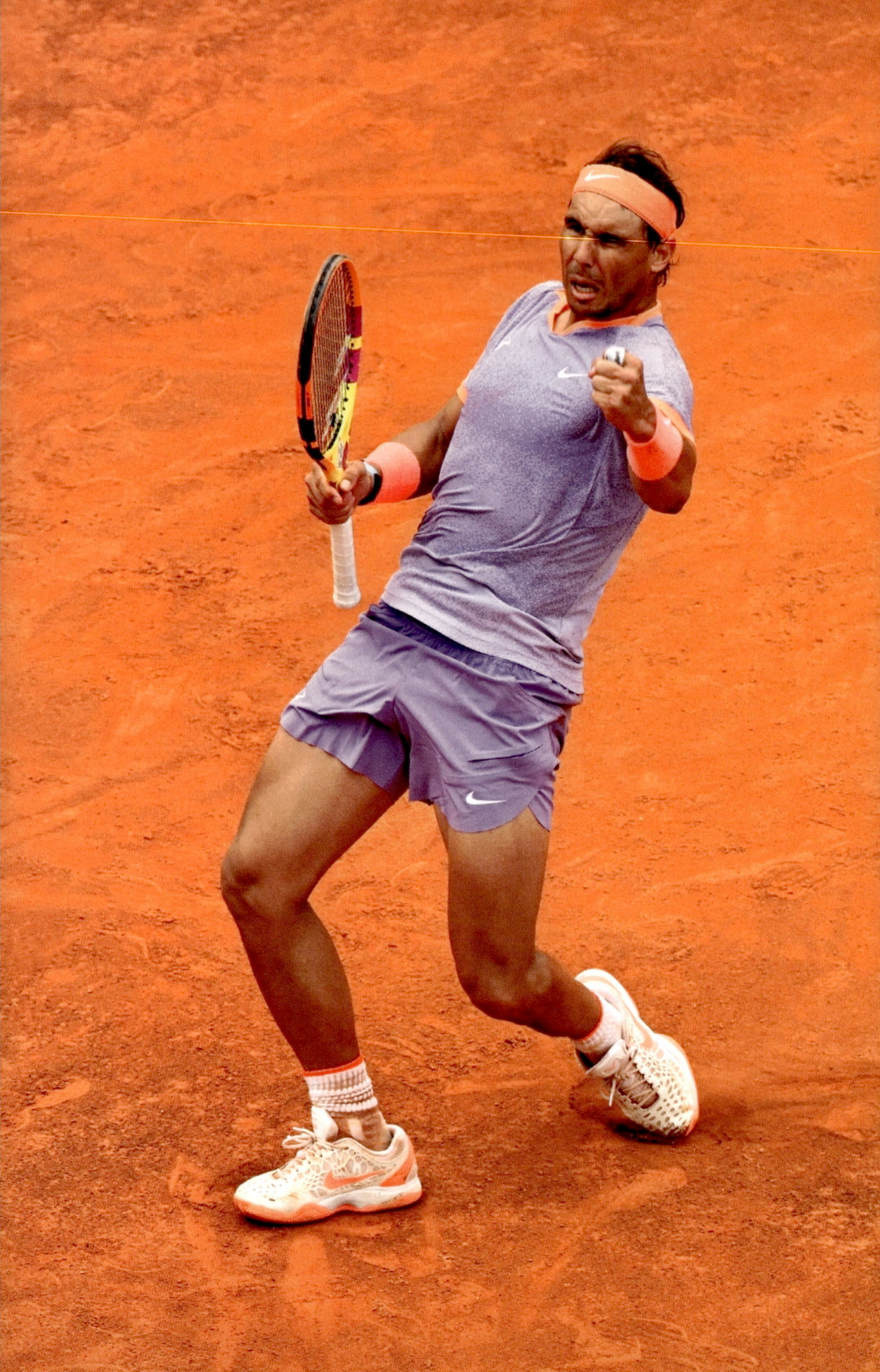

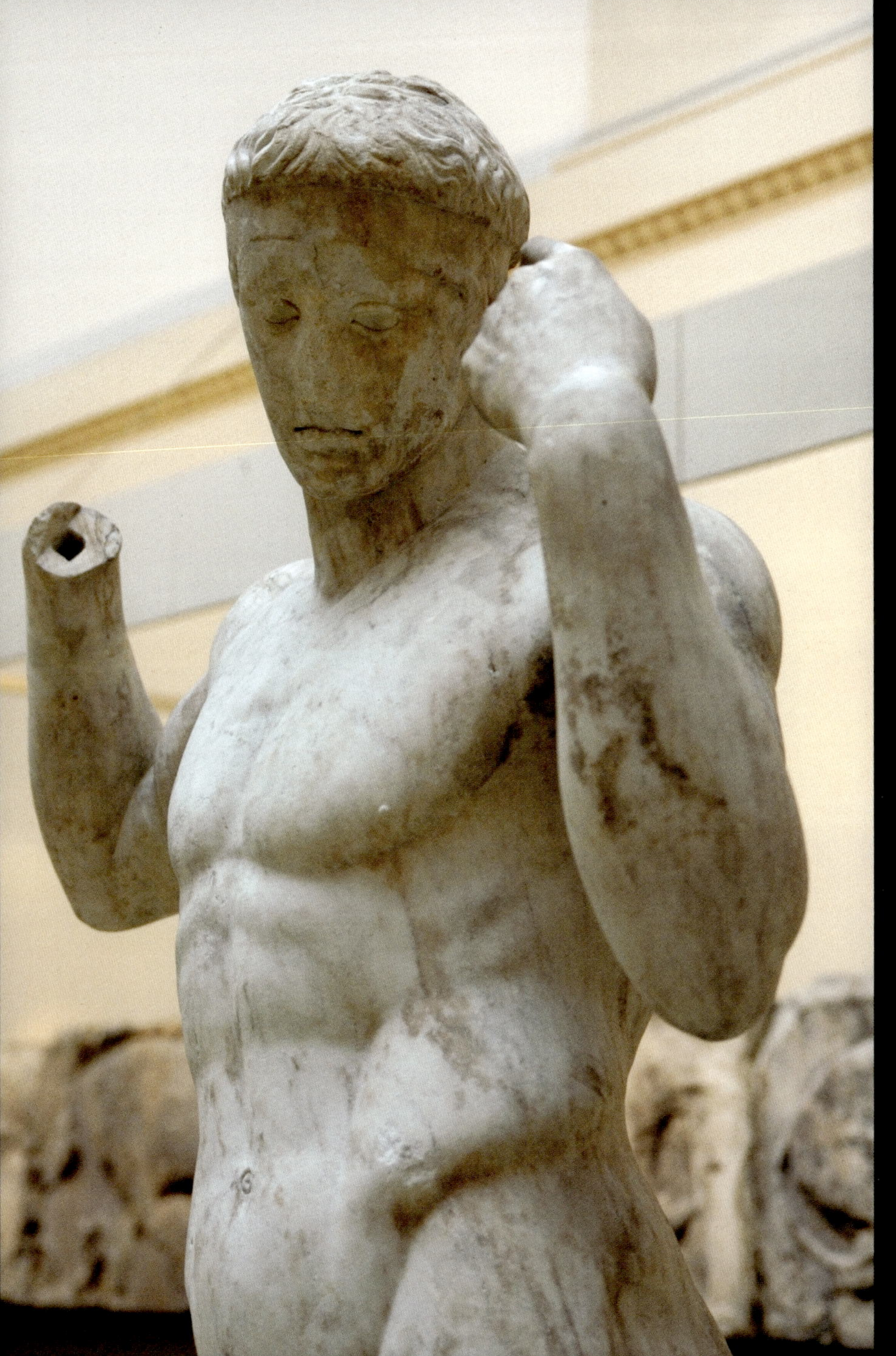

Opposite page: Rafael Nadal of Spain celebrates a point against Thierry Ascione of France during Day Four of the Australian Open Grand Slam at Melbourne Park on January 22, 2004, in Melbourne, Australia. Photo by Nick Laham/Getty Images.

This page: *Vaison Diadumenos*, Roman copy circa 50 AD after a Greek original circa 440 BC, unknown artist copy after Polykleitos. Digital image by Marie-Lan Nguyen. British Museum. Flipped from the original.

THE CARRYING OF THE KING

My hometown museum, the Met, has a supremely underrated section of Cycladic art, from the Leonard N. Stern collection on permanent loan, tucked in just to the left of the Great Hall. Roberta Smith's profile on it in *The New York Times* convinced me to take a closer look, and I fell into a deep rabbit hole on the genre. There's something chilling but oddly comforting about the "modern" composition of these figures made over 4,500 years ago. The more things change, the more they stay the same. It's partly why I thought it was an apt pick for the Battle of the Sexes, where 29-year-old women's star Billie Jean King beat a then 55-year-old man, Bobby Riggs—6–4, 6–3, and 6–3. The victory was a watershed moment in the movement for gender equality in sports.

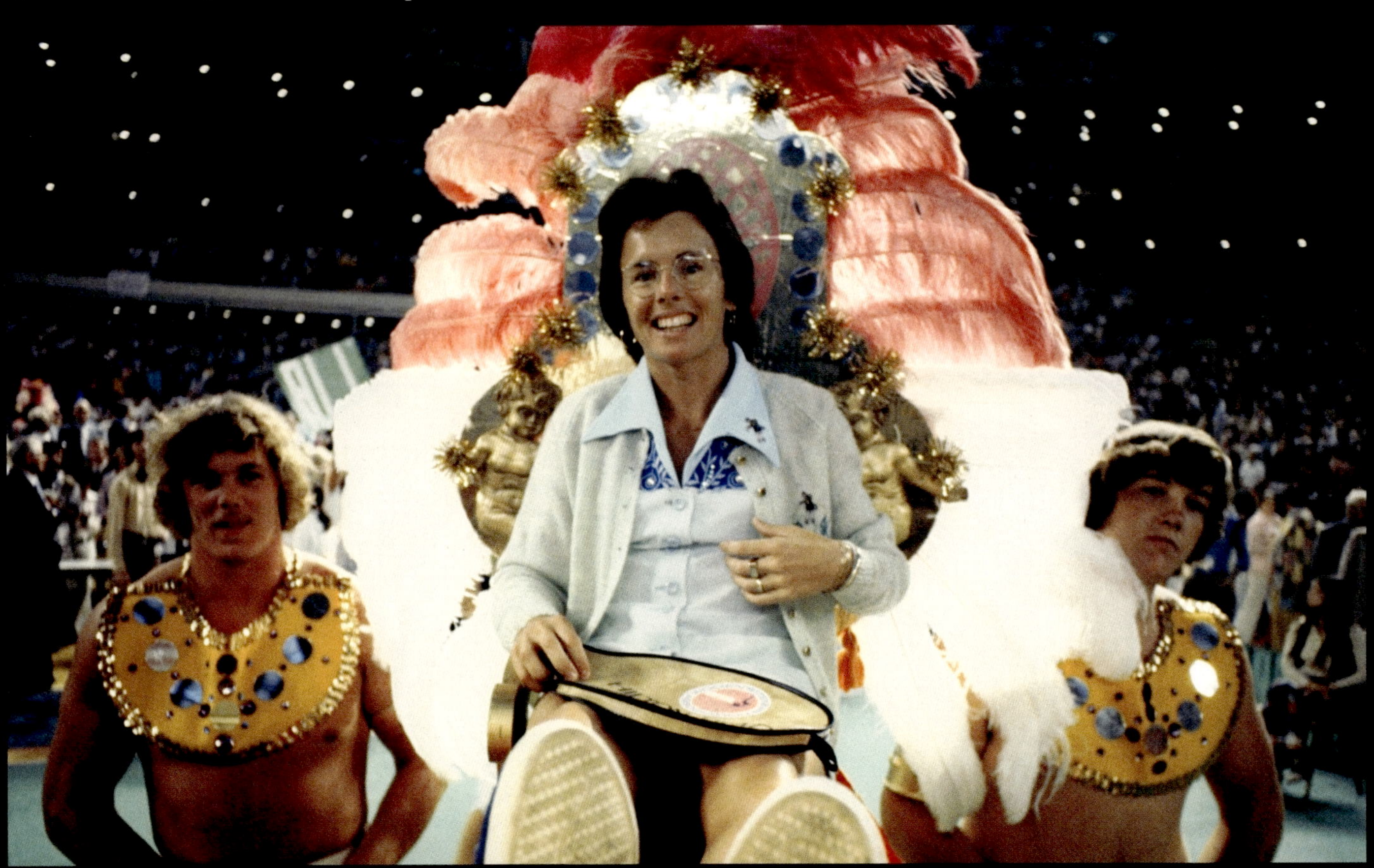

Opposite page: Tennis star Billie Jean King is carried to the court by four men for the Battle of the Sexes tennis match with 55-year-old tennis star Bobby Riggs on Thursday, September 20, 1973. Photo by Bettmann via Getty Images.

This page: *Group of two male figurines carrying a female figurine of the early Spedos variety,* circa 2600–2500 BC, unknown artist. Baden State Museum.

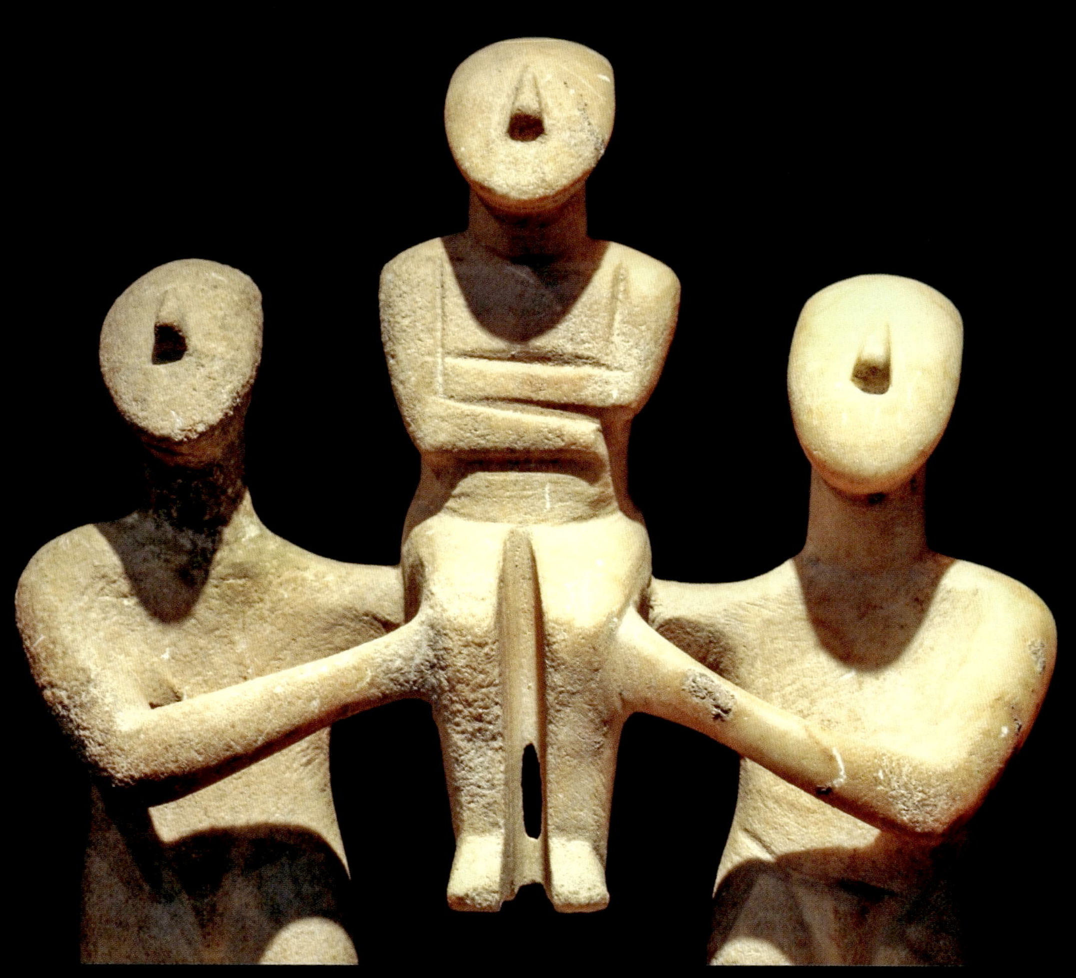

ALCARAZ ART

Carlos Alcaraz can hardly be considered a fashion icon, but these threads from the 2023 US Open were a work of art.

Carlos Alcaraz of Spain celebrates a point against Dominik Koepfer of Germany during their Men's Singles First Round match on Day Two of the 2023 US Open at the USTA Billie Jean King National Tennis Center on August 29, 2023, in Flushing, New York. Photo by Clive Brunskill/Getty Images.

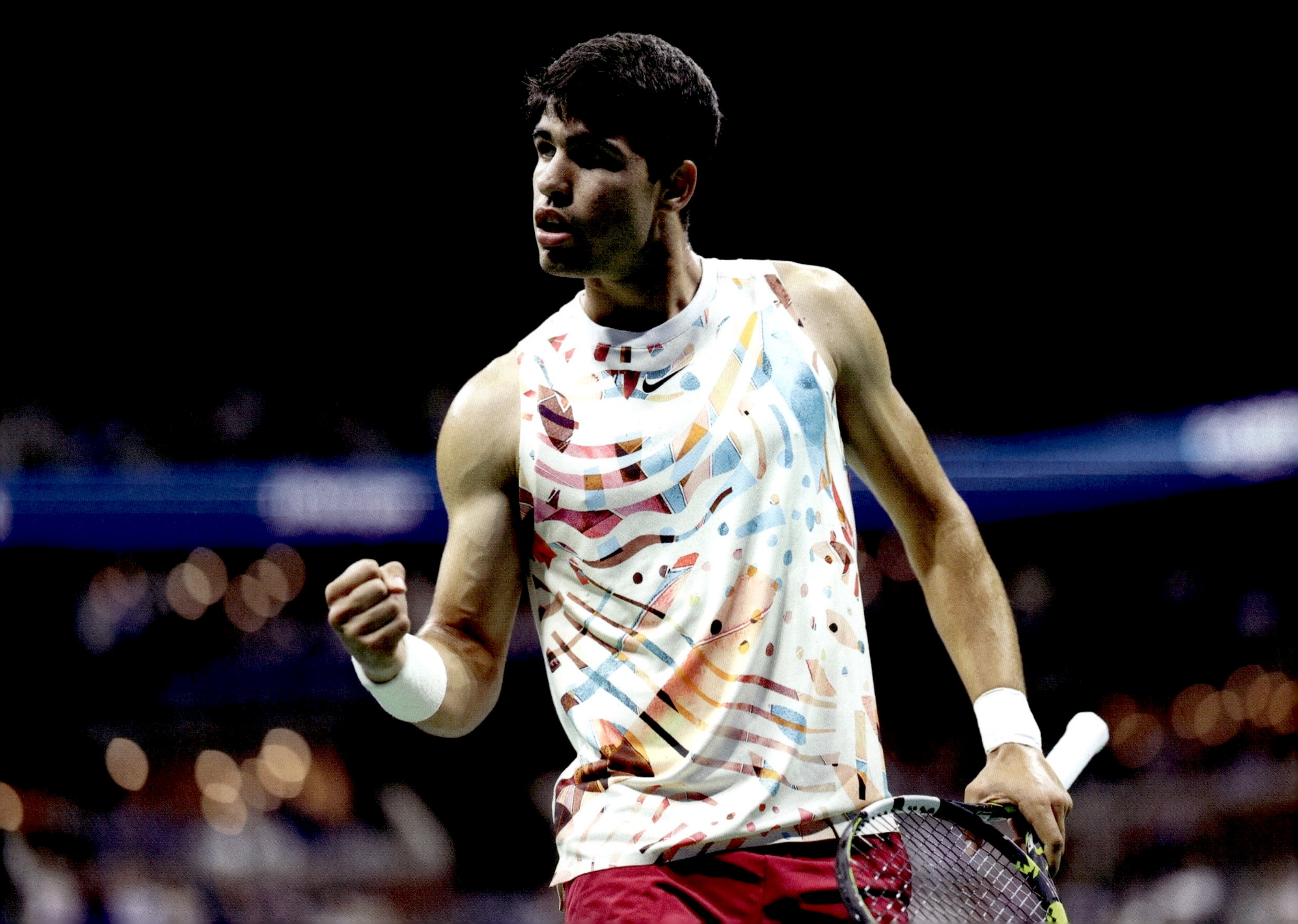

Blue Segment, 1921, Wassily Kandinsky. Digital image by Éternels Éclairs. Solomon R. Guggenheim Museum.

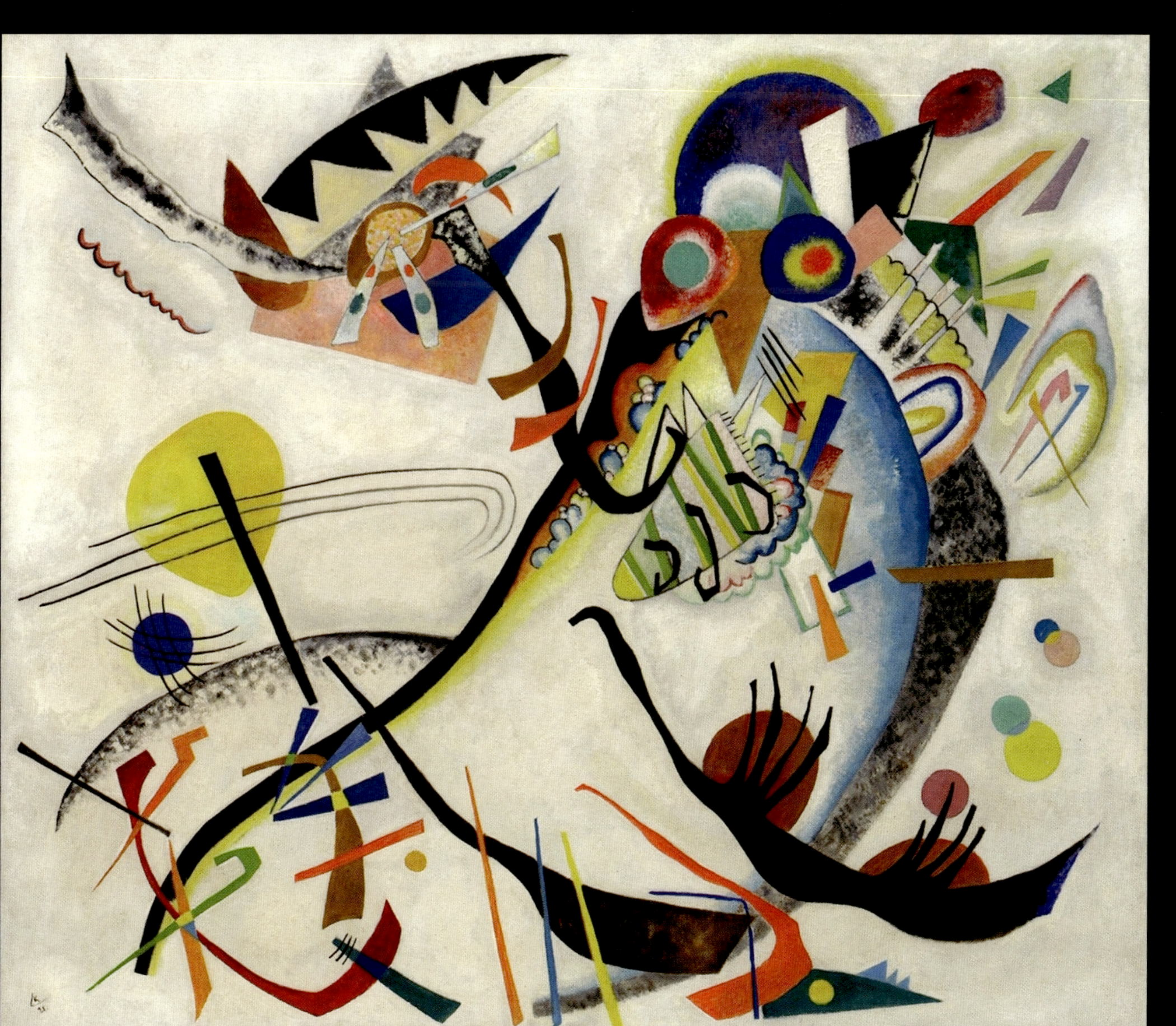

FINAL FEDERER

Despite a career chock-full of gravity-defying shots and championship moments, the lasting image of Roger Federer, at least for me, is from the 2022 Laver Cup, his final competitive event. The entire tennis world gathered to send off the GOAT, turning the match into a celebration of Fed's career and producing this gem of a photo, as the people's champion was hoisted into the air by his peers. It's a fitting parallel to the fifth-century BC Greek boxer Diagoras, a champion who was carried off by his sons and the adoring public.

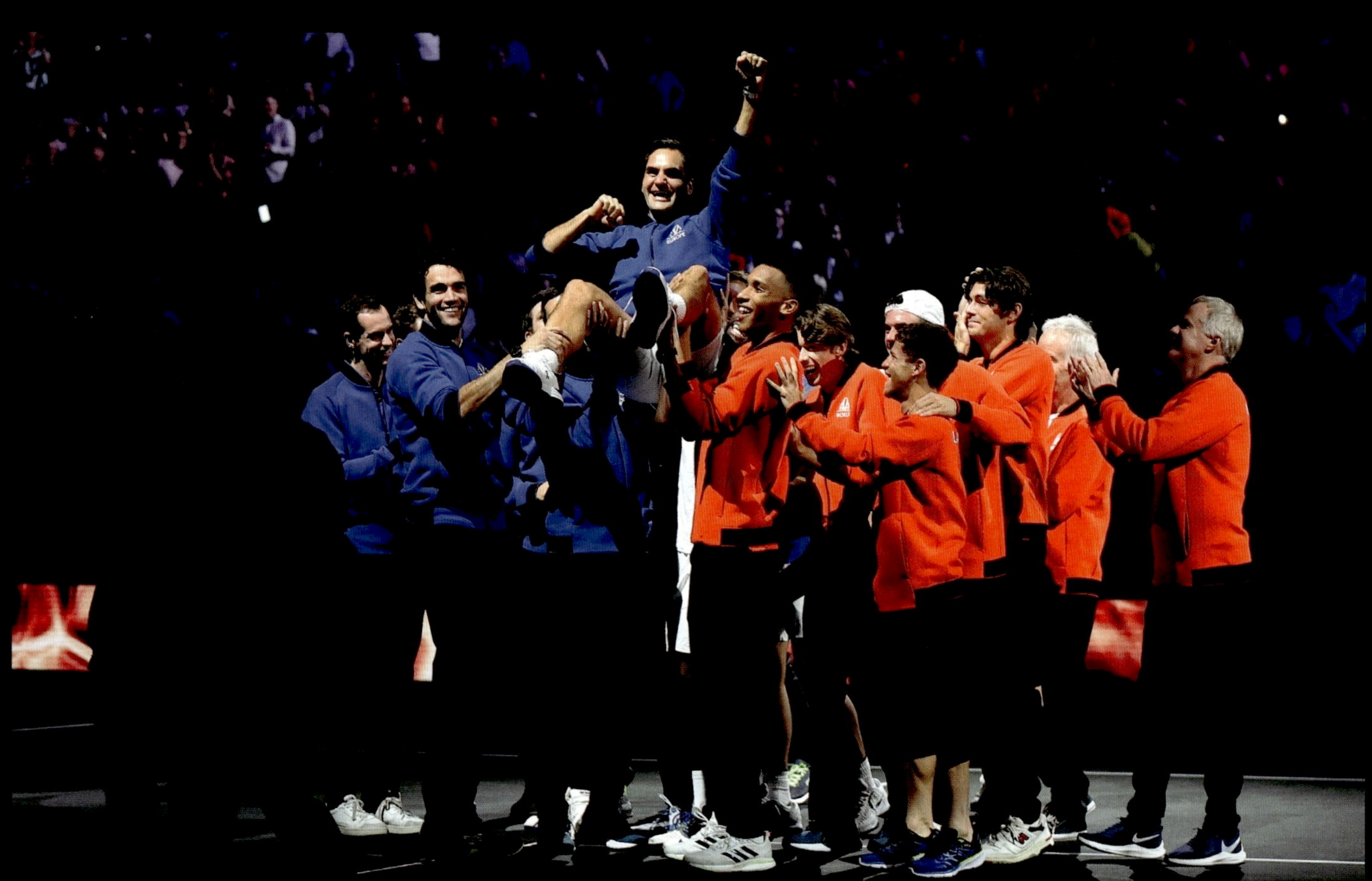

Opposite page: Roger Federer of Team Europe is lifted up after his last match in the doubles between Jack Sock and Frances Tiafoe of Team World and Roger Federer and Rafael Nadal of Team Europe during Day One of the Laver Cup at the O2 Arena on September 23, 2022, in London, England. Photo by Julian Finney/ Getty Images for Laver Cup.

This page: *Diagoras carried in triumph by his sons to Olympia* (detail), 1814, Christophe Thomas Degeorge. Musée d'art Roger-Quilliot.

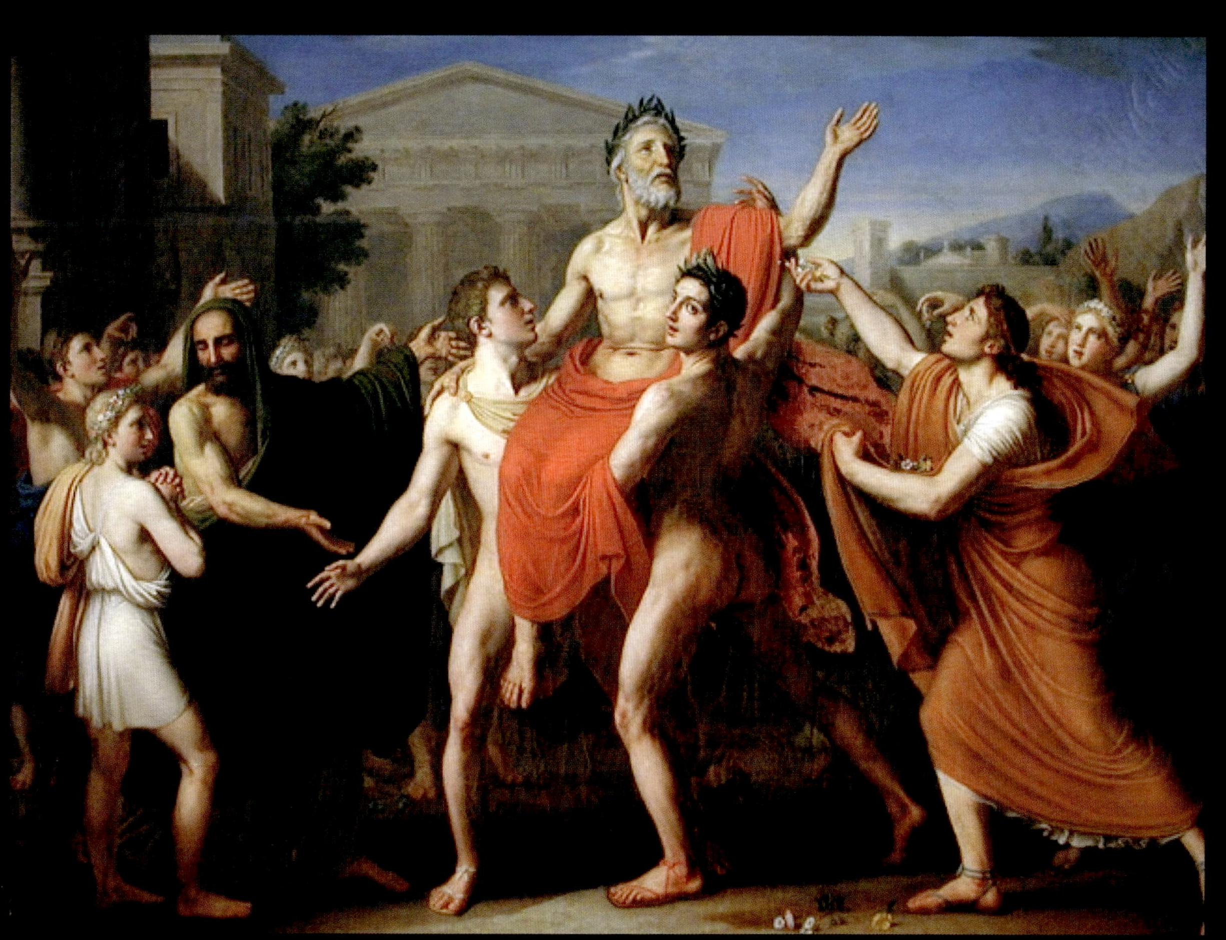

HOCKEY

Hockey has by far the most fervent fan base online, and the passion on the ice translates directly into art, with fights, scrums, and celebrations all dripping with heightened emotion. Sticks also play a starring role, which is why this gem from the Musée d'Orsay is always where my mind goes when I think of hockey. It also goes to abstract expressionism paintings, which unfortunately aren't aged enough to be a part of the public domain. Joan Mitchell, Lee Krasner, and Helen Frankenthaler are all extremely hockey-coded. I'll just have to wait twenty-five years and write a sequel that includes them!

Le Prévôt des marchands Ĕtienne Marcel et le dauphin Charles (detail), 1879, Lucien Mélingue. Digital image by Mysterious Art Century. Musée d'Orsay.

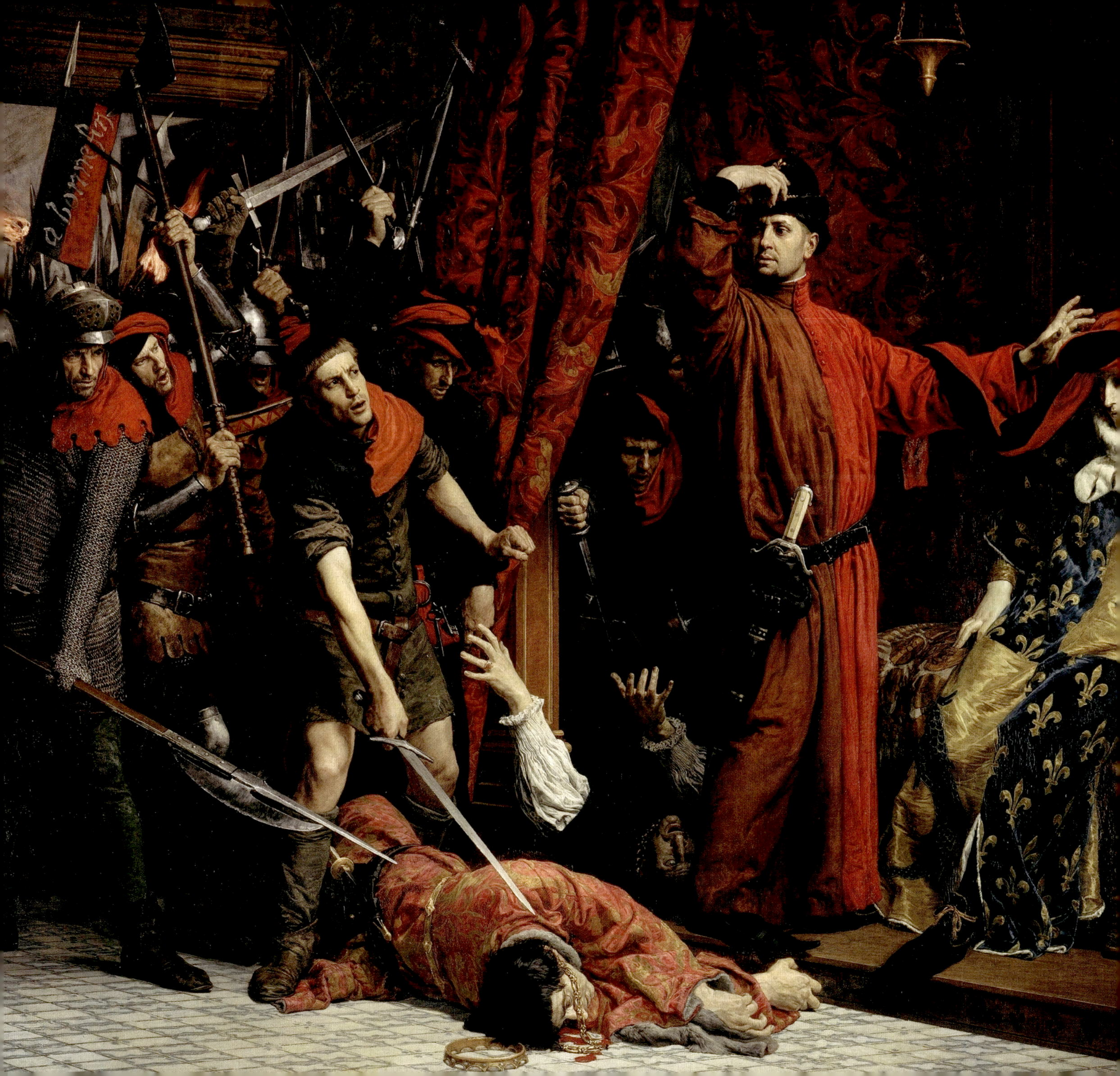

ST. LOUIS RECEIVING THE STIGMATA

I wouldn't be able to use the word *sports* in the title of this book in good faith if I didn't include the shot of Boston Bruin Bobby Orr's overtime goal to win the Stanley Cup in 1970 against the St. Louis Blues.

Saint Francis Receiving the Stigmata is a common theme in art history, and in Lorenzo Ghiberti's version, the seraph (the flying figure) is especially horizontal, matching Orr's position in the air.

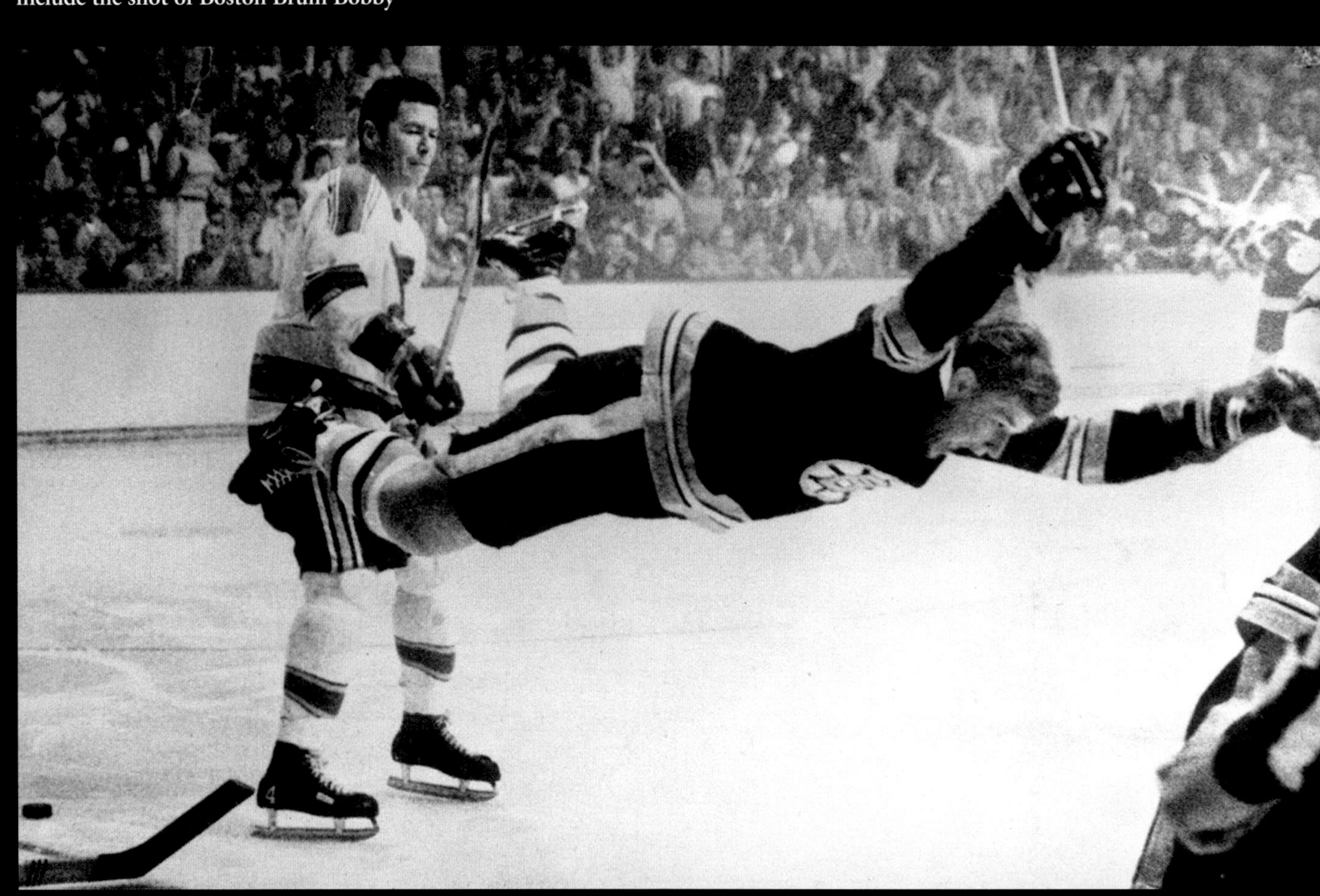

Opposite page: Boston Bruin Bobby Orr's overtime goal that won the Stanley Cup, beating the St. Louis Blues at the Boston Garden, in Boston, Massachusetts, on May 10, 1970. Photo by MediaNews Group/Boston Herald via Getty Images.

This page: *Saint Francis Receiving the Stigmata* (detail), circa 1400–05, Lorenzo Ghiberti. Yale University Art Gallery.

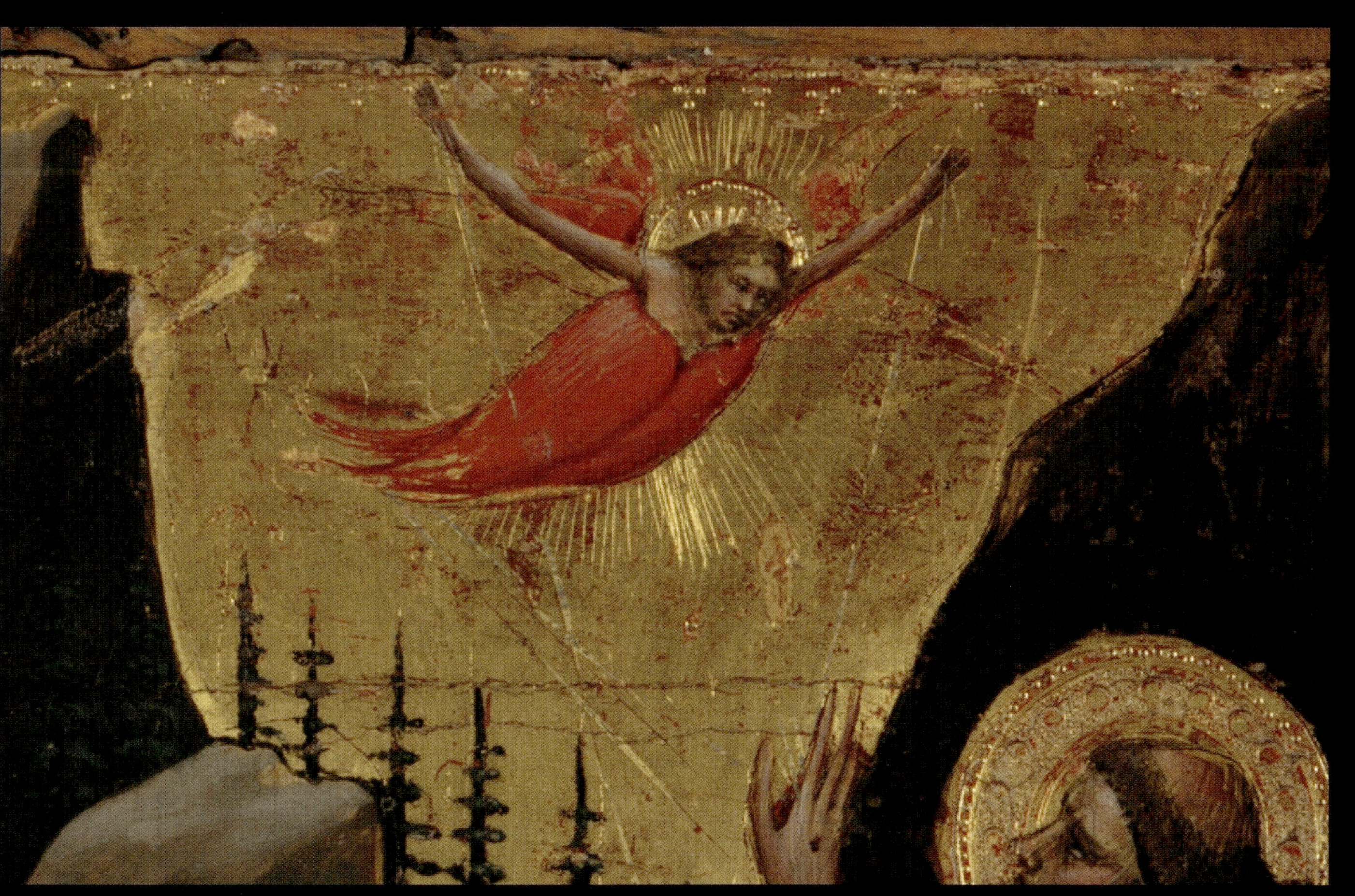

THE CUP RUNNETH OVER

When the Avalanche won the Stanley Cup in June 2022, I knew I had to jump on the opportunity. The visual composition is all there: the Stanley Cup is the goblet and the Avalanche logo (an ode to the Rockies) is the exact shape of the mountain range. The composition works on its own, but there's a deeper thread: Thomas Cole was known for allegorical scenes, with *The Titan's Goblet* serving as his best example. It's a small work, but if you look closely, there's a whole world inside the chalice. Separate from the rest of the landscape, it sits above the oceans, on top of the land, and elevated above the mountains. The Stanley Cup—the most recognizable trophy in sports—features the names of all those who have earned it, a private community that is elevated, both figuratively and literally, above all the rest. It's a fun little detail that can easily get lost, and I really wanted to call attention to it here.

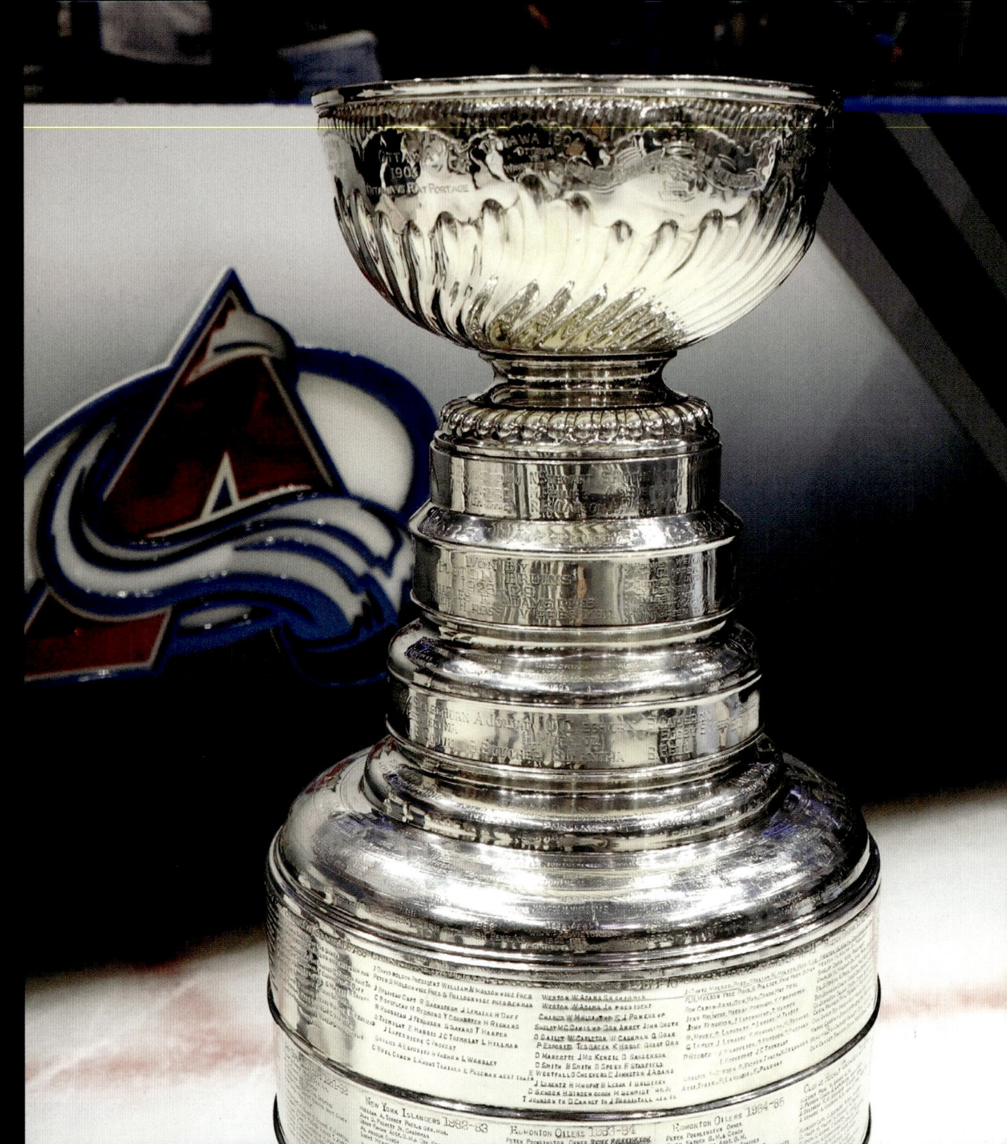

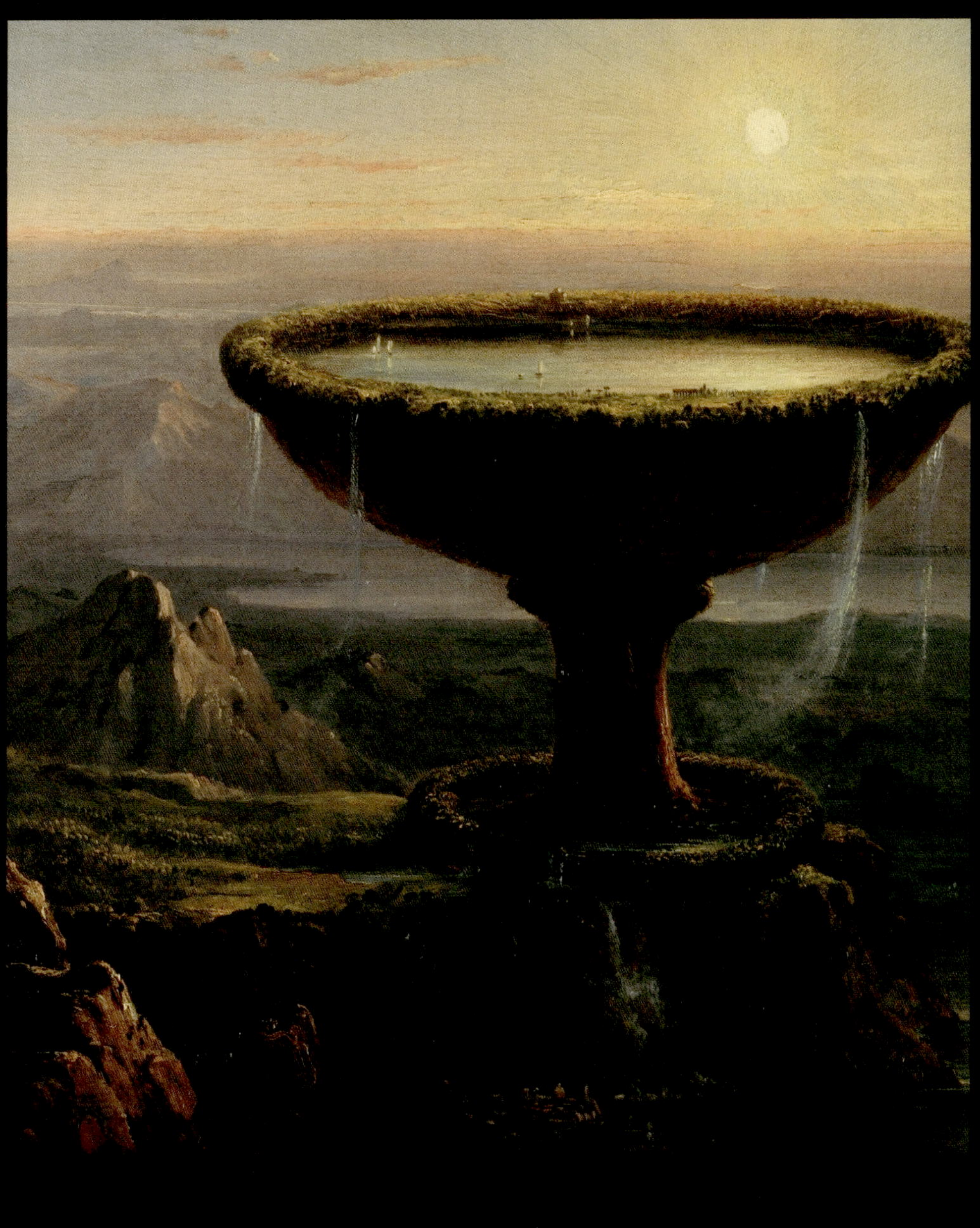

Opposite page: The Stanley Cup sits on the ice after the Colorado Avalanche defeated the Tampa Bay Lightning 2–1 in Game 6 of the 2022 NHL Stanley Cup Final at Amalie Arena on June 26, in Tampa, Florida. Photo by Christian Petersen/Getty Images.

This page: *The Titan's Goblet*, 1833, Thomas Cole. The Metropolitan Museum of Art.

THE BATTLE FOR VICTOIRE

While there's a Monet haystacks element to this one (see page 47), with a central group of figures and a triangle shape on top, what makes the photo so visually pleasing is the sticks—without the sticks represented, there is no match. *The Battle of San Romano* is a series of three paintings, all by Paolo Uccello. I've seen two in person, the ones at the National Gallery and Louvre, but ended up using the third, which is housed at the Uffizi. Likely intended to be the central panel of a triptych composed of the three pieces, it had the highest concentration of lances.

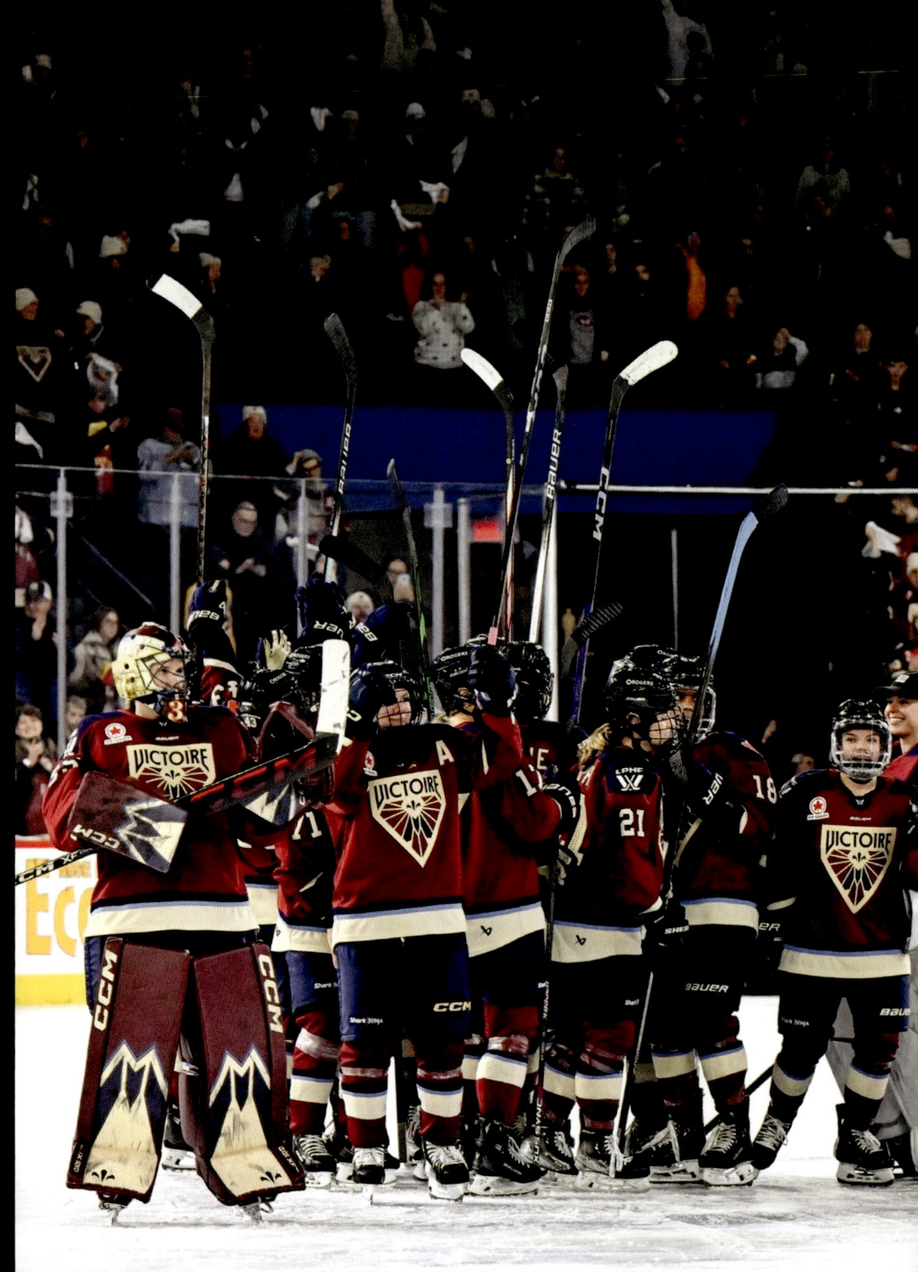

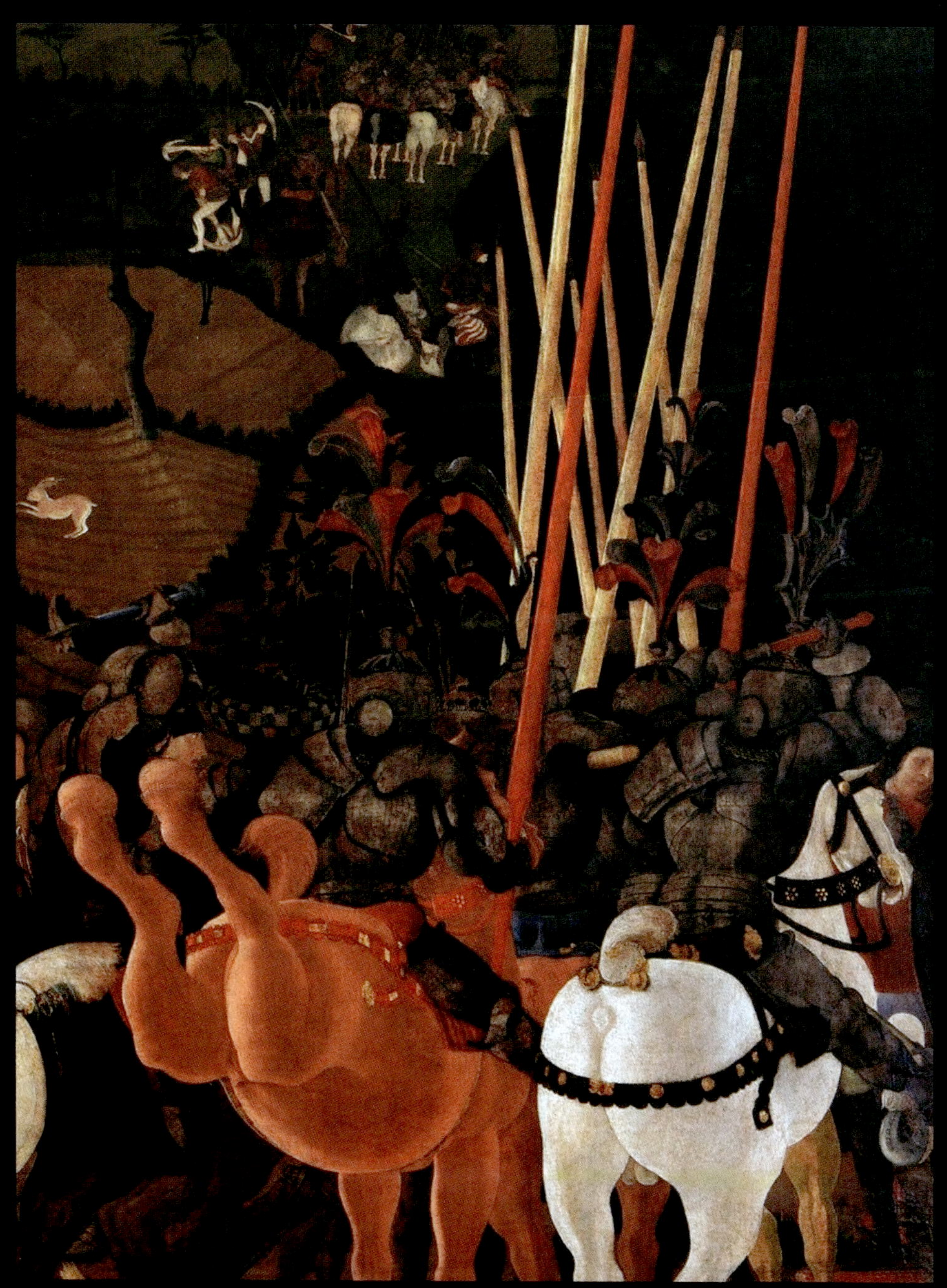

Opposite page: The Montréal Victoire celebrate a goal during a 3–1 win over the Boston Fleet on December 31, 2024. Photo by Minas Panagiotakis/ Getty Images.

This page: *Niccolò Mauruzi da Tolentino unseats Bernardino della Carda at the Battle of San Romano* (detail), circa 1436–40, Paolo Uccello. Digital image by Gleb Simonov. Galleria degli Uffizi.

GOPHERS HOCKEY

El Lissitzky—alongside Kazimir Malevich, whom we saw with the Fernando Tatis Jr. slide on page 52—was a fundamental figure in suprematism, a movement under the umbrella of the Russian avant-garde that took place from 1890–1930. It's a rough generalization, but Malevich's deconstructed, abstract works of shapes and lines tend to be more colorful, while Lissitzky's catalog is much more muted, with a heavy reliance on blacks, grays, whites, and reds.

Here we see a nice play on those colors, with the red central figure and the off-white ice background. It's always fun when shapes can represent people, and if you stretch your imagination enough, each of the four players in the image has a corresponding presence in the canvas.

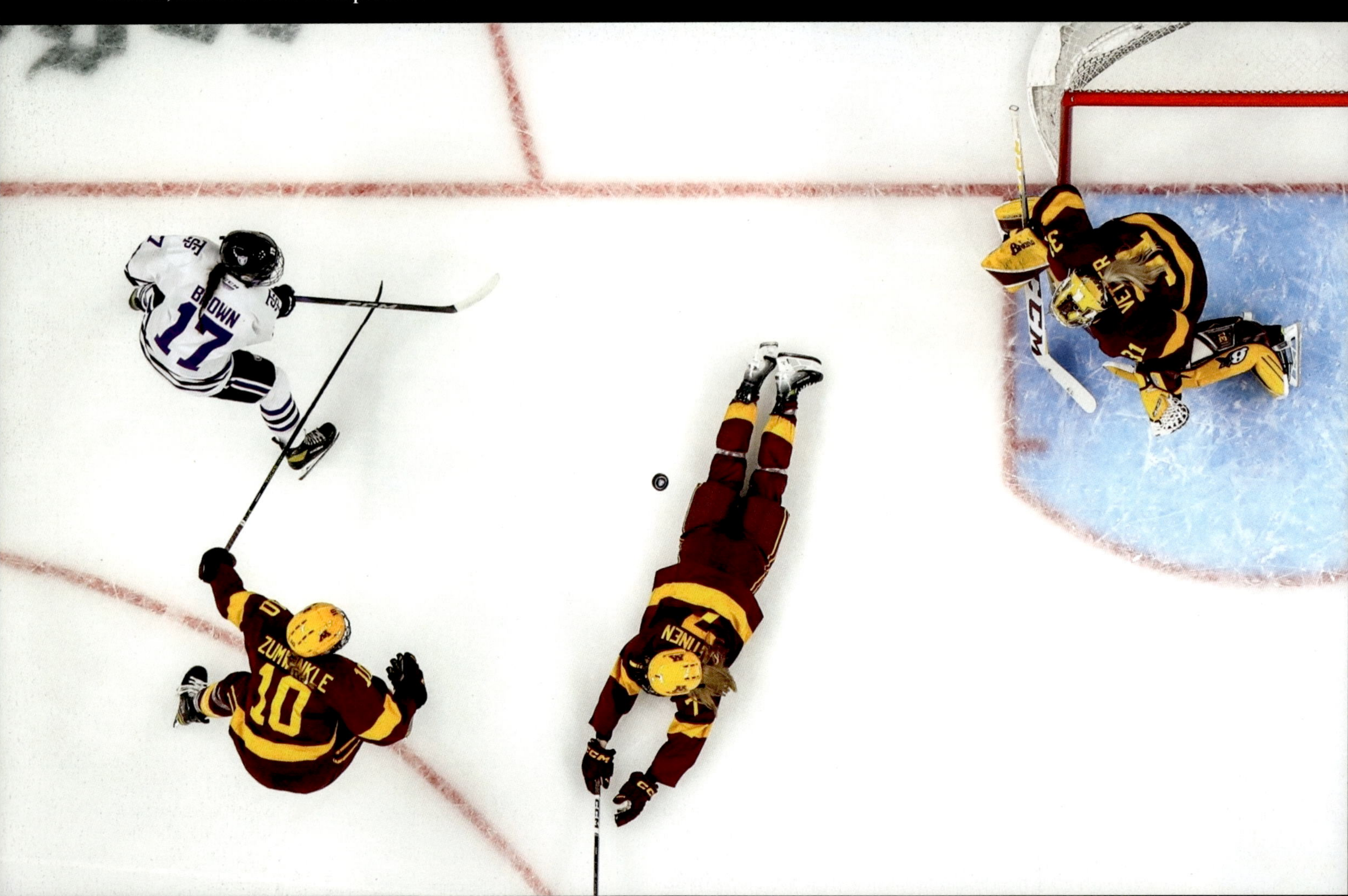

Opposite page: University of Minnesota women's hockey defender Nelli Laitinen blocks an incoming shot in a game against the University of St. Thomas during the 2023–24 season. Photo by Matt Krohn (University of Minnesota).

This page: *Troublemaker (plate seven from Figurines),* 1923, El Lissitzky. Brooklyn Museum. Rotated and flipped from the original.

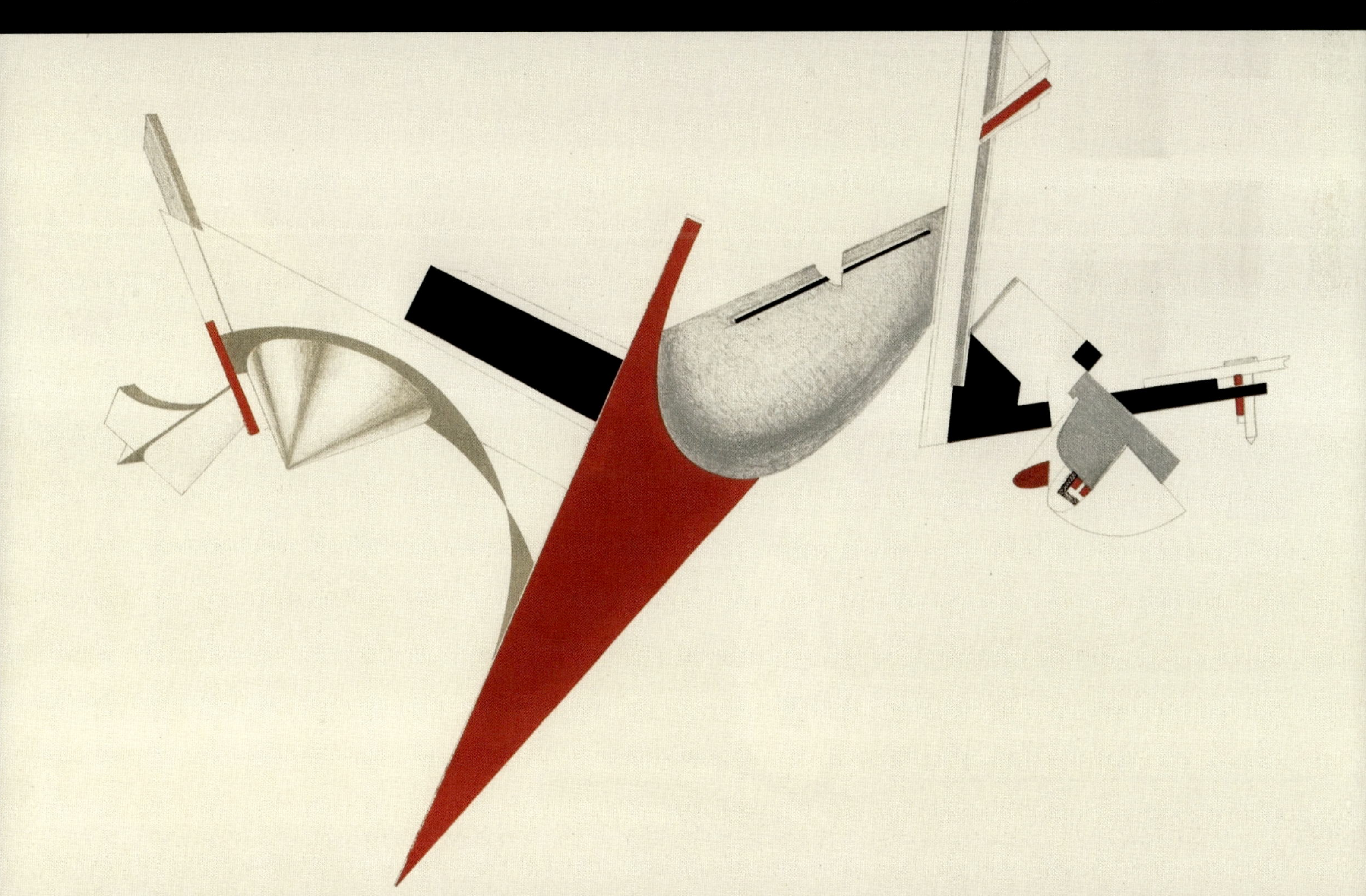

A GAME OF KNUCKLEPUCKS

Here the title works just as well as the visual, as *The Game of Knucklebones* (which turns out is the same as jacks or jinks) sounds appropriate for the physical sport that is hockey.

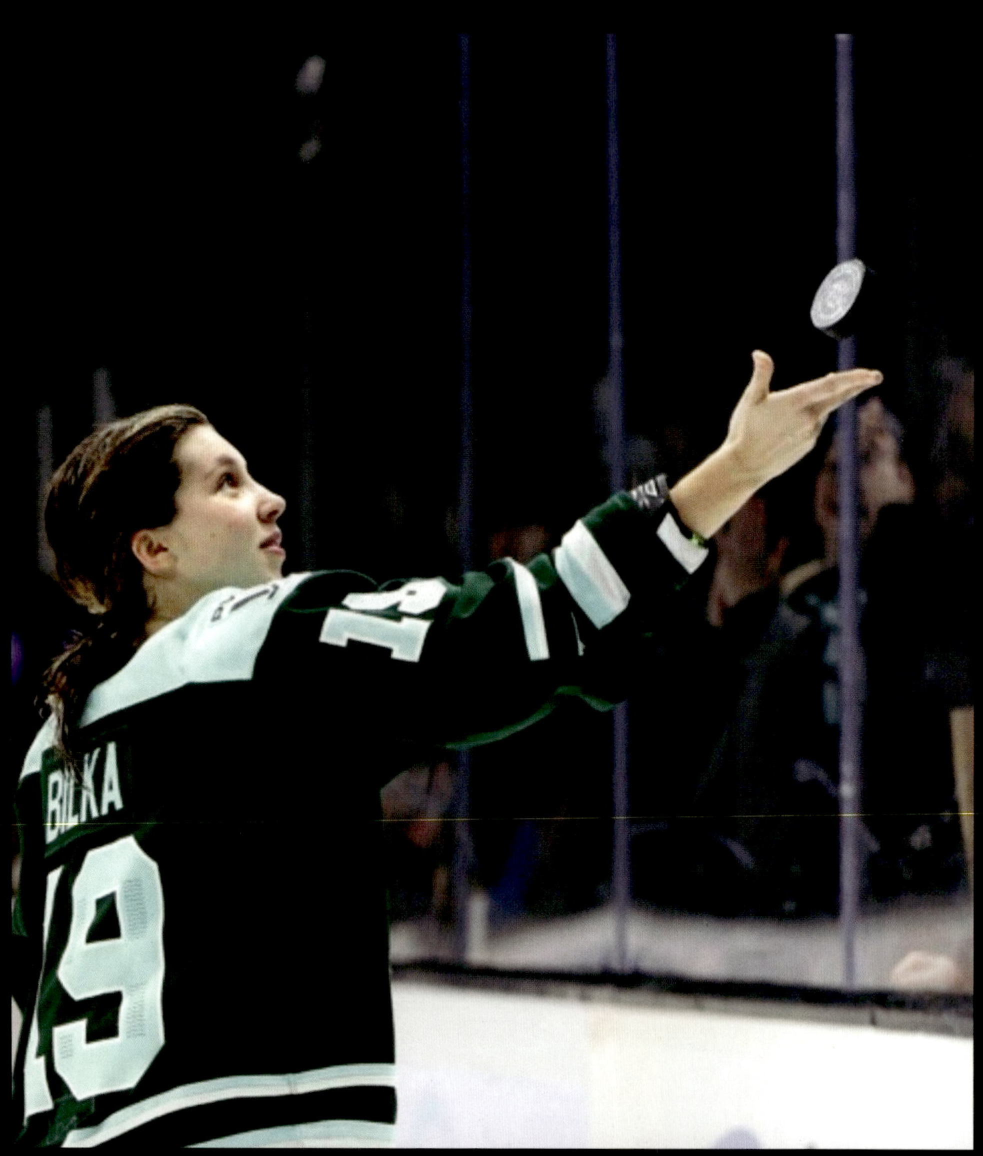

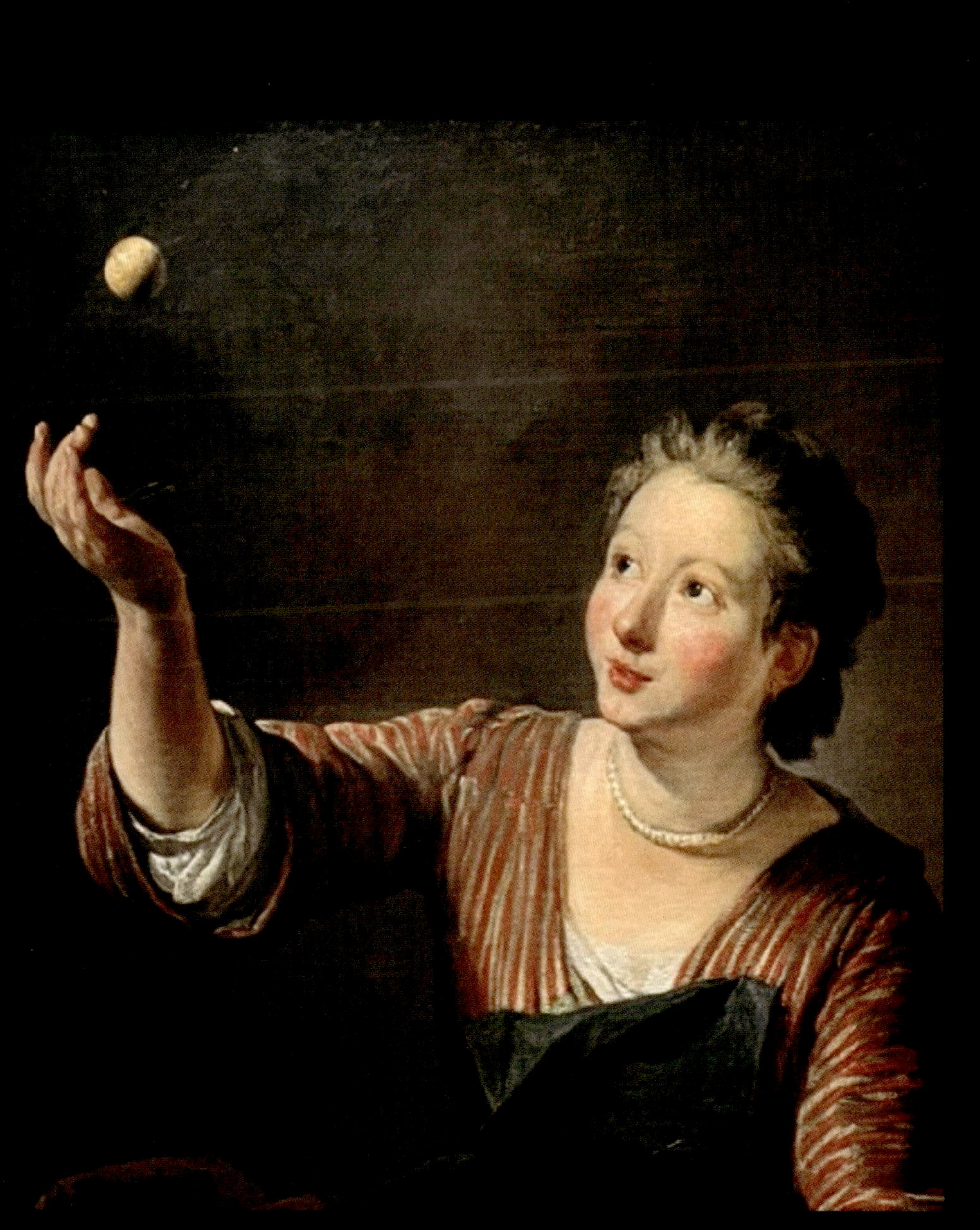

Opposite page: Hannah Bilka (#19) of the Boston Fleet tosses a puck after being named the first star of the game against Montréal Victoire during a PWHL Takeover Tour game at Climate Pledge Arena on January 5, 2025, in Seattle, Washington. Photo by Steph Chambers/ Getty Images.

This page: *The Game of Knucklebones* (detail), circa 1734, Jean-Baptiste-Siméon Chardin. Digital image by Google Arts & Culture. The Mary Frick Jacobs Collection.

BOURQUE CARRIES THE KINGDOM

Ray Bourque, a legendary defenseman, at long last breaking through after a twenty-two-year wait at the age of forty, is arguably the most iconic Stanley Cup lifter in NHL history. Though Bourque didn't quite grow the playoff beard to match, this Chagall seems more than fitting for the moment, especially given the physical and emotional weight of the cup. It must have felt like holding a literal palace overhead.

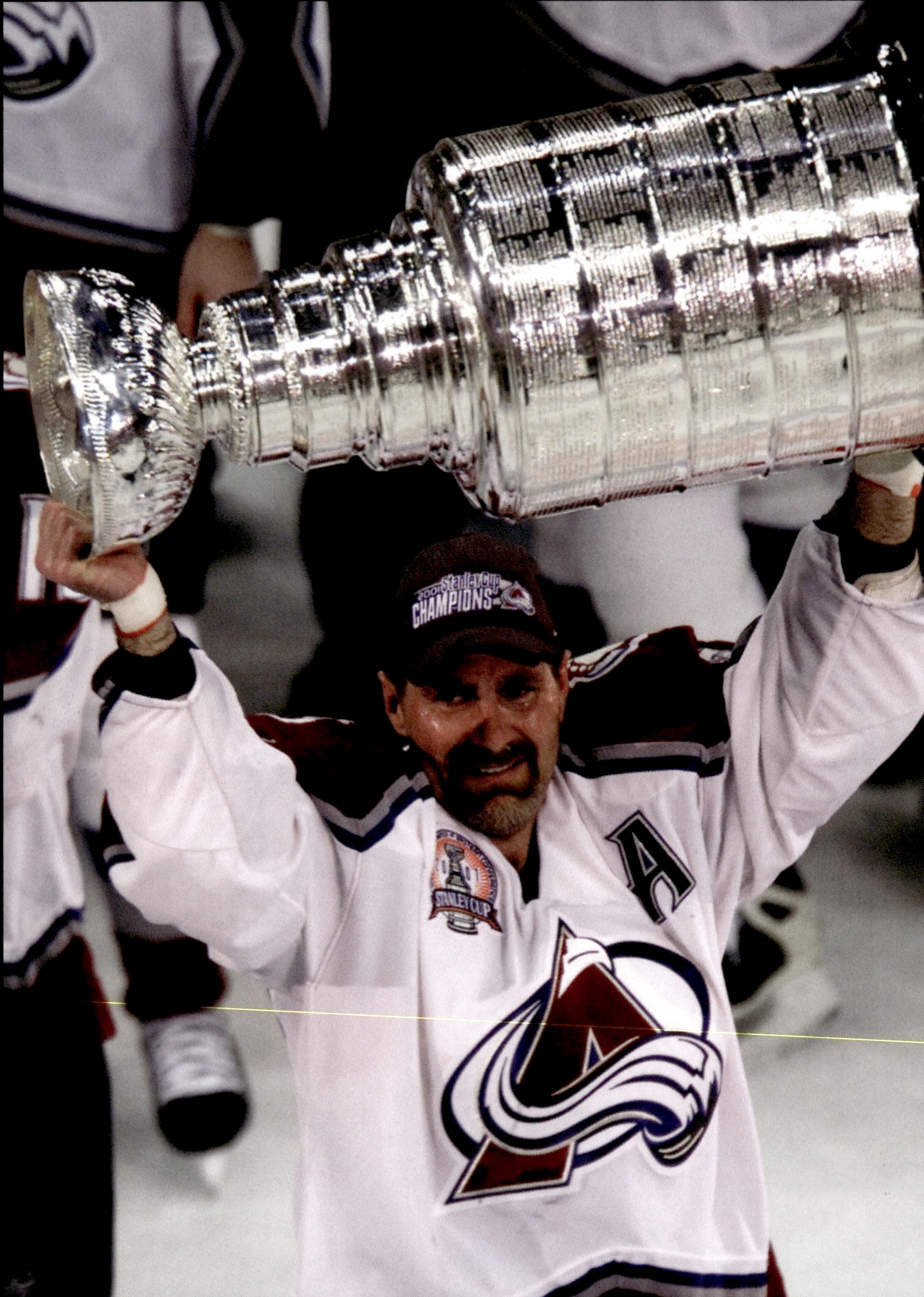

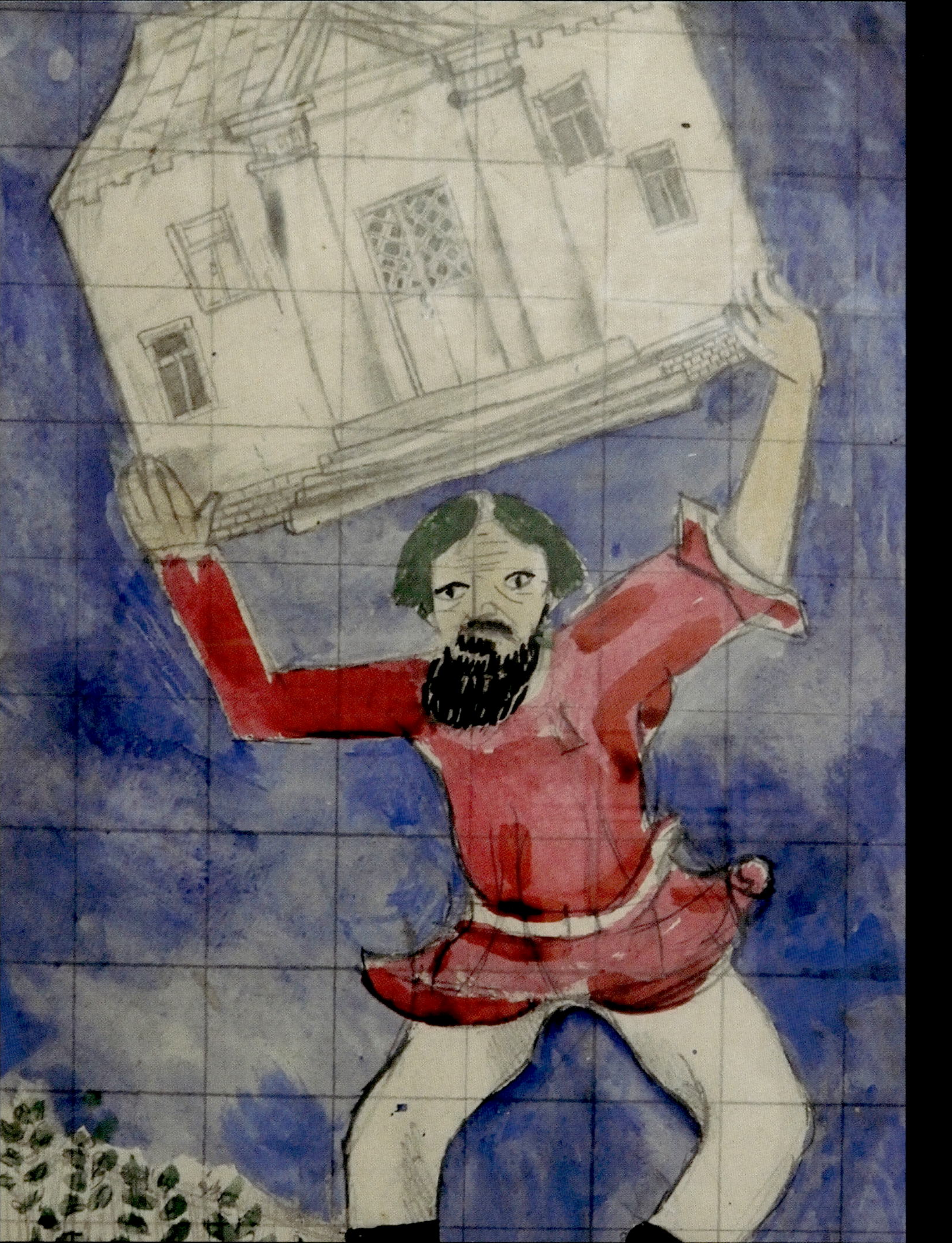

Opposite page: Ray Bourque (#77) of the Colorado Avalanche hoists the Stanley Cup after defeating the New Jersey Devils during the Stanley Cup finals at the Pepsi Center on June 9, 2001, in Denver, Colorado. The Avalanche defeated the Devils 3–1 to win the series 4–3. Photo by Brian Bahr/ALLSPORT.

This page: *Paix aux chaumières – guerre aux palais*, 1918, Marc Chagall. State Tretlatkov Gallery. Flipped from the original.

MALKIN AND ZETTERBERG

What's a hockey section without a good old-fashioned scrum?!

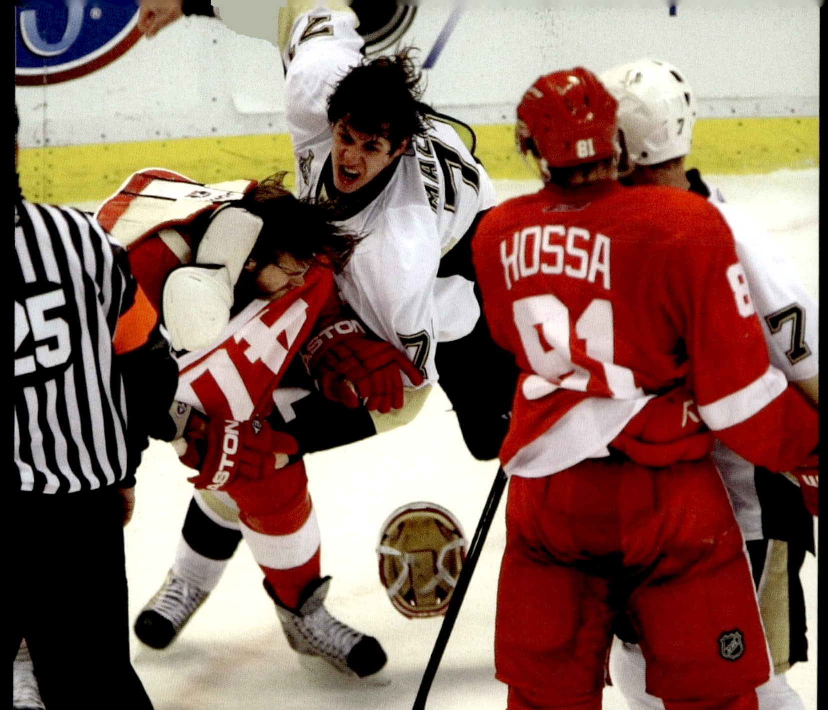

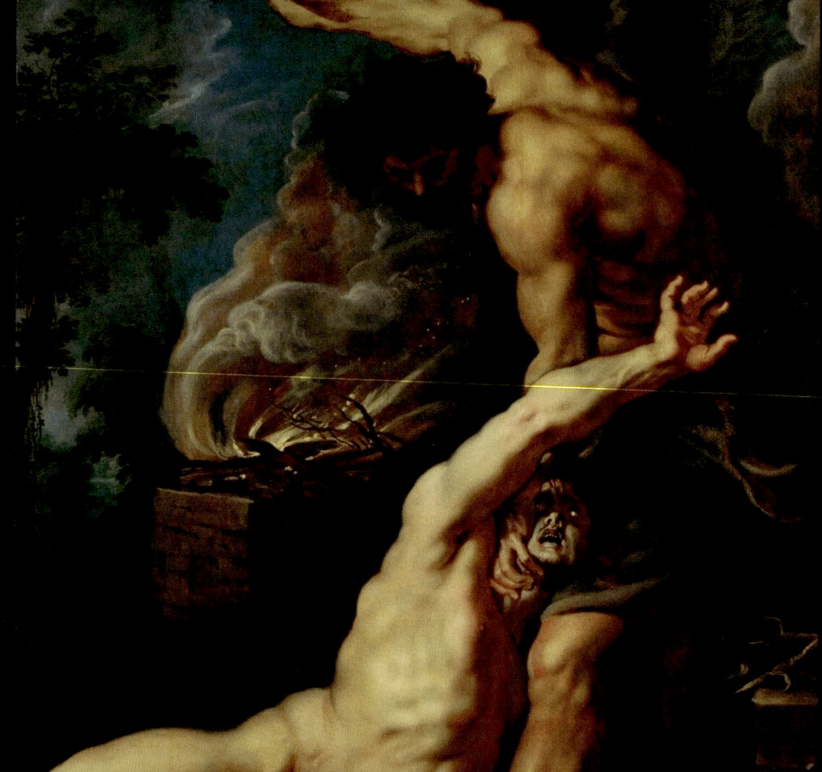

Top: Evgeni Malkin (#71) of the Pittsburgh Penguins fights Henrik Zetterberg (#40) of the Detroit Red Wings during Game 2 of the 2009 Stanley Cup finals at the Joe Louis Arena on May 31, in Detroit, Michigan. Photo by Claus Andersen/Getty Images.

Bottom: *Cain Slaying Abel* (detail), 1608–09, Peter Paul Rubens. Digital image by Google Arts & Culture. The Courtauld Institute of Art.

THE MASK

"Meet James Ensor, Belgium's famous painter!" As extolled by They Might Be Giants in their appropriately titled 1994 track "Meet James Ensor," the Belgium painter was most famous for illustrating skeletons and masks, making him especially appropriate to put alongside Tony Esposito and his early goalie face shield.

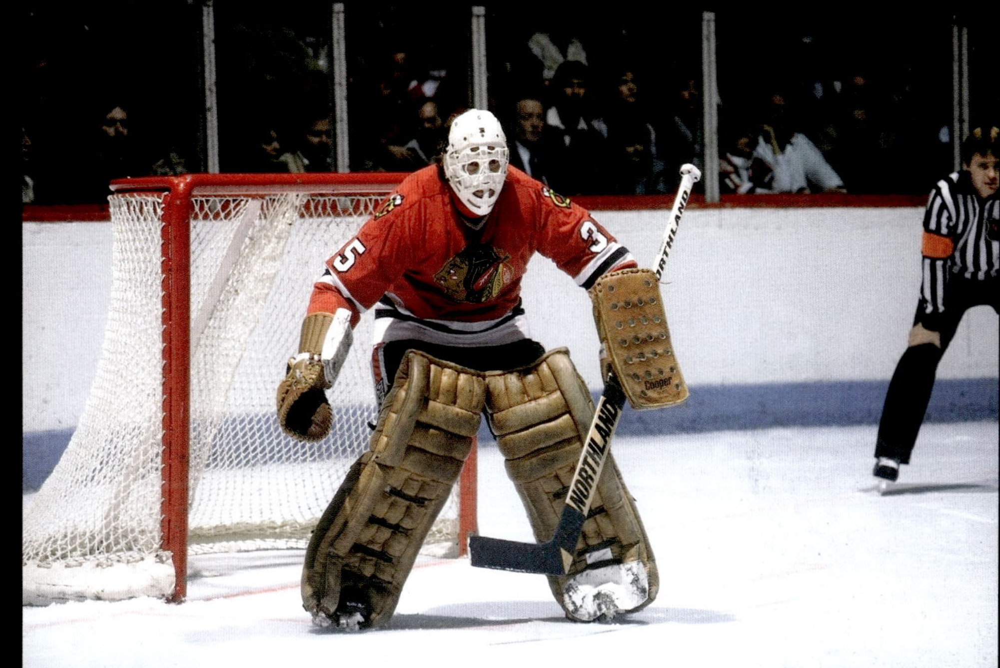

Top: Goaltender Tony Esposito (#35) of the Chicago Blackhawks prepares to defend the net against the Montreal Canadiens in the 1980s. Photo by Denis Brodeur/NHLI via Getty Images.

Bottom: *Masks*, 1925, James Ensor. Digital image by PubHist. Tel Aviv Museum of Art.

THE GREAT ONE(S)

There's a long history of portraits featuring sitters holding objects, and these are two of my favorites. On one hand, Botticelli's *Portrait of a Young Man Holding a Roundel* captures the Great One's immaculate flow, but van Honthort's *Smiling Girl, a Courtesan, Holding an Obscene Image* has better puck placement and matches Gretzky's enthusiasm. Choose your fighter!

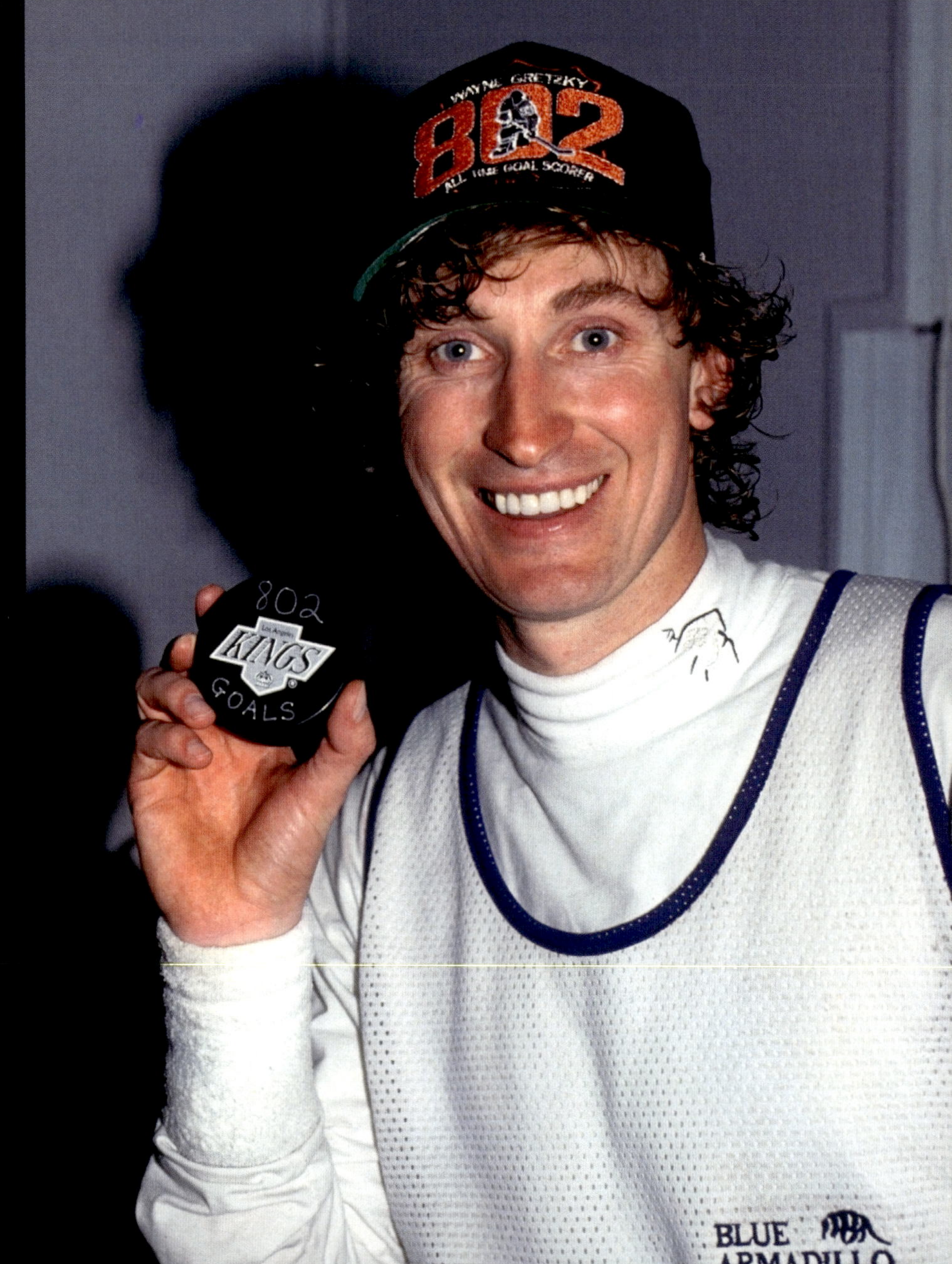

Wayne Gretzky (#99) of the Los Angeles Kings poses with the puck he scored his 802nd career goal with after the game against the Vancouver Canucks on March 23, 1994, at the Great Western Forum in Inglewood, California. Photo by Bruce Bennett/ Getty Images.

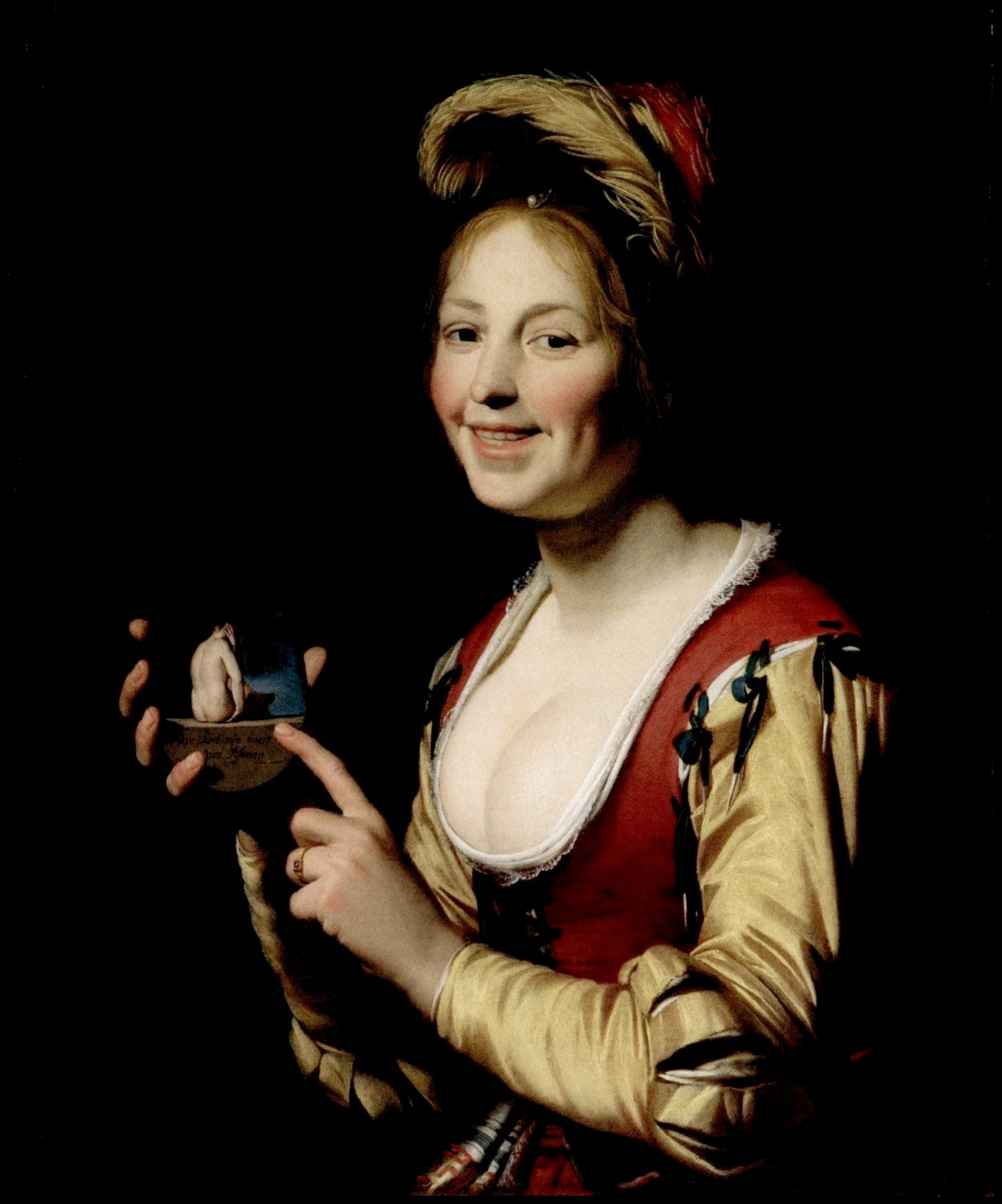

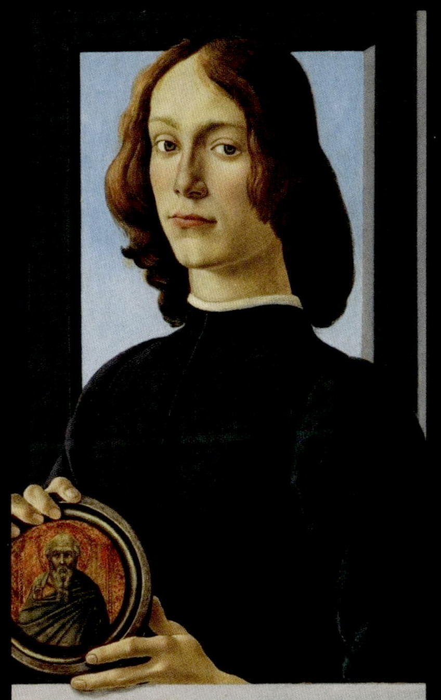

Left: ***Smiling Girl, a Courtesan, Holding an Obscene Image***, **1625, Gerrit van Honthorst. Saint Louis Art Museum.**

Right: ***Portrait of a Young Man Holding a Roundel***, **circa 1480–85, Sandro Botticelli. Private collection.**

GOLF

Playing golf is a lot like putting this book together. One good shot has you thinking you finally know what you're doing. Then your next swing ends with a mulligan and leaves you deeply humbled. But you keep chasing that initial high, and you grab it just often enough to start the cycle all over again.

The Golfers (detail), 1847, Charles Lee. National Galleries Scotland.

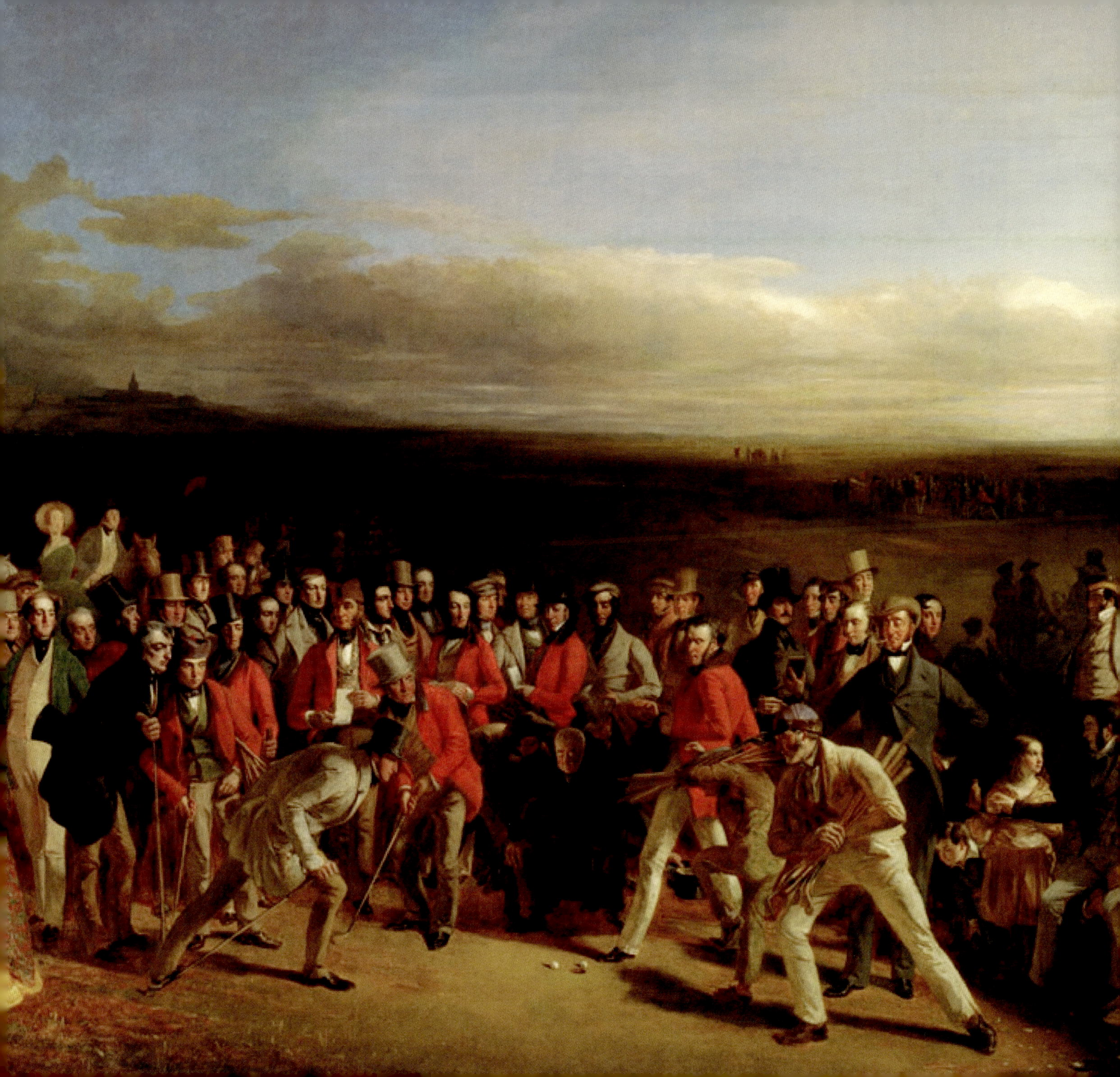

THE ANNIKA EFFECT

Golf is hard. It's hard to play. It's hard to stay awake while watching it at 3:00 p.m. on a Sunday afternoon when you're comfortable on the couch. And above all, it's hard to meme. Golfers can be milquetoast, and their moments of victory and defeat tend to be repetitive—there's only so much that's acceptable on the course.

I knew I wanted to feature a photo of Annika Sörenstam, and what struck me about this Mike Mulholland shot is that it's just so different from the normal golf photos I've seen. I also consider Sörenstam to be a matriarchal figure in golf, with her dominance clearing a path for the women's game to be taken seriously.

Mary Cassatt is *the* modern painter when it comes to depicting motherhood, and her standing makes her the perfect complement to Sörenstam. Career oriented, Cassatt defied traditional gender roles and let her viewpoint be known through her artwork. In a similar fashion, Sörenstam bucked the norm and played in the 2003 Bank of America Colonial, a PGA Tour event, becoming the first woman to compete with the men in over fifty years. Though she missed the cut, she finished above eleven male competitors.

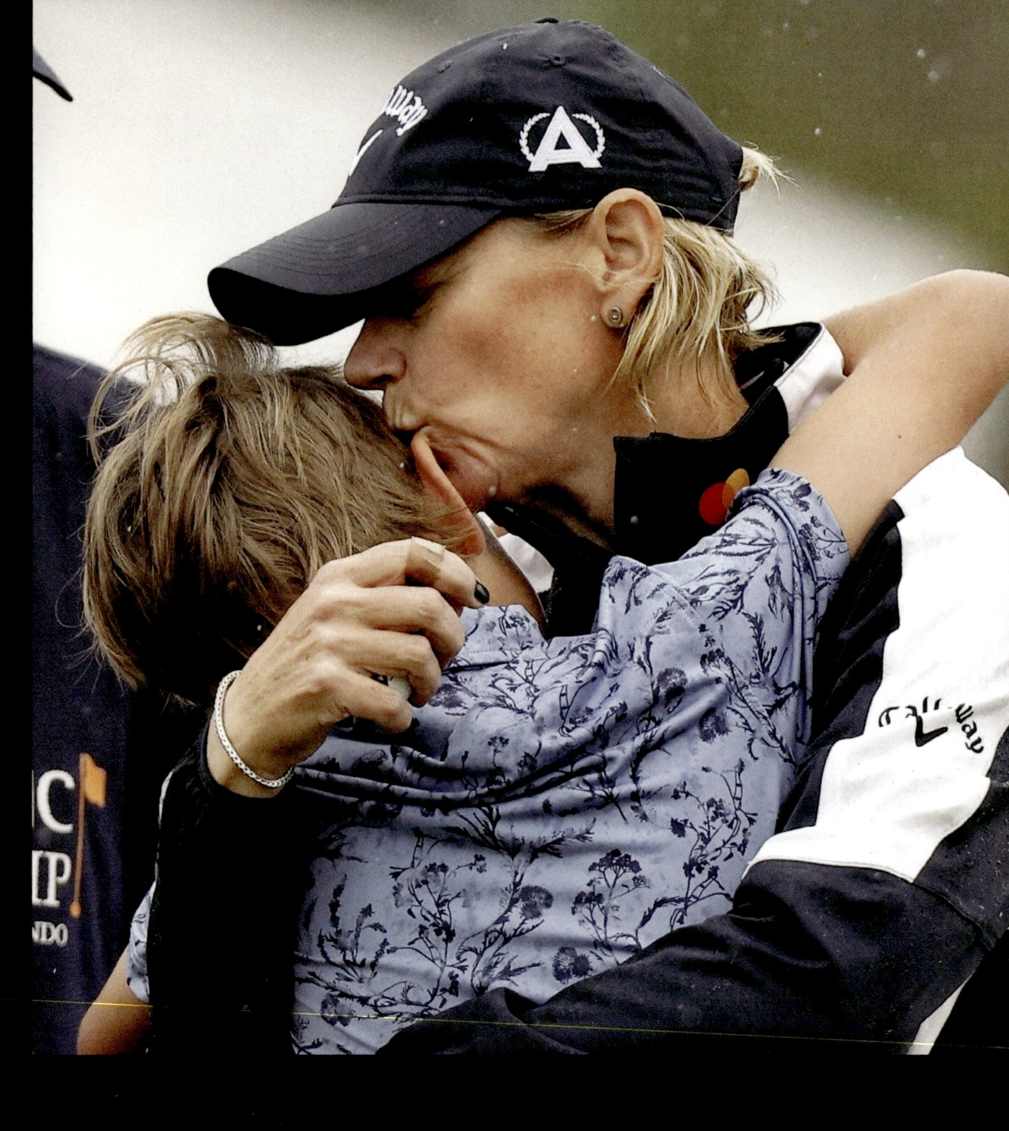

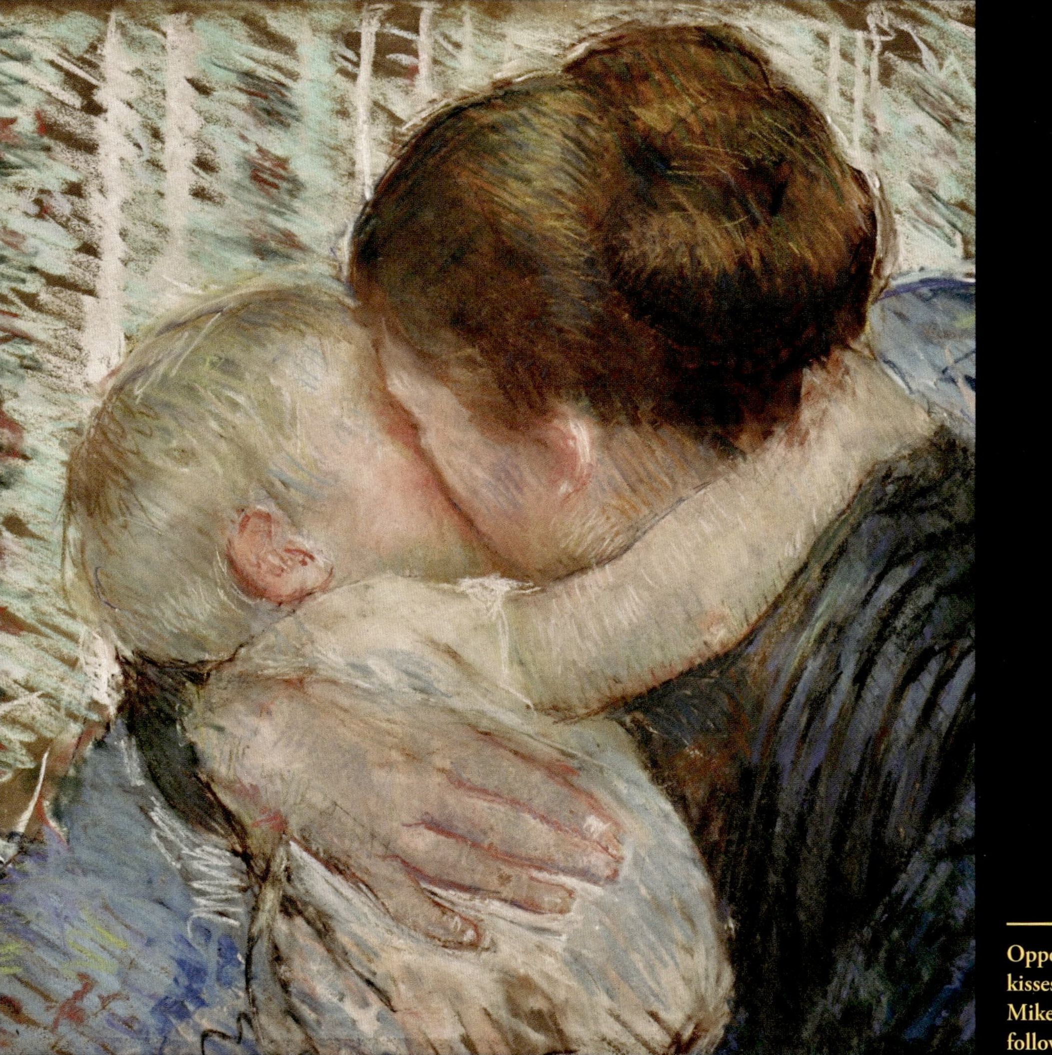

Opposite page: Annika Sörenstam of Sweden kisses her son Will McGee as her husband, Mike McGee, looks on from the 18th green following the first round of the PNC Champi-

PAYNE STEWART

Payne Stewart tragically passed away in an airplane accident at the age of forty-two, just months after this photo of him celebrating his third major championship was taken at the 1999 U.S. Open. Stewart was stylish and graceful, and this photo of him is as iconic as a similarly elegant Degas dancer.

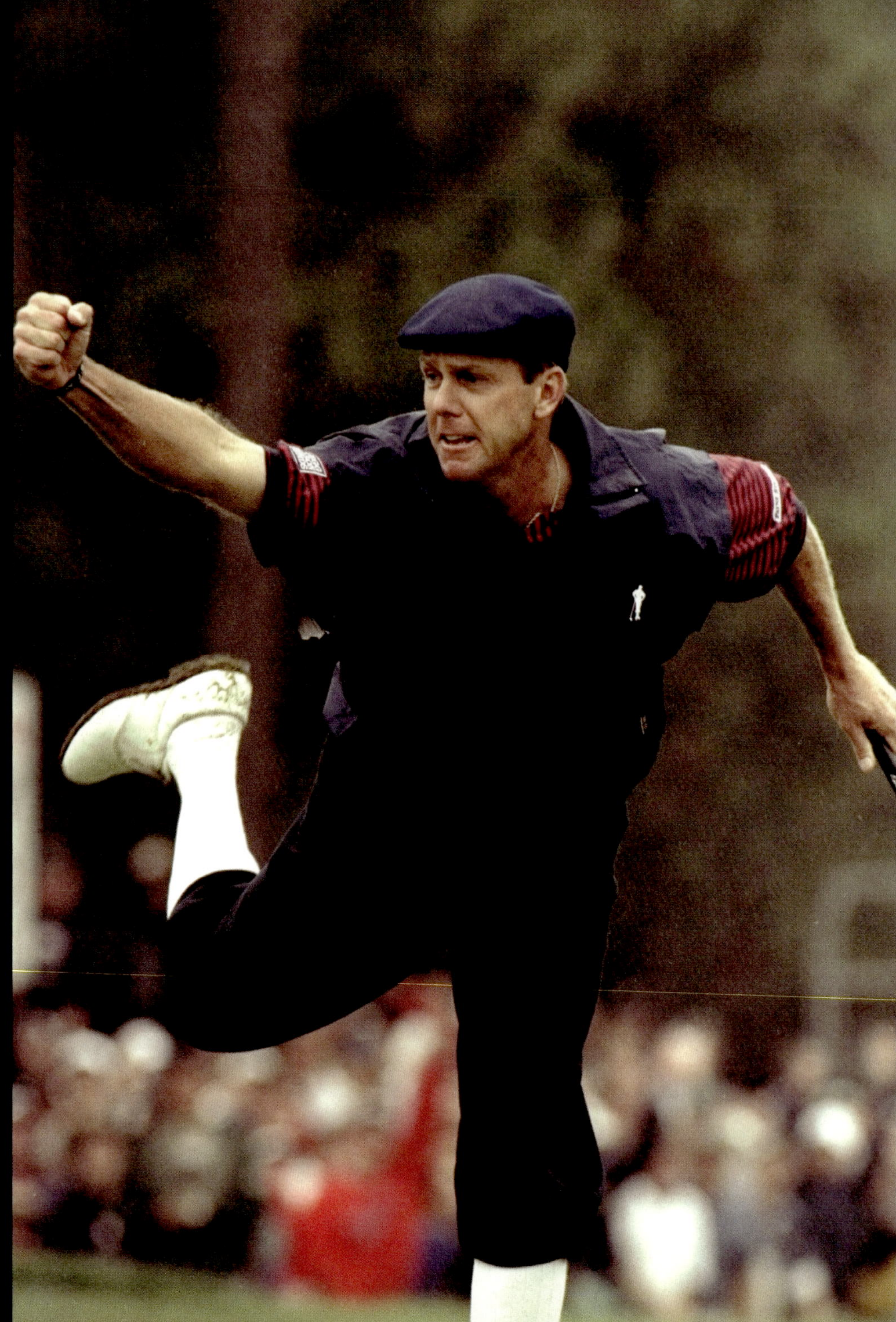

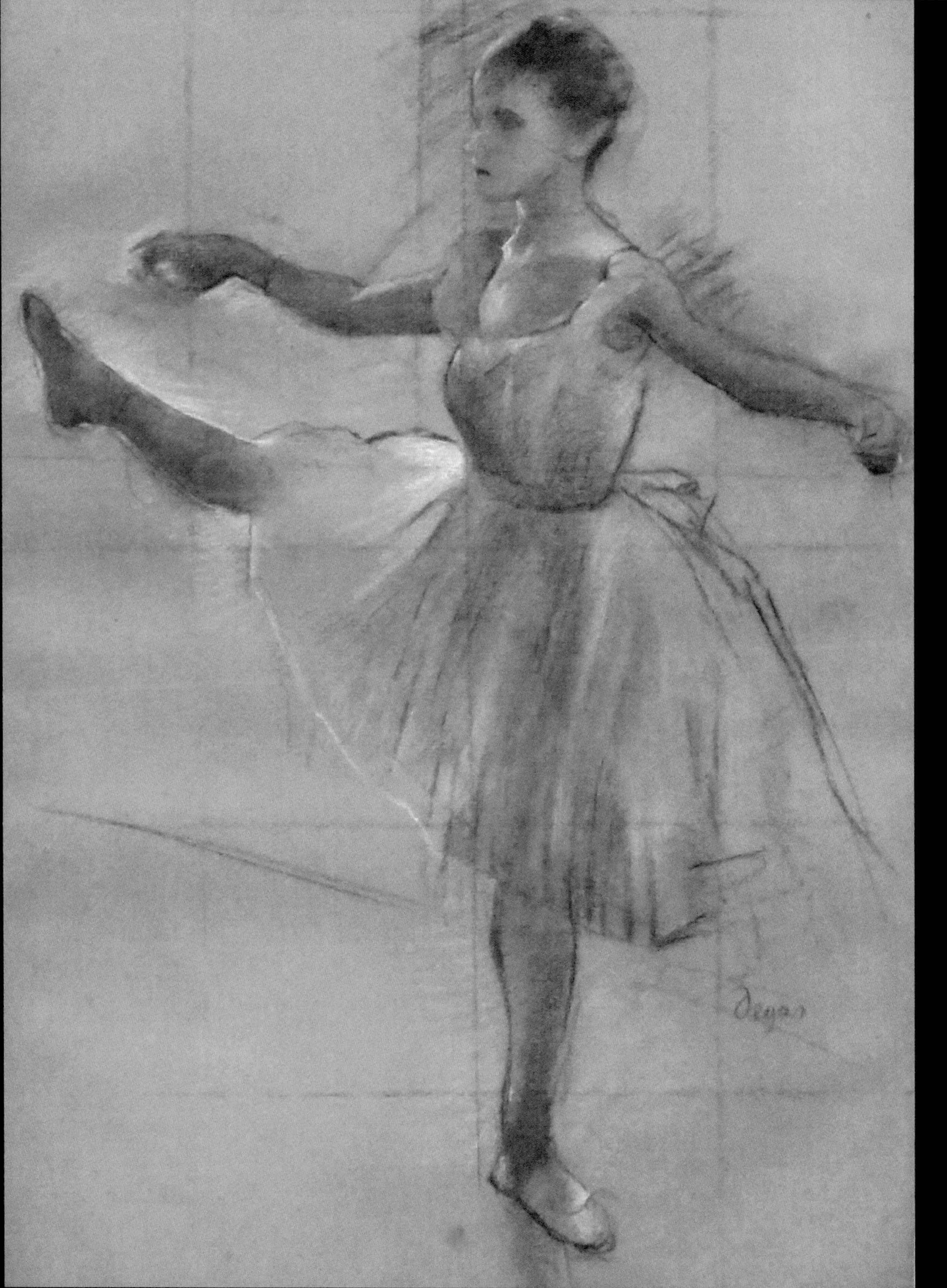

Opposite page: Payne Stewart of the United States celebrates victory after sinking his final putt during the last day of the 1999 U.S. Open played on the number two course at Pinehurst on June 20, 1999, in North Carolina. Photo by Craig Jones/ALLSPORT.

This page: *Dancer (Battement in Second Position)*, 1874, Edgar Degas. Norton Simon Museum.

TIGER AND CHARLIE

Seeing the kin of your favorite athletes compete in their own right is both humbling and oddly inspirational. My favorite athlete growing up—Ken Griffey Jr.—was potentially the most famous nepo baby athlete of them all, so I've always taken a shine to players whose parents also competed. Seeing Charlie Woods start his own career makes me feel my age, but it also warms my heart. There's always the concern that following in a parent's footsteps creates overwhelming, unwarranted pressure, especially with a father who has the stature of Tiger Woods. But from the outside, it seems like Tiger has instilled a genuine love of the game into Charlie. That being said, I couldn't help myself making a comparison to Rosa Bonheur's *Two Goats*, with Tiger, the GOAT, carving a path of greatness for his son to follow.

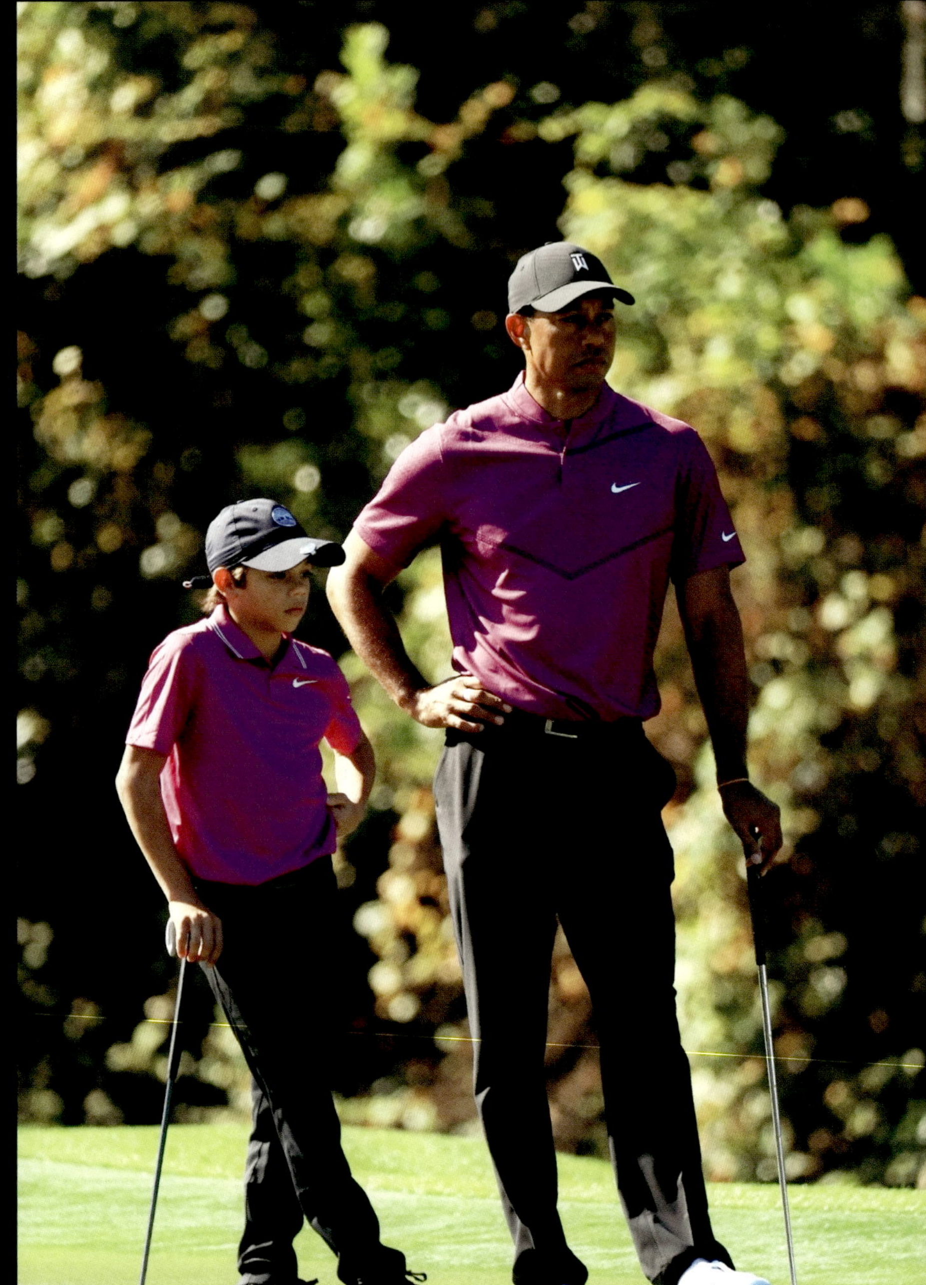

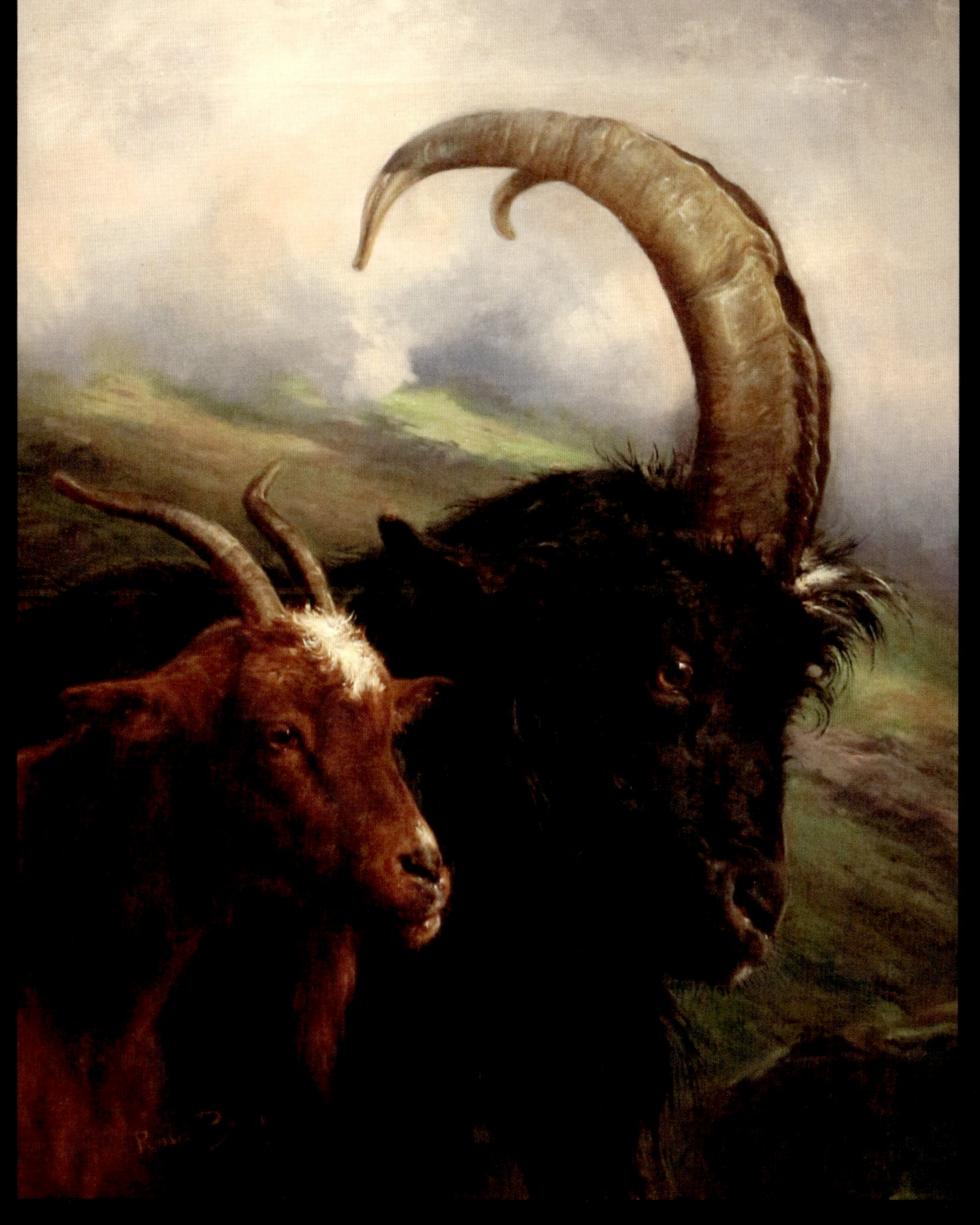

Opposite page: Tiger Woods and Charlie Woods look on from the 1st green during the first round of the PNC Championship at the Ritz-Carlton Golf Club Orlando on December 19, 2020, in Orlando, Florida. Photo by Mike Ehrmann/ Getty Images.

This page: *Two Goats*, circa 1870, Rosa Bonheur. Digital image by Sailko. Milwaukee Art Museum.

RORY MASTERS AUGUSTA

"Der Gestürzte" translates to Fallen Man, which sums up the cathartic release we saw from Rory McIlroy when he dropped to all fours after winning the 2025 Masters. It was a moment over fifteen years in the making, during which McIlroy came painfully close on multiple occasions to donning the Green Jacket.

His breakthrough wasn't any less stressful, as it took a sudden death playoff against Justin Rose to finally complete the career grand slam.

As an added Easter egg, this photo was shot by baseball legend Ken Griffey Jr., who, like his former teammate Randy Johnson, took up sports photography post-playing career.

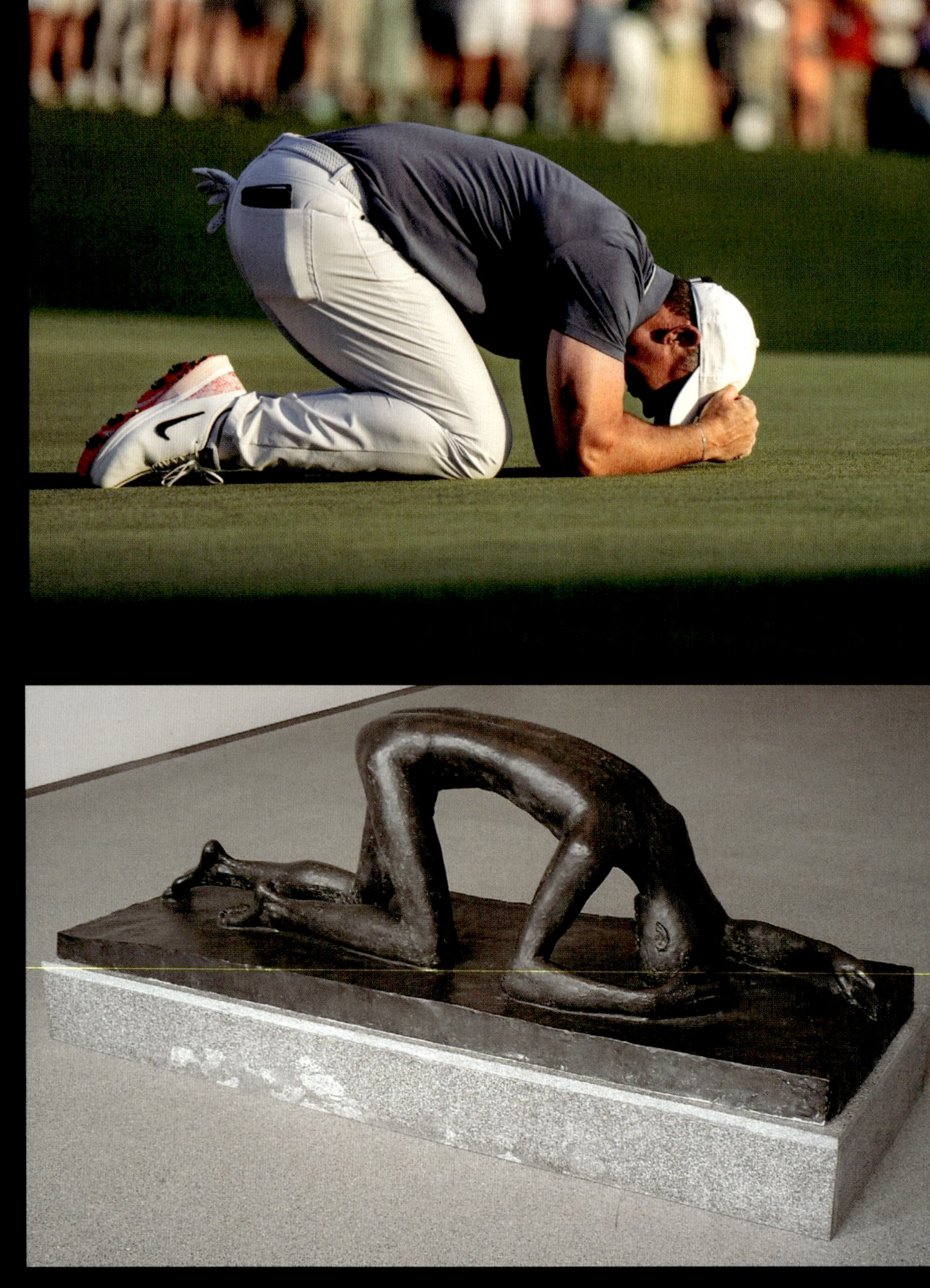

Top: Masters champion Rory McIlroy of Northern Ireland celebrates on the No. 18 green after a sudden death playoff against Justin Rose of England to win the Masters at Augusta National Golf Club, Sunday, April 13, 2025. Photo by Ken Griffey Jr./Augusta National/Getty Images.

Bottom: *Der Gestürzte*, 1915–16, Wilhelm Lehmbruck. Digital image by Oliver Kurmis. Pinakothek der Moderne. Flipped from the original.

JACK

A Jack vs. Tiger debate feels a lot like MJ vs. LeBron, at which point you probably just want to take a step back and appreciate greatness. It's those vibes that come from this photo and Manet's painting: a salute to the fans from a seasoned champion.

Left: Honorary starter Jack Nicklaus holds up his hat during the first tee ceremony prior to the first round of the 2017 Masters Tournament at Augusta National Golf Club on April 6, 2017, in Augusta, Georgia. Getty Images.

Right: *A Matador*, 1866–67, Édouard Manet. Digital image by the Metropolitan Museum of Art. H. O. Haveymeyer Collection.

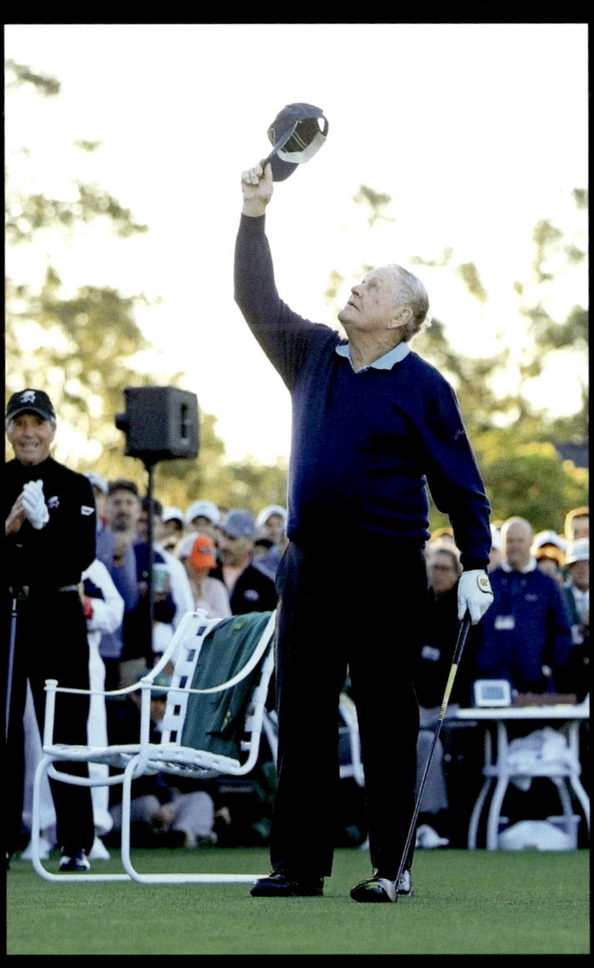

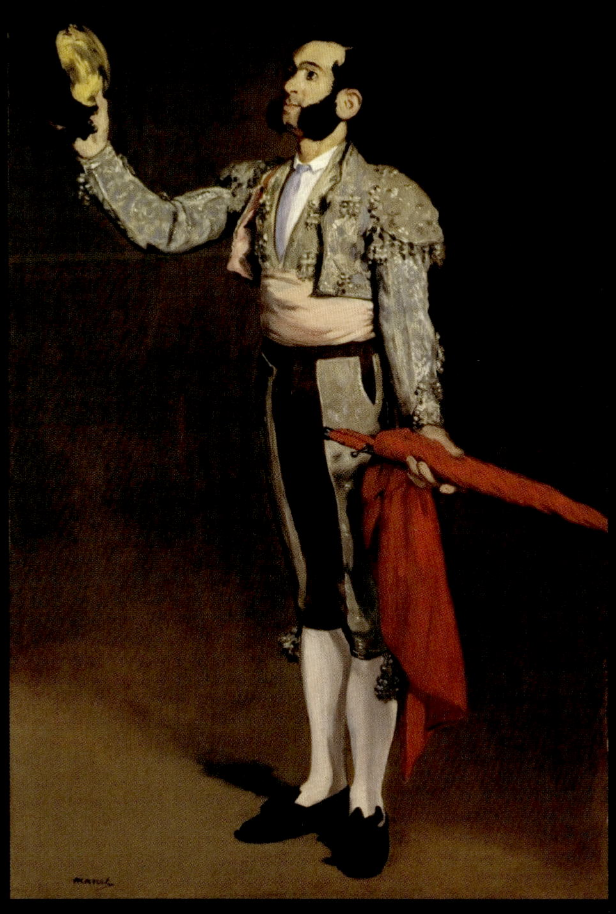

THE OLYMPICS

I had the honor of directly working on two Olympics. I was the digital producer of boxing, fencing, judo, taekwondo, and wrestling for London 2012, and helped run the live-streaming app for Sochi 2014. The Olympics are near and dear to my heart, and my absolute favorite sport to see reflected in artwork.

Marble relief fragment depicting athletic prizes (detail), second century CE, unknown Roman artist. Metropolitan Museum of Art.

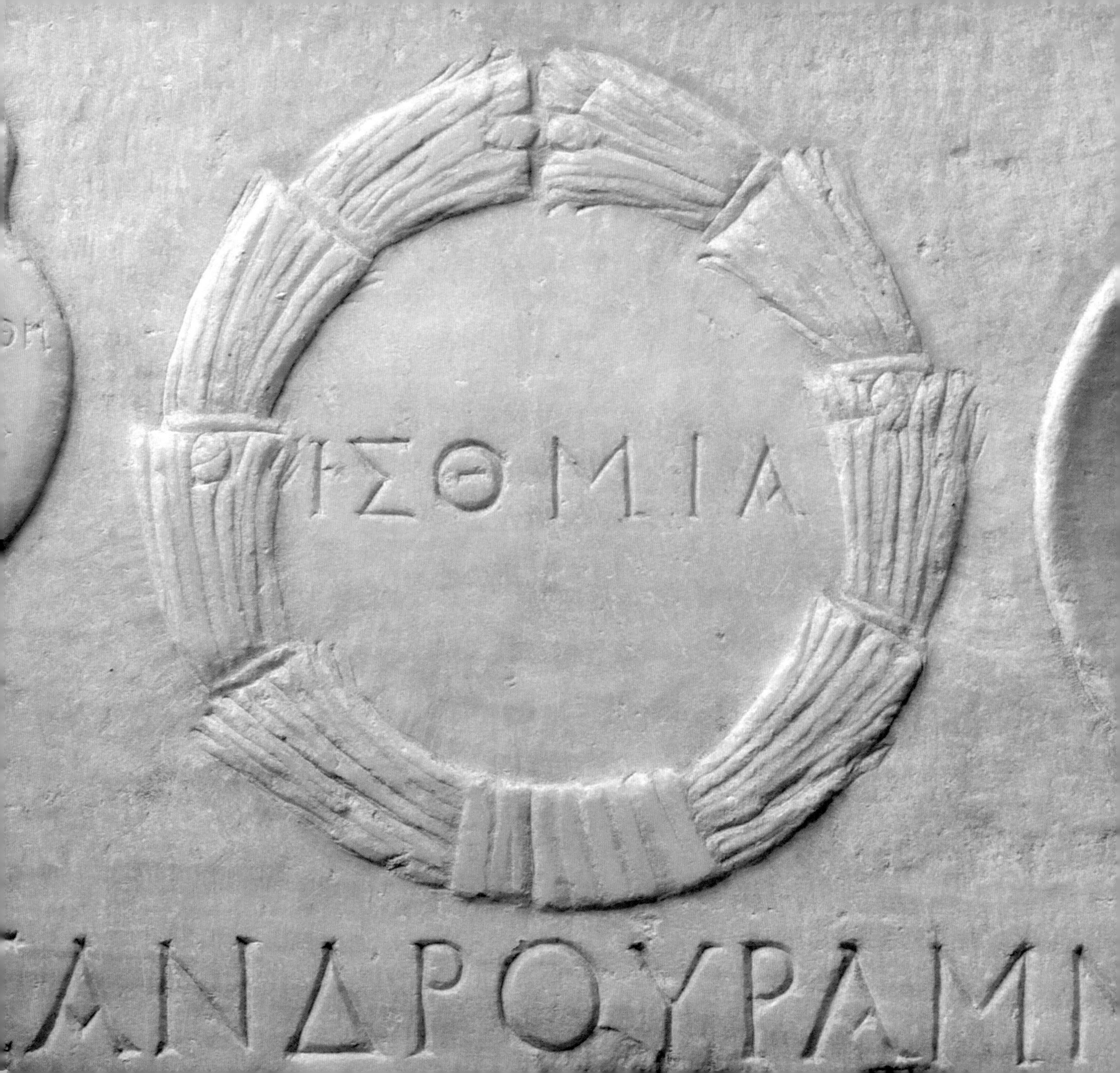

ΙΣΘΜΙΑ
ΑΝΔΡΟΥΡΑΜΙ

THE INEVITABLE LEBRON

There was nothing particularly special about the Puerto Rico vs. United States Group C game at the 2024 Paris Olympics, as the latter routed the former 104–83. And while some of the best sports images earn their status because of the ramifications surrounding the play at hand, some of my favorites are those where the photographer captures a seemingly innocuous moment that I can make metaphorical. This frame comes from a run-of-the-mill dunk attempt by Ismael Romero that had no larger consequence, but it's clear why it went viral: it's the look on his face, knowing there's the potential of impending doom (one of LeBron's signature moves is the chase-down block), juxtaposed against LeBron's extreme calm.

I initially thought of paintings with a central theme of an animal/hunter targeting their prey—a Peter Paul Rubens or Jean-Léon Gérôme, perhaps. But the extra layer here is that LeBron represents a "Father Time" type; in a basketball sense, he's cheated death (aging) to the point where he's become the inevitable. And I think that's what Böcklin's piece offers: the matching faces, the same position, the deeper theme, but also the parallel to who LeBron is.

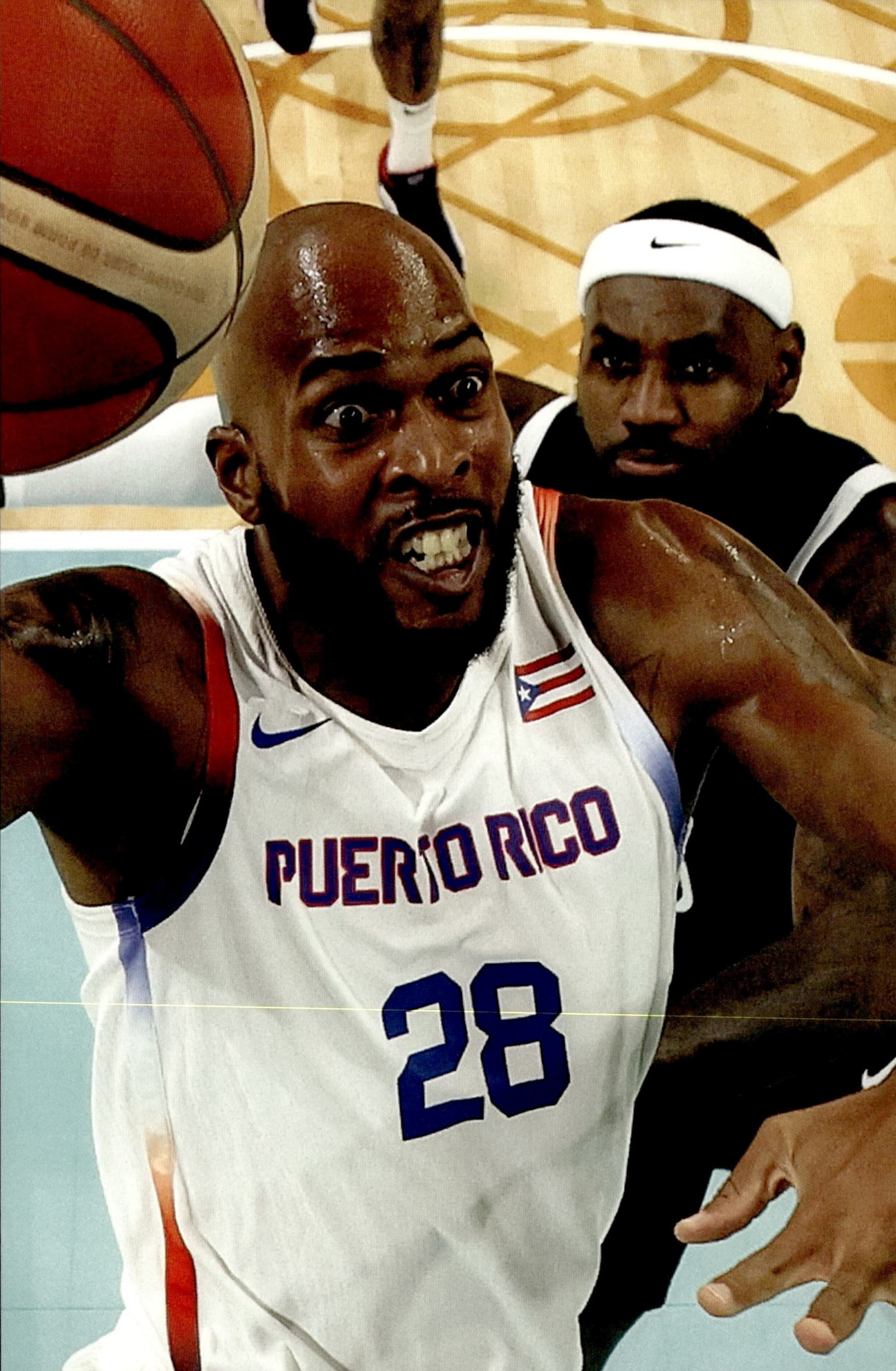

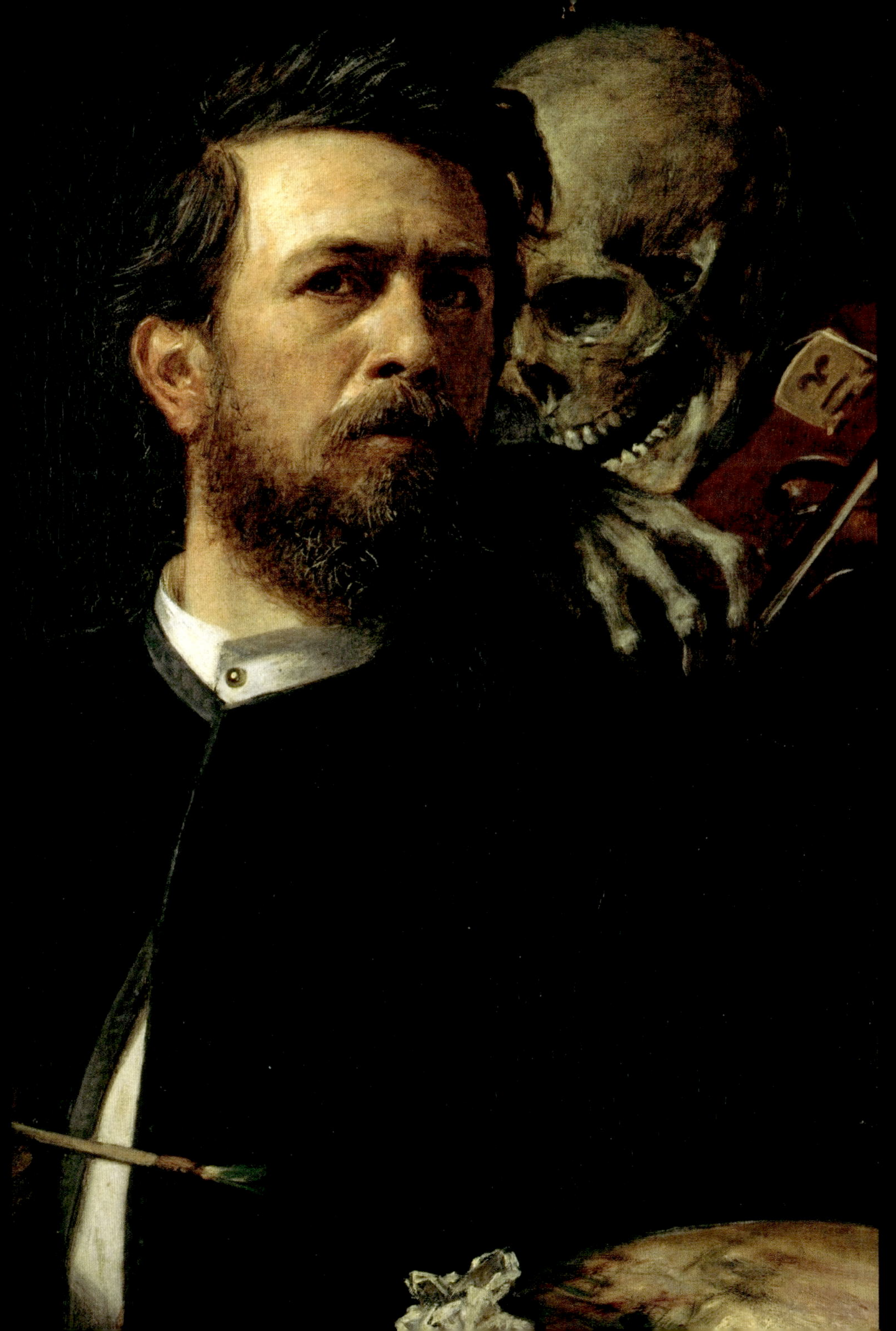

Opposite page: Ismael Romero (#28) of Team Puerto Rico goes up for a dunk past LeBron James (#6) of Team USA during a men's basketball Group C game on Day Eight of the Olympic Games at Stade Pierre-Mauroy on August 3, 2024, in Lille, France. Photo by Gregory Shamus/ Getty Images.

This page: *Self-Portrait with Death Playing the Fiddle* (detail), 1872, Arnold Böcklin. Digital image by Google Arts & Culture. Alte Nationalgalerie.

BILES BY MILES

The figure in Degas's masterpiece—his lone circus painting—is Miss La La, a high-flying performer with the Troupe Kaira, a traveling circus act during the late 1800s. There's a weightlessness to how Miss La La is depicted, and while her body and the background don't exactly match, you get a sense of artistry and power—the same characteristics we undoubtedly see in Biles—that you wouldn't get from, say, a Chagall, who often painted flying figures.

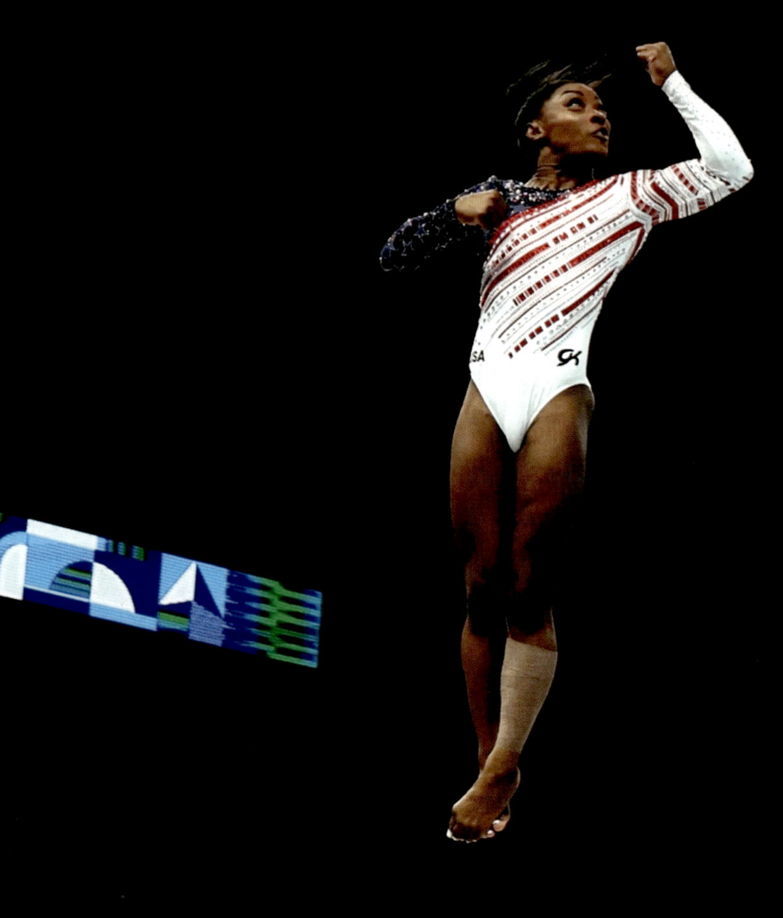

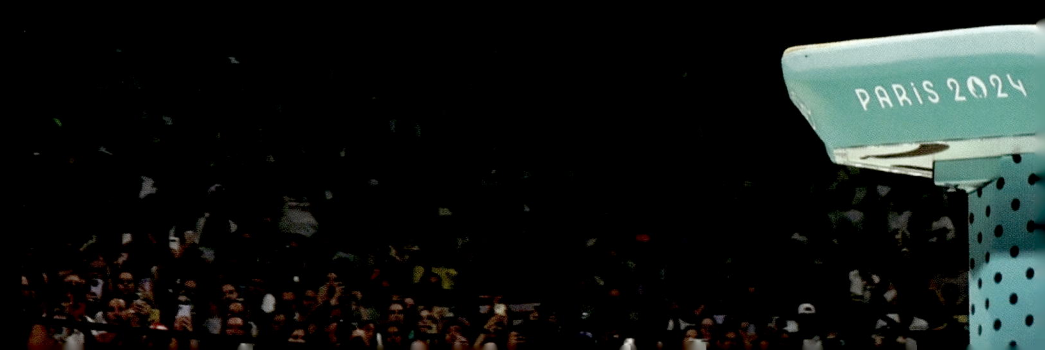

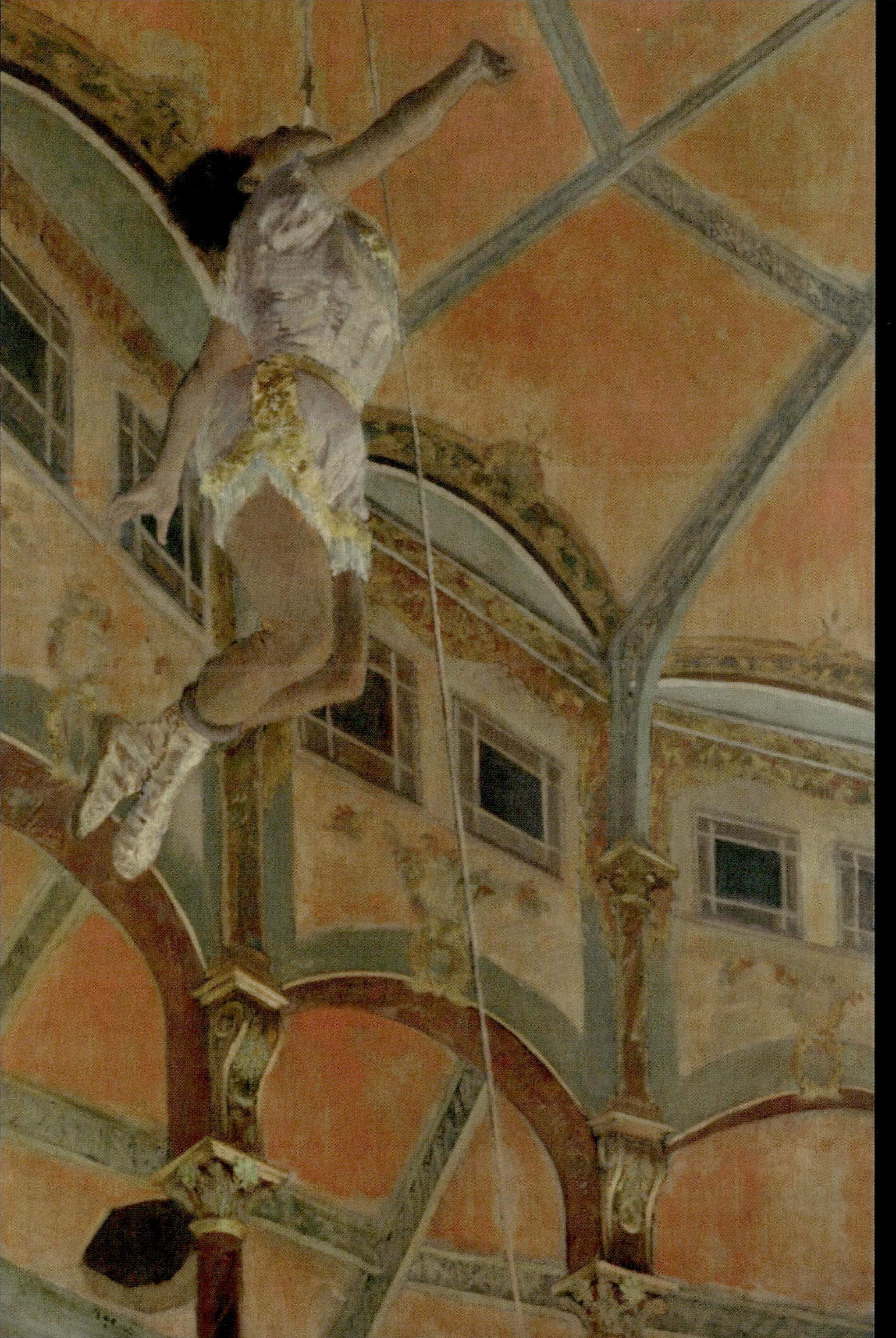

Opposite paget: Simone Biles of Team USA competes on the vault during the women's artistic gymnastics team final on Day Four of the Paris Olympic Games at Bercy Arena (now the Accor Arena) on July 30, 2024. Photo by Naomi Baker/Getty Images.

This page: *Miss La La at the Cirque Fernando*, 1879, Edgar Degas. National Gallery, London.

HIDDEN JEWEL

I knew I wanted to use this painting in the book. There are very few tasteful artistic depictions of people of color in the public domain, which is partly why this work feels special to me. Furthermore, it's an awesome painting, as it very much feels like a gesture ripped directly from an athlete's celebration. After a bit of searching (shout-out to the massive Getty Images library), I landed on a shot of one of my favorite ballers and one of the most entertaining hoopers in the game, Jewell Lloyd, shushing the crowd at the 2024 Olympic Games.

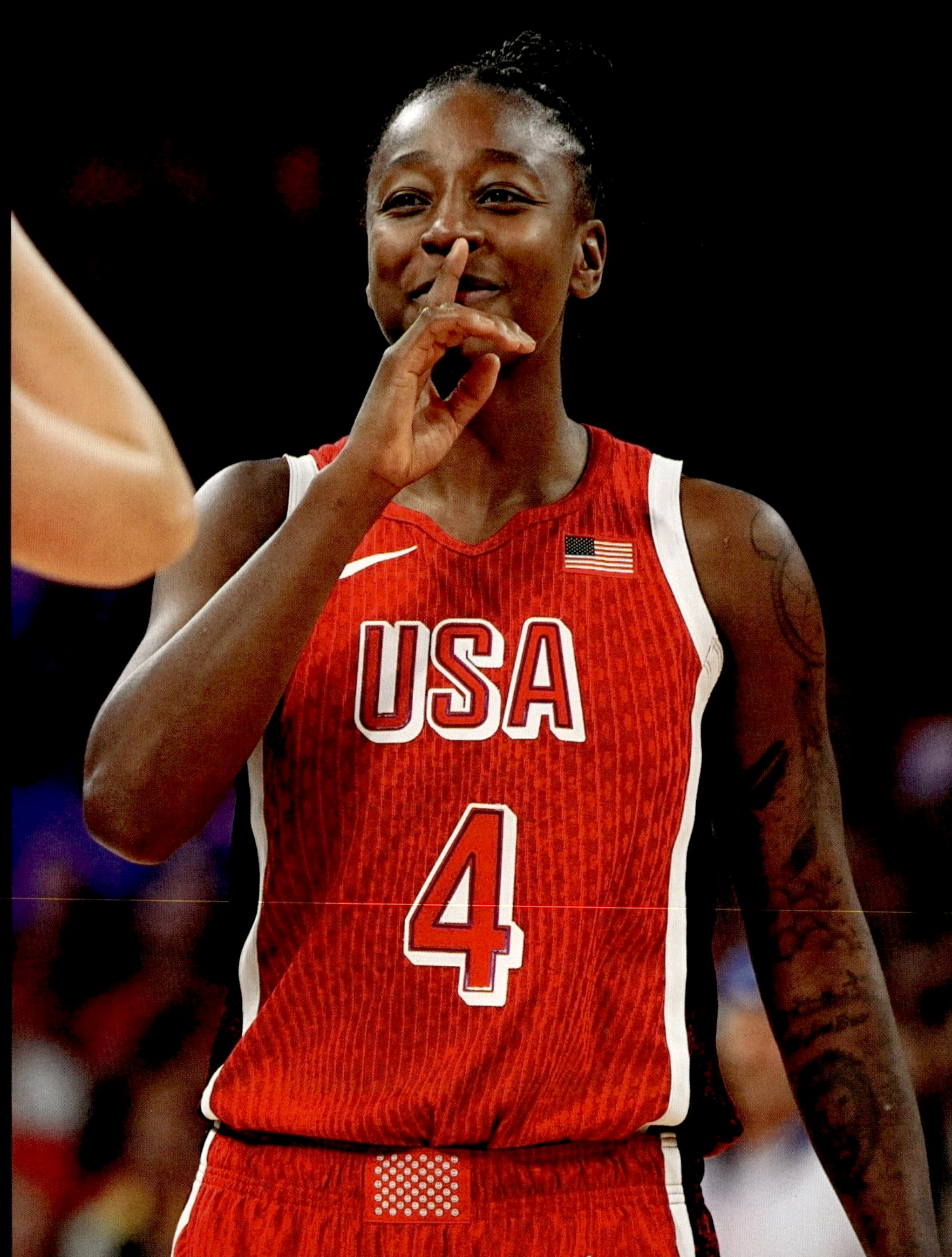

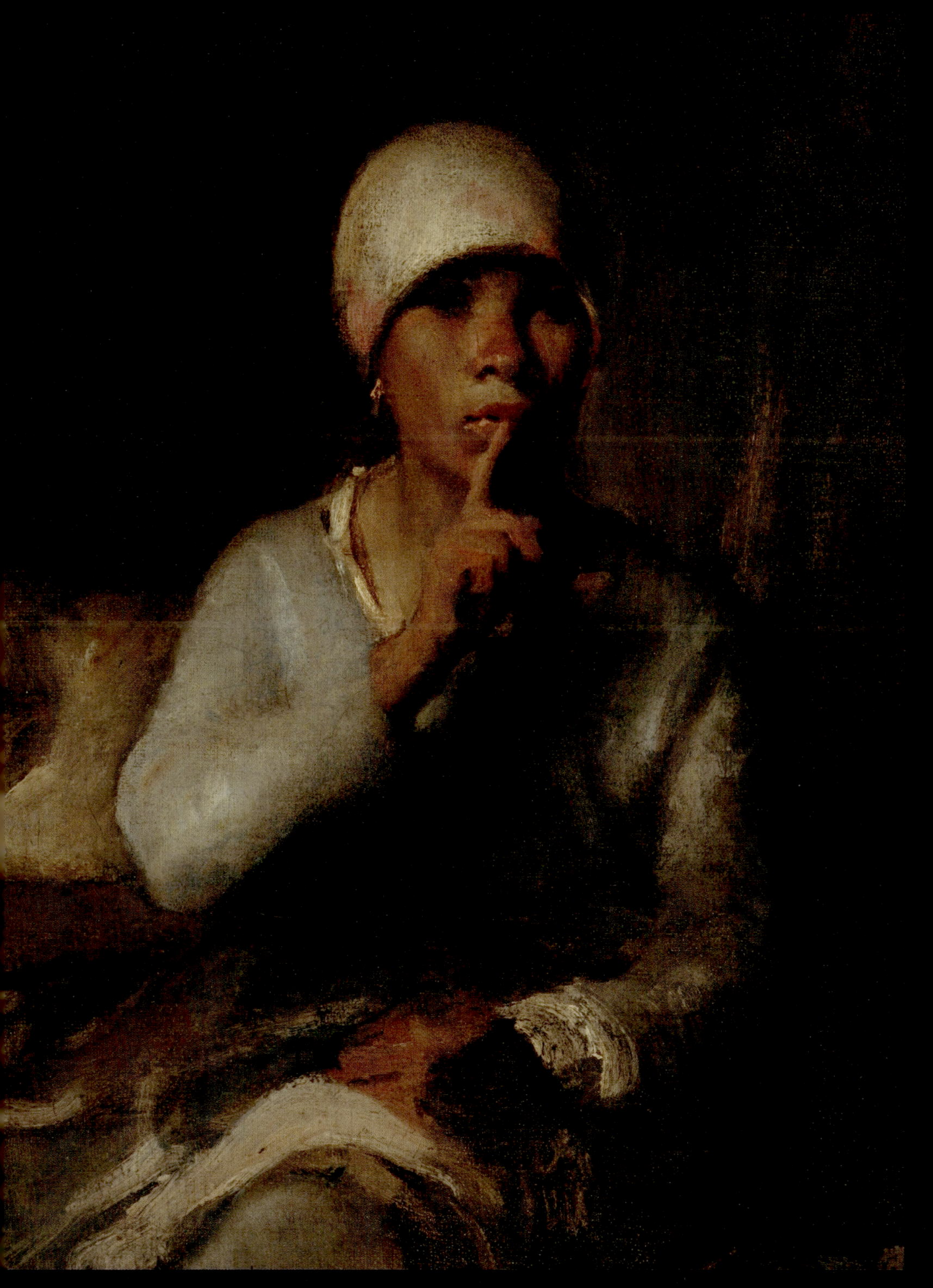

Opposite page: USA's Jewell Loyd (#4) reacts at the end of the women's preliminary round Group C basketball match between Belgium and USA during the Paris 2024 Olympic Games at the Stade Pierre-Mauroy in Villeneuve-d'Ascq, northern France, on August 1, 2024. Photo by Sameer Al-Doumy/AFP.

This page: *Woman and Child (Silence)* (detail), 1855, attributed to Auguste Boulard, the Elder. Private collection.

queen of women's swimming, and one of America's most heralded Olympians. So I thought it apt to find artwork alluding to the permanence of stone. The Asclepios pillar is from the Acropolis, and it mimics how Ledecky is constantly lurking, eyeing down her inferior competition.

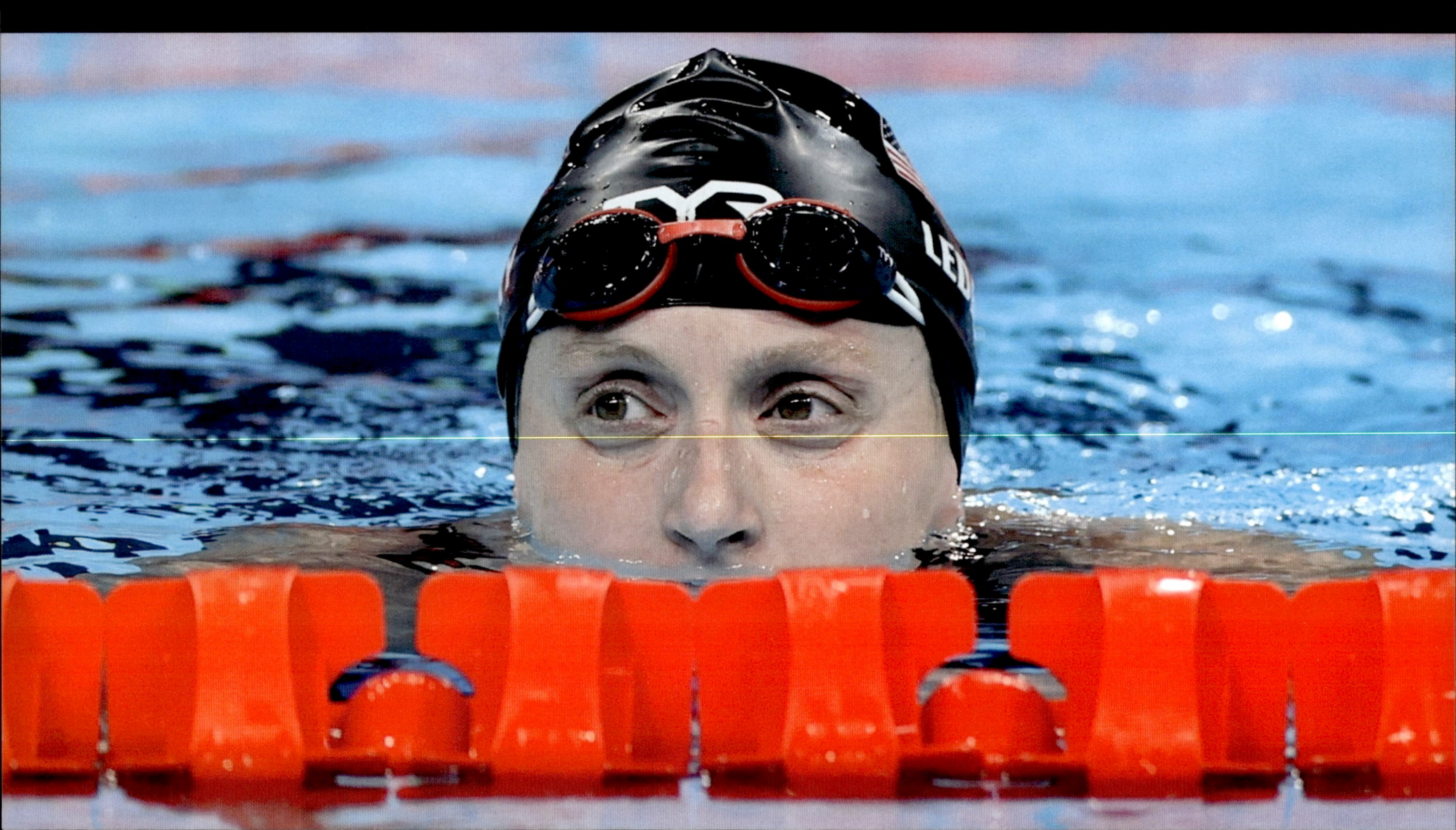

Opposite page: Katie Ledecky of Team USA looks on after winning gold in the Women's 800-meter freestyle final on Day Eight of the Olympic Games at Paris La Defense Arena on August 3, 2024, in Nanterre, France. Photo by Adam Pretty/Getty Images.

This page: *Ancient Greek Votive offering* (detail), late fourth century, unknown artist (likely Praxias). Acropolis Museum.

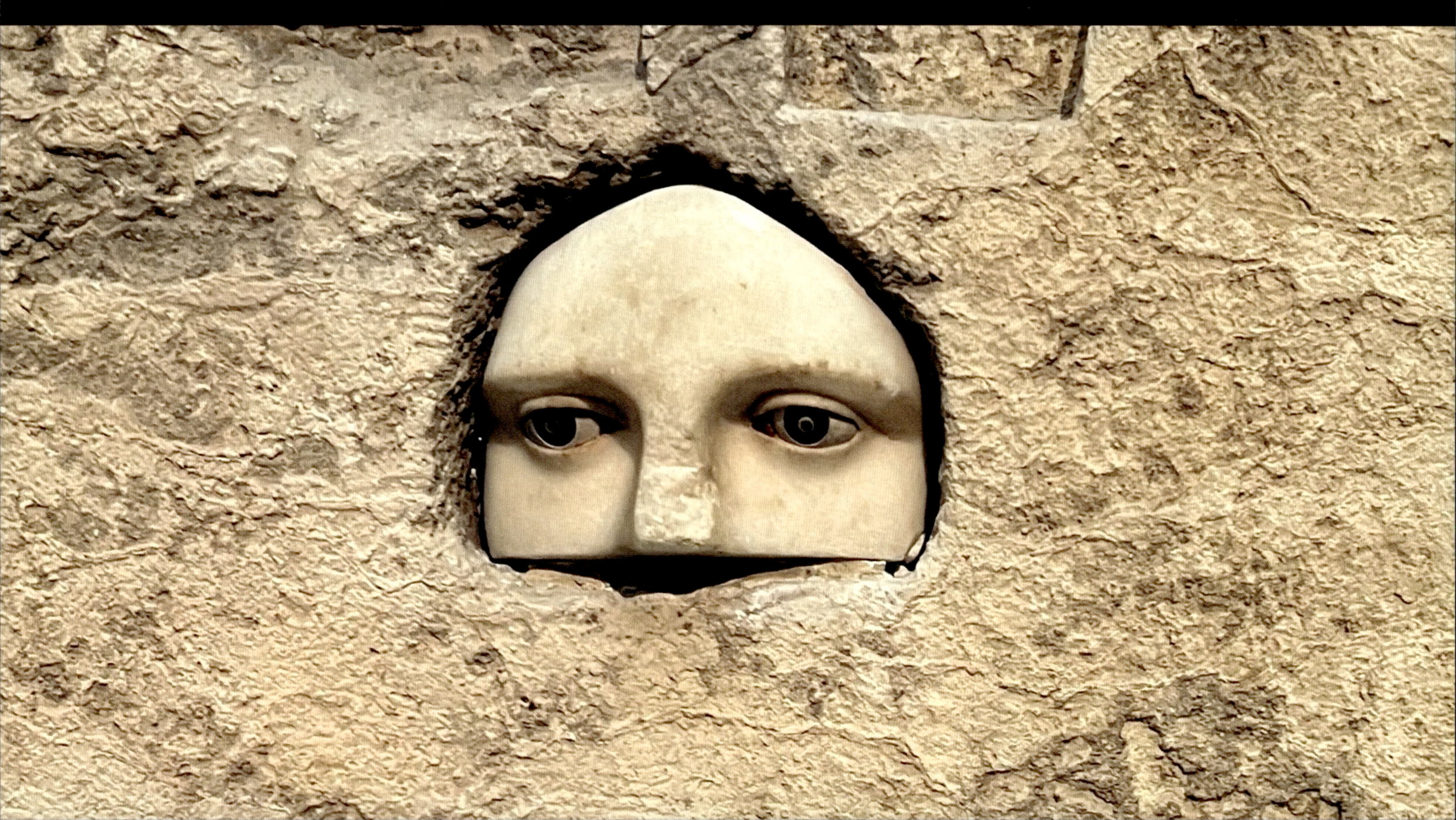

BOLT

Another William Blake! An artist and poet, Blake was *the* figure of the Romantic age and was so prolific that I could probably do an entire ArtButMakeItSports book featuring just his work. He's an especially appropriate dance partner for Usain Bolt, the eight-time Olympic gold medalist for Jamaica who dominated his era across multiple events: the 100-meter, 200-meter, and relays.

This particular photo is indisputably the hardest from Bolt's vast portfolio to pair, as Cam Spencer managed to perfectly capture Bolt's superiority and infectious personality in a single frame, with the blurred, Gerhard Richter–like background and feet of the runners representing speed while still managing to keep Bolt's expression in focus.

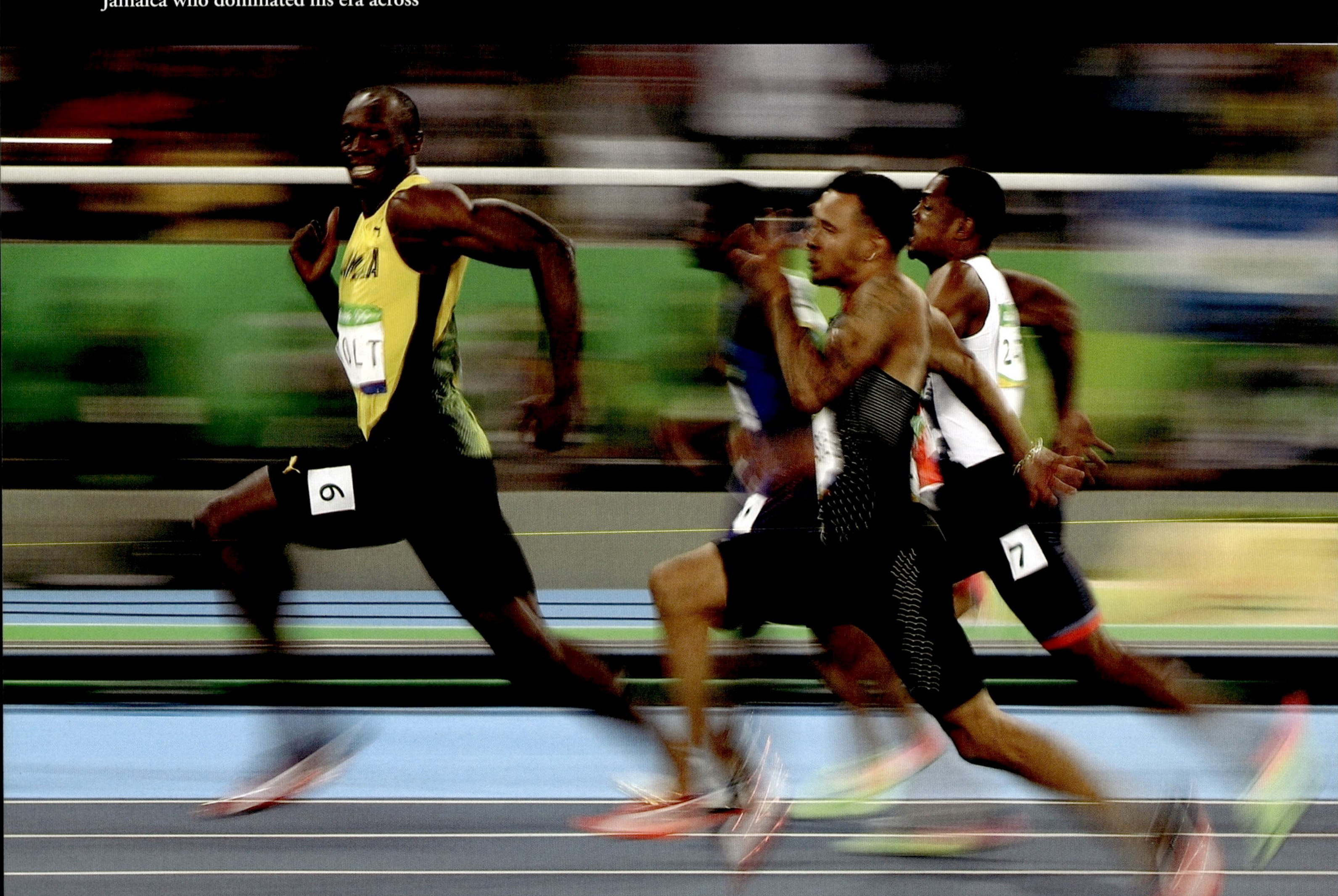

This page: *Dante running from the three beasts* (detail), 1824–27, William Blake. Digital image by Google Cultural Institute. National Gallery of Victoria.

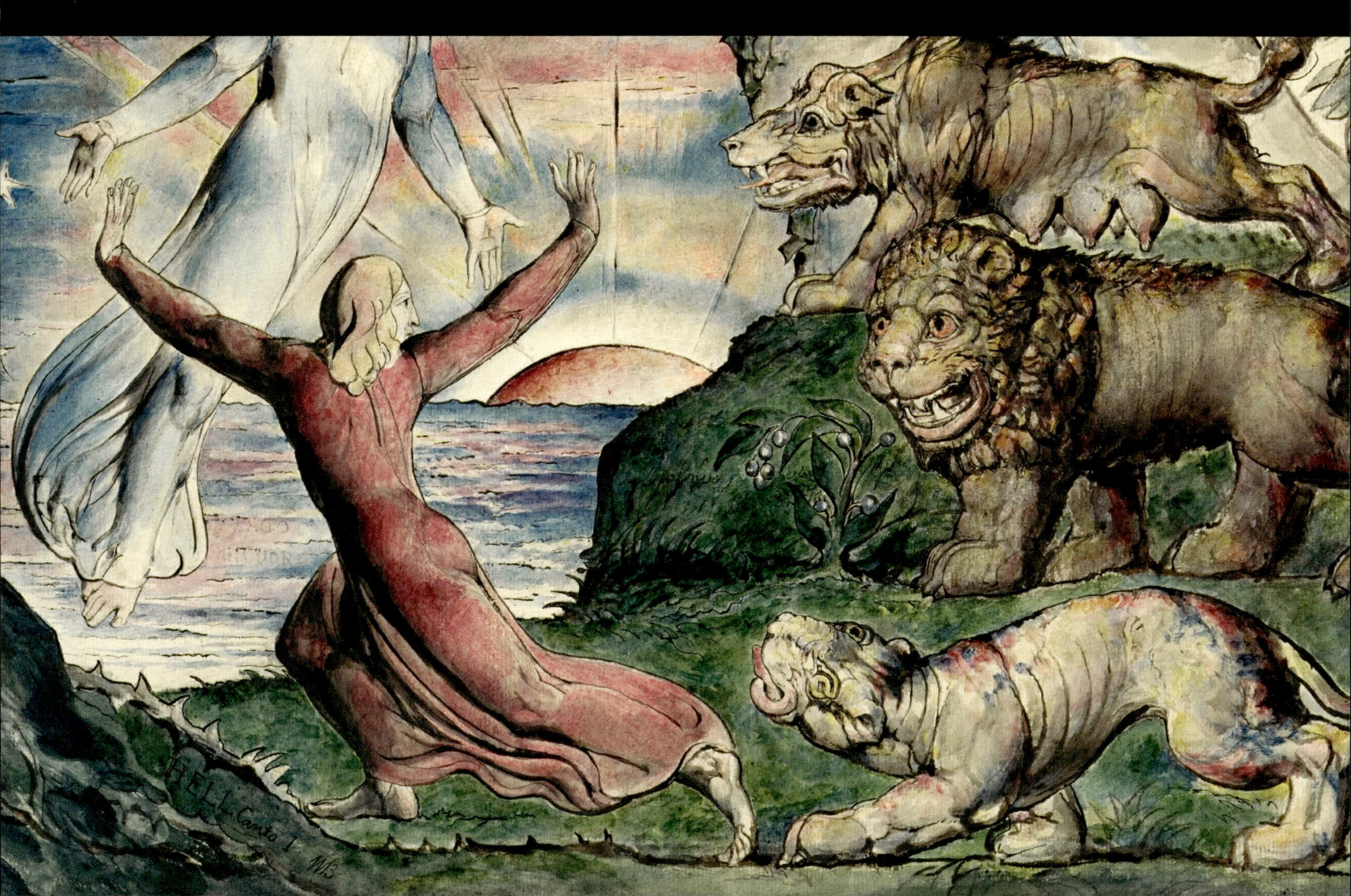

This snap from the 2024 Paralympic Games was so good that I decided to embargo it until now, as I wanted to give it its proper shine. It reminded me immediately of the two suspended figures in Segantini's *Punishment of Lust*, a painting that doesn't match on meaning (scholars suggest it touches on themes of motherhood, abortion, and religion) but does so on composition.

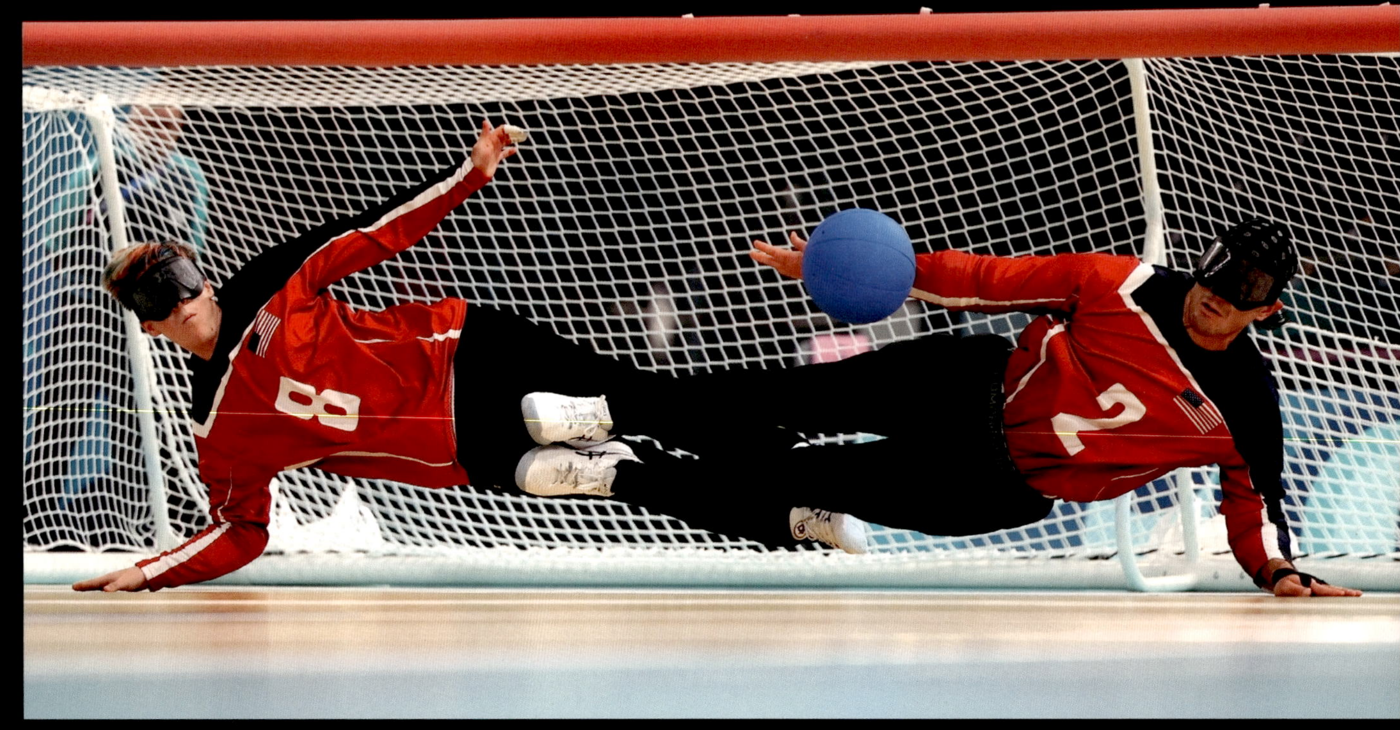

Opposite page: Christian King and Tyler Merren of Team USA make a save during the men's 5/6 goalball playoff match against Iran on Day Six of the Summer Paralympic Games on September 3, 2024, in Paris, France. Photo by Alex Davidson/Getty Images.

This page: *The Punishment of Lust*, 1891, Giovanni Segantini. Digital image by Google Cultural Institute. Walker Art Gallery.

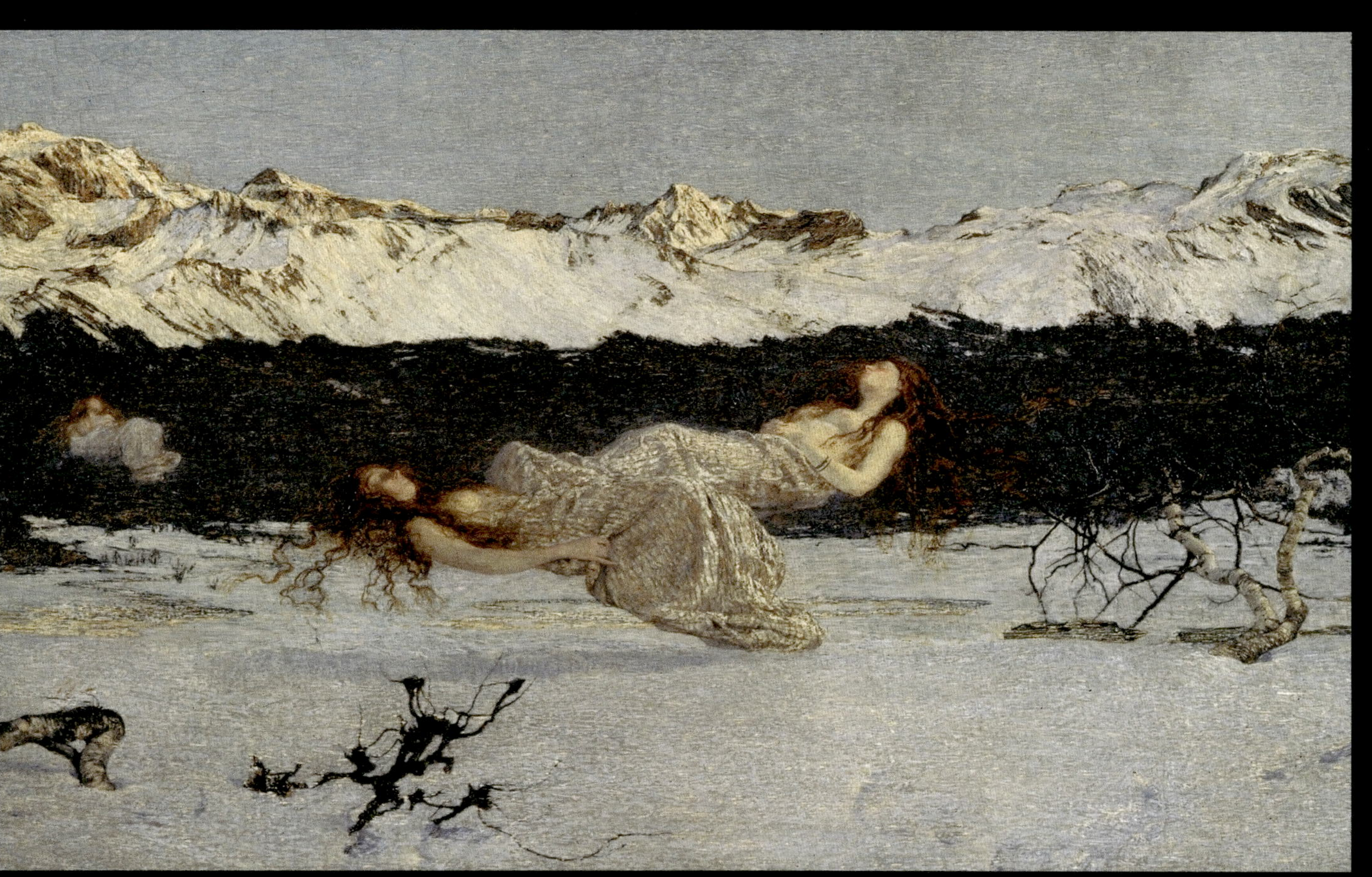

LEE KIEFER

There's the obvious visual match in expression and emotion, as well as the armor and sword. But Lee Kiefer also fenced at Notre Dame, so there's a Catholic connection, and Joan of Arc is a patron saint of France. Lee is also dominating in what was previously a sport only for men, breaking barriers in the same way that Joan did when she dressed as a man to battle, because it was not proper for women to fight.

I'm also excited to feature Lee, as I covered her back in 2014 when I was a combat sports producer for NBCSports.com. She was gracious with her time and easy to root for—and while she ended up just missing out on a medal in London (placing 5th in the individual), she went on to win individual gold in Tokyo 2021, and then gold in both the individual and team categories in Paris 2024, making her the most decorated foil fencer in Team USA history.

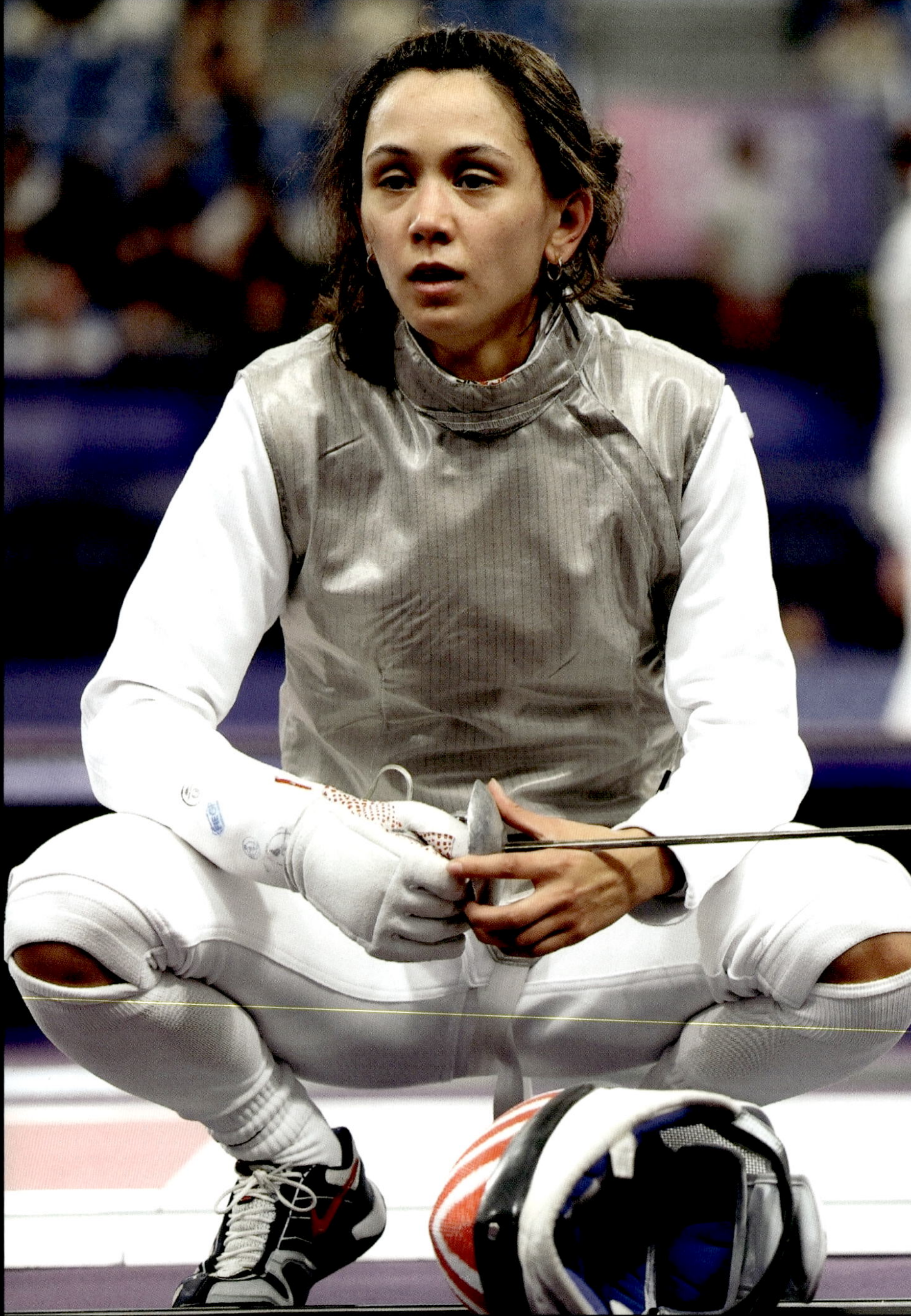

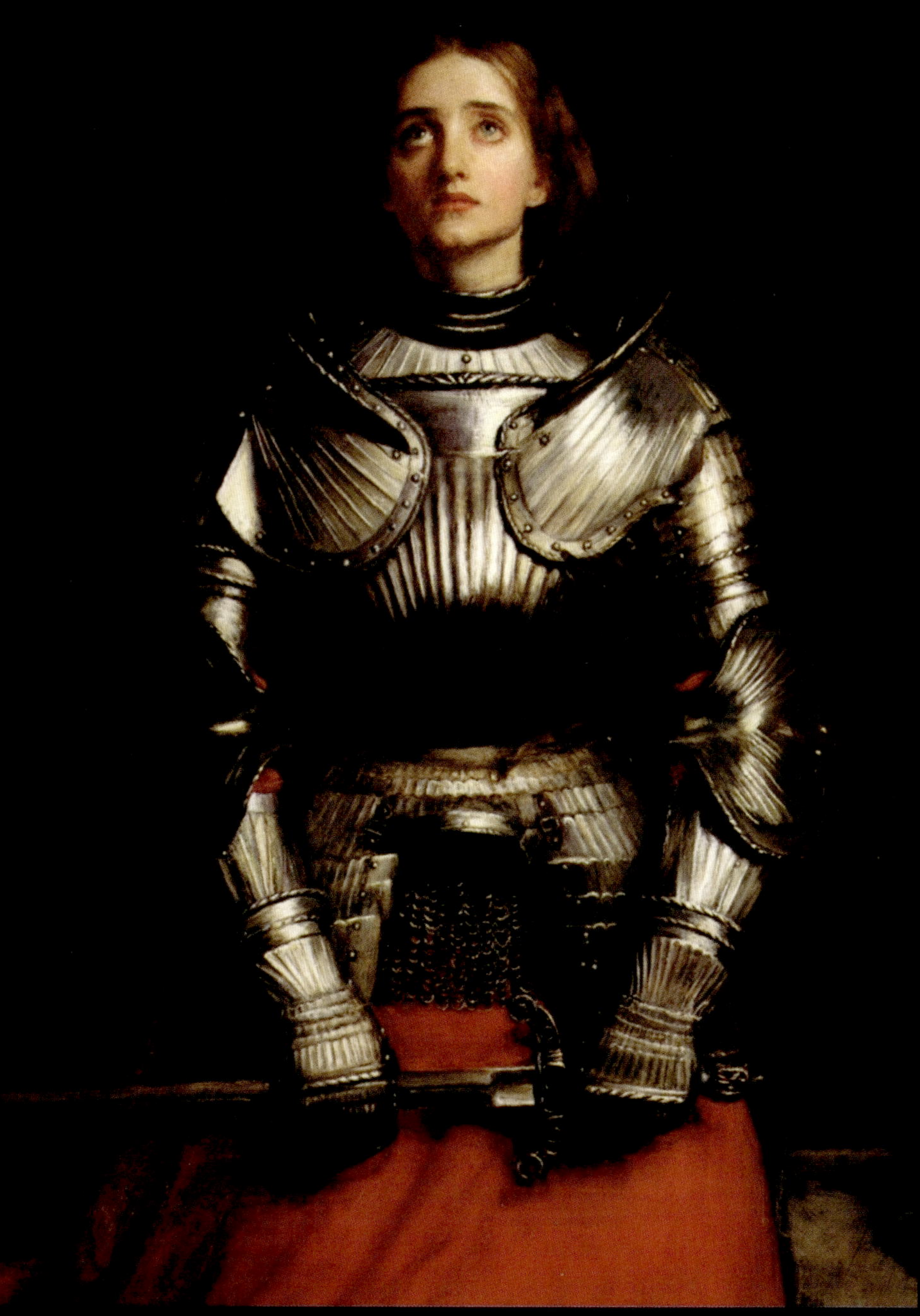

Opposite page: Lee Kiefer of Team USA looks on while competing against Martyna Jelińska of Team Poland (not pictured) in the women's foil fencing individual table of 32 match on July 28, 2024, in Paris, France. Photo by Patrick Smith/Getty Images.

This page: *Joan of Arc* (detail), 1865, John Everett Millais. Digital image by Art Renewal Center. Private collection. Flipped from the original.

REBECA'S REDEMPTION

There are so many sports moments that can be compared to the *Assumption of the Virgin*, as plenty feature hovering figures with their arms outstretched. So I try to be conservative about using it, reserving it for only the most important and compelling instances.

This image of Rebeca Andrade celebrating her gold for the women's floor exercise at Paris 2024 felt worthy of the occasion, partly because of the weight of the moment—you could build a case that it was the shot of the Olympics—but also because Simone Biles and Jordan Chiles play a key role in the storytelling behind what makes the photo so memorable.

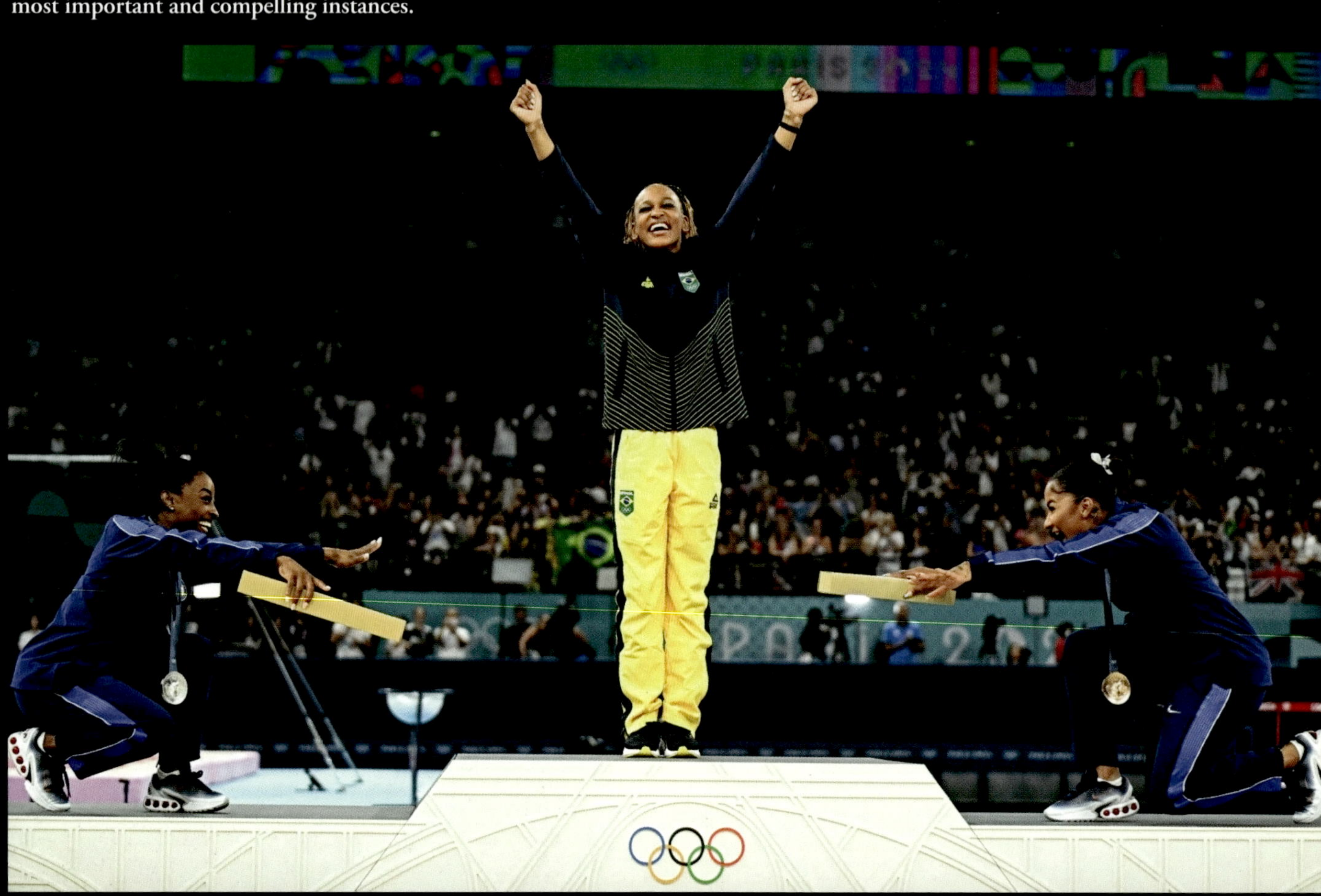

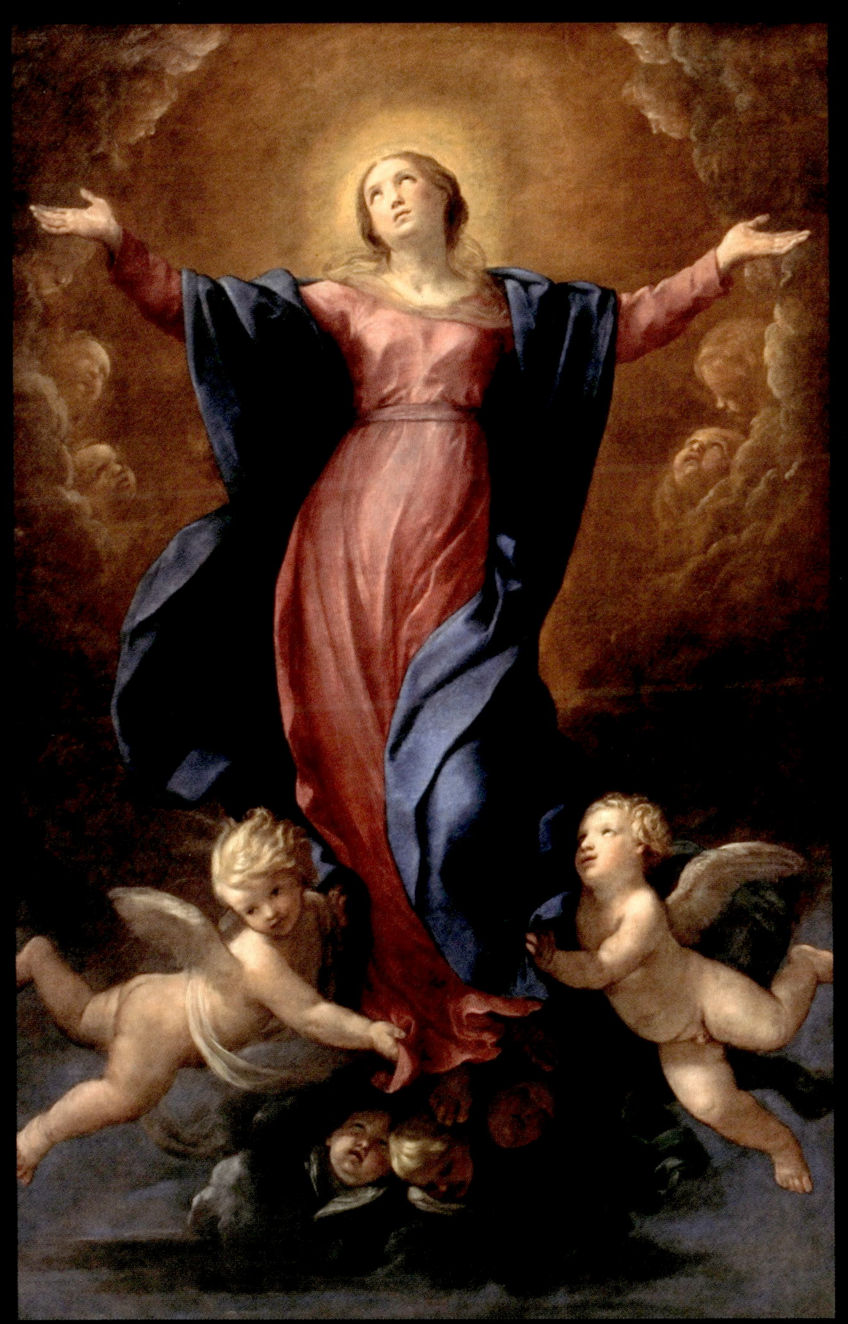

Opposite page: Team USA's Simone Biles (silver), Brazil's Rebeca Andrade (gold), and Team USA's Jordan Chiles (bronze) pose during the podium ceremony for the artistic gymnastics women's floor exercise event of the Paris 2024 Olympic Games at the Bercy Arena on August 5, 2024. Photo by Gabriel Bouys/AFP via Getty Images.

This page: *Assumption of the Virgin*, 1637, Guido Reni. Digital image by Rama. Museum of Fine Arts of Lyon.

MIRACLE ON ICE

The "beheading" portion that's seen in both images is the obvious link, especially with the matching colors, but I particularly like how the two onlookers/fans are accurately framed up. It gets better when you look below the surface. This motif, which was popular among Caravaggio and other Italian artists of the time, was inspired not by the Bible but by a collection of over 150 hagiographies (writings about the lives of saints) chronicled by Jacobus de Voragine between 1259 and 1266. This compilation was referred to as the "Golden Legend," a nice correlation to the eventual victory by the US team.

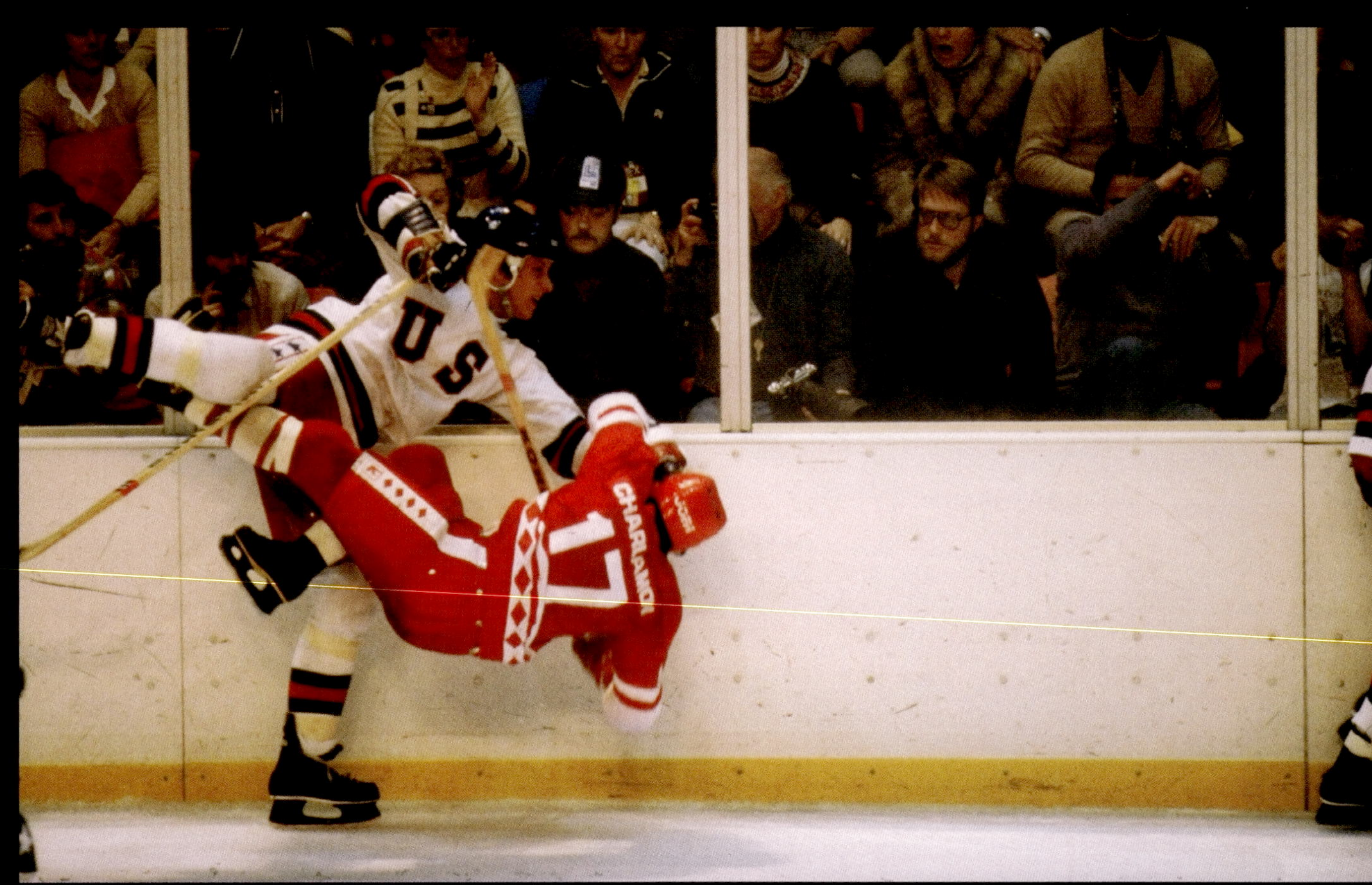

Opposite page: Mike Ramsey (#5) of the United States checks Valeri Kharlamov (#17) of the Soviet Union during the Winter Olympic Games on February 22, 1980, in Lake Placid, New York. The United States won 4–3. Photo by Tony Duffy/Getty Images.

This page: ***The beheading of St. John the Baptist*** **(detail), 1608, Caravaggio. St. John's Co-Cathedral. Flipped from the original.**

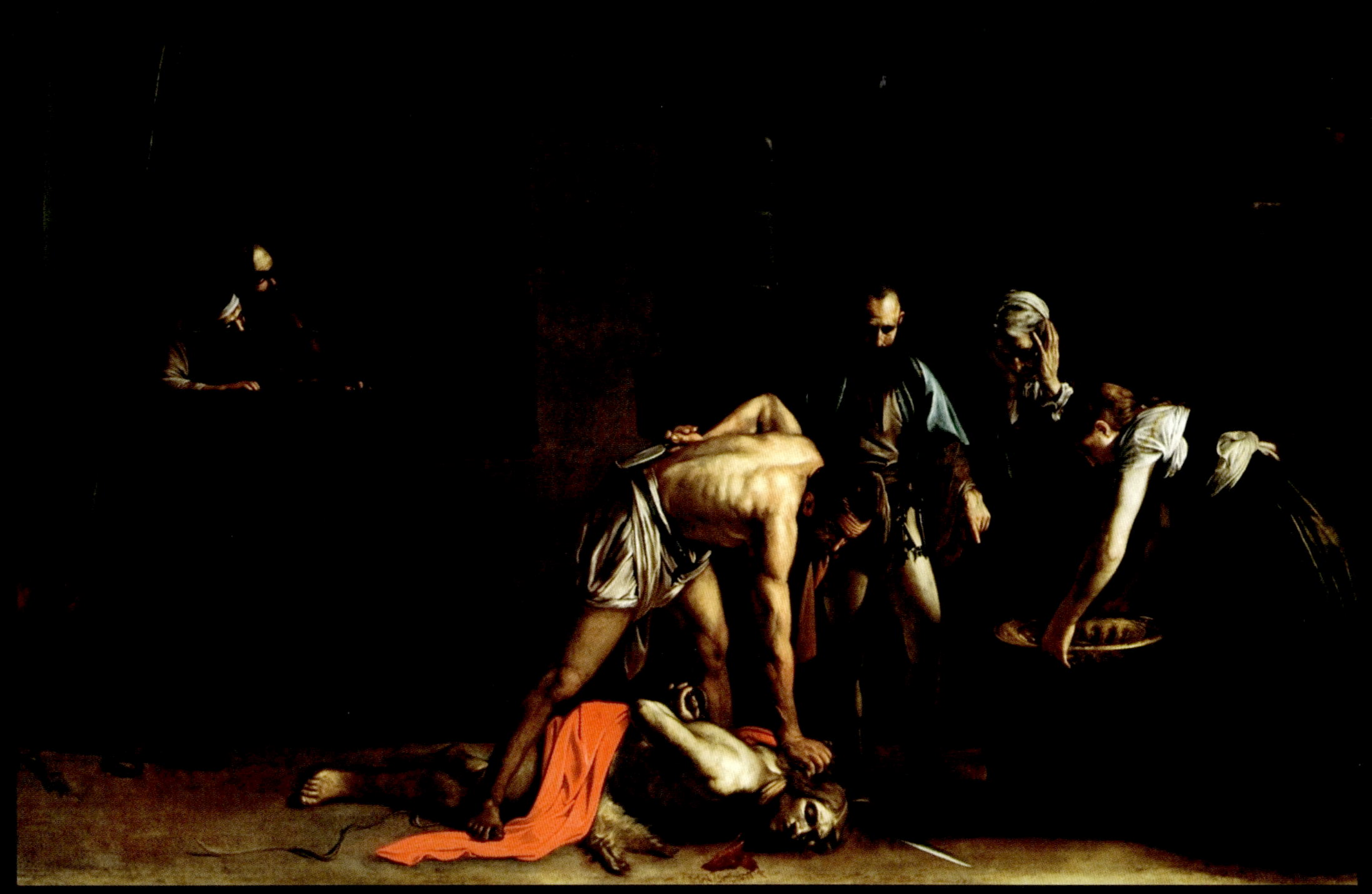

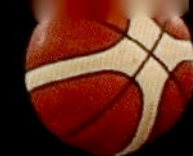

STEPH ANNUNCIATION

In an Olympics chock-full of timeless images, this one could take the cake. Pairing it with the Archangel Gabriel fit the vibe, and being able to capture the basketball that mimics the bird in Venusti's painting is what made this one worthy of inclusion.

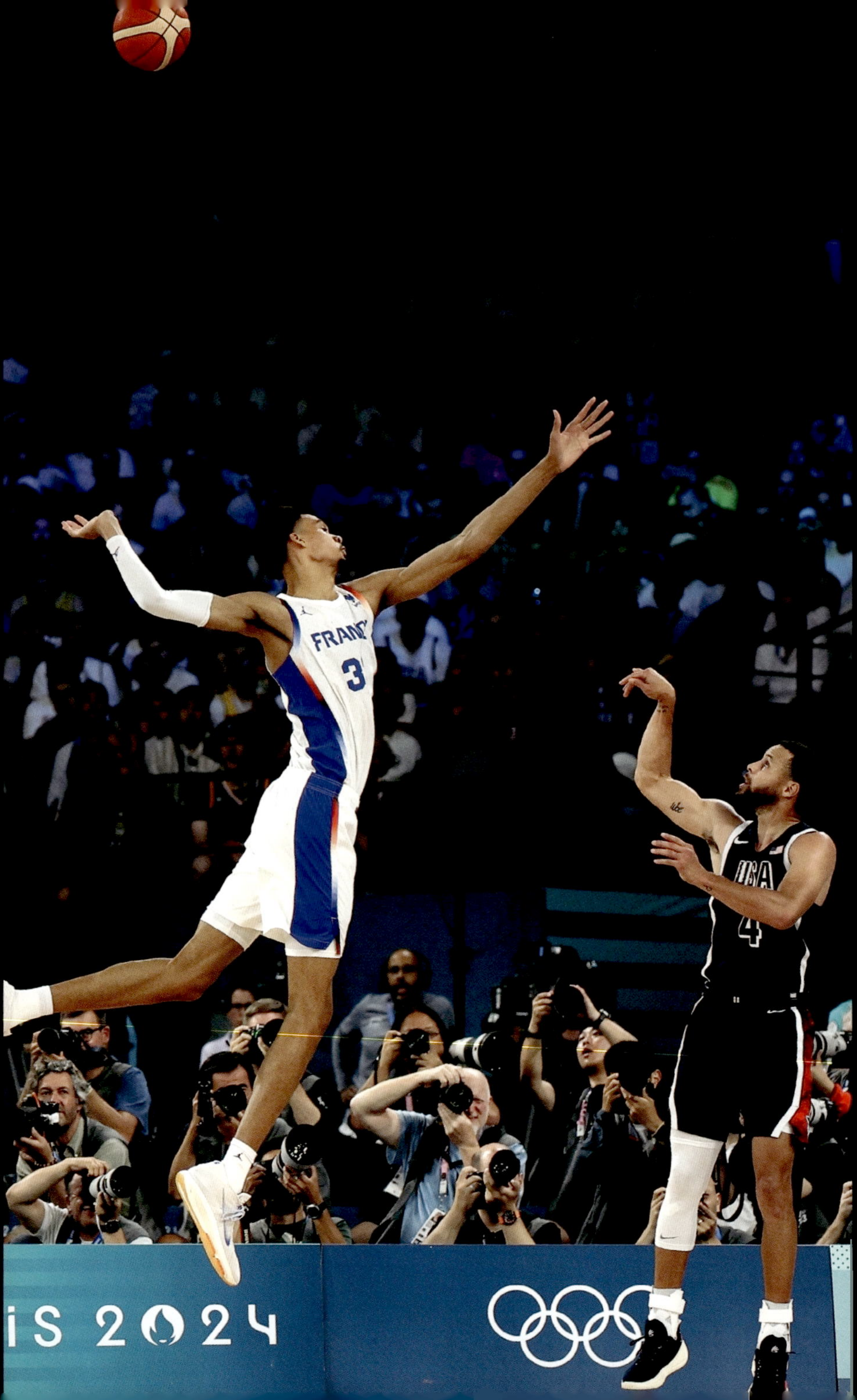

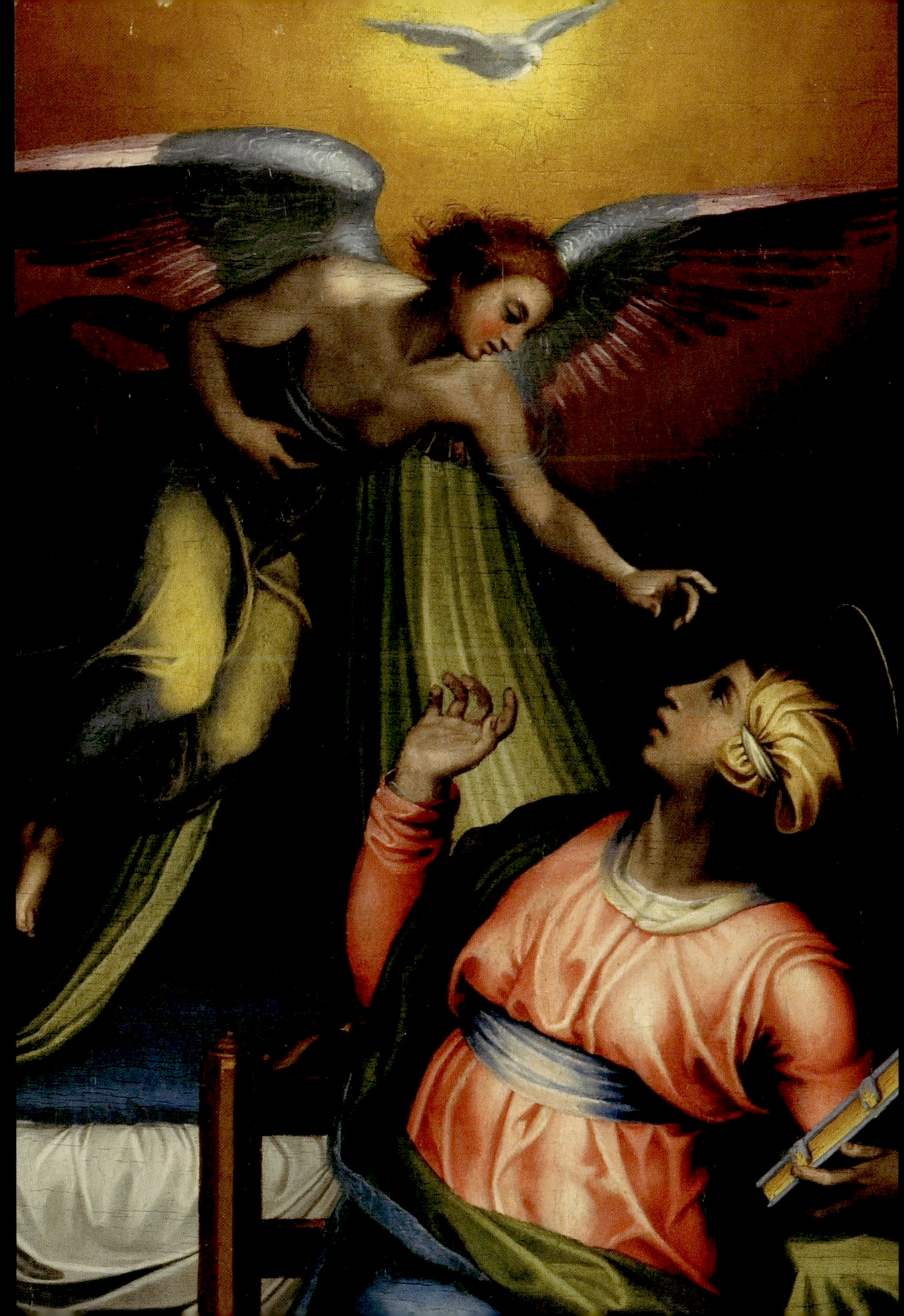

Opposite page: Stephen Curry (#4) of Team USA shoots over Victor Wembanyama (#32) of Team France during the men's gold medal game on August 10, 2024, at Bercy Arena in Paris, France. Photo by Ezra Shaw/Getty Images.

This page: *The Annunciation* (detail), 1550, Marcello Venusti. Digital image by Geheugen van Nederland. Rijksmuseum. Flipped from the original.

DOROTHY BLOOMS

If this is your first time coming across Agnes Pelton's work, I encourage you to take a major deep dive, as discovering her catalog was a seminal moment in my journey with art. Her paintings are deeply spiritual and ethereal, and many use light and brush-strokes to evoke wisps of movement. 1929's *Sand Storm* is the perfect encapsulation of her style, and it reminded me of a Dorothy Hamill spin—with the added bonus of the flowing skirt mimicking the blooming lotus.

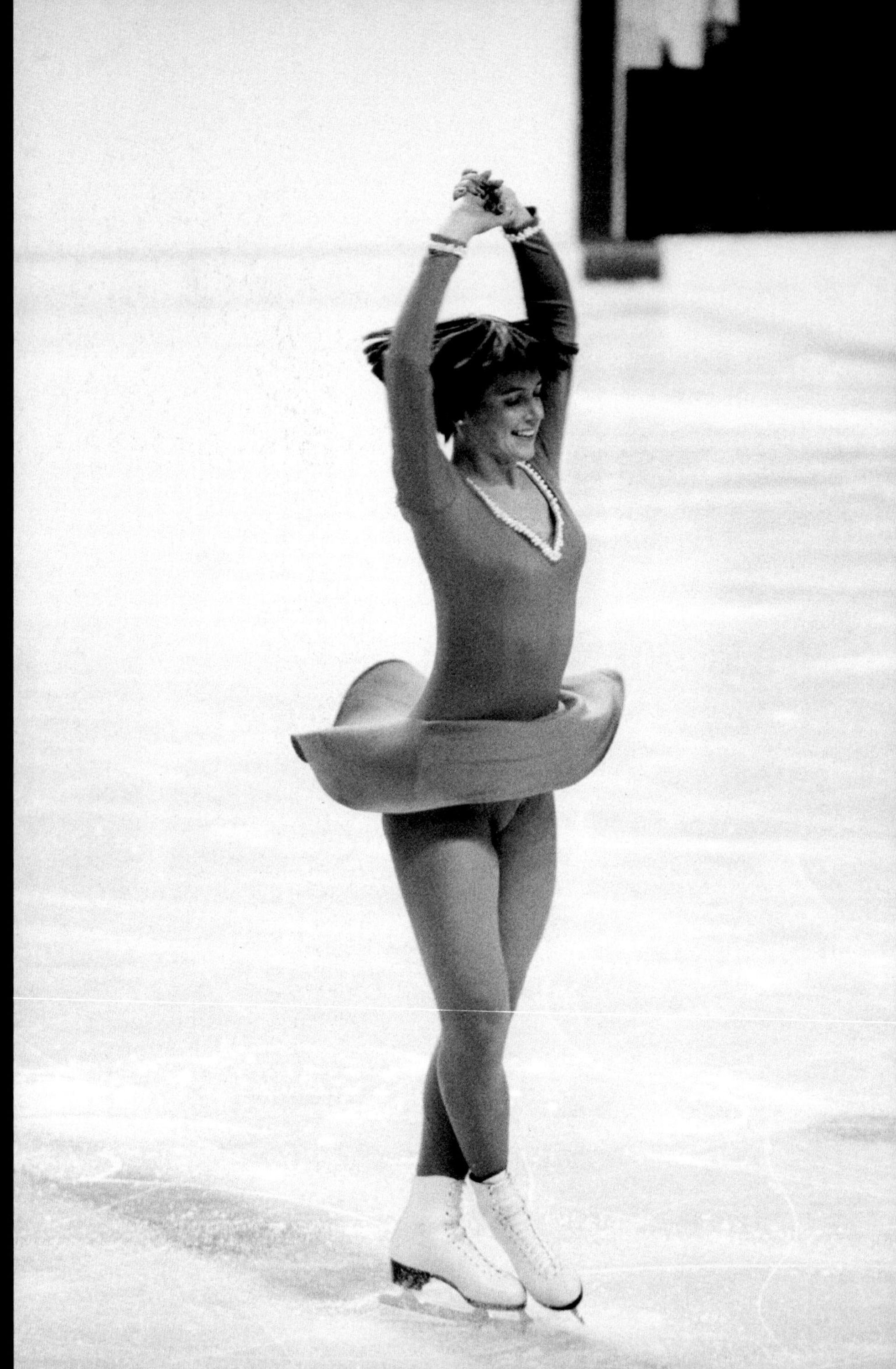

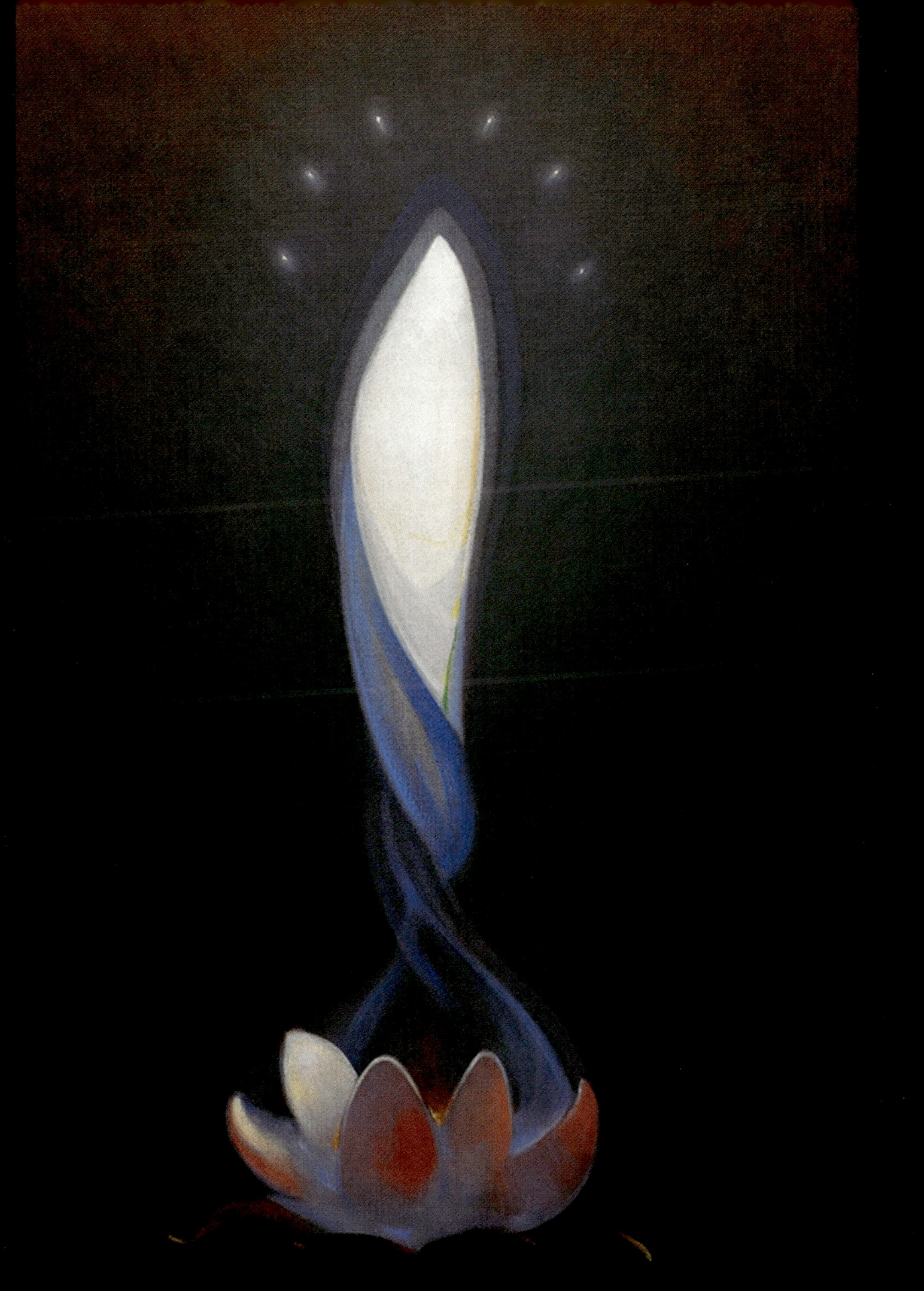

Opposite page: Dorothy Hamill of Chicago, Illinois, has a look of confidence during the Women's Olympic free skating event, while on her way to a gold medal at the 12th Winter Games in Innsbruck, Austria, on February 13, 1976. Photo by Bettmann via Getty Images.

This page: *Divinity Lotus*, 1929, Agnes Lawrence Pelton. Crystal Bridges Museum of American Art.

MISCELLANEOUS

This 1908 Henri Rousseau fever dream felt appropriate for the Miscellaneous chapter because, well, they aren't football players, they're rugby players. But they're also wearing pajamas, punching each other, and in the middle of a tree-lined park that is certainly not a sporting pitch. It's a little bit of everything in one, a fitting lead-in.

The Football Players (detail), 1908, Henri Rousseau. Solomon R. Guggenheim Museum.

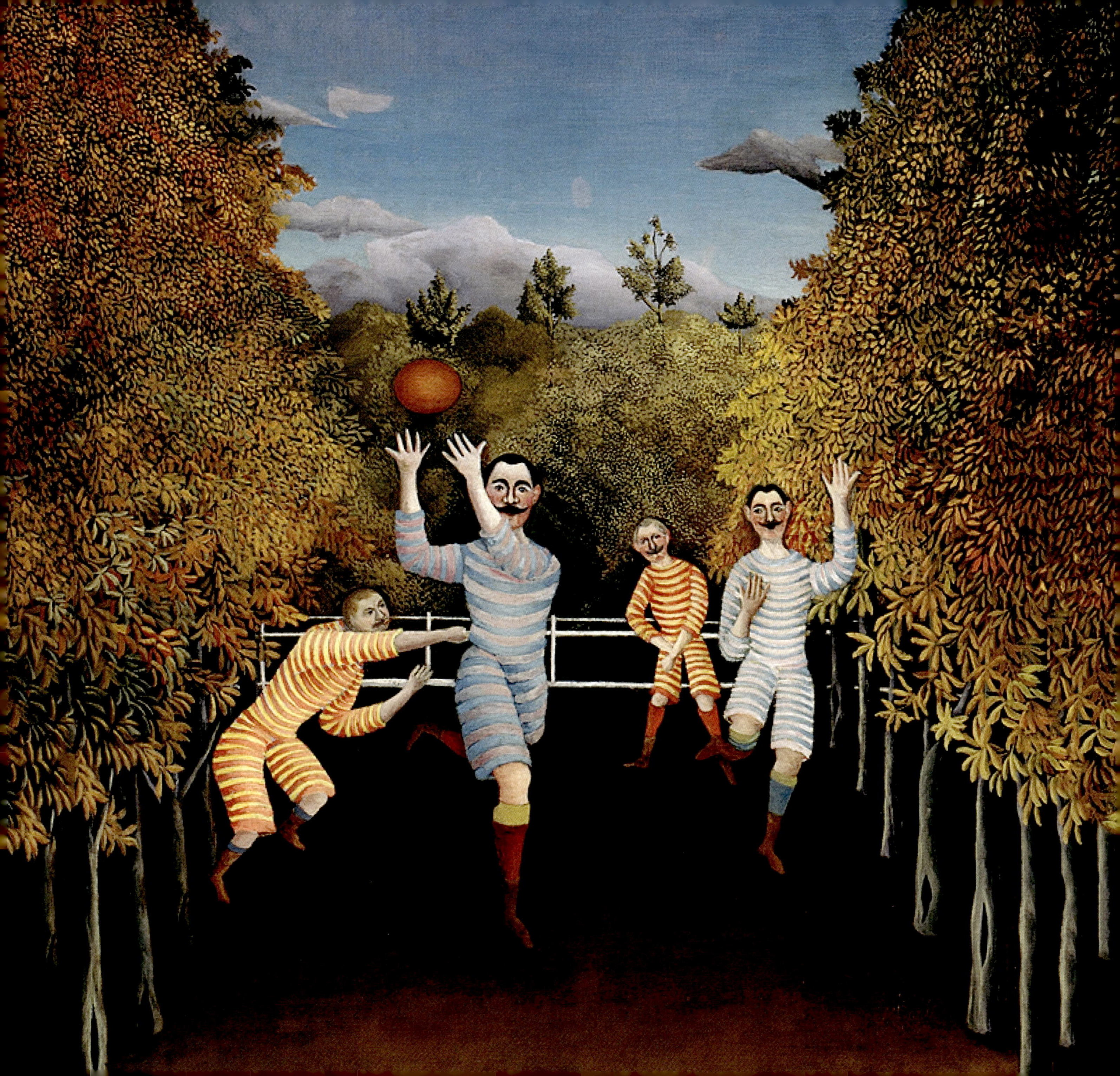

HAMILTON VS. VERSTAPPEN

While F1 has long been a powerhouse on the global stage, the release of Netflix's *Drive to Survive* in 2019 brought the sport into the mainstream in the United States.

The 2021 F1 season ended in a perfect confluence: interest in *Drive to Survive* peaked, ESPN's television and connected device coverage made the sport extremely accessible, social media usage and chatter were at an all-time high, and the battle between drivers Lewis Hamilton and Max Verstappen ping-ponged throughout the duration of the championship push. *BBC Sport*'s Andrew Benson called it "one of the most intense, hard-fought battles in sporting history."

At the Italian Grand Prix, a crash between the two nearly crushed Hamilton's head, which was saved by the protective halo in place. The shapes and palette immediately brought to mind Wassily Kandinsky, whose signature works feature colorful circles, here representing the various components of the wheel and Hamilton's head and helmet.

Left: Mercedes's British driver Lewis Hamilton and Red Bull's Dutch driver Max Verstappen collide during the Formula 1 Italian Grand Prix at the Autodromo Nazionale circuit in Monza, on September 12, 2021. Photo by Andrej Isakovic/AFP via Getty Images.

Right: *Several Circles* (detail), 1926, Wassily Kandinsky. Solomon R. Guggenheim Museum.

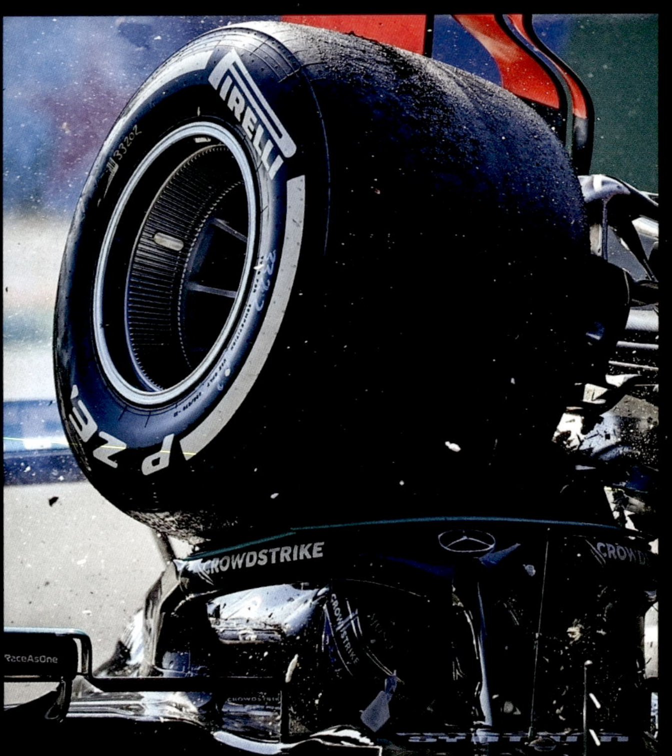

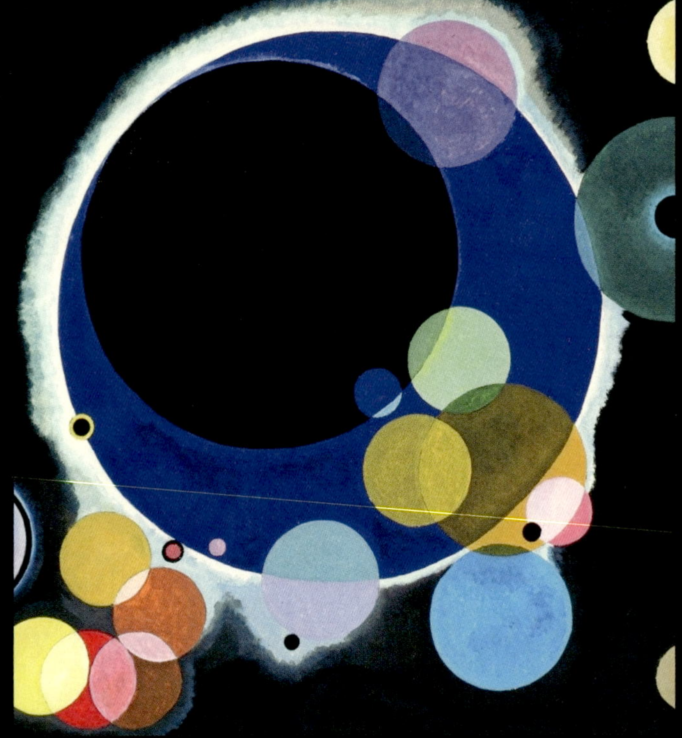

In the final reach of the season, a shot of the two racing neck-and-neck served as the perfect summation of the Hamilton and Verstappen rivalry—paralleled by the symmetry and color patterns in Hilma af Klint's *Altarpiece, No. 1, Group X.*

A cult figure in the art world, af Klint was not widely known until her 2018/19 retrospective "Paintings for the Future," at the Guggenheim New York, after which interest in her work exploded. It's not a dissimilar path that F1 took after *Drive to Survive* in 2019, bringing the connections truly full circle (another Kandinsky moment).

Top: Max Verstappen of the Netherlands, driving the (#33) Red Bull Racing RB16B Honda, and Lewis Hamilton of Great Britain, driving the (#44) Mercedes AMG Petronas F1 Team Mercedes W12, battle for track position at the start of the F1 Grand Prix of Emilia Romagna at Autodromo Enzo e Dino Ferrari on April 18, 2021, in Imola, Italy. Photo by Bryn Lennon/ Getty Images.

Bottom: *Altarpiece, No. 1, Group X, Altarpieces* (detail), 1907, Hilma af Klint. WikiArt. Flipped from the original.

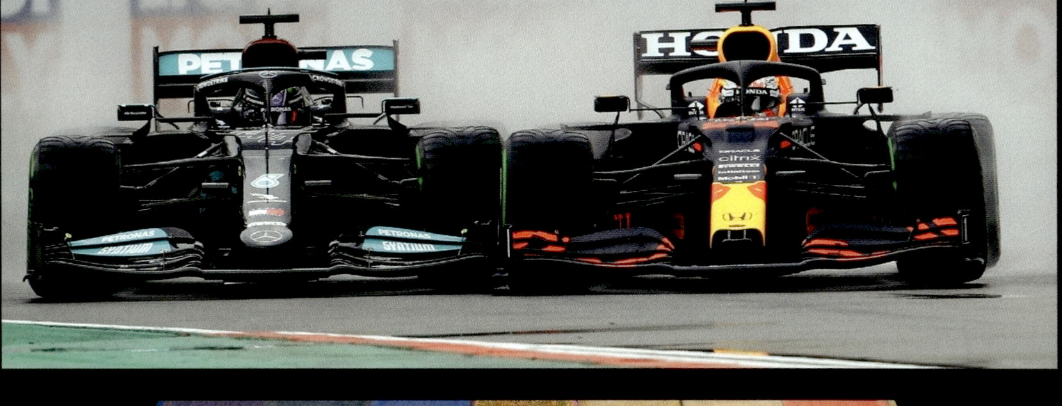

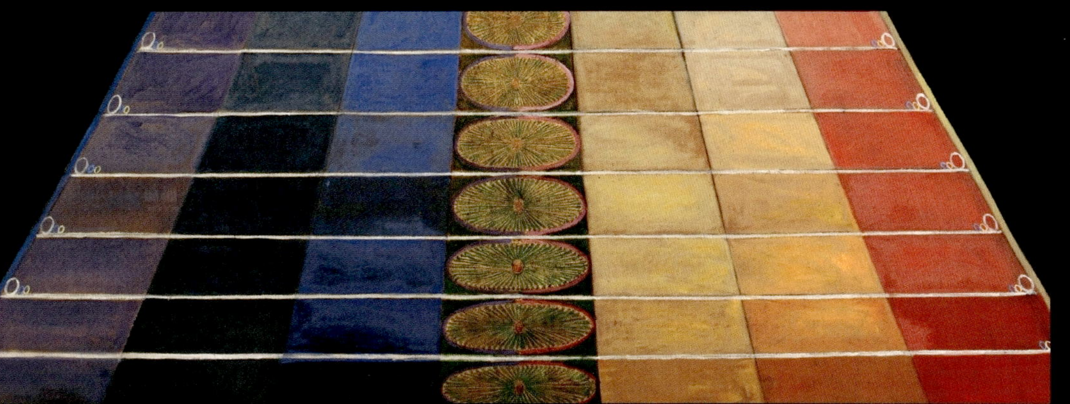

CRICKET PARTY

I'm flattered that folks think I know a significant amount more about art than I do sports, though I'd chalk it up to it being a numbers game; there are a lot more people out there that know more about sports than art.

It's one thing to make a 1:1 visual comparison, but there's so much more there when you have an understanding of the context and underlying storylines within the sports image.

All of this to say, I don't have a lick of context when it comes to cricket. And it pains me, because it seems like a fun sport with an undeniably massive fan base, plus the obvious similitude with baseball. I just no longer possess the mental storage (or, frankly, time) to onboard another sport, and because I don't have the context, I tend to move on whenever I'm tagged in a

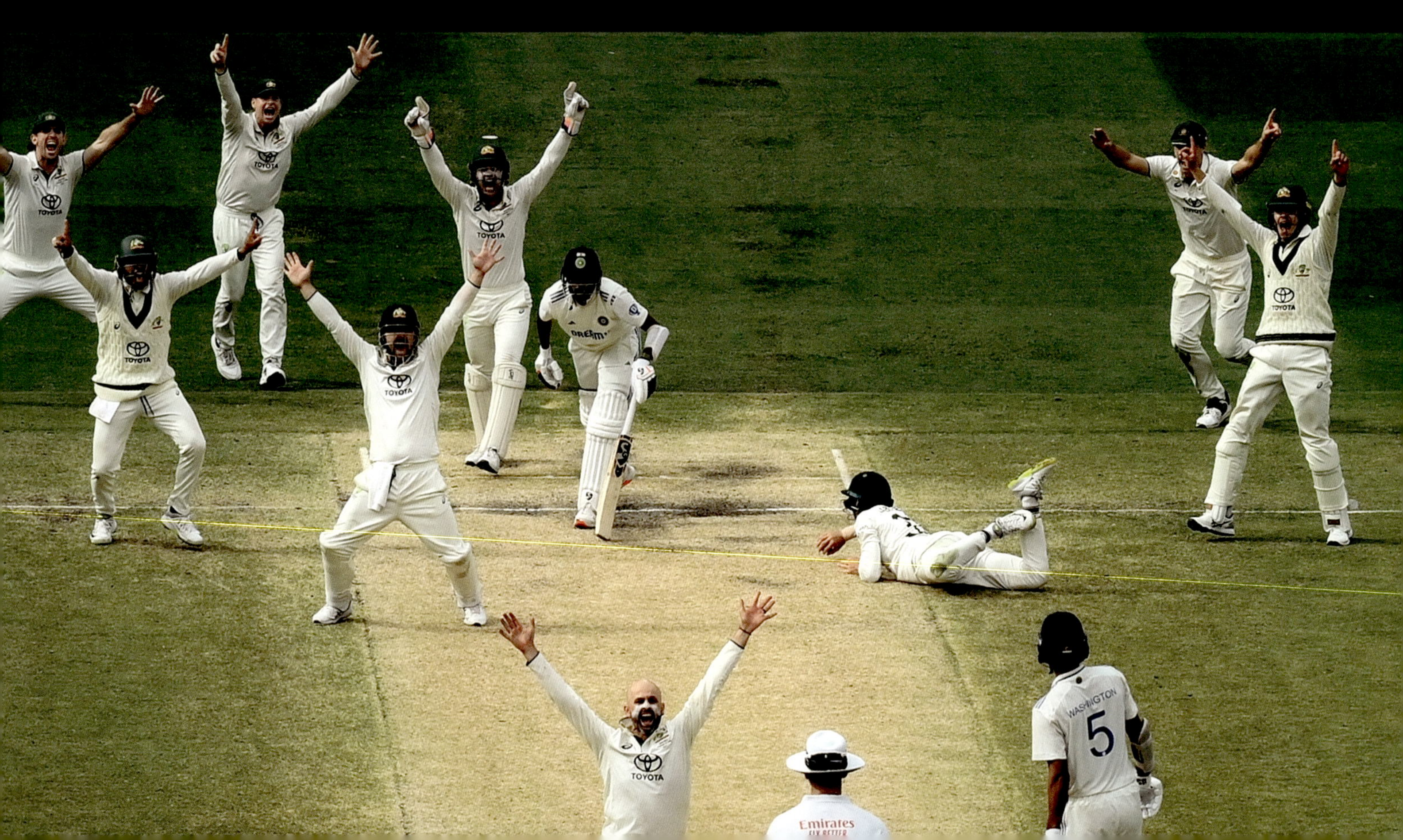

cricket image. However, around one hundred accounts tagged me in this moment, which I later learned was Australia sealing the deal vs. India during Day Five of the Men's Fourth Test Match. So while I didn't—and still don't—know much about cricket, the soul of the image has all the characteristics of the thrill of victory and agony of defeat, which form the foundation of any good sports moment.

Opposite page: Nathan Lyon celebrates after trapping Mohammed Siraj LBW (Leg Before Wicket) as Australia won the match during Day Five of the Men's Fourth Test Match in the series between Australia and India at Melbourne Cricket Ground on December 30, 2024, in Melbourne, Australia. Photo by Quinn Rooney/Getty Images.

This page: *The Youth of Bacchus* (detail), 1884, William-Adolphe Bouguereau. Digital image by Erik Cornelius. Nationalmuseum.

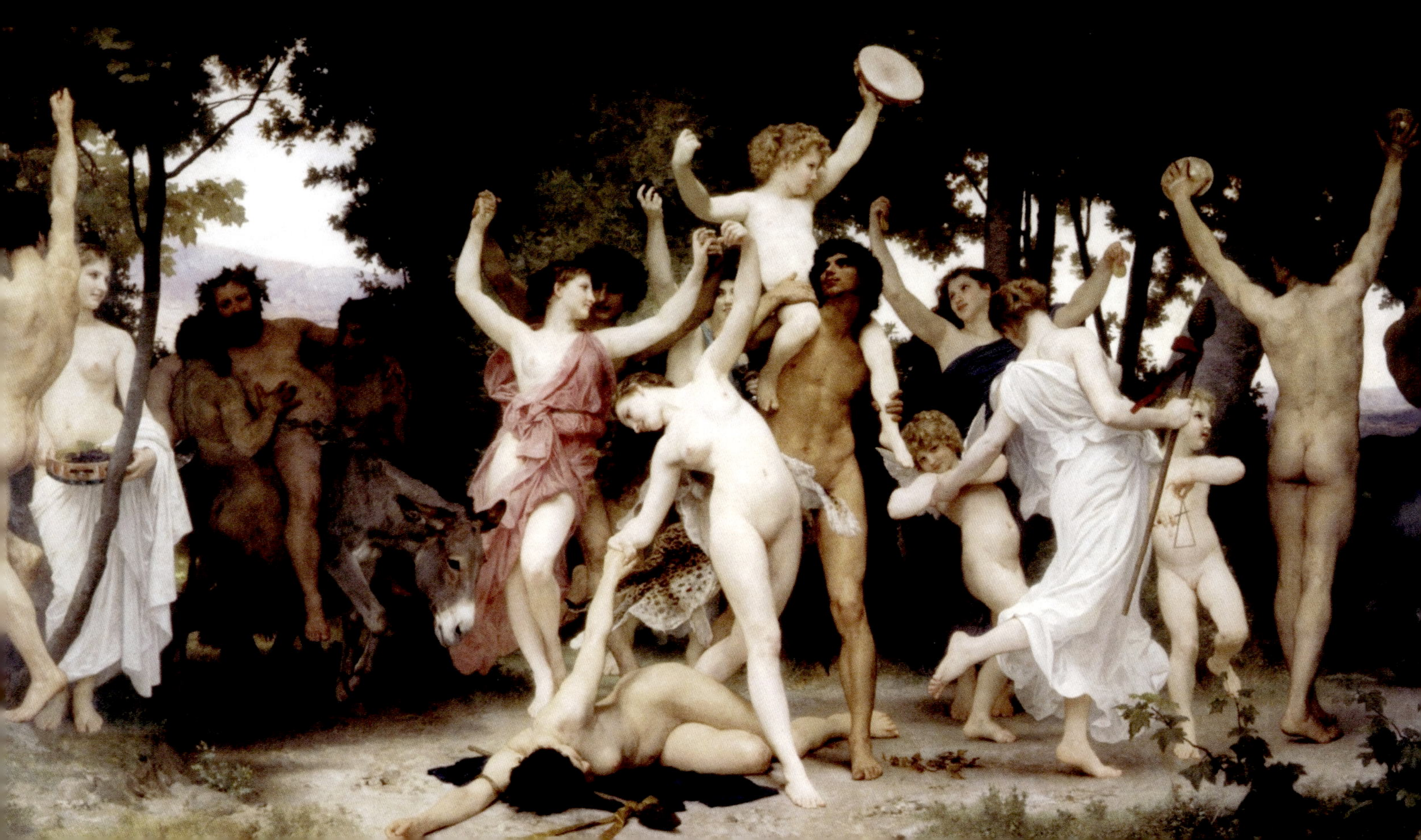

Fall of the Rebel Angels again, but this time Pieter Bruegel the Elder's chaotic version. Claire Chaussee's insane vertical is on display, and whenever you have a chance to compare a volleyball to a weird little pufferfish figure, you have to pull the trigger.

Center Omaha on December 15, 2022, in Omaha, Nebraska. Photo by C. Morgan Engel/ NCAA Photos via Getty Images.

Right: *The Fall of the Rebel Angels* (detail), 1562, Pieter Bruegel the Elder. Royal Museums of Fine Arts of Belgium.

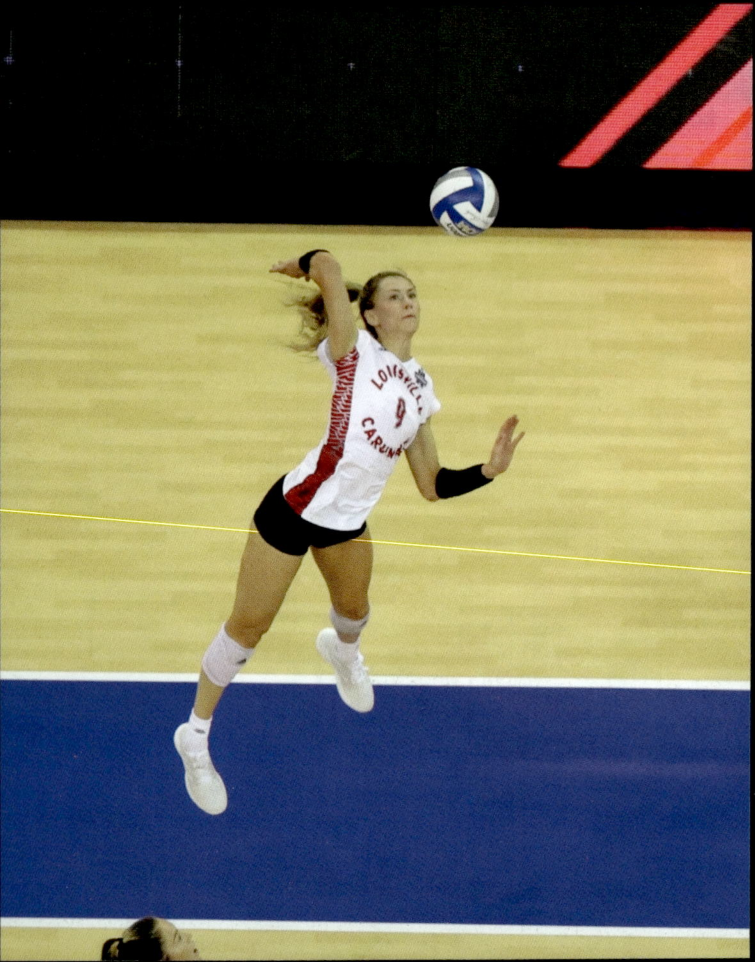

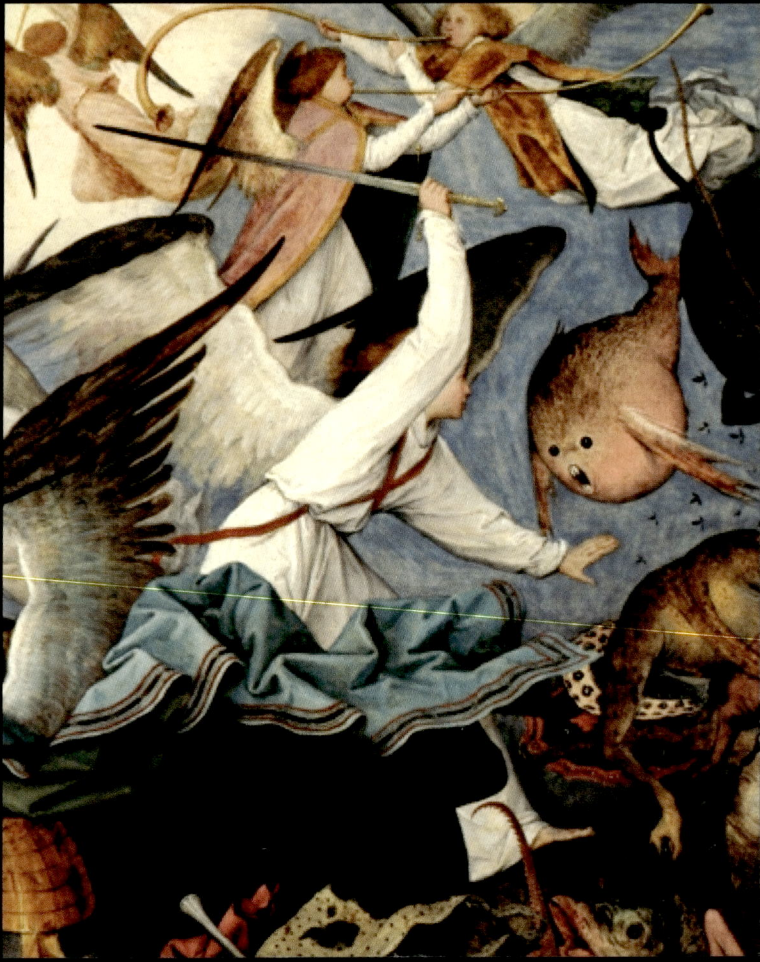

THE FAMOUS EARS

This one's a bit(e) of a before and after, from the immediate moments following Mike Tyson taking a chunk of Evander Holyfield's ear during their Heavyweight title fight on June 28, 1997. Vincent van Gogh also lost his ear in a "fight" of sorts, his following an argument with artist Paul Gauguin.

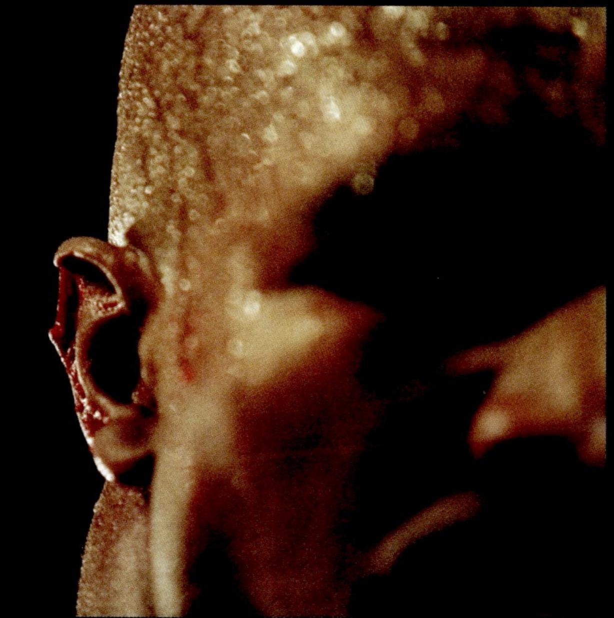

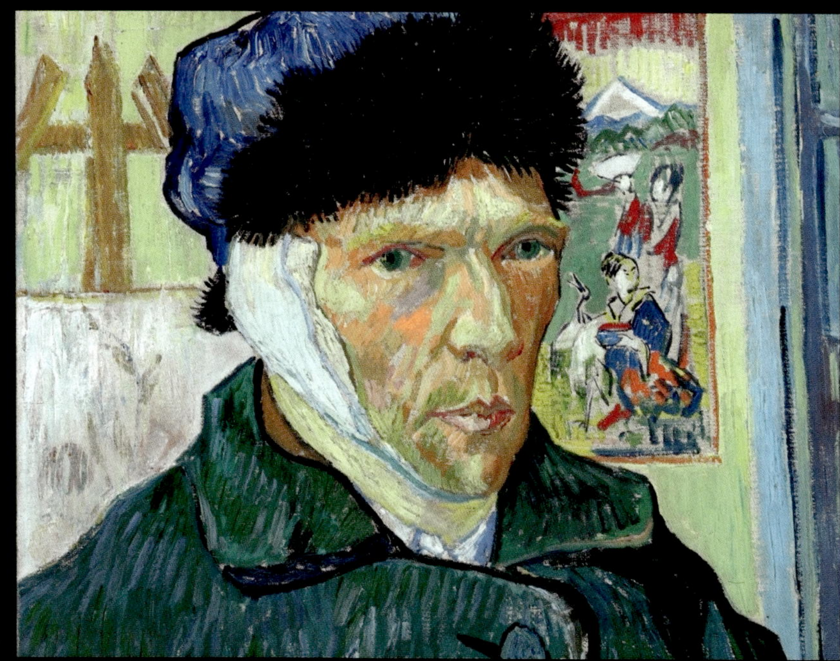

Top: A close-up of the injury to the right ear of Evander Holyfield after Mike Tyson bit off a piece of it in the third round of their World Boxing Association Heavyweight title fight on June 28, 1997, at the MGM Grand Garden Hotel in Las Vegas, Nevada. Mike Tyson was later disqualified. Photo by Jed Jacobsohn/ ALLSPORT/Getty Images.

Bottom: *Self-Portrait with Bandaged Ear* (detail), 1889, Vincent van Gogh. Courtauld Institute of Art.

MUNCH ADO ABOUT WINNING

Edvard Munch is so, so much more than just *The Scream*, with a portfolio that goes toe-to-toe with any of the all-time greats. *Ashes* is among my favorites of his, and perfectly captures this stage win by Mark Cavendish.

You could also use the painting for any "Surrender Cobra" scene (a term coined by the fantastic writer Holly Anderson for when fans in the stands put their hands on their head in disbelief after their team falls apart), but featuring patrons at their lowest seemed like something I should probably avoid.

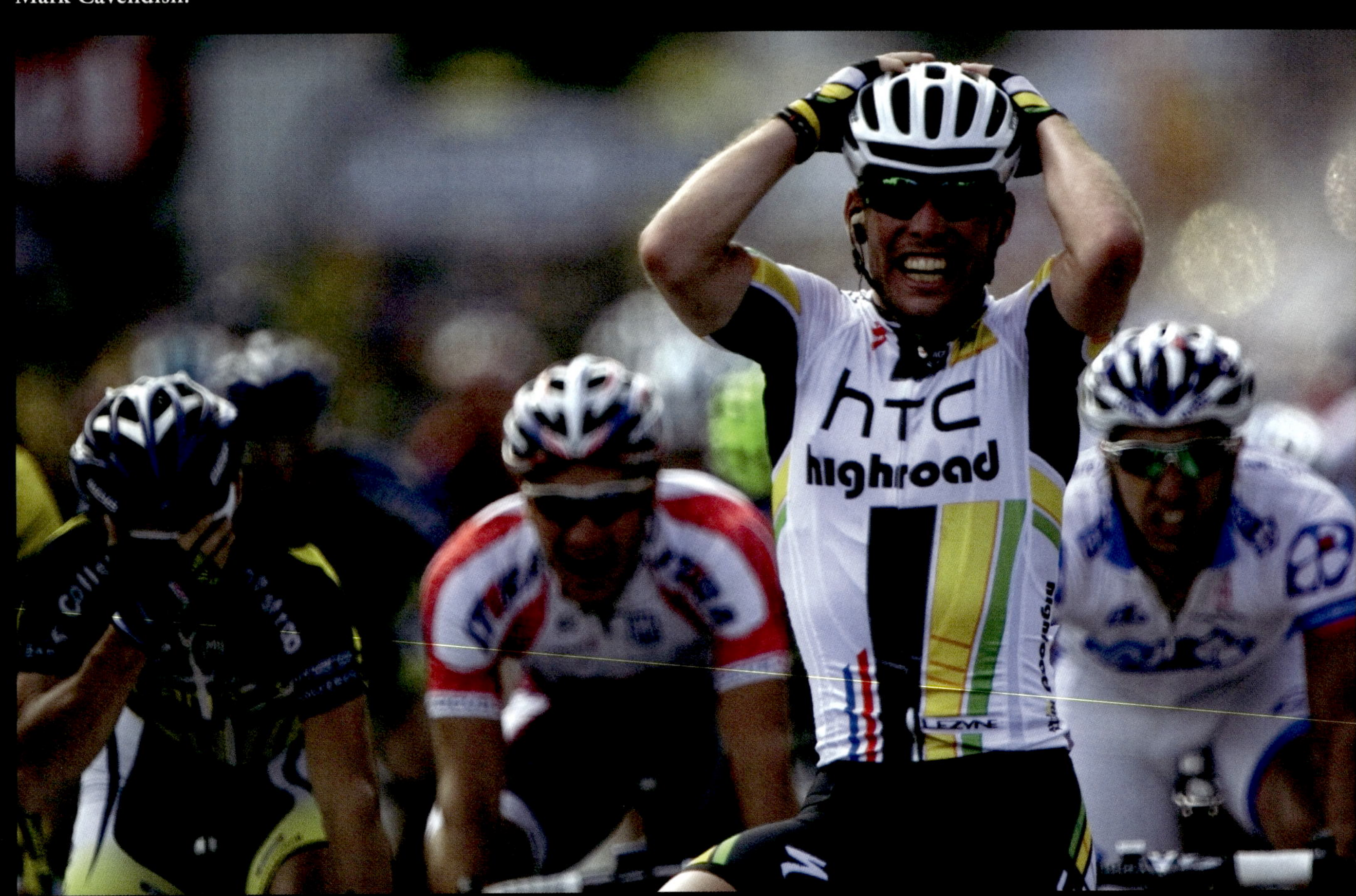

Opposite page: Britain's Mark Cavendish celebrates on the finish line as he wins the 218 km and seventh stage of the 2011 Tour de France cycling race run between Le Mans and Chateauroux, center France, on July 8, 2011. Photo by Lionel Bonaventure/AFP via Getty Images.

This page: *Ashes* (detail), 1895, Edvard Munch. Digital image by Flickr. National Museum of Art, Architecture and Design.

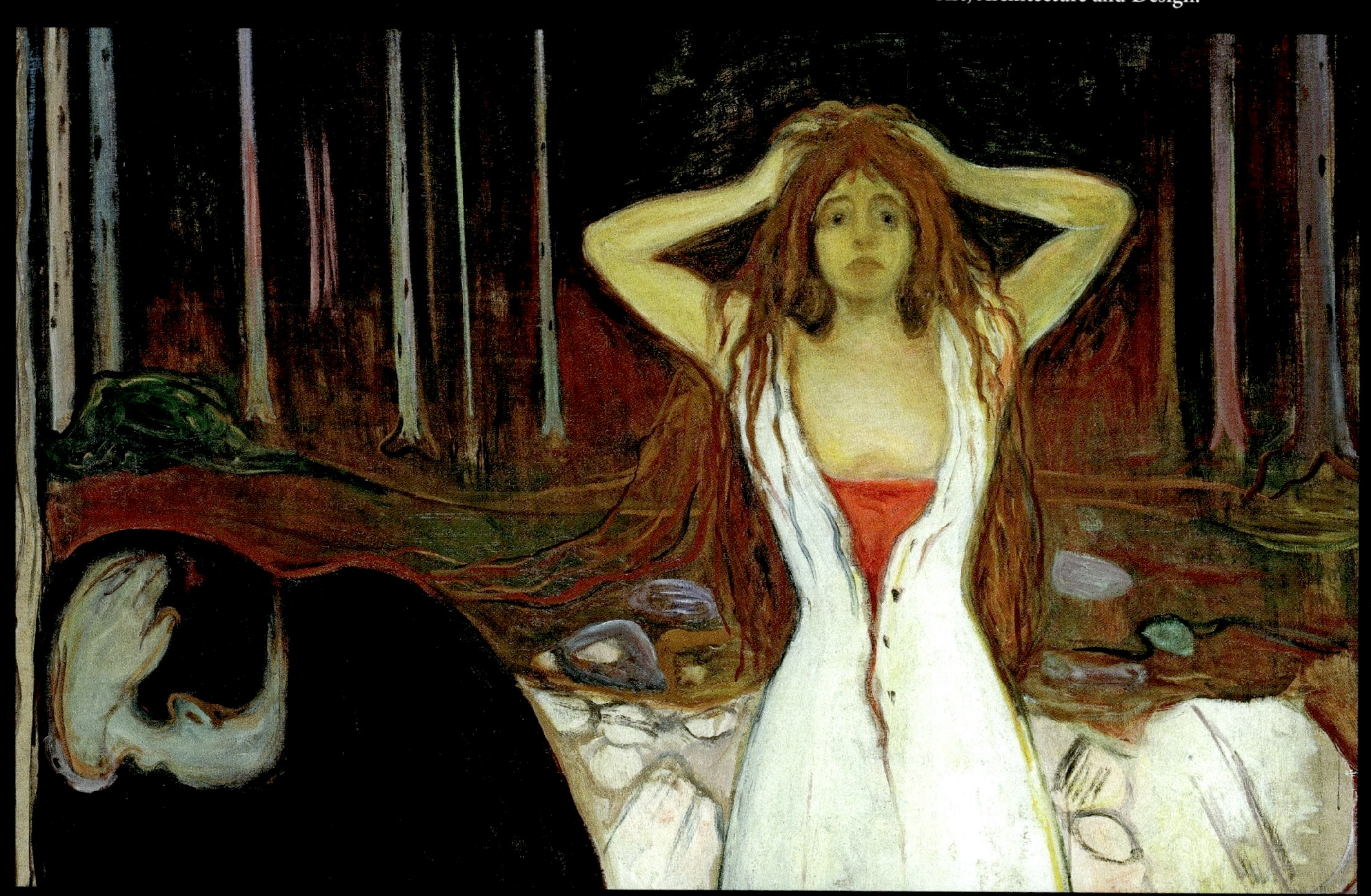

LACROSSE BATTLE

Do yourself a favor and watch lacrosse and the PLL. It has the just the right amount of scoring where goals actually matter, but a comeback is doable even if a team is down a handful. There's drama, constant movement, and, as seen above, hits! Despite the action, it's not the easiest to meme, as sticks tend to play an important role. It's why the section of this Tiepolo, with the concentrated sword fighting, felt apropos. This work fills a prominent position at the Met, hanging right above the main staircase at the entrance of European Paintings. It's weight also matches the moment, as it set the tone for an eventual 12–11 Archers victory.

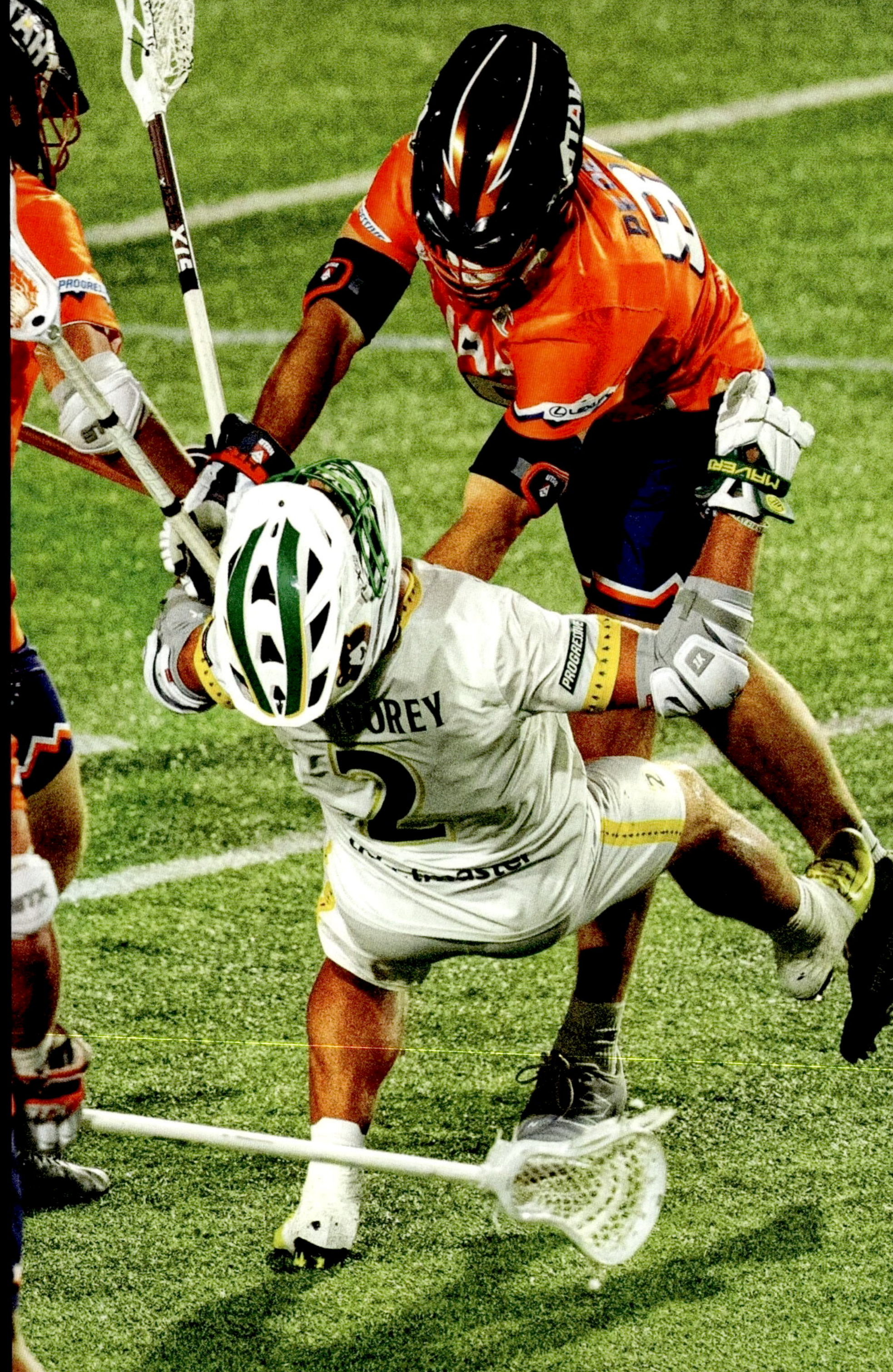

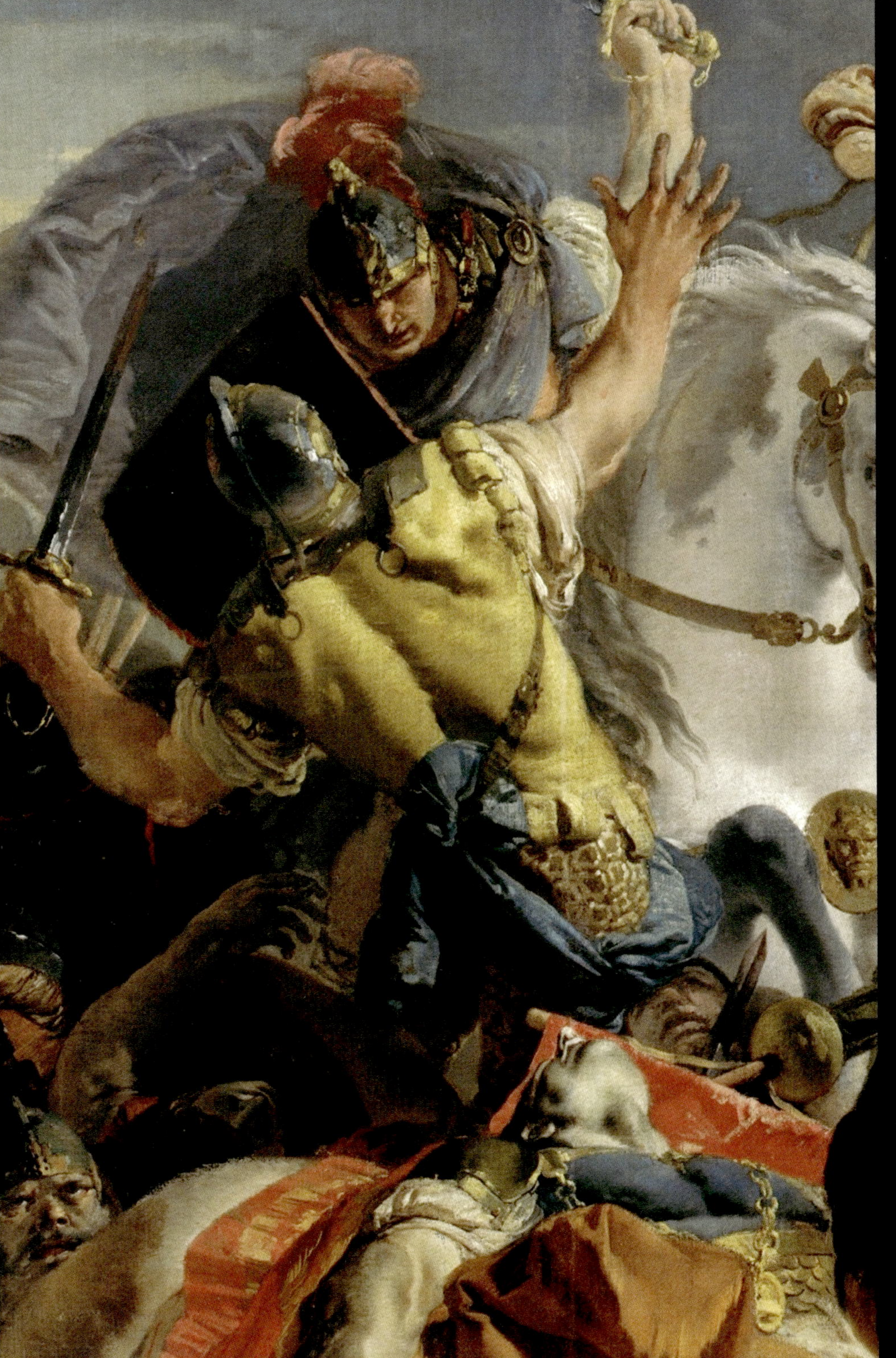

Opposite page: Beau Pederson (#89) of the Utah Archers lays a hit on Andrew McAdorey (#8) of the California Redwoods on June 13, 2025, the third weekend of the 2025 Premier Lacrosse League (PLL) season, in Philadelphia, Pennsylvania. Photo via PLL/ by Nick Ieradi (@n18productions).

This page: *The Battle of Vercellae* (detail), 1725–29, Giovanni Battista Tiepolo. The Metropolitan Museum of Art. Flipped from the original.

THE LAST JUDGMENT

We've reached the end, so let's close things out with *The Last Judgment*, which sits behind the altar in the Sistine Chapel and is so grand and detailed that it should be looked at as a hundred paintings in one.

I did a post of an awkward tackle in an NFL game compared to two figures on the bottom right (can't show it here because of copyright), and received the following response from a Twitter (now X) user named Holly (@amnapping): "I used to feel like it was cheating when you cropped a piece of art to fit a picture, but then I realized it means you're recalling all these tiny details instead of just the 'main' themes and shapes. Incredible. Like, it's one thing to see a picture and remember the famous Christ figure here. It's entirely another thing to see a picture and remember some random guy way off to the lower right side."

This feels like a fitting piece to conclude with, partly because of the title, but mostly because I hope this book has shown that inspiration and connections can be pulled from all corners. Go out and find the artistic parallels in your life and make something fun and beautiful.

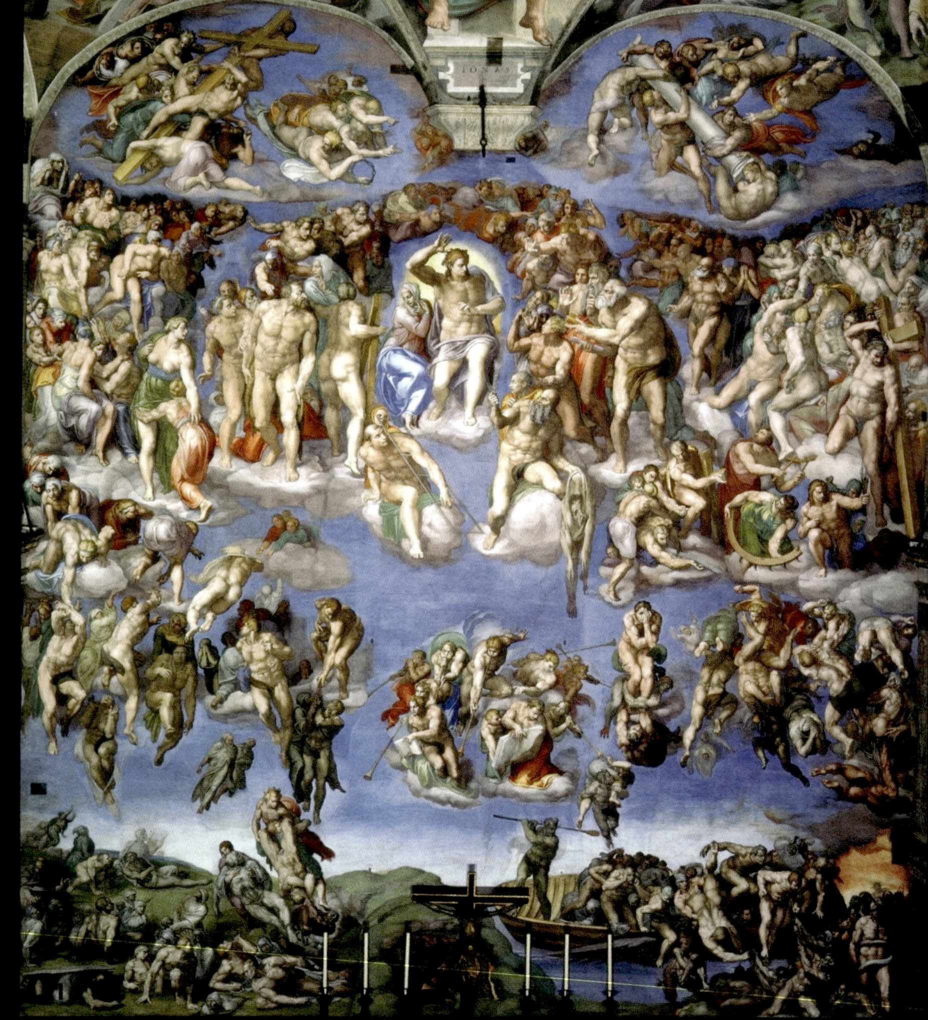

All paintings in this section are details from *The Last Judgment*, 1536–41, Michelangelo. Digital image by Alonso de Mendoza. Sistine Chapel.

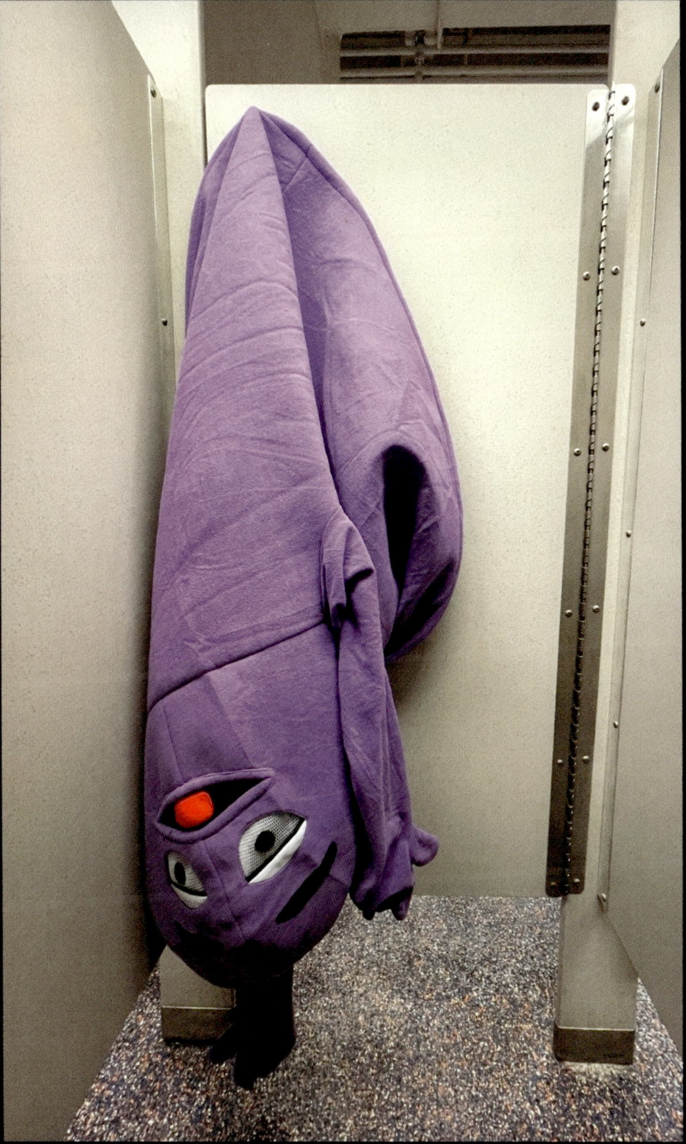

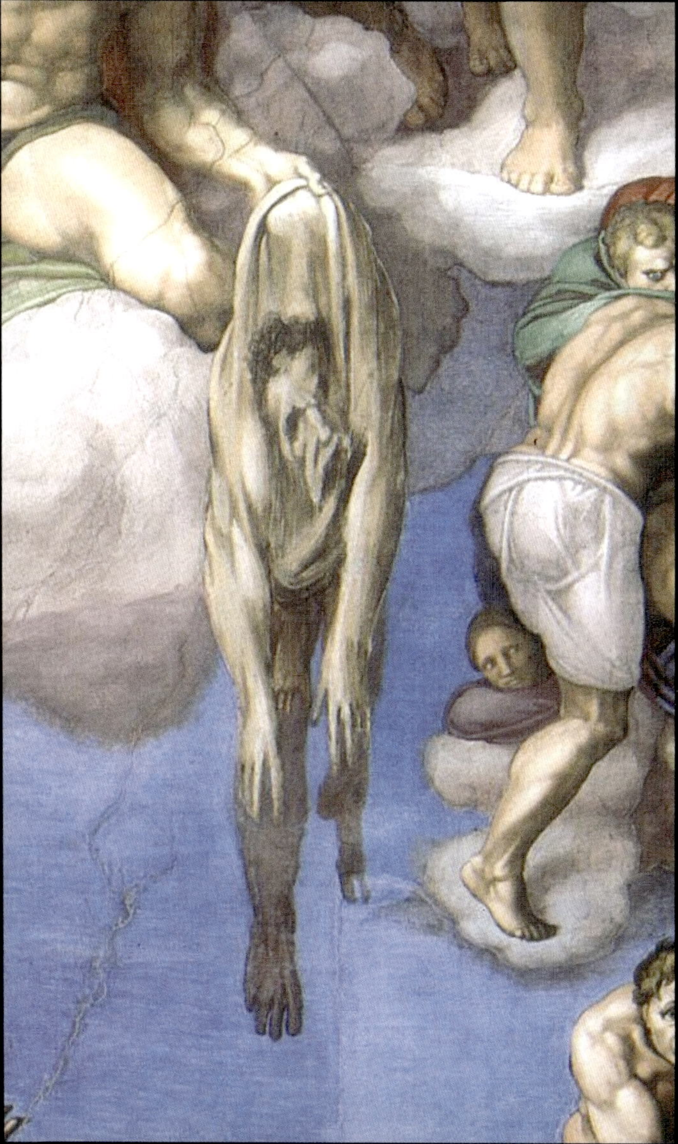

Left: This photo by Twitter (now X) user @krissyy_elyse, taken during a bathroom break after doffing a Grimace costume, went viral during the Mets' 2024 season.

for a loose ball against Camryn Brown (#35) of the UCLA Bruins during the first half of their game at Jon M. Huntsman Center on January 22, 2024, in Salt Lake City, Utah. Photo by Chris Gardner/Getty Images.

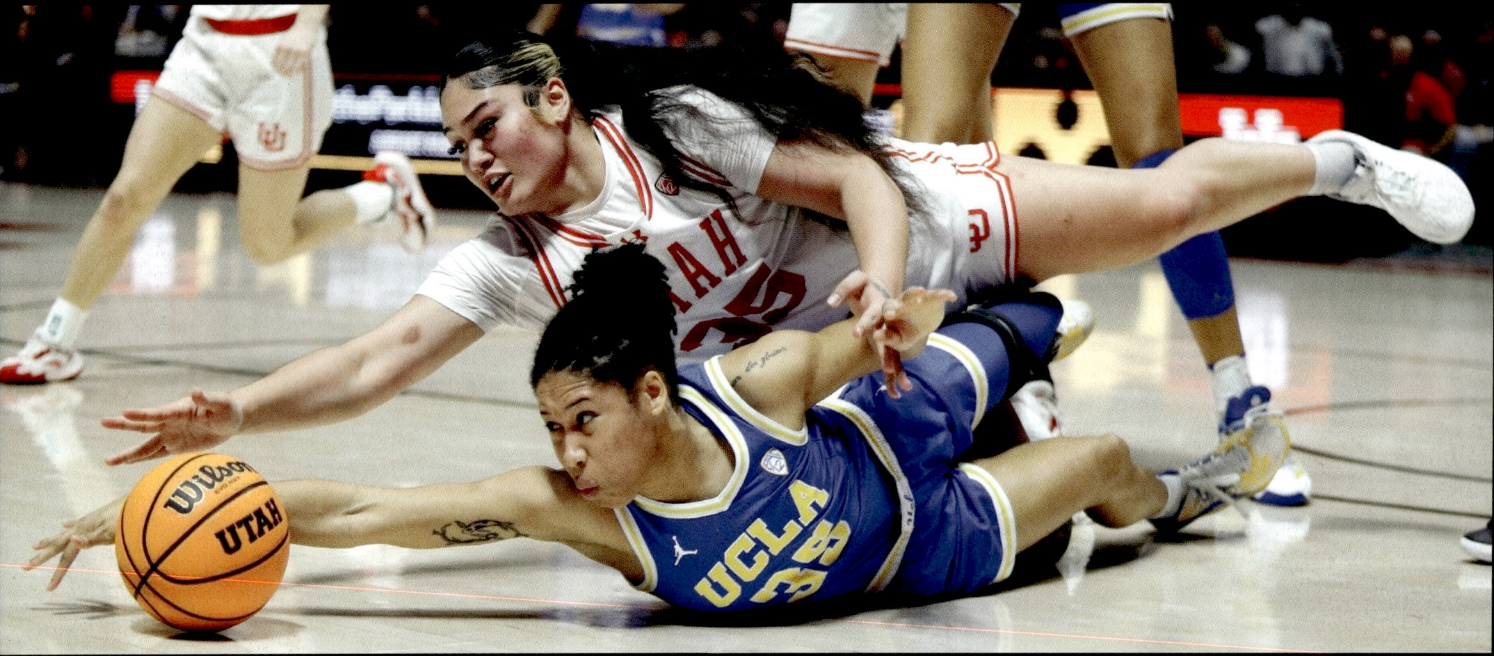

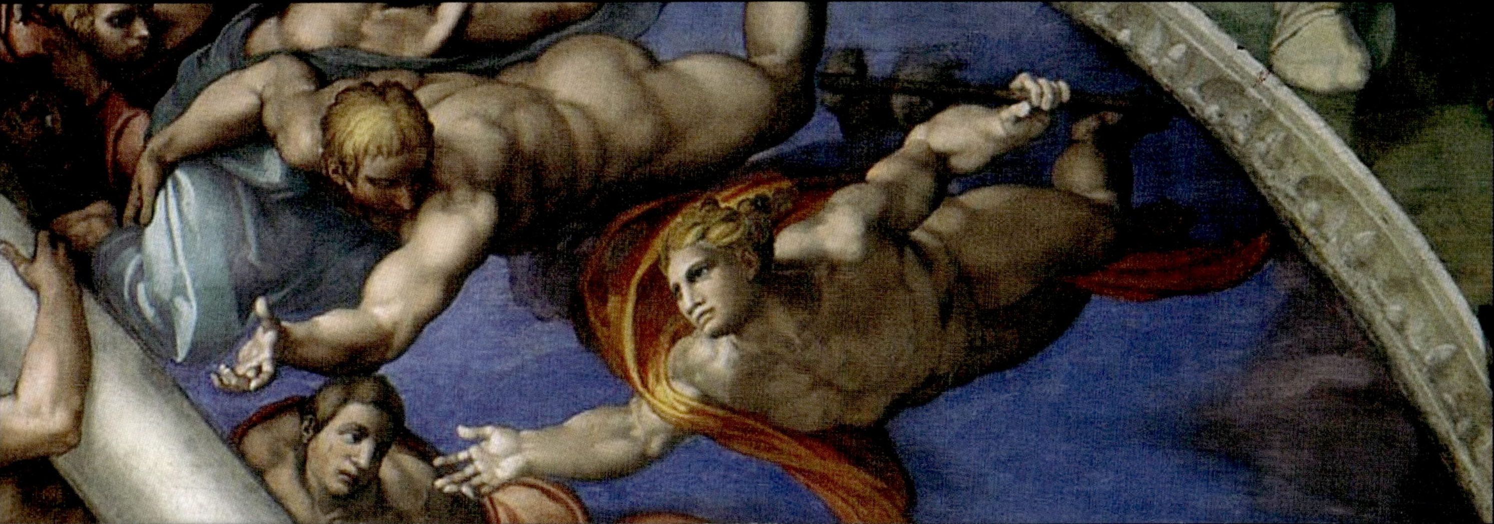

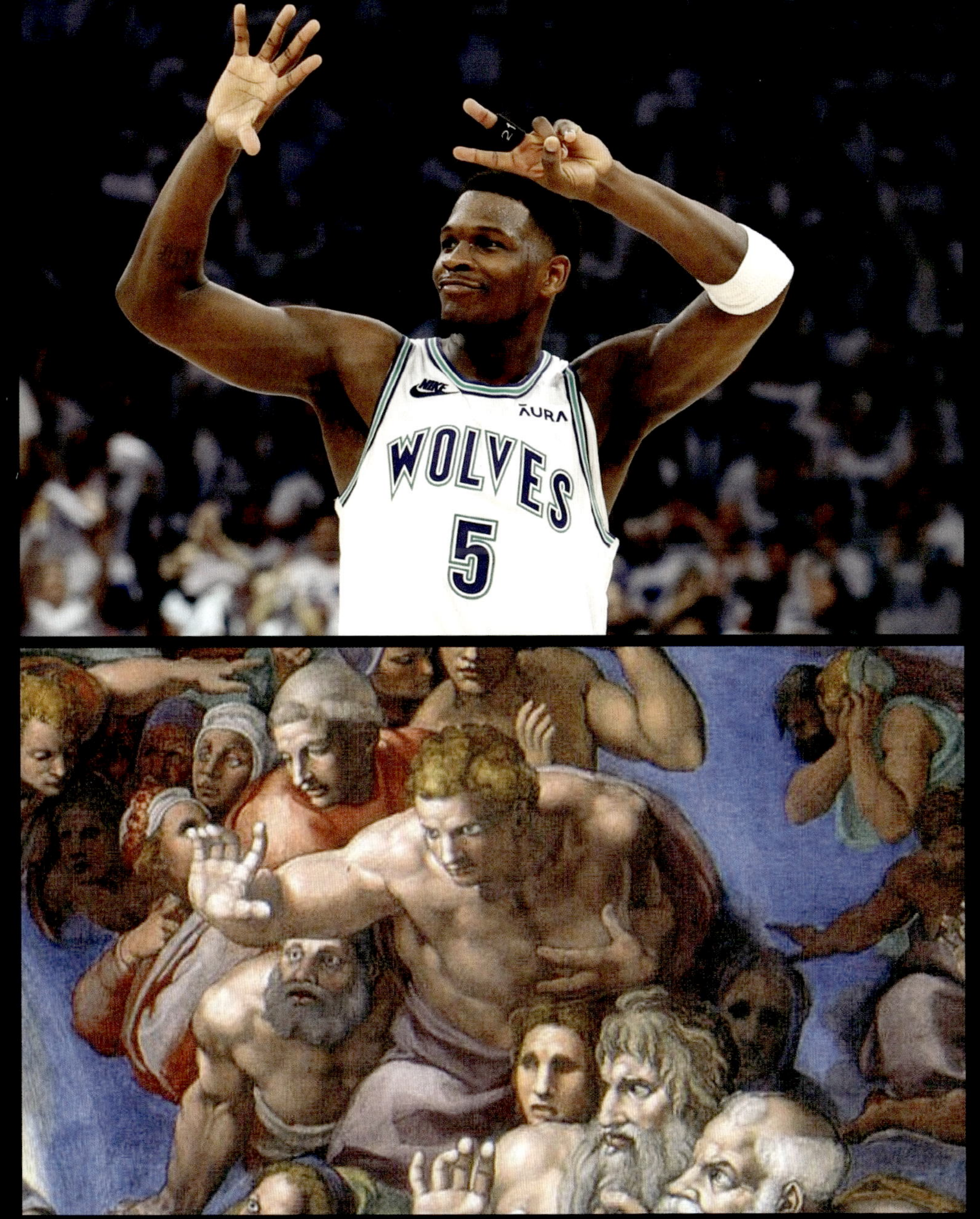

Top: Anthony Edwards (#5) of the Minnesota Timberwolves celebrates against the Denver Nuggets during the fourth quarter in Game 6 of the Western Conference Second Round Playoffs at Target Center on May 16, 2024, in Minneapolis, Minnesota. Photo by David Berding/ Getty Images.

ABOUT THE AUTHOR

LJ Rader is the founder and one-man operation behind the social media account ArtButMakeItSports. A graduate of Vanderbilt University, he is a lifetime sports professional, starting his career at NBC Sports, where he won an Emmy Award for his work on the XXII Olympic Winter Games. LJ was on the product team at DraftKings and is currently the head of the Broadcast Product Group at Sportradar. He's also a diehard sports fan and passionate about art (go figure), spending free time at games, museums, galleries, and auction houses. In addition, he's recently become obsessed with propagating plants, as well as dipping his toes into art collecting. He lives in New York City with his wife, son, and their dog, Rosie (shout-out to the ASPCA).

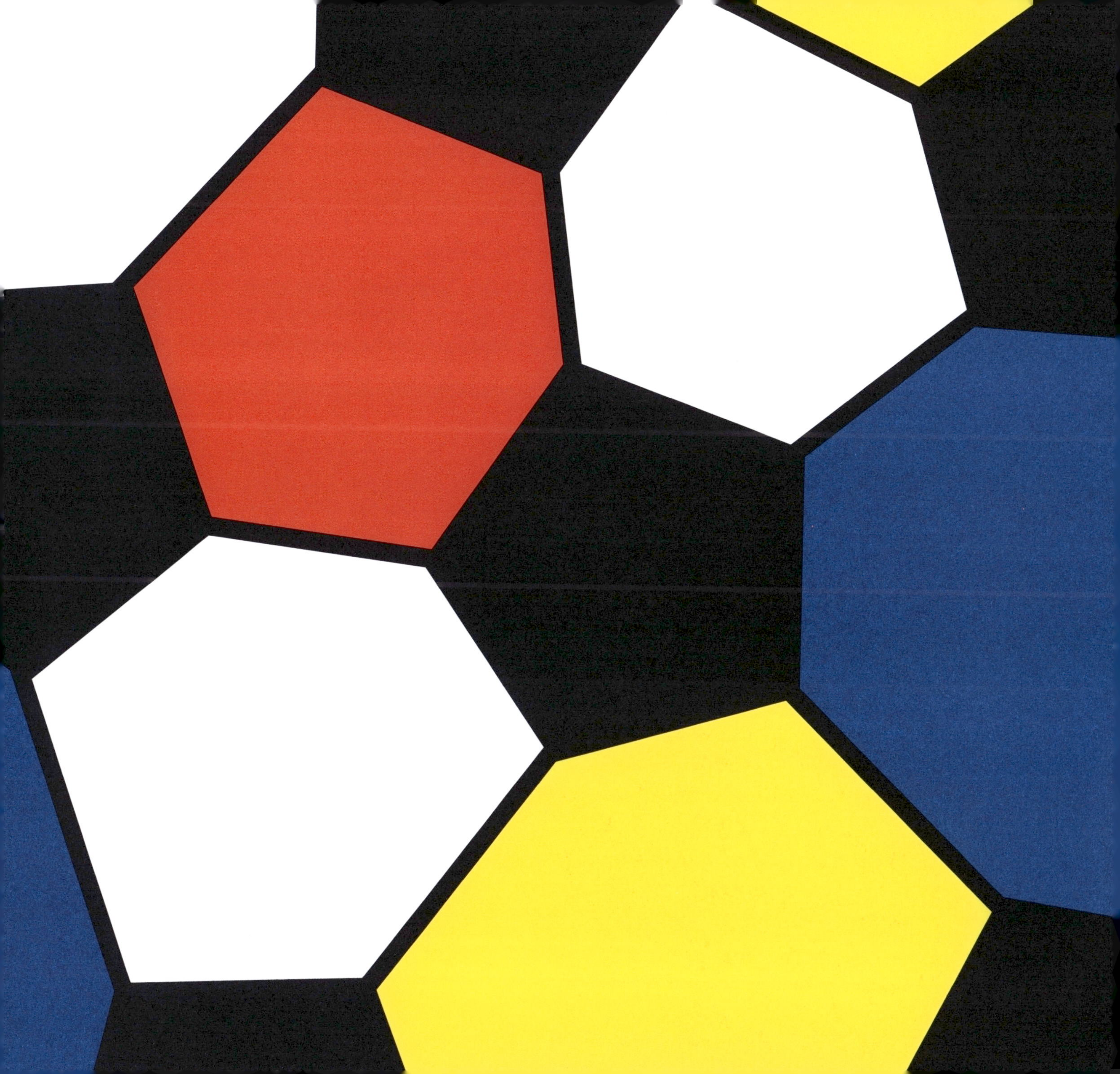

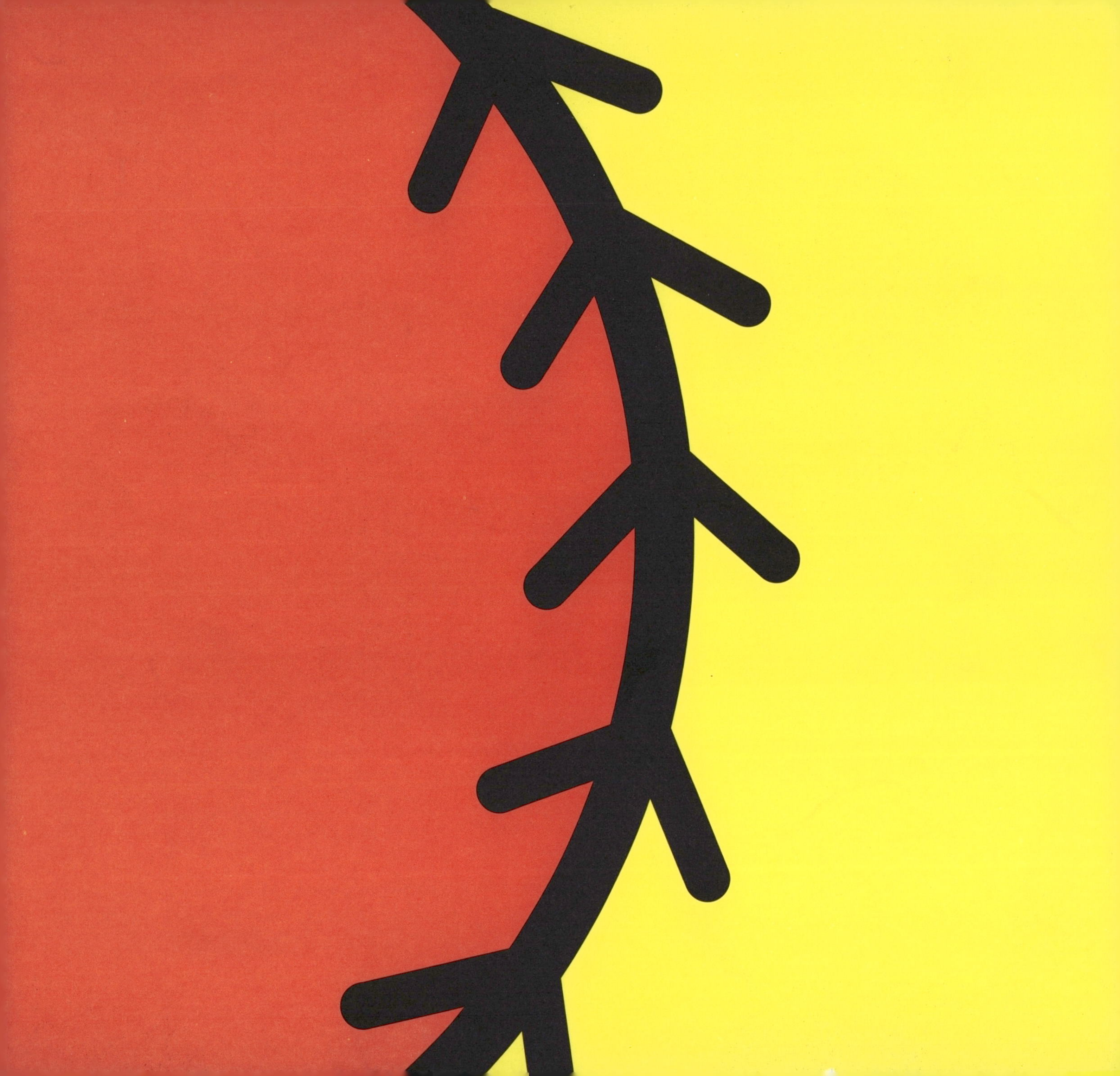